CAROL AGOCS
CATHERINE BURR
FELICITY SOMERSET

Employment Equity

CO-OPERATIVE STRATEGIES FOR ORGANIZATIONAL CHANGE

0   57812 74010   5

CAROL AGOCS
CATHERINE BURR
FELICITY SOMERSET

Employment Equity

CO-OPERATIVE STRATEGIES FOR ORGANIZATIONAL CHANGE

Prentice-Hall

Canadian Cataloging in Publication Data

Agocs, Carol
    Employment equity: cooperative strategies
for organizational change
Includes bibliographical reference and index.

ISBN 0-13-274010-9

    1. Discrimination in employment.   2.
Affirmative action programs.   3. Organizational
change.   I. Burr, Catherine   II. Somerset,
Felicity.   III. Title.

HD4903.A46 1992   331.18'3   C92-093171-2

Prentice-Hall, Inc., Englewood Cliffs, New Jersey
Prentice-Hall International, Inc., London
Prentice-Hall of Australia, Pty., Ltd., Sydney
Prentice-Hall of India Pvt., Ltd., New Delhi
Prentice-Hall of Japan, Inc., Tokyo
Prentice-Hall of Southeast Asia (Pte.) Ltd., Singapore
Editora Prentice-Hall do Brasil Ltda., Rio de Janeiro
Prentice-Hall Hispanoamericana, S.A., Mexico

ISBN 0-13-274010-9

ACQUISITIONS EDITOR: John Wray
DEVELOPMENTAL EDITOR: Joe March
PRODUCTION EDITOR: Dick Hemingway
PRODUCTION COORDINATOR: Lisa Kreuch
COVER AND INTERIOR DESIGN: ArtPlus Limited/Brant Cowie
PAGE LAYOUT: ArtPlus Limited/Valerie Phillips
TECHNICAL ILLUSTRATION: ArtPlus Limited/Cathy Campion

Printed and Bound in U.S.A. by R. R. Donnelley & Sons Company

1 2 3 4 5 RRD 96 95 94 93 92

To Action Travail des Femmes and all
equality seekers who work for change

Contents

CHAPTER 14

Tracking Progress Toward Equity: Monitoring, Evaluation and Organizational Learning 373

Preface

THIS BOOK HAS BEEN WRITTEN as events crucial to the development of equality policy in Canada are unfolding. Findings will soon be reported from a large scale evaluation of the primary federal employment equity policy instruments, the Legislated Employment Equity Program and the Federal Contractors Program. The government of Ontario is undertaking public consultation to prepare for legislation that will make action toward employment equity mandatory for most employers, and there is speculation that other provinces may follow suit.

While there is some public debate about the need for employment equity legislation, the weight of evidence demonstrates that entrenched patterns of discrimination in the Canadian workplace remain unchanged, and that effective action must be taken if equality in employment is to be a reality. The structures of inequality remain intact after a generation of experience with legislative and policy approaches that are limited to responding to incidents of discrimination against individuals. Patterns of inequality that affect individuals because they are members of categories they did not choose to "join" can only be changed by policies that deal with individuals as members of groups, and with the structural arrangements that perpetuate group-based inequality.

The Canadian policy and legislative framework is only beginning to come to terms with the implications of the concepts of
group rights and structural inequality. There is as yet no map of the
unknown territory that lies beyond liberal individualism and
"equality of opportunity." But there is dissatisfaction and anger on
the part of the new majority in the workplace—women, racial
minorities, aboriginal peoples, and persons with disabilities—that a
commitment to undertake a journey toward equality of results has
been so long in coming.

A growing commitment to develop policies that deal successfully
with the complex realities of discrimination in Canada is part of a
global concern for human rights and social justice for all groups.
Canadian employment equity policy is evolving within a context of
worldwide demographic change that is giving rise to an increasingly
diverse work force of women and men in many parts of Europe and
North America. In a global economy, people find themselves working and living side by side with others very different from themselves. Yet recent violence and conflicts based on gender, ethnicity
and race in Canada, Europe and the United States make it clear that
the significance of gender, and of cultural and racial diversity, is not
diminishing, nor are these differences tolerated more easily as the
world becomes smaller. Furthermore, as more women, people with
disabilities, aboriginal peoples and racial minorities enter the workplace, the traditional concentration of these groups in job ghettos,
and their lack of representation in higher paying jobs with decision-
making power, shows few signs of changing.

As each workplace becomes more like a microcosm of the globe,
it is essential that on this small scale, people learn new ways to
acknowledge, appreciate, and build upon human differences. We
can no longer afford to use those differences as excuses for oppression, or for restricting the opportunities of some human beings
while preserving the privileges of those who have traditionally
enjoyed them. As economic challenges become more pressing it is
tempting to set aside the hard work of taking down the walls of
discrimination and inequality stone by stone. Yet in a difficult economic environment it is all the more vital to ensure that full use is
made of the talents, skills, knowledge and energy of all who want
to participate in economic life, and that no arbitrary barriers prevent some from contributing fully to our common well-being.

This book is part of an ongoing discussion of the difficult issues involved in bringing about the social reconstruction of the Canadian workplace. It objectives are

- to acquaint the reader with the Canadian policy, legislative and judicial framework within which we work toward equity in employment, and with the principles and some of the evidence on which that framework rests;
- to raise issues and propose suggestions about how to approach the long and complex process of changing the workplace to make its structural arrangements and culture fair to all, and able to accommodate diversity;
- to examine the implementation of employment equity policy in the light of what is known about how large scale changes in the structure and culture of the workplace can be effectively guided and encouraged, and how resistance to organizational change can be analyzed and addressed; and
- to view employment equity as a fundamental part of a productive and progressive approach to the entire spectrum of human resource management functions and decisions within organizations.

In the broadest sense, the objective of this book is to help to realize the purpose of the federal Employment Equity Act (1986), as stated in Section 2:

> To achieve equality in the workplace so that no person shall be denied employment opportunities or benefits for reasons unrelated to ability and in the fulfilment of that goal, to correct the conditions of disadvantage in employment experienced by women, aboriginal peoples, persons with disabilities and persons who are, because of their race or colour, in a visible minority in Canada by giving effect to the principle that employment equity means more than treating persons in the same way but also requires special measures and the accommodation of differences.

Legislation and regulations, and the polices based upon them, cannot be effective unless they are translated into action. It is the application and practice of the principles of employment equity in the workplace that concerns us in this book. We present a way of thinking about employment equity implementation strategies and issues. Our objective is to help equality seekers to define and set appropriate goals, work effectively toward those goals, and get results.

Although Canada's employment equity regulations and legislation are based upon some sound principles, progress toward equity has been slow and disappointing. In our view, an important reason for the failure to get results is that the issues involved in implementing this form of organizational change have yet to be examined and faced. Our reading of the available literature on employment equity, and our observations and experiences as change agents, have convinced us that employment equity practitioners will not get results by adopting a top-down, control oriented approach in which employment equity is viewed as a series of technical tasks to be performed. Certainly it is important to secure support for employment equity from top executives, complete a work-force census and analyze those data in comparison with labour market statistics, review employment systems, and complete a work plan with goals and timetables. Yet performing these tasks required by federal regulations does not in itself lead to greater access to jobs, career opportunity, decision-making power, and an improved working environment for women, minorities, aboriginal peoples, and persons with disabilities.

There is evidence in the theoretical and research literature on organizational change that such changes in the workplace are most likely to be brought about through a goal-oriented process that involves key stakeholder groups who have an interest in employment equity implementation, and who see themselves as having something to gain or lose. Through the participation and commitment of stakeholders, policy objectives can be set and attained in a manner appropriate to the social, cultural and task environment of the workplace. The various stakeholders — for example, members of designated groups inside the organization, associations in the community that represent those groups, senior management, human resource professionals, first line supervisors, bargaining agents, non-unionized employees, and representatives of governments — have interests that need to be identified and acknowledged, so that common ground can be found and resistance to change can be successfully addressed.

The approach to implementing change that is developed in this book rests on the assumption that there is no single "best way" to work toward equity in the workplace: organizations differ greatly, and a strategy that works in one may be ineffective in another. In most workplaces, employment equity is a process of large-scale change that involves the transformation of the organization's culture and structures. Yet the change process can be expected to occur in various ways in different organizations: there is no standard set of rules or sequence of tasks that will result in equity. The change agent is thus advised to approach the task as a series of organizational choices that grow out of a careful analysis of the prevailing realities in a particular organizational context, and that are guided by a vision of a desired end state, and a strategy for getting there.

The term "employment equity" is confusing, since it appears to refer both to a process of change, and to an end state — to the goals of that process. In this book we are concerned with both dimensions of employment equity, and we attempt to make a case for stakeholder participation both in setting goals for change, or defining desired outcomes, and in carrying out the organizational change processes and the tasks that move the organization toward those goals. The organization's employment equity goals generally include:

- removing discriminatory barriers and obstacles to the full participation of women, aboriginal peoples, persons with disabilities and racial minorities in the workplace;
- providing remedies for the long standing disadvantage and discrimination those groups have historically experienced and still experience; and
- attaining more equitable representation, distribution and participation of those groups in all aspects of working life.

The employment equity implementation processes that move an organization toward these goals include identifying and removing (or revising) human resource management practices and policies that result in inequities; preventing future discrimination through education, training, and enforcement of sound policies; taking initiatives that respond to the special needs of designated group members; creating and maintaining a workplace free of harassment and conducive to the integration, development and retention of designated group members; and making hiring and promotion decisions in ways that increase the representation and distribution of designated group members throughout the organization. The organizational change processes that are needed to ensure that employment equity implementation actually occurs, and gets results, include identifying and empowering change agents, identifying and working with stakeholders and their interests, facilitating negotiation and cooperation among stakeholders in addressing their interests, creating appropriate ways to encourage stakeholders to participate in change, providing needed resources, developing a change strategy, identifying and managing sources of resistance to change, and evaluating and making appropriate revisions to the change strategy.

Employment equity is an issue that is now high on the human resource management agendas of many public and private sector employers. Federally regulated private sector employers and crown corporations must comply with the Employment Equity Act of 1986, and employment equity regulations apply to contractors with the federal government and with some local governments. Public sector employers including governments at all levels, universities and colleges, police services, boards of education and hospitals are undertaking employment equity initiatives, as are many private sector employers. Pay equity legislation in some provinces has created awareness among some employers of the issues of gender inequality in the workplace. Employment equity is increasingly regarded as an important element of an advanced and productive approach to human resource management, and is being initiated voluntarily by progressive employers. The emergence of a new organizational position, that of the employment equity specialist, testifies to the investment employers are beginning to make in this form of change in Canada.

Organizations representing the designated groups and labour have raised the public profile of equity issues and created pressures for response from employers and policy makers. Government agencies, sector-wide organizations of employers and trade unions, associations of human resource and legal professionals, and advocacy organizations representing the designated groups, are among the stakeholders who are attempting to influence the emerging policy framework.

This book is addressed to all who are interested in acquiring relevant information and addressing the complex issues involved in employment equity policy development and implementation. This group includes equality seekers, managers, human resources professionals, human rights professionals, and officers and members of trade unions, employee associations and advocacy organizations representing the designated groups. We hope that employment equity practitioners and those in government who are responsible for policy development and implementation will find the book useful. Students in courses dealing with human resources management, organizational behaviour, sociology of work, labour relations, women's studies, race relations, human rights law, social policy, or public administration will find this book relevant to their concerns. We have made an effort to communicate in the language of the practitioner and general reader, but the discussion is informed by what we have learned from the research and theoretical literature on organizational change, workplace democracy, human rights law, and discrimination in employment.

In the United States, public and private sector employers have been required to comply with affirmative action regulations for almost a generation, and for many, affirmative action is a firmly established component of human resource management systems. While there is a large literature on the American experience with affirmative action, few publications have dealt with the process of implementing this form of organizational change. Moreover, the American literature provides little guidance for working toward equality in the workplace within the distinctive Canadian legal, institutional and cultural milieu. Few Canadian discussions of employment equity have dealt with the role of stakeholder participation in change, or with the separate and unique circumstances that each of the four designated groups — women, aboriginal peoples, persons with disabilities, and members of racial minorities — bring to the process of planning and implementing organizational change. Employment equity has yet to be analyzed as a cornerstone of a comprehensive human resource management strategy for the contemporary Canadian organization. This book begins to address some of these gaps in the existing literature.

We have not attempted to repeat what is contained in sources that are generally available, for example, from government agen-

cies. This book is not a handbook of instructions on how to implement government regulations, although practitioners will find useful suggestions regarding compliance. Nor have we attempted a
comprehensive review of the impact of employment equity policy
thus far, since the evidence required to support such an evaluation
is not yet available. Furthermore, we obviously cannot provide an
up-to-the- minute account of a rapidly evolving field; other
sources, including publications of government agencies and
newsletters such as *Managing Diversity* or *The Canadian Human Rights
Reporter* are valuable sources of information about changing legislation, regulations, government policy, and case law. There is unfortunately no substitute for keeping in touch with new developments
in the field as they unfold. We have not attempted to review initiatives undertaken by major employers, though we cite some as
examples of points under discussion. Indeed, we have seen few
applications of the stakeholder-based, strategic approach to
employment equity that we are suggesting.

One more disclaimer is in order. Employment equity policy as it is
presently conceived does not deal with the fundamental issues of
racism and sexism in society, nor does it address poverty and social
inequality, particularly for those who are not in the labour force. Nor
is employment equity the only available strategy for working toward
fundamental change in the world of work. For example, rather that
seeking to be full and equal participants in mainstream organizations,
some individuals and groups may choose to work together to establish separate enterprises, cooperatives, or other types of organizations to work toward their collective goals as women, or people with
disabilities, or aboriginal peoples, or members of an ethnic or racial
group. Employment equity policy is essentially a strategy designed
to integrate historically disadvantaged groups into the existing
opportunity structure, but not to assimilate them by obliterating
what makes them distinctive.

However, some groups — notably aboriginal peoples — may not
share the goal of integration, although some individual members
may, and can therefore benefit from employment equity policy. The
First Nations are seeking economic and political self-determination,
in addition to full and equal participation in the opportunity structure of Canadian society. Employment equity policy must be developed and implemented through joint decision making, as part of a

broader response to the priorities of economic development and self government by the First Nations.

In writing this book, we have approached our task from varied but complementary perspectives and experience. Carol Agócs teaches organizational behaviour and public administration in a university, does research on employment equity and on women's career progression in management, and chairs the university's employment equity committee. Catherine Burr is a private consultant on employment equity and organizational change. In her previous work as a human resources manager, she directed the implementation of an employment equity program in a large municipality, and prior to that she was responsible for the analysis of systemic discrimination and other compliance matters in two human rights commissions. Felicity Somerset has a background in training, consulting and policy development on race relations issues and anti-racist organizational change in the public, private, and community sectors. We all have experience in education, training and policy development for employment equity as well as experience as employment equity practitioners and change agents within the workplace and in community and advocacy settings; we are thoroughly familiar with the frustrations and exhilaration of working for change. We wrote this book as a means of increasing our understanding of how to make equity a reality in the workplace, and during the two years we have been writing we feel we have learned much from each other and accomplished our purpose.

We owe a large debt of gratitude to those who have taught, inspired and helped us, and to those who have been patient and encouraging as the project evolved — slowly! Most of all, we thank Rosalie Silberman Abella, the Royal Commissioner whose work is the foundation of employment equity policy in Canada. Rosie has been our inspiration, role model, and intellectual and ethical pathfinder, and we are honoured by her encouragement of our project. Flora McDonald has our gratitude and respect for her political courage and commitment in championing the Employment Equity Act and Federal Contractors Program. In her many writings, Rosabeth Moss Kanter helped us to see equity issuses in structural and cultural perspective, and guided our efforts to understand employment equity as a process of organizational change.

We thank Dick Hemingway, our editor, for his skill and good-natured hard work in seeing the manuscript through to completion. Joe March and John Wray of Prentice-Hall Canada saw the project's potential and provided us with the opportunity to carry it out, and didn't give up on us when the going was slow. Wendy Bichard gave invaluable help in producing the text, and Brant Cowie of ArtPlus designed the cover. The staffs of the Industrial Relations Library at the University of Toronto, and of the Business Library, Law Library, and the D.B. Weldon Library at the University of Western Ontario, gave indispensable assistance in locating sources we needed. Ursula Moore, night supervisor for Priority Post, always seemed to have a truck ready to take manuscripts to our editor in Toronto. We appreciate the helpful comments, suggestions, and criticisms of those who reviewed the book proposal and various parts of the manuscript, including Sándor Agócs, Neil Gavigan, Jeannette Lavell, Susan Lewis, Carrie MacKinnon, Shirley Murray, Bob Noftall, Paul Scott, Marie Tellier, Nan Weiner, and Bill Wilkinson. The authors are grateful for the assistance provided by small research grants from the Social Sciences and Humanities Research Council of Canada. Finally, we thank the members of our families and our close friends for their encouragement, support and fortitude.

London, Ontario, November 1991.

1

Employment Equity: The State of the Art

I N AUGUST 1986, Canadian banks, airlines, railways and shipping companies, together with Bell Canada, Canada Post, the Canadian Broadcasting Corporation, and other federally regulated employers and crown corporations, were legally required to take steps toward employment equity for women, aboriginal peoples, racial minorities and people with disabilities.

The legislative purpose, eloquently and concisely stated in section 2 of the Employment Equity Act, is

> to achieve equality in the work place so that no person shall be denied employment opportunities or benefits for reasons unrelated to ability and, in the fulfillment of that goal, to correct the conditions of disadvantage in employment experienced by women, aboriginal peoples, persons with disabilities and persons who are, because of their race or colour, in a visible minority in

Canada by giving effect to the principle that employment equity means more than treating persons in the same way but also requires special measures and the accommodation of differences.

Federally regulated organizations employ approximately ten percent of the Canadian workforce. Although not numerous, these firms in the federal jurisdiction are often large, visible and geographically dispersed across the country. Furthermore, provincially regulated employers, who account for about 90% of Canadian workers, are not "off the hook" regarding employment equity. The Canadian government used its buying and contracting power to create the Federal Contractors Program, which established a policy, enforced by regulations, that requires provincially regulated employers bidding on federal government goods and services contracts worth at least $200,000 to demonstrate a commitment to employment equity by complying with eleven employment equity criteria (Box 1.2).

BOX 1.1
Requirements Under the Federal Employment Equity Act

PROGRAM NAME:
> Legislated Employment Equity Program (LEEP). Before passage the Act was known as Bill C-62.

EFFECTIVE DATE:
> August 13, 1986. First reports, covering 1987 work-force data, were due on or before June 1, 1988, and are submitted annually thereafter.

APPLIES TO:
> Federally regulated employers with 100 employees or more.
> Examples: Bell Canada, Bank of Montreal, CP Rail, Canadian Airlines, Saskatchewan Wheat Pool, other employers in banking, interprovincial transportation and communications.
> Federal crown corporations such as Canada Post, Air Canada, CBC.

DOES NOT APPLY TO:
> Federal/Canadian government departments and agencies.
> Provincially regulated employers.

REQUIREMENTS:

Submission of annual statistical reports by the employer to Employment and Immigration Canada. These reports use standardized forms showing the number of employees and workforce representation of women, aboriginal peoples, racial minorities and people with disabilities in specific salary ranges and occupational groups in the company, as well as annual counts of hirings, promotions and terminations. Employees who are permanent full-time, permanent part-time, and temporary employees where they comprise 20% or more of the total number of employees, are included. An optional executive summary of no more than four pages may be submitted with the reports to describe special efforts, exceptional situations or problems related to employment equity implementation.

Annual reports are compiled and published by CEIC, and individual employers' reports are public documents available on microfiche in public libraries and other depositories of government documents. Copies of employers' reports are submitted by CEIC to the Canadian Human Rights Commission.

The Act requires the employer to prepare and retain a plan setting out goals and timetables for employment equity implementation. This plan is not submitted to the government. The Act states that it is the duty of the employer to: consult with employee representatives or bargaining agents, and to implement employment equity by:

- identifying and eliminating discriminatory barriers in its employment practices;
- instituting positive policies and practices and making reasonable accommodation to improve the representation of the designated groups.

There is no reporting to the government or compliance audit by the government regarding such consultation or implementation.

SANCTIONS:

There is a fine of up to $50,000 for failing to file reports. Three employers have been charged or prosecuted. There are no sanctions for failing to implement other provisions of the Act.

(SOURCE: Employment and Immigration Canada, *Employment Equity Act and Reporting Requirements*, Ottawa: Minister of Supply and Services, 1986.)

BOX 1.2
Requirements Under the Federal Contractors Program

PROGRAM NAME:
Federal Contractors Program (FCP), or contract compliance.

EFFECTIVE DATE:
August 13, 1986. First certificates were signed in 1986. New bidders continue to sign. Compliance reviews commenced in 1987.

APPLIES TO:
Organizations that bid on Canadian government goods and services contracts worth $200,000 or more, and which have 100 or more employees.
Examples: Northern Telecom, General Motors, Beaver Foods, Queen's University, Dorothea Knitting Mills.

DOES NOT APPLY TO:
Federally regulated employers and federal crown corporations which are covered by the Employment Equity Act, even if they bid on or supply goods and services to the Canadian government.
Federal departments and agencies.
Provincially regulated employers that do not bid on federal contracts.
Bidders and suppliers of goods and services under $200,000 in value, or that have fewer than 100 employees.
Sub-contractors and contractors that bid on construction, real estate and legal services contracts are not covered.

REQUIREMENTS:
Bidders and suppliers must sign a certificate of commitment to implement employment equity.
They must implement an employment equity program comprising 11 criteria:
1. Communicate commitment by the chief executive officer.
2. Assign responsibility for employment equity to senior personnel.
3. Collect and maintain workforce statistics related to the designated groups. (Note: Unlike LEEP there is no standardized format for such data, and data are not collected by the government or made public.)
4. Analyze designated group representation in relation to availability.

4

5. Review and change human resource systems to remove barriers.
6. Establish goals for hiring, training and promotion of designated groups.
7. Establish a work plan.
8. Adopt special measures and provide reasonable accommodation.
9. Establish a climate favourable to integration.
10. Adopt monitoring procedures.
11. Permit access of FCP officials to the employment equity records of the supplier in order to measure progress.

Suppliers/contractors covered under the FCP are selected at random for audits to ensure compliance with the eleven implementation criteria.

An unfavourable compliance review can be appealed by the contractor to the Minister of Employment and Immigration and an independent review will be undertaken.

SANCTIONS:

If, on appeal, an independent review finds a failure of the contractor to comply with the criteria for implementation under the FCP, then the contractor may be excluded from bidding on future federal government contracts. Two companies have been subject to this sanction as of June 1991, and both were reinstated after introducing programs.

(SOURCE: Employment and Immigration Canada, "Employment Equity, Federal Contractors Program," n.d.)

Approximately 370 employers and 632,000 employees are affected by the Legislated Employment Equity Program (LEEP) under the Act, and approximately 1350 employers and over a million employees are covered by the Federal Contractors Program (FCP). (Employment and Immigration Canada, 1990: 2, 17). Although the 1986 legislation and regulations represented Canada's first move to make employment equity mandatory for private sector and quasi-public employers, there were precedents. Since the mid-1970s many private and public sector employers have undertaken various forms of employment equity on a voluntary basis, often under incentive programs of the provincial or federal governments, or under policies applied by governments to their own ministries, departments and agencies.

Employment equity legislation applying to most Ontario public and private sector employers has been promised by the Government of Ontario by the end of 1991 (*Globe and Mail,* May 16, 1991: B7). Some provincial public service domains, such as education and policing, have been subject to employment equity requirements. For example, under the Police Services Act (1991), Ontario police departments and agencies are required to implement employment equity, including numerical targets, to improve the employment opportunities and representation of the four designated groups.

Chapter 4 discusses in more detail the legislative and policy responses of governments to disadvantage in the Canadian workplace. The pay component of employment systems has been addressed for women under various provincial and federal pay equity statutes and government initiatives. Box 1.3 outlines how pay equity is complementary to, but distinct from, employment equity.

BOX 1.3
Employment Equity and Pay Equity: What's the Difference?

It is not unusual for people to confuse employment equity and pay equity. However, the two have distinctly different goals and processes. Here are some of the distinctions:

✓ EMPLOYMENT EQUITY

- covers all employment systems, such as recruitment, selection, training, development, promotion; all terms and conditions of employment including compensation, lay-off and disciplinary action

- addresses discrimination and disadvantage in employment affecting women, aboriginal peoples, racial minorities, and people with disabilities

✓ ...WHEREAS PAY EQUITY

- covers compensation only

- addresses discrimination in earnings affecting women

✓ EMPLOYMENT EQUITY

- applies to all jobs

- current and continuing

- is based on an analysis of unequal treatment, adverse impact, lack of accommodation and under-utilization (Chapter 5 explains these terms)

- typical activities include:
  work-force and availability analysis of representation and distribution

  employment systems review covering formal and informal policies, practices and decision-making, and organizational culture

  goals and action plans

  training and communication

  policy statements

  monitoring

...WHEREAS PAY EQUITY

- applies to jobs where females predominate, and where there are male comparator jobs within the employer's "establishment"

- generally a "one-time" analysis and remedy

- is based on an analysis of unequal treatment

- typical activities include:
  analysis of male and female predominance of jobs/job groups

  evaluation of jobs using a gender-neutral job evaluation plan

  comparison of pay lines or of comparator groups

  pay adjustments

Workplace Disadvantage as a Public Issue, and the Policy Response

During the seventies and eighties, and into the nineties, organizations representing designated groups, human rights commissions and associations, trade unions, the legal profession, and other stakeholders have pressed for legislation and regulations that would bring about equity in the workplace. In the early eighties the issues of inequality and systemic discrimination in employment were raised with growing urgency, and a number of public enquiries resulted in reports that documented the need for remedies and policy responses (e.g. House of Commons, 1980; Employment and Immigration, 1981; House of Commons, 1981; House of Commons, 1984; Abella, 1984).

These thorough investigations questioned the effectiveness of a human rights anti-discrimination approach, based on responding to complaints of individuals, and of voluntary employment equity, as ways to reduce disadvantage and discrimination in the workplace, and recommended mandatory affirmative action legislation with enforcement provisions. With these public enquiries, the reports they produced and the policy debates that followed, the problem of disadvantage in the workplace emerged as a public issue. The federal government's response — the Employment Equity Act and the Federal Contractors Program — reflects the principle that conditions of disadvantage in the workplace must be corrected.

The foundation document of Canadian employment equity policy was the 1984 report of the Royal Commission on Equality in Employment (Abella, 1984). In her landmark report, Judge Rosalie Silberman Abella, the one-person Commission, set out many of the principles that underlie employment equity policy, and which distinguish the Canadian approach from affirmative action as it has evolved in the United States. Abella's report does compare Canada and the U.S. and tries to cut employment equity in Canada loose from the damaging baggage of reaction against affirmative action in the U.S.(e.g. quotas and reverse discrimination). We discuss this further in Chapter 4. The principles that Judge Abella set out include the following:

- the purpose of employment equity is to correct the disadvantage and discrimination in employment that affects women, racial minorities, aboriginal peoples and persons with disabilities (see Box 1.4);
- employment equity should be mandatory for most employers, at least in the federal jurisdiction, and there should be appropriate arrangements to ensure compliance;
- diversity exists and will increase among groups in the workplace, and differences must be recognized and accommodated rather than ignored.

The Federal Contractors Program, announced five months after the Abella report was published, reflected both the spirit and the substance of many of Abella's most important recommendations. But the Progressive Conservative government's legislative response to the Report did not include many of the elements Abella and others had suggested were necessary if employment equity is to be effective — such as measures, targets or timetables that employers would be required to adhere to, specific guidelines for defining systemic discrimination, formal employee and designated group participation in planning, or the need for an enforcement agency and for sanctions in the event of failure to implement employment equity (House of Commons, 1985). The sound principles and analysis presented in Abella's report were compromised by the political process.

BOX 1.4:
The Designated Groups for Employment Equity

PEOPLE WITH DISABILITIES

For purposes of reporting under the Employment Equity Act, Employment and Immigration Canada defines persons with disabilities as persons who:
- have any persistent physical, mental, psychiatric, sensory or learning impairment;
- consider themselves to be, or believe that an employer or a potential employer would be likely to consider them to be, disadvantaged in employment by reason of an impairment; and
- identify themselves to an employer, or agree to be identified by an employer, as persons with disabilities.

People with disabilities make up approximately 13% of Canada's population. The terms "impairment," "disability," and "handicap" should be distinguished from each other. The concept of disability implies that a person's "prospects of securing, training and advancing in suitable employment are substantially reduced as a result of a duly recognized physical or mental impairment." Impairment refers to a medical condition or loss or absence of bodily structure or function that can lead to a disability. A handicap arises for a person who has a disability when the workplace or other setting poses barriers that exclude that person from full participation, or hinder the person from attaining their goals. A handicap, then, is not a condition of a person, but of the environment within which the person must function.

RACIAL (VISIBLE) MINORITIES

Under the Employment Equity Act, visible minorities are defined as persons "other than aboriginal peoples, who are, because of their race or colour, in a visible minority in Canada," and/or who identify themselves to their employer as such. Examples may include Blacks and persons of Chinese, Japanese, Korean, Filipino, Indo-Pakistani, West Asian, or Southeast Asian ancestry. About 6% of Canada's population are members of racial minorities.

PERSONS OF ABORIGINAL ANCESTRY

Under the Employment Equity Act, aboriginal persons are defined as persons who identify themselves to the employer as Indian, Inuit or Metis. Aboriginal people comprise about 2.8% of Canada's population.

WOMEN

Women make up about 51% of Canada's population. It is important to note that women may also fall into any of the other employment equity categories and therefore be doubly or triply disadvantaged. Employers' work-force audits should report separately on the designated group status of male and female employees. About 12% of women in the Canadian labour force are also members of another designated group.

(SOURCES: Employment and Immigration Canada, *Employment Equity Act and Reporting Requirements*, Minister of Supply and Services Canada, 1986: sec. B., Glossary and Technical Paper No.2; Abt Associates of Canada, "Evaluation of the Legislated Employment Equity Program and the Federal Contractors Program, Methodology Report," November 1990, 40-41; Employment and Immigration Canada, "Employment Equity Act, Annual Report to Parliament," 1988, p. 27 and 1990, 29.)

The government's response to the Report focused on its "technical" aspects — the reporting of data and formal reviews of employment systems — rather than upon outcomes, change and consultation. Procedures and structures for assuring consultation in employment equity planning and implementation are not required, and designated group involvement is not even mentioned, although the importance of such participation was raised repeatedly during the Commons debates on Bill C-62 (House of Commons, 1985). However, while we are critical of the limitations of the legislation, we believe that the principles that underlie the Canadian approach to employment equity, as developed in the Abella report, are fundamentally sound, and provide a solid foundation for realizing our national goals for equality in employment.

Employment Equity Goals

In reflecting on the goals Canadian policy is attempting to achieve through employment equity, our starting point, like Judge Abella's, is the historical and current experience of disadvantage and discrimination in the workplace and labour market faced by Canadians because of their gender, disability, race and colour. Clearly there is great variation among women in regard to employment experience, as is true of the other three designated groups. However, we know that in the aggregate, members of groups designated for employment equity experience disproportionate disadvantages, such as higher unemployment rates and lower pay for the same educational attainment, when compared with the male, able-bodied, white population (Abella, 1984). Chapter 2 examines evidence for disadvantage in employment faced by these groups, and some of the dynamics of discrimination that lead to disadvantage.

The legislative purpose of employment equity contained in the Act, cited at the beginning of this chapter, provides a concise statement of the goals of employment equity. But we need a more concrete and complete understanding of what equity in the workplace would look like. We turn now to a discussion and critique of some of the typical formulations of goals for employment equity.

Are "Good Numbers" a Sign of Equality?

Some may define equality as "quantity": the presence, representation and distribution of the designated groups within an employer's work force. From this perspective, a compelling measure of inequality occurs when there are "zeros" — where no designated group members are present in certain jobs or at higher levels of the organization. Similarly, if women, racial minorities, aboriginal peoples and people with disabilities are present only in certain occupations or, as is likely, at lower levels of the organization, then we are also likely to perceive inequality.

However, to focus on *presence* as the goal of employment equity may be to treat the symptom (and symbol) of disadvantage and discrimination, not the cause. We know that without access, without the opportunity to "be there," members of the designated groups cannot succeed economically in our society. They cannot experience job satisfaction, career development and mobility. Neither will they be able to participate in decision-making or wield influence and power if they are not a part of organizational life in Canadian society. Yet presence alone does not necessarily translate into employment opportunity, power, and influence. Simply put, numbers are a necessary but not sufficient measure of equality — it is not just a matter of increasing the numbers and changing the distribution of designated groups, but also a matter of changing the systems and culture of the workplace. Access to employment opportunities is but one focus for change.

Without change in the composition of the work force, and in particular the composition of groups in positions of power and decision-making authority, there is not likely to be fundamental change in the allocation of organizational resources. However, to be present but unable to progress in organizational careers is not equality; nor is mere survival in a hostile environment. Equality is not a reality in an organization that marginalizes people by its insensitivity to matters of disability, work and family responsibilities, or cultural and religious differences, or by biased communications and truncated networks of information and professional relationships, or by tolerating racism. No matter how we shuffle the players, unless the systems and organizational structures of decision-making are fundamentally changed in order to reflect the life experiences of designated groups, we will be forcing disabled persons, racial minorities, aboriginal peoples and women who seek access and opportunity to conform to an organization that remains dominated by white, male, able-bodied values, norms, interests and perspectives. We will simply force the designated groups to change, not the organizations. This will not lead to true equality in employment.

Envisioning Equality

It is not easy to define equality or to describe what an equitable workplace would be like. It is often easier to be specific about what constitutes discrimination and disadvantage — at least in regard to particular employment practices. For example, we know that requiring police officer applicants to be at least five feet ten inches in height has an adverse and disproportionate impact on women and people of Asian ancestry. Yet we know that employment equity is more than identifying and changing such practices. Employment equity aims to take a comprehensive, holistic view of organizations as managers of human resources on society's behalf, and as a key part of the opportunity structure for individuals and groups in our society. Thus in order to take action, get results and evaluate these results, we need to know what we want to achieve regarding an organization's management of human resources. This is not an easy task as it requires us to envision equality. If we look to government policy and the human rights case law for clarification and direction we are likely to remain uncertain about the goals of employment equity, at least in an operational sense. The following examples illustrate this.

"Employment Equity: A Guide for Employers," a current and concisely titled pamphlet of the Canada Employment and Immigration Commission (CEIC), the federal government department overseeing the implementation of both LEEP and the FCP, provides the following answer to the question, "What is employment equity?"

> Simply put, employment equity means ensuring that all job applicants and employees have a fair chance in the workplace. It is achieved when no person is denied employment opportunities or benefits for reasons unrelated to ability.

This innocuous definition is no more than a statement of non-discrimination. Fortunately, CEIC's "Employment Equity: A Guide for Employers" (1987), addressed to firms covered by LEEP and FCP, moves the definition forward step by step. In the Introduction to the Guide it is said that

> Employment Equity is an action-oriented approach that identifies the existence of specific employment barriers to certain groups of people and provides a number of practical and creative remedies (p. 1).

Here we begin to understand that employment equity is related to employment barriers and remedial initiatives. In the Guide's Glossary we find a more expansive definition of employment equity:

> a comprehensive planning process adopted by an employer to: identify and eliminate discrimination in the organization's employment procedures and policies; remedy the effects of past discrimination; and ensure appropriate representation of designated groups throughout an employer's work force. (p. 3)

This definition is more helpful: it talks about eliminating as well as identifying current employment barriers, it addresses the remedial purpose of employment equity, and it includes attention to representation and distribution. However, it does not talk about the need to prevent barriers in the future. The entry in the Glossary that explains the "employment equity plan" appears to equate equality goals with quantity and measurement. A plan contains

> the employer's goals, timetables and strategies for improving the representation of each of the designated groups in various occupations according to availability and qualifications. Plans also assign clear responsibility and accountability for each activity, and describe the monitoring and evaluation procedures to be used. (p.4)

Numerical representation as the prime goal of employment equity is also implied in the sole compliance focus of the federal Employment Equity Act: the annual statistical reporting of work-force data. The FCP broadens this focus by including "non-numerical" goals as a component of goal setting, along with employment systems review, special measures and the establishment of a favourable climate. (See Boxes 1.1 and 1.2).

If we look to the case law for help in defining our goals for employment equity we again find a variety of definitions with differing emphases. A 1989 Ontario human rights board of inquiry, *Roberts vs. Ontario (Ministry of Health)*, examined at length the concept of affirmative action, including differing definitions, concluding that an "open" definition is most beneficial:

> A more comprehensive definition of affirmative action might be cast as follows: 'any program or policy that attempts to assist disadvantaged groups improve their position.' ... The concept of 'disadvantage' should be left open so that it can accommodate the needs of groups which may emerge in the future as we peel more and more layers off the surface of discrimination. Much the same can be said about the mechanisms adopted to reduce disadvantage. This will be a process of trial and error, and we would do well to permit a wide diversity of programs and policies as we

experiment in determining how best to alleviate the disparities.
(10 CHRR D/6359, para.45084)

Although we agree in principle with the Board's evolutionary notion of how to perceive disadvantage, again we are left without a clear understanding of what employment equity aims to achieve.

By contrast, the Supreme Court of Canada in the 1987 Action Travail des Femmes (ATF) human rights case *(Canadian National Railway Co. vs. Canadian Human Rights Commission [Action Travail])* offers the following description:

> An employment equity programme thus is designed to work in three ways. First, by countering the cumulative effects of systemic discrimination, such a programme renders further discrimination pointless. ... Secondly, by placing members of the group that had previously been excluded into the heart of the workplace and by allowing them to prove ability on the job, the employment equity scheme addresses the attitudinal problem of stereotyping.... Thirdly, an employment equity programme helps to create what has been termed a 'critical mass' of the previously excluded group in the work place. *(Action Travail des Femmes v. C. N. Rail.* [1987], 40 D.L.R. [4th] 193 [S.C.C.].)

The Supreme court's notion of employment equity is helpful because it is specific, addressing what the employer is to achieve and how. Nevertheless, employers and other equality seekers might well say, "These definitions help, but I still do not understand what employment equity is. What is it supposed to achieve? Tell me, what am I supposed to do to make it happen?"

Three Goals of Employment Equity
We propose the following three-fold statement of goals for employment equity action, based on the Supreme Court's statement of purpose:
  1. to *eliminate* current employment barriers caused by discrimination and disadvantage,
  2. to *remedy* the effects of past disadvantage and discrimination, and *prevent* future disadvantage and discrimination, and
  3. to *improve* the representation, access and distribution of designated groups in the work force and labour market.

1. Eliminate Current Employment Barriers   Employment equity aims to eliminate discriminatory barriers currently experienced by women, aboriginal peoples, racial minorities and people with disabilities, both as employees and as prospective employees. These barriers may include unequal treatment, inhospitable organizational cultures, organizational practices applied to everyone that negatively affect members of designated groups (differential adverse impact), and the lack of accommodation of diversity in employment, policies and practices, whether these are formal or informal.

2. Remedy Past and Prevent Future Discrimination and Disadvantage   Employment equity aims to remedy the effects of past disadvantage and discrimination, and prevent future disadvantage and discrimination that disabled people, racial minorities, aboriginal peoples and women experience or are likely to experience in employment or in gaining access to employment.

3. Improve Numerical Representation (Access and Distribution) Employment equity aims to provide job and career opportunities so that aboriginal peoples, women, racial minorities and people with disabilities are better represented and distributed throughout an employer's work force and the Canadian labour market.

BOX 1.5
Examples of the Goals of Employment Equity from Action Travail des Femmes vs. CN Rail

In 1987 the Supreme Court of Canada upheld the earlier decision of a Canadian Human Rights Tribunal which ordered CN Rail to implement an employment equity program related to women in certain non-traditional, blue-collar jobs at the CN rail yards in Montreal.

To illustrate the goals of employment equity, this decision yields some concrete examples of changes an employment equity program may introduce.

ELIMINATE CURRENT EMPLOYMENT BARRIERS

• **Unequal treatment**
-in selection, discontinue the physical tests required by foremen and others of female candidates yet not required of male candidates, such as the lifting of a brakeshoe with one arm

-employment office to give female candidates complete, specific and objective information on the real requirements of non-traditional positions

-direct foremen that no one shall be rejected on the basis of sex

-continue to implement measures to eliminate sexual harassment and discrimination in the workplace

• **Adverse impact**

-in selection, discontinue the use of the Bennett test (except for apprentice positions) and all mechanical aptitude tests that have a negative impact on women and are not warranted by the aptitude requirements of the position being applied for

-discontinue the requirement for welding experience for all entry level positions (except apprentice positions)

• **Lack of accommodation of diversity**

-no accommodation issues were found requiring remedy

REMEDY THE EFFECTS OF PAST BARRIERS

-undertake an information and publicity campaign inviting women in particular to apply for non-traditional positions

PREVENT FUTURE BARRIERS

-measures to eliminate sexual harassment

NUMERICAL REPRESENTATION

-hire at least one woman for every four non-traditional positions filled in the future, over each quarterly period, until the desired objective of having 13% of non-traditional positions filled by women is achieved.

(SOURCE: *Action Travail des Femmes vs. C.N. Rail.* [1987], 40 D.L.R. [4th] 193 [S.C.C.])

In thinking about how these three goals are realized in the workplace, it is useful to consider two kinds of outcomes:

1. **Results outcomes**, which focus on the changes we want to achieve in employment systems, culture and numbers (such as those illustrated in Box 1.5 and further discusssed in Chapter 12.); and
2. **Process outcomes**, which focus on the process of change itself, and which produce the desired results.

Perhaps the processes we develop to work toward our employment equity goals are as important as the results. Enhancing support and minimizing resistance, involving people and their differing experiences and perspectives rather than excluding them and forcing change on them, may be approaches to change that explicitly recognize diversity in the workplace, and use it to advantage.

The Employment Equity Process

In this book we present the case for a dual focus on results and change processes, combining a discussion of *what* we do with considerations of *how, when* and *with whom* we undertake change projects. We believe that an employment equity program cannot be viewed in isolation from the employment equity **process**: how we implement a program has a significant impact on the results we get. At the end of this chapter we show how a process model relates to the usual elements of an employment equity program, but first, let us briefly assess the results to date in Canada under the legislative, regulatory and policy frameworks currently in place.

Research on Employment Equity Activity: What Can We Learn?

The Canadian employment equity policy framework has been in place since 1986; this is not long enough to observe and evaluate its results. The legislation provides for a review of the Act in 1991, and a large scale evaluation of the LEEP and FCP initiatives is currently in progress. Until reports on the evaluation and review become available there is very limited information upon which to base an assessment; hence our suggestions are tentative.

The FCP regulations contain some elements of a mandatory approach to employment equity. Voluntary employment equity has been permitted since 1978 in the federal jurisdiction, and even longer in the provincial domain, but few employers initiated programs until they were required to do so. From 1978 until March 1983, consultants from the Canadian Employment and Immigration Commission approached approximately 900 firms to encourage them to sign agreements to undertake voluntary affirmative action programs. Only 34 employers signed, despite the fact that the commitment was voluntary, and there were no sanctions for non-fulfillment (Agòcs, 1986: 154).

There is little research evidence regarding impacts of voluntary programs, and virtually none regarding the linkages between specific employment equity measures and outcomes in the form of increased rates of representation and retention. The reporting requirements of the Employment Equity Act do not cover employment equity activities by employers. There is also an absence of evidence on how to assess and improve the workplace culture for the designated groups.

Some indications about employer response to the FCP regulations are available in findings of a survey of 99 Ontario employers participating in the Federal Contractors Program. These employers showed little employment equity activity six to eight months after the regulations were introduced (Agócs, 1989). Only 17 of the 99 companies indicated that they had an employment equity program. Only 13 companies had started voluntary programs before the FCP took effect, despite almost ten years of federal efforts to encourage voluntary affirmative action. However the FCP, as a mandatory program, was evidently having an impact: 50 companies were starting or planning to start employment equity initiatives.

Respondents who reported having employment equity programs already in place were engaged in very few specific activities, and these were not the kinds of projects that could be expected to lead to changes in organizational structures and cultures. Their efforts were devoted primarily to developing policy statements, reviewing recruitment and selection practices for barriers to women, and appointing someone to be responsible for employment equity, which are among the requirements of the FCP. But only one company had set goals and timetables, and eleven had employment equity committees. Few employers kept counts of the representation in their work force of designated groups other than women, and there was very little effort to develop initiatives for people with disabilities, racial minorities or aboriginal peoples. Two other investigations of Canadian employment equity activity confirm the observation of a low level of commitment by employers in the late 80s, and very little initiative in relation to any group except women (Jain and Hackett, 1989; Blakely and Harvey, 1988).

Given the low level of employment equity activity among employers it is not surprising that there has been little change in the representation of the four designated groups since 1987, the first year covered by employers' reports submitted under the Employment Equity Act. Data contained in the 1988, 1989 and 1990 compilations of employers' reports filed under the Act show consistent patterns of inequality among the federally regulated workforce, and even the slight improvements that occurred are partially due to increases in self-identification by employees who are members of designated groups. The data show:

- **Marked underrepresentation of aboriginal peoples and people with disabilities in federal sector employment relative to their presence in the Canadian labour force.** Aboriginal and disabled employees numbered only one third of their respective representation levels in the Canadian labour force in 1987. By 1989 people with disabilities improved their representation slightly but some of the change was due to more self-identification. There was very little improvement for aboriginal peoples.
- **Marked underrepresentation of aboriginal peoples, people with disabilities and racial minorities in decision making positions, with women from these groups virtually absent from upper management.** For example, in 1987, of a total of 4465 permanent full-time upper level managers working in federally regulated firms, 1 was an aboriginal woman and 11 were aboriginal men; 3 were women with disabilities and 67 were men with disabilities; and 10 were racial minority women and 107 were racial minority men. By 1989 the number of women who were also members of the other designated groups had increased by 5, although the total number of employees classified as upper level managers had grown by almost 1000.
- **Concentration of women in a narrow range of jobs,** and even higher levels of concentration for women who are also members of another designated group. For example, in the federal sector as a whole, 62% of women were clerical workers in 1987 and 1989.
- **Absence of women from decision-making positions even in settings where women are the majority of the workforce.** For example, in banking women held about 73% of all full time jobs in 1987 and 72 % in 1989, but only 3% of upper level management jobs in 1987 and 6 % in 1989. In the federal sector as a whole, one tenth of one percent of women were upper level managers, compared with 1.3% of

men in 1987; in 1989 the proportions in upper level management were 0.17% of women and 1.51% of men.
- **A substantial salary gap between women and men in the white able-bodied population and in all designated groups.** For example, in banking, women made 56% of men's average salary for full time work in 1987 and 58% in 1989. Women who are also aboriginal, or disabled, or minorities, are paid less than all women and less than men who are members of these designated groups. For example, in 1987, aboriginal women were paid 10% less that other women working full time, and only 73% of the average annual salary for aboriginal men; aboriginal men were paid 10% less than all men. By 1989 aboriginal women's salaries had dropped slightly relative to all women, and aboriginal men's salaries dropped slightly compared to those of men's.

(Employment and Immigration, 1988: 30, 33, 36, 40, 42, 50; Table 4.1; 1989, Table 4.2; 1990: 29, 33, 38, 40, 48,; Table 5.1, 5.4, 6.4).

Research on Affirmative Action in the U.S.: What Can We Learn?

The United States has had roughly a quarter century of experience with affirmative action. There is a substantial research literature assessing the impacts of contract compliance under Executive Order 11246, and of court ordered remedies under Title VII of the Civil Rights Act (1964), on the representation of women, Blacks, Asians and Hispanics in the workplace. There is also a research literature that assesses the relative importance of various program elements to the effectiveness of affirmative action programs. Both bodies of research are instructive for employment equity in Canada. The U.S. studies suggest that the following are among the essential elements of an effective affirmative action strategy that gets results. These results take the form of increased representation of women and Blacks in jobs and sectors where they have been underrepresented, and a lessening of the wage gap relative to white males:

1. Top Management Commitment and Accountability of Decision Makers for Results   An affirmative action or employment equity initiative is often officially launched with a public statement of commitment by top management. If this symbolism is backed up by allocation of resources, systematic monitoring and assignment of responsibility and accountability to line management, and on-going public support of efforts to bring about change by top management, the employment equity program is more likely to be effective in getting results (Shaeffer and Lynton, 1977; Marino, 1982; Vernon-Gerstanfeld and Burke, 1985). Hitt and Keats (1984: 215) found "commitment from higher administration" to be the strongest predictor of the effectiveness of affirmative action programs, followed by "receptive attitude" among key personnel, credibility of programs and officers, and provision of resources.

2. Mandatory Policy Framework with Effective Enforcement and Sanctions Studies of the impact of class action litigation and contract compliance have shown that regulation and enforcement have prompted employers to act (O'Farrell and Harlan, 1984). Results have included increases in the employment and integration of Black males (Ashenfelter and Heckman, 1976; Leonard, 1984c), reduction in women's quit rates (Osterman, 1982), and gains in numbers of Hispanic, Asian and American Indian males in white collar and skilled jobs (Leonard, 1984b). These effects have not been accompanied by depressed productivity or profits (Leonard, 1984a), and they are augmented in growing establishments (Leonard, 1984b). Johnson and Salon (1986) suggest that a combination of pay and employment equity policies, effectively implemented, could reduce the gender gap in wages.

A number of studies have confirmed the importance of effective compliance audits and sanctions in improving the representation and compensation of the designated groups in firms subject to affirmative action enforcement in the U.S. For example, Beller (1979) found that women's earnings increased the most when the Title VII legislation was more stringently enforced, and when there was a higher probability of an investigation. Another study by Beller (1984) found that contract compliance regulations increased the likelihood of women being employed in male-dominated occupations. Studies by Leonard (1983, 1984c) and the U.S. Department of Labour (1984) reported that the representation and career progression of minorities and women increased more rapidly in contractor firms than in those that were not contractors, and in firms that had been subject to compliance reviews as compared with firms that had not. Leonard (1983) also found that employers that had set affirmative action hiring goals had actually hired more women and minorities than those that had not set goals. Osterman (1982) reports that penalties and compliance reviews have the effect of reducing women's quit rates.

3. Integrating Employment Equity/Affirmative Action into Human Resource Management A large number of studies have confirmed the discriminatory impact on the designated groups of many common and customary personnel decision making practices. Decisions about hiring, performance appraisal, job assignment, compensation, and promotion may create and perpetuate discrimination (Billingsley and Muszynski, 1985; Henry and Ginzberg, 1985, Hitt and Keats, 1984; Bielby and Baron, 1984; Treiman and Hartmann, 1981; Roos and Reskin, 1984). This research suggests the importance of building equity into decisions across the entire spectrum of human resource policies and practices, and of diagnosing and removing the systemic discrimination that is too often built into such decision making.

There is also research evidence that effective government policies to reduce discrimination affect personnel decision-making at the level of the workplace. This has resulted in more equity-conscious human resource practices such as initiating minority recruitment programs, and using the performance appraisal process to hold managers accountable for meeting corporate affirmative action goals (Freeman, 1981). Gottschalk (1990) found that the gap in earnings between men and women, and between whites and racial minorities, narrowed as a result of the anti-discrimination programs and the investment in human capital that took place in the U.S. in the 60s, 70s and 80s.

In Chapters 2 and 5 we discuss in greater detail the meaning of discrimination, how it can be part of human resource management systems, and how it results in disadvantage for members of the designated groups in the workplace. Throughout the book the reader will find suggestions as to how to make human resource management practices more equitable.

Research on Organizational Change: What Can We Learn?
As we will discuss in detail in Chapter 6, employment equity is an example of large-scale organizational change that depends on the involvement of employees at all levels of the organization, the associations that represent them, members of the designated groups, and community organizations that work in their behalf. Research in a variety of contexts for organizational change, including the introduction of new technology, as well as employee involvement and other approaches designed to increase employee participation in decision-making, suggests that arrangements to ensure widespread involvement of stakeholders in the change process are important ingredients for success. This is particularly true when a change project is a large scale and complex intervention whose goals are rather vague, where there is an absence of consensus about goals, and where there is likely to be substantial resistance to the change (e.g. Covin and Kilmann, 1988; Kanter, 1983; Nightingale, 1982; Pettigrew, 1985). The implementation of employment equity is certainly this kind of change project (Agócs, 1992).

Expectations and Accomplishments — Why the Gap?

As we have noted, currently available evidence suggests that results of Canadian employment equity policy and implementation so far have been limited, and many individuals and organizations representing designated groups have been disappointed in the rate of progress. There may be several reasons why progress to date in improving the representation, distribution and compensation of women, aboriginal peoples, people with disabilities, and racial minorities in the workplace has been slow.

First, employment equity involves large-scale change in the ways people are managed and treated in the workplace. Changes of this magnitude take time — case studies of large projects have suggested that five years is a reasonable minimum to institutionalize new patterns of behaviour on a large scale (Kanter, 1983; Pettigrew, 1985).

Second, employment equity change is complex, involving many interdependent activities and elements that mutually support and reinforce each other. For example, senior managers usually move into their positions as a result of a sequence of promotions within an organization. Employment equity prompts a reassessment of this traditional practice. If there are few members of designated groups in developmental positions at lower levels of management, there is no "feeder pool" from which to draw top executives who are women, people with disabilities, aboriginal peoples, or racial minorities. In order to improve the representativeness of senior management and attain a "critical mass" of designated group members in decision making, the organization might undertake management development, fast tracking, mentoring, and other measures to prepare members of designated groups to move into executive roles, in addition to recruiting them externally.

Third, Canadian employment equity legislation and regulations have shortcomings that may limit the results that can be expected. Political compromises occurred when the recommendations of the Abella Report were translated into the Employment Equity Act, and the resulting policy and implementation arrangements do not provide for effective enforcement and sanctions when employers fail to implement employment equity measures (Bevan, 1987). The Federal Contractors Program does provide for compliance reviews and sanctions, but its coverage is limited, as noted in Box 1.2. Many Canadian organizations are still operating within an environment in which employment equity is a voluntary activity, and we have seen that the level of employment equity initiative is very low when employers are not required to act.

Fourth, we believe that a major reason for limited results from employment equity so far is that the implementation process — the practice of employment equity — has not received adequate thought and attention. In particular, we argue that thinking about employment equity as a form of organizational change will make the implementation process more effective. In the chapters that follow, we suggest that employment equity, whether it is undertaken voluntarily or because of legal or government requirements, is more likely to get results if we develop an implementation process that is:

- **strategic** — planned, goal-oriented, and based on clearly articulated values;
- **participatory** — involving all the key stakeholders throughout the process by providing ways and means for them to contribute and be rewarded;

- **open and accountable** — so that those responsible for managing people and using organizational resources act on the principle that employment equity is a priority;
- **based on a sound analysis of how organizational change happens,** how and why change is resisted, and how resistance can be effectively managed, and
- **based on a sound diagnosis of the organization's employment equity issues** that rests on accurate and relevant information, and on a clear understanding of the nature of discrimination and disadvantage in the workplace, especially from the perspectives of those who have experienced it — members of the designated groups.

Employment Equity: Another Approach

In this chapter we have introduced the reader to employment equity, its purpose and goals, and the tasks and processes of implementation. We outlined the generally accepted ways of thinking about employment equity policy and practice. After reviewing experience with implementation to date, we concluded that the results have been disappointing. Briefly we examined what the research literature tells us about the results of American experience with affirmative action through contract compliance policies and court ordered quotas.

We also looked at implications for employment equity of research on the introduction and maintenance of large-scale organizational change. Employment equity practitioners attempt to change the structure and culture of the workplace in significant ways. There is much to be learned from experience with other forms of organizational change such as introducing new technology, developing more participative decision-making and management structures, or implementing employee involvement or customer/client service programs. In this book we draw on theory and research about affirmative action and organizational change, to suggest an approach to the change process that depends on stakeholder participation to strategically plan and implement employment equity.

Stakeholders are those groups and individuals affected by employment equity change. They may include:

- the designated groups,
- equality seekers and special interest or advocacy groups who may be external or internal to the organization,
- employees who are or will become the co-workers of the designated groups, especially in work places or work groups undergoing integration for the first time,
- representatives of employees, including union officials and leaders of employee associations,
- all levels of management including top executives, middle managers, supervisors and forepersons,
- the staff support functions such as human resources, strategic planning, public relations, information systems and legal counsel, and
- government officials, including employment equity compliance officers, policy-makers, consultants and educators.

Simply put, we suggest that employment equity can be effectively implemented through a planned process of organizational change that involves stakeholders in all the conventional employment equity activities. The traditional ingredients of employment equity — the policy statement, work-force analysis, employment systems review and goal setting — can be situated within an organizational change framework. We invite you to think about and implement the usual elements of employment equity in this new way in order to bring about effective change in an organization in ways defined by stakeholders. In Chapter 6 we discuss stakeholder participation in employment equity in terms of the dynamic processes of conflict and collaboration, bargaining and negotiation, leading to identification of shared interests and action to achieve results.

Our central belief is that employment equity must achieve results that are meaningful to the work life and experience of those groups who are ultimately to benefit from it. To do less will not fulfill the promise of employment equity. Moreover, to do less is likely to result in a perception of failure, regardless of the good faith efforts, energy and resources the employer commits to employment equity.

Women, people with disabilities, racial minorities and aboriginal peoples are the "designated groups" for employment equity. Clearly they must be part of the process and have a say in how results are defined and assessed. Only if they perceive and experience progress and authentic outcomes of employment policies, practices and decision-making will employment equity become a reality. They must perceive and experience a work environment and organizational culture that includes them and acts to value their contributions — a workplace that does not exclude, marginalize, stereotype or stigmatize them for their gender, ability, racial and cultural differences, or confine them to short-term and static roles. They must be able to work, contribute, make decisions, develop and progress in an atmosphere where the diversity they represent is valued and accepted as an integral part of organizational life.

The designated groups are not the only organizational stakeholders who must become part of the process of change. Without the involvement of the line mangers, unions, employees and human resources practitioners in diagnosing what needs to change and how, there will be active or passive resistance, and the resulting employment equity initiatives may not be appropriate and effective. The involvement of these particular stakeholders is critical in the identification and implementation of realistic solutions to real and perceived barriers to designated group participation and opportunity in the organization. Without their input we are likely to see a backlash and a further marginalization and stigmatization of the designated groups as the employment equity process moves beyond its initial stages.

We believe that most stakeholder groups will benefit when the organization undergoes a process of employment equity change. In Chapter 3 we discuss the benefits of employment equity to employers facing a changing demographic composition in their labour markets or client or customer populations. Employment equity is part of the momentum towards more progressive approaches to managing people and organizations, a more "rights seeking" environment in society and the workplace, and a legal and constitutional framework increasingly supportive of equality.

Equity Program versus Organizational Change

Box 1.6 compares and contrasts the conventional program approach with a stakeholder organizational change process approach. We believe that an integration of both approaches is needed to achieve results.

Box 1.6

Comparison of Conventional and Stakeholder Organizational Change Approaches to Employment Equity

PROGRAM **Conventional Approach**	PROCESS **Stakeholder Organizational Change Approach**
Policy statement	Securing commitment and resources through a "triggering" process
Assignment of top management responsibility	Identification of change agents and stakeholders and their interests
Data collection and analysis — work-force audit — availability analysis — employment systems review	Stakeholder diagnosis of — systems — culture — numbers using various sources of information, including designated group members' experience
Training and awareness	Education and structures to deal with resistance
Setting centralized goals and timetables	Developing a goal-oriented change strategy — predominantly decentralized, with centralized support available
Special measures and accommodation	Initiatives designed to change organizational structures and culture, with attention to integration and "critical mass"
Reporting	Organizational learning and diffusion as an outcome of monitoring and evaluation

The current and what we will call the conventional program-oriented approach to employment equity has several characteristics:

- It is top management focused and led.
- It is oriented to the completion of certain specific tasks, and these tasks are conceptualized as occurring in a linear sequence.
- Each task is seen as a discrete activity to complete, so the next task marks a new beginning, not part of an ongoing process, or a cycle that needs to be repeated.
- The tasks are corporate or organization-wide, and appear to be primarily initiated by top management and centralized in their implementation.
- The program of employment equity is data driven, and specifically driven by statistical or numerical data reflecting utilization rates of the designated groups.
- It is assumed that interests are shared by managers, employees, unions and others within the organization, and that everyone wants what is best for the organization as a whole.
- Above all, the conventional approach reflects a rational, optimizing model of decision-making. This decision-making model assumes that there is a single, well defined goal to be maximized; that all options are identified and clearly defined; that the outcomes desired by all parties to the decision are clear, constant, and held in common; and that the decisions made will maximize these desired outcomes (Robbins, 1988:64-65). The implication is that once top management decides to undertake employment equity or is required by government or the courts to do so, then goals are defined, roles are assigned and "technology" is applied to produce results. A rational problem-solving approach, based on quantitative data analysis, is assumed to convince organizational participants that change is needed and in the organization's best interests, and they are expected to simply carry out decisions made at a higher level.Often this approach is supplemented with some of the human relations and organizational development interventions, which may include:

- awareness and sensitivity training for managers and employees;
- attitude and behavioural change projects directed to the designated groups, such as assertiveness training or career planning for women;
- analysis of the forces creating resistance to employment equity, with training given to help overcome these impediments to change by modifying the attitudes of those who are resisting.

These interventions complement the rational-optimizing approach in that they are top-down and aimed at creating a consensus on goals and actions. Training and other attitude change activities occur only if initiated and sanctioned by management, although frequently management is not targeted for these interventions.

The stakeholder approach to organizational change proposed in this book is not intended to wholly replace more typical ways of thinking about employment equity, but rather to supplement them and to emphasize how we go about the process of employment equity change. We are suggesting that attention to the change **process** is just as important as the completion of the tasks that make up an employment equity **program**. Our approach has these features:

- Elements of an employment equity program are not necessarily sequential, although some activities may need to build on others. The change process clearly is not linear. Often, several things are best done at the same time or in a coordinated fashion to capitalize on synergies.
- The change process may be most realistically portrayed as a dynamic cycle or web. It is messy: there is no lock-step sequence or blueprint to follow, but there are principles to guide the process of change.
- Change is usually a continuing process, without a clear beginning or end.
- Successful organizational change initiatives are often characterized after the fact as corporate, centralized, or organization-wide. Yet during the process of development, change is often carried out in an *ad hoc*, localized, experimental fashion (using pilot projects), until success can

be demonstrated and then publicized. Change seems to develop and thrive in small pockets on the periphery of the organization, where innovation and unconventional approaches are allowed.

- Information and a good diagnosis of the problems are needed, but enormous amounts of detailed statistical data are not required in order to develop and implement solutions. A useful information base consists of qualitative data concerning how things work or do not work well, combined with a limited amount of good quantitative data. Information about perceptions and experience are at least as valuable to the analysis and evaluation of change as statistical data. Quantitative data may be especially useful after the fact to justify and explain what was done or accomplished, and why.

- Above all, this approach is political: it recognizes a diversity of interests, perspectives and needs at play in an organization. It sees the introduction of employment equity change as raising fundamental issues of power, with inevitable conflict and concerns about the distribution — or redistribution — of opportunities and resources that are perceived as either scarce, unconditionally "deserved" by those who now have them, or both.

- Therefore, a stakeholder approach to the change process is characterized as an array of tasks and activities that are set in motion in various parts of the organization once change agents are able to secure sponsorship, resources, and the freedom to try new things. It involves a process of negotiation, bargaining, and conflict among differing interests, and the development of cooperation and coalitions among shared interests.

Conclusion

As the Report of the 1984 Royal Commission on Equality in Employment (the Abella Report) said, "employment equity won't happen unless we make it happen." Our concern is how to make it happen. Based on our own experience and on research we propose a different way of thinking about, planning, implementing and assessing employment equity change because, like other employment equity practitioners, human resources professionals, researchers, managers and equality seekers, we want our efforts, energy and resources to result in enduring, positive employment benefits for aboriginal peoples, racial minorities, people with disabilities and women. We want Canadian employers and unions to develop the insight, knowledge and competencies they require in order to respond appropriately to the demographic, legal, social and human resources management changes occurring now and in the future. We believe that the designated groups, employment equity and human resources practitioners, managers, union officials, co-workers, government bureaucrats and the other employment equity stakeholders have much to offer to the process of employment equity planning, diagnosis, problem-solving, decision-making, communication, education and evaluation.

REFERENCES

Abella, Rosalie Silberman. *Equality in Employment: A Royal Commission Report.* Ottawa: Minister of Supply and Services, 1984.

Agócs, Carol. "Affirmative Action, Canadian Style: A Reconnaissance," *Canadian Public Policy*, 12, 1986, 148-62.

Agócs, Carol. "Employment Equity Activity Among Federal Contractors in Ontario." *Industrial Relations Issues for the 1990s* Proceedings of the 26th Conference of the Canadian Industrial Relations Association, Quebec, 1989.

Agócs, Carol. "Implementing Employment Equity: The Role of Participation in Organizational Change." In William Lafferty and Eliezer Rosenstein (eds.), *International Handbook of Participation in Organizations*, vol. III. New York: Oxford University Press, 1992, Ch. 1.

Ashenfelter, Orley, and James Heckman. "Measuring the Effect of an Anti-Discrimination Program." In O. Ashenfelter and James Blum (eds.), *Evaluating the Effects of Social Programs.* Princeton: Princeton University Press, 1976, 46-89.

Beller, Andrea. "The Impact of Equal Opportunity Laws on the Male-Female Earnings Differential." In Cynthia Lloyd, E. Andrews and C. Gilroy, *Women in the Labor Market.* New York: Columbia University Press, 1979.

Beller, Andrea. "Trends in Occupational Segregation by Sex and Race, 1960-1981." In Barbara Reskin (ed.), *Sex Segregation in the Workplace: Trends, Explanations, Remedies.* Washington, D.C.: National Academy Press, 1984, 11-26.

Bevan, Lynn. "Can Federal Employment Equity Initiatives Be Enforced?" In Harish Jain (ed.), *Emerging Trends in Canadian Industrial Relations*. Proceedings of the 24th annual meeting of the Canadian Industrial Relations Association, Hamilton, 1987, 295-328.

Bielby, William, and James Baron. "A Woman's Place is With Other Women: Sex Segregation Within Organizations." In Barbara Reskin (ed.), *Sex Segregation in the Workplace*, Washington, D.C.: National Academy Press, 1984, 27-55.

Billingsley, Brenda, and Leon Muszynski. "No Discrimination Here? Toronto Employers and the Multiracial Workforce." Toronto: Social Planning Council and Urban Alliance on Race Relations, May 1985.

Blakely, John, and Edward Harvey, "Socioeconomic Change and Lack of Change: Employment Equity Policies in the Canadian Context", *Journal of Business Ethics*, 7 (1988), 133-50.

Covin, Teresa, and Ralph Kilmann. "Critical Issues in Large-Scale Change." *Journal of Organizational Change Management*, 1(2), 1988, 59-72.

Employment and Immigration Canada. *Employment Equity Act and Reporting Requirements*. Ottawa: Minister of Supply and Services, 1986.

Employment and Immigration Canada, *1988 Annual Report, Employment Equity Act*, Ottawa: Minister of Supply and Services, 1988.

Employment and Immigration Canada, *1989 Annual Report, Employment Equity Act*, Ottawa: Minister of Supply and Services, 1989.

Employment and Immigration Canada. *1990 Annual Report, Employment Equity Act*. Ottawa: Minister of Supply and Services, 1990.

Employment and Immigration Canada. Task Force on Labour Market Development. *Labour Market Development in the 1980s* (Dodge Report), Ottawa: Minister of Supply and Services, 1981.

Freeman, Richard. "Black Economic Progress After 1964: Who Has Gained and Why?" In Sherwin Rosen (ed.), *Studies in Labor Markets*. Chicago: Univ. of Chicago Press, 1981, 247-285.

Gottshalk, Peter. "Reducing Gender and Racial Inequality — The Role of Public Policy." In Katherine Abraham and Robert McKersie (eds.), *New Developments in the Labor Market: Toward a New Institutional Paradigm*. Cambridge, Mass.: MIT Press, 1990, 241-274.

Harvey, Edward B. *Information Systems for Employment Equity: An Employers Guide*. Don Mills: CCH Canadian Ltd., 1988.

Henry, Frances, and Effie Ginzberg. "Who Gets the Work? A Test of Racial Discrimination in Employment." Toronto: Social Planning Council and Urban Alliance on Race Relations, 1985.

Hitt, Michael, and Barbara Keats. "Empirical Identification of the Criteria for Effective Affirmative Action Programs." *Journal of Applied Behavioral Science*, 20 (3), 1984, 203-222.

House of Commons. Commons Debates, October 3 and Nov. 23, 1985, "Bill C-62, An Act Respecting Employment Equity," 2nd Reading.

House of Commons. "Minutes of Proceedings and Evidence on the Legislative Committee on Bill C-62, An Act Respecting Employment Equity," First Session of the 33rd Parliament, 1984-85, Dec. 10,12, 16, 17, Jan. 14, 16, 21, 22, 1986.

House of Commons. Special Committee on Participation of Visible Minorities in Canadian Society (Daudlin Committee). *Report: Equality Now!* Ottawa: Queen's Printer, 1984.

House of Commons. Special Committee on the Disabled and the Handicapped (Smith Committee). *Obstacles*. Ottawa: Minister of Supply and Services, 1981.

House of Commons. Task Force on Employment Opportunities for the 80s. *Work for Tomorrow: Employment Opportunities for the 80s*. Ottawa: Minister of Supply and Services, 1980.

Jain, Harish, and Rick Hackett. "Measuring Effectiveness of Employment Equity Programs in Canada: Public Policy and a Survey." *Canadian Public Policy*, 15 (2), 1989, 189-204.

Johnson, George, and Gary Solon. "Estimates of the Direct Effects of Comparable Worth." *American Economic Review*, 76(5), 1986, 1117-1125.

Kanter, Rosabeth Moss. *The Change Masters*. New York: Simon and Schuster, 1983.

Leonard, Jonathan. *The Impact of Affirmative Action*. Washington D.C.: U.S. Department of Labor, 1983.

Leonard, Jonathan. "Anti-Discrimination or Reverse Discrimination: The Impact of Changing Demographics, Title VII, and Affirmative Action on Productivity." *Journal of Human Resources*, 19 (2), 1984(a), 145-174.

Leonard, Jonathan. "Employment and Occupational Advance Under Affirmative Action." *Review of Economics and Statistics*, 66(3), 1984(b), 377-385.

Leonard, Jonathan, "The Impact of Affirmative Action on Employment," *Journal of Labor Economics*, 2(4), 1984c, 439-63.

Marino, Kenneth. "Structural Correlates of Affirmative Action Compliance." *Journal of Management*, 8(1), 1982, 75-93.

Nightingale, Donald. *Workplace Democracy*. Toronto: University of Toronto Press, 1982.

O'Farrell, Brigid, and Sharon Harlan. "Job Integration Strategies: Today's Programs and Tomorrow's Needs." In Barbara Reskin (ed.), *Sex Segregation in the Workplace*. Washington D.C.: National Academy Press, 1984, 267-291.

Osterman, Paul. "Affirmative Action and Opportunity." *Review of Economics and Statistics*, 64 (4), 1982, 604-612.

Pettigrew, Andrew. *The Awakening Giant: Continuity and Change in ICI*. Oxford: Basil Blackwell, 1985.

Robbins, Stephen, *Essentials of Organizational Behavior*, Englewood Cliffs: Prentice Hall, 1984.

Roos, Patricia, and Barbara Reskin. "Institutional Factors Contributing to Sex Segregation in the Workplace." In Barbara Reskin (ed.), *Sex Segregation in the Workplace: Trends, Explanations, Remedies*. Washington, D.C.: National Academy Press, 1984.

Schaeffer, Ruth, and Edith Lynton. *Corporate Experiences in Improving Women's Job Opportunities*. New York: Conference Board, 1979.

Tremain, Donald, and Heidi Hartmann (eds.). *Women, Work and Wages: Equal Pay for Jobs of Equal Value*. Washington, D.C.: National Academy Press, 1981.

U.S. Department of Labor. *Employment Patterns of Minorities and Women in Federal Contractor and Noncontractor Establishments, 1974-1980*. Washington, D.C.: Office of Federal Contract Compliance, 1984.

Vernon-Gerstanfeld, S. and E. Burke. "Affirmative Action in Nine Large Companies: A Field Study." *Personnel*, April 1985, 54-60.

2

Employment Equity: The Remedy for Workplace Disadvantage

THE 1984 REPORT OF THE ROYAL COMMISSION on Equality in Employment recommended mandatory employment equity legislation and regulations as a remedy for deeply entrenched patterns of disadvantage in the Canadian workplace. While Judge Abella's report marked a watershed in the public acknowledgement of disadvantage, it was by no means the first or last research to document the inequalities in employment suffered by women, aboriginal peoples, racial minorities and people with disabilities (see Chapter 1, Box 1.4 for descriptions of these groups). Although other groups such as francophones (Weinfeld, 1981), youth, and older workers have also been subject to unequal access to employment opportunities, the weight of evidence has shown that patterns of disadvantage for the four groups designated in employment equity policy are particularly pronounced and persistent. This chapter discusses some evidence of the disadvantage these groups confront and outlines ways in which discrimination creates and perpetuates inequality in employment. It is important to understand what disadvantage is, and how it arises, in order to:

- appreciate the need for employment equity policies and practices;
- understand how to identify and diagnose disadvantage and discrimination in the workplace and the labour market; and
- design appropriate remedies to deal with discrimination and the disadvantage it causes.

In later chapters we address these topics in detail.

The identification of the designated groups for employment equity hinges on evidence of long-standing and intractable disadvantage, such as high and persistent rates of unemployment, relative absence from large sectors of the economy and from decision-making positions, and wage disparities that remain after such factors as educational level and work experience are taken into account. The designation of employment equity target groups may also be influenced by their relative numbers, how organized they are, and how strongly they share a common group identity. In addition, the choice may be influenced by public perceptions of who is "deserving," and by official definitions of the groups that constitute Canada's pluralistic society. The identification of the designated groups is a product of demonstrated disadvantage and public acknowledgement of that inequity within a political context. Therefore, the list of designated groups could conceivably alter as times change and as better data on patterns of inequality become available.

The four designated groups identified by Abella and by other government reports share an historical experience of inequality and disadvantage in the Canadian economic, political and social structure. Census data and a large body of research on the history and present status of the designated groups in Canada have documented the subordinate role of women in economic life, the colonial oppression of racial minorities and aboriginal peoples by European and North American settler societies, and the negative stereotypes that persist in public attitudes toward mental and physical disability and which manifest themselves in discriminatory behaviour. These historical dimensions of inequality are embedded in the social structures and cultural patterns of our contemporary society, creating a cumulative cycle of disadvantage for people with disabilities, aboriginal peoples, women, and racial minorities. The result for members of these groups when they enter the labour market and the workplace is a work experience, and an opportunity and reward structure, that is different from and unequal to that encountered by able-bodied white male workers (see Box 2.1). It is this structure of disadvantage that employment equity is intended to acknowledge and remedy.

BOX 2.1
In Comparison to Women and Racial Minorities, White Males Have...

- higher pay
- more promotions
- more economic and decision making power
- higher rank in the hierarchy
- lower unemployment
- lower educational levels
- access to a diversity of occupations
- higher labour force participation rates
- higher unionization rates

It is important to note that the four groups are not mutually exclusive, and that individuals may have a double or even triple designated group membership that has the potential to create multiple disadvantage. Of course, it is also true that there is enormous variation within each of the designated groups, and not all individual members feel that they have experienced the disadvantages that are evident in the indicators for the group. Moreover, because of their distinctive historical and contemporary experiences, each of the four groups is disadvantaged in different ways, and these differences must be recognized in an employment equity change strategy.

The Experience of Disadvantage

What are the measures of disadvantage that demonstrate inequality of employment opportunities and experiences for the designated groups? Disadvantage can be seen on two dimensions:

Access to employment opportunities, as shown by indicators such as:

- labour force participation rates;
- unemployment rates; and
- rates of representation in the various occupations and sectors of the economy.

Disadvantage experienced by employees who do gain access to employment, as shown by such indicators as:

- income levels;
- occupational concentration and segregation;
- rates of promotion;
- turnover;
- harassment and other adverse experiences in the workplace.

Indicators of Disadvantage in Access to Employment

Individuals must enter the labour market in order to be employed, but labour force participation does not ensure success in being hired. Relatively high unemployment rates, then, are clearly evidence of disadvantage. In addition, a relatively low participation rate may indicate a lack of suitable job opportunities for which designated group members may apply — or lack of success over a long period of time in competing for job opportunities. For example, aboriginal peoples living in communities far from the larger cities where jobs are most plentiful may not have jobs in their area for which to apply. And repeated rejection when they do apply for steady work that pays a living wage may eventually discourage further attempts to seek employment. Thus a high unemployment rate and a low participation rate may be complementary indicators of disadvantage in access to employment.

Disadvantage in the labour market is also indicated when members of a group do not gain access to the jobs they are qualified for, given their educational and experience levels. Access to employment for the designated groups may be limited to job ghettos; if so, we see concentrations in certain employment sectors, and very low rates of representation in others.

BOX 2.2

Labour Force Participation Rates and Unemployment Rates, 1986, Canada

	LABOUR FORCE PARTICIPATION RATE	UNEMPLOYMENT RATE
Women[1]	55.9%	11.2%
Aboriginal Peoples[1]	60.3%	22.7%
Racial Minorities[1]	72.1%	10.8%
Persons with Disabilities[1] (aged 15-64)	37.7%	20.0%
Men (age 25-64, Canadian born, not racial minorities)[2]	90.2%	8.2%

(SOURCE: [1]Data Development and Systems Analysis, Employment Equity Branch, Employment and Immigration Canada, February 7, 1991. [2]Boyd (1992), Table 2.)

For example, Box 2.3 shows that women are concentrated in clerical and service jobs, and underrepresented in managerial positions, as compared with men. Men's distribution across the occupational groups is much more even than that for women, who are virtually absent from some occupational categories. We also see differences based upon racial minority status. For Canadian born men who are not racial minorities, the managerial category is the leading occupational group. The strong representation of racial minority persons in professional and semi-professional occupations reflects the facts that the average educational level of racial minorities is higher than the Canadian population, and that racial minority women are concentrated in health care occupations. Minority women and men are overrepresented in service jobs compared with people who are not minorities.

Various theories have been put forward to explain disadvantage in the labour market and to suggest how it might be eliminated. One of these theories proposes that there is a dual labour market that is segmented into primary and secondary sectors, based upon the division of labour and skill levels (Baron and Bielby, 1984; Osterman, 1984; Edwards, Reich and Gordon, 1975). Jobs in the secondary labour market are characterized by less favourable rates of pay, types of work and working conditions, little job security, and low rates of unionization. Examples include many part-time jobs and many jobs in fast-food and other service establishments and in small businesses. Women and minorities tend to be overrepresented in this sector, and employers tend to use traits such as gender or race as signals of individuals' suitability for jobs. The indicators of disadvantage for the designated groups are the same features that characterize the secondary labour market.

BOX 2.3

Occupational Distribution of Visible Minority (VM) and Other Men and Women, Age 25-64, Canada, 1985, by Place of Birth

	WOMEN				MEN			
	CANADIAN BORN		FOREIGN BORN		CANADIAN BORN		FOREIGN BORN	
Occupation:	NOT VM	VM	NOT VM	VM	NOT VM	VM	NOT VM	VM
Managerial, administrative	9.1	10.1	8.6	6.6	15.0	15.9	15.5	12.9
Professional, semi-professional	23.4	27.2	18.7	21.0	13.3	19.8	15.4	19.3
Clerical & related	34.1	33.4	27.5	26.5	6.1	9.6	4.1	8.1
Sales	8.5	9.0	9.3	5.6	8.4	10.2	7.0	7.2
Service	13.5	12.4	16.8	17.1	7.8	8.5	8.7	14.0
Primary	2.7	1.1	2.6	1.8	8.1	4.7	3.8	1.1
Processing	2.0	2.0	2.5	2.5	4.5	2.6	4.4	5.2
Machining, fabrication	3.4	2.7	10.1	14.6	12.8	9.8	17.9	20.2
Construction	0.4	—	0.4	0.2	10.5	7.3	13.5	3.4
Transportation	0.8	0.3	0.4	0.2	7.2	5.0	3.9	3.0
Other	2.1	1.8	3.2	3.9	6.3	6.7	5.6	5.6

(SOURCE: Boyd (1992), Table 2, from 1986 Census, Public Use Sample.)

The dual labour market model suggests that there are institutional barriers between the two sectors so that it is difficult for people to move from the secondary to the primary sector: there are in reality two separate labour markets. One of the aims of employment equity, then, is to remove barriers that limit the access of designated group members to jobs in the primary labour market.

Indicators of Disadvantage within the Workplace

Within the hierarchy of the workplace, the *distribution* of the designated groups may also demonstrate their relative disadvantage. There may be patterns of segregation, resulting in job ghettos, across the horizontal dimension of the organization. For example, in hospital settings women may be overrepresented in nursing and food services and underrepresented in physicians' or administrators' roles. Minorities may be overrepresented in food and housekeeping services. In addition, there may be disadvantage on the vertical dimension of the organization if designated groups are not represented at upper levels, and therefore lack access to decision making roles, and when members of the designated groups encounter a "glass ceiling" which limits their upward mobility. They may receive fewer opportunities to be promoted or to benefit from the training and career development opportunities that lead to promotion. An example of this can be seen in the educational system where women fill only 22% of principals' jobs, but are a majority of the teaching staff in elementary schools, and a majority of those completing the supervisory officers' certificate course in Ontario (*Globe and Mail*, Nov., 3 1990).

Yet another indicator of disadvantage may be lack of equal access to rewards within the organization. Disparities in income levels, given equivalent qualifications and experience, may indicate that designated group members receive unequal returns for the investment they make in education (e.g. Box 2.4). Boyd (1992) found that racial minority men and women have higher educational levels than the general population, and are much more likely to live in large cities where earnings are higher. But when the influence of these factors on earnings is taken into account, racial minority employees earn less than employees who are not members of racial minorities, in both the foreign born and Canadian born populations.

BOX 2.4
Unequal Returns to Investment in Education

AVERAGE ANNUAL EARNINGS OF FULL TIME
YEAR ROUND WORKERS, CANADA, 1982:

EDUCATIONAL ATTAINMENT:	WOMEN	MEN	WOMEN'S EARNINGS AS % OF MEN'S
less than grade 9	$11,804	$20,073	58.8%
high school (attended or completed)	14,087	22,778	61.8
some post-secondary	16,577	24,662	67.2
post-secondary certificate or diploma	17,607	26,123	67.4
university degree	24,380	36,266	67.2
Total	16,056	25,096	64.0

(SOURCE: Statistics Canada, Women in Canada, A Statistical Report, Ottawa: Supply and Services, 1985, Table 13.)

• • • • • • •

"...if we control hourly earnings by education level, men with less education consistently make more than do women with more education. Thus a man with secondary schooling or less makes more than a woman with a non-university diploma or certificate or some university training, while a man with similar educational qualifications makes more than does a woman with a bachelor's degree or certificate; in turn, a man with a bachelor's degree makes more than does a woman with a postgraduate degree. These figures suggest forcefully that the problem is not primarily one of training, for with the same amount of training, women make substantially lower hourly wages. (This means that the overall wage difference cannot be explained by the fact that women may potentially work fewer hours than men because the comparison is based on hourly, not weekly or monthly, earnings)."

(SOURCE: Margrit Eichler, *Nonsexist Research Methods, A Practical Guide*, Boston: Unwin Hyman, 1988, p. 33.)

" The potential average lifetime earnings of a female university graduate (even if other factors like the interruption of her employment because of domestic responsibilities are taken into account) are equal to those of a male high school graduate."

(SOURCE: Pat Armstrong, "Women's Work: Women's Wages," in Greta Hofmann Nemiroff (ed.), *Women and Men, Interdisciplinary Readings on Gender*, Montreal: Fitzhenry and Whiteside, 1987, p. 370.)

Disadvantage also manifests itself when the environment of the workplace is not as supportive or welcoming for members of the designated groups as it is for white, able-bodied males. For example, working conditions may include harassment because of an employees' race, gender or disability, or designated group members may experience a "chilly climate" when they are excluded from social networks or made to feel unwelcome. It may be difficult to measure the impact of the workplace environment on members of the designated groups, but such indicators as higher turnover rates may signal problems.

There are many differences in ability, education, skills and other factors among individuals who are members of a designated group, and the employment experiences of these individuals vary greatly. However, the evidence of inequality is there for the group as a whole even if some individuals in the group have not experienced the same level of disadvantage, or do not perceive that they are disadvantaged in the workplace. We will briefly discuss some indicators of disadvantage for each of the designated groups, and some of the limitations of available data about each.

BOX 2.5
Gender Harassment: Would You Want to Work in an Environment Like This?

(A) FACTORY WORK

"Several foremen ganged up to force Stelco's first female stationary engineer to quit after she complained to management that a foreman molested her, an Ontario Labor Relations Board hearing has been told.

Bonita Clark said yesterday that after she reported a foreman's attack on her in 1980, several other foremen ostracized her, refused to acknowledge her presence, refused to give her direction or training, assigned her work to others, and generally tried to make it impossible for her to perform her duties in the central boiler station at Stelco's Hilton Works in Hamilton.

Clark said she tried to escape the campaign by applying for a transfer to the open hearth department of the steel mill, although this involved dirtier working conditions, lower pay and reduced opportunities for training and advancement.

Her foreman at the open hearth utility station seldom spoke to her, and then only to shout with a swing of obscenities that he `hated women', Clark said.

Another foreman ordered her to clean the men's washroom or be suspended, she said.

The walls of the men's room were plastered with explicit obscene pictures of women, but when Clark complained to higher management about the pornography, the only result was that `large pictures of penises were posted on the walls'.

Clark said that although she was put through the humiliating cleaning duty, Stelco foremen consistently refused her access to convenient washroom facilities. She had to leave the building to wash or use a toilet, she said, thus breaking the Operating Engineers Act by leaving equipment untended too long.

Clark described the alleged harassment campaign at a hearing that will decide whether a work environment poisoned by sexual harassment is a health and safety hazard, with victims entitled to the protections of the Occupational Health and Safety Act.

The board has agreed to hear evidence covering Clark's employment at Stelco since 1979, before deciding whether a climate of sexual harassment was encouraged or condoned by the corporation." (*The Toronto Star*, Wednesday, April 8, 1987, A23.)

The case ended with a settlement between Clark and Stelco, although the outcome did not establish that sexual harassment is a health and safety issue under Ontario law. In addition, as a result of a separate complaint to the Ontario Human Rights Commission, Stelco was ordered to pay Clark $5,000 for failing to provide washroom facilities at the workplace, and required to build a washroom for women employees at a cost of approximately $20,000. (*Globe and Mail*, Sept., 13, 1988.)

In 1984, the Quebec Workers' Compensation Commission recognized stress resulting from sexual harassment as a compensable injury and awarded compensation to a woman (Labour Canada, 1991:53).

In a 1990 landmark ruling by the Ontario Workers' Compensation Board, a woman was awarded workers' compensation benefits for the disability — workplace stress — she suffered as the result of persistent and vexatious sexual harassment by co-workers. Lack of response to her appeals for help from management and her union contributed to the harassing and stressful environment. The victim, a 44-year old Black woman, was employed for six years by Colgate-Palmolive Canada at their Toronto factory, and was the lone woman and one of only two Blacks working in a department packing soap and detergent into boxes. (*Toronto Star*, November 6, 1990, A1; Lancaster Labour Law Reports, October 1990, vol. 6, no. 10.)

(B) ENGINEERING

"A recent grad attended her first technical conference, where she was the only woman among several hundred men. At dinner she was told by the waiter that she was in the wrong place because `this is an engineering meeting.'

`You have a choice between feeling proud and wanting to crawl under the table,' she recalls. `I chose to feel proud.'

`The real problem came at the hospitality suites. This is where all the networking is done, so I went to the first one. I stood around talking for awhile, sipping my ginger ale. Then my problems began.

First, they wanted to freshen my drink. Next, the propositions started. I soon realized they thought I came with the room! I left and didn't go to another hospitality suite.

I'm older now, and I know what I'd say if the situation arose again; but I'm still mad about it'."

(SOURCE: *Mechanical Engineering*, May, 1988, p. 2.)

Aboriginal Peoples　Accurate statistical information about aboriginal peoples in Canada is difficult to obtain because of data collection and validity problems associated with the census in 1981 and 1986 (e.g. Bagley, 1988). Disadvantaged sectors of the population in general tend to be under-counted in censuses (Gleick, 1990). There was under-counting, misunderstanding of questions, and resistance to the collection of census data in their communities by some aboriginal groups (Statistics Canada, 1989:xiii). There were also discrepancies between 1981 and 1986 census questions. Census data therefore underrepresent and to some extent misrepresent the size and nature of the aboriginal population of Canada and its provinces, territories, and municipalities.

However, the data that are available show clear evidence of considerable disadvantage. For example, aboriginal peoples have a lower level of educational attainment than the total population (Employment Equity Branch, Employment and Immigration Canada, 1991), although educational levels are rising among aboriginal youth. Disadvantage in educational attainment contributes to aboriginal disadvantage in employment, as is clear from a 1991 study of Indian education. Only a quarter of the Indian population completes high school, compared to half the non-Indian population, and only 25% of Indians who enter university earn a degree, compared with 55% of non-Indians. For Indians who graduate from university, labour force participation is identical to that of non-Indians, but an income gap remains. Indians with university degrees earn about a third less than non-Indians with the same educational qualifications (*University Affairs*, April 1991, 11).

Racial Minorities   The term "minority," when used by social scientists who study race and ethnic relations and discrimination, refers not just to the size of the group, but to their relative powerlessness and exclusion from the opportunities generally available in a society. The issue, then, is not the relative number of people in a group, but their relative position in the social, political and economic structures of society, and the quality of their life experience.

One of the difficulties in identifying disadvantage and discrimination for racial minorities is the great diversity among the groups and individuals to which this label is applied. This diversity encompasses not only race, ethnicity, national origin and culture, but also language, religion, education and skill levels, previous employment experiences outside Canada, and employment outcomes in Canada. About 89% of the racial minority population aged 25-64 are immigrants to Canada (Boyd, 1992:14), but many members of racial minorities come from families that have been in Canada for many generations.

Levels of education are higher for the racial minority population compared to the total population, as are labour force participation rates. Yet a number of research studies have provided evidence of lower incomes than comparable white groups (Ramcharan, 1976; Shepard and Levin, 1973; Zureik and Hiscott, 1983; Muszynski and Reitz, 1982). A recent examination of census data on income (Beaujot, Basavarajappa and Verma, 1988) found that the incomes of immigrants to Canada generally catch up relatively quickly to incomes earned by those born in Canada. However, immigrants from non-European sources, generally racial minorities in Canada, can take up to 20 years to earn comparable incomes.

BOX 2.6
Educational Levels, 1986, Canada Population Age 15+

	RACIAL MINORITIES	TOTAL POPULATION
Less than grade 9	14.4%	17.3%
University degree	17%	10%

(SOURCE: Employment Equity Branch, Employment and Immigration, Canada, 1991.)

The pattern of disadvantage in employment for racial minority groups is particularly evident for Nova Scotia's Blacks, many of whom trace their ancestry in Canada to the early 1600s. A study sponsored by the provincial Human Rights Commission found that the average income of Blacks was only 57% of the income of white Nova Scotians. The unemployment rate for Black males was 22% — three times the rate for whites. Blacks make up only about 12 of the province's 1,200 lawyers, 85 of Nova Scotia's 11,000 teachers, and 5 of the 275 police officers in Halifax (*Globe and Mail*, July 24, 1990; July 23, 1991).

In The Prestons, a Halifax suburb first settled in the 1780s by Black Loyalists and still a predominantly Black community, more than 75% of the work force was found to be unemployed in 1985. A changing economy in which credentials have become all-important in access to employment has brought hardship to this community, where trades such as carpentry, masonry, plastering and bricklaying have traditionally been passed down from fathers to sons, rather than learned in vocational schools (*Globe and Mail*, Feb., 8, 1985:4).

People with Disabilities   Statistical data on the employment of people with disabilities are limited. Abella (1984) suggested that one of the difficulties is a lack of precision in the use of the term "disability." It is estimated that one in ten Canadians has a disability of some kind, and that only half of those who are employable, find employment (OFL/FTO, 1987). The 1986 National Health and Activity Limitation Survey (HALS) found that 7.3% of the Canadian population between the ages of 15 and 64 had a disability that constituted a limitation in the workplace (Employment Equity Branch, Employment and Immigration Canada, 1991). Work-force participation rates for this population are considerably lower than the total population, as are educational levels (Box 2.7). A 1984 national survey found that 46% of persons with disabilities between the ages of 35 and 64 were not in the labour force, compared with 23% of the able-bodied population, and only 39% of persons with disabilities had jobs, in contrast to 72% of the non-disabled (*Globe and Mail*, April 29, 1988).

BOX 2.7
Educational Levels, 1986, Canadian Population Age 15-64

	PERSONS WITH DISABILITIES	TOTAL POPULATION
Less than grade 9	33.%	17%
University degree	4.4%	11.5%

(SOURCE: Employment Equity Branch, Employment and Immigration, Canada, 1991.)

Disadvantage is clear when we compare employment outcomes for the population with university degrees: 26.3% of people with disabilities having such qualifications remain unemployed, compared with 2.7% of the able-bodied (Abella, 1984).

Women   Information about the labour force experience of women is much more extensive than it is for the other three designated groups. In 1989, women made up 44% of Canada's employed labour force and about 40% of total union membership — but women were 46%

of the unemployed. Women's unemployment rates are consistently higher than men's (Labour Canada, 1991: 39). Although women's participation in the labour force has steadily grown over the years, there is little evidence that their earnings are catching up to men's, or that women are gaining access to a broader range of jobs or to decision making positions. It has been estimated that seven out of ten women experience sexual harassment at some time in their working lives (OFL/FTO, 1987). There is a highly persistent pattern of disadvantage on the basis of a person's sex in employment in Canada.

Women remain concentrated in a narrow range of occupations and sectors of the economy, where they outnumber men. In 1989, 57% of women were in clerical, sales and service occupations, as compared with 25% of men (Labour Canada, 1991: 19). In the service sector, 63% of employees were women: 47% of women but only 22% of men worked in this sector of the Canadian economy (Labour Canada, 1991: 16).

Increasingly, part time work is women's work. In 1989, women made up 88% of the part time work force aged 25 to 44 years (Labour Canada, 1991: 30). A quarter of all working women, but only 8% of men, worked part time in 1989 (Labour Canada, 1991: 27,28). For about 22% of both women and men, part time jobs were the only work they could find. But women were much more likely than men to work part time because of family or personal responsibilities, while men were twice as likely as women to work part time because they were going to school (Labour Canada, 1991: 29). Earnings, benefits, job security, and rates of unionization are much less favourable for part time than for full time workers. The results for many working women are inadequate earnings, and poverty among those who are retired.

For full time workers, too, the gap in earnings between men and women is still wide. In 1988, women employed full time for the full year earned 65 % of mens' average earnings. In all occupational categories and at all levels of educational attainment, women's earnings were markedly less than men's (see Box 2.4 for examples). Women who were university graduates earned 63% of the income of men with university degrees (Labour Canada, 1991: 41, 42, 43, 59).

Women are also disadvantaged when it comes to benefits. For example, about 56 % of men, but only 47 % of women who worked full time in 1987 belonged to a pension plan, and only

16% of women working part time were covered by a pension plan (Labour Canada, 1991: 95-96).

Yet women, and particularly those who are racial minorities, represent a highly qualified labour force. The higher a woman's educational level, the more likely she is to participate in the labour force. Almost 80% of women with university degrees were in the labour force in 1989 (Labour Canada, 1991: 19). Women are now over-represented among university graduates: in 1988, women received 54% of all bachelor's and first professional degrees, 45% of master's degrees, and 31% of Ph.D.s, and women were 57% of community college graduates. Women are increasingly acquiring higher education in scientific and technical specialties including natural and applied sciences, engineering, mathematics, and agricultural and biological sciences (Labour Canada, 1991: 70, 71, 72).

Women are also a reliable labour force. It is clearly a myth, for example, that women are highly likely to leave their jobs because of pregnancy. In 1986–89, the number of initial maternity claims granted under the Unemployment Insurance program represented less than 3% of all women in the labour force (Labour Canada, 1991: 93).

BOX 2.8
The Gap Between Men and Women: Some Canadian Examples

	(As % of Population age 15+)	
	MEN	WOMEN
% of labour force in medicine and health occupations, 1987	19.9%	80.1%
Full year, full time employment, 1985: % of physicians and surgeons	83.4%	16.6%
Average earnings: physicians and surgeons	$90,562	$57,126
general managers and other senior officials	$60,327	$34,096
% of general managers and other senior officials	87.5%	12.4%
% of labour force in the top 10 highest paid occupations	86.7%	13.3%

(SOURCE: Labour Canada, 1991: 20, 36, 54.)

Women who are also members of the aboriginal, racial minority or disabled population suffer multiple disadvantage. Aboriginal women are particularly at risk, experiencing an unemployment rate nearly double the aboriginal male level, and disadvantages in pay (Employment Equity Branch, Employment and Immigration, Canada 1991). Racial minority women are disadvantaged both in access to employment and in pay, in comparison with minority men or with white women (Proceedings, 1983). Boyd (1992: 19) found that women who are members of visible minorities and who are foreign born had lower average earnings than all men, and than Canadian born and foreign born women who are not members of visible minorities. If the effects of such characteristics as residence in large cities, occupation, birthplace, education, work experience, and age are statistically controlled, visible minority women have lower earnings than all other women and men — clear evidence of the double disadvantage suffered by minority women. As Box 2.9 shows, women with disabilities also pay a heavy cost because of their double disadvantage.

BOX 2.9
Average Annual Earnings of Men and Women With and Without Disabilities, Canada, 1986

	WOMEN	MEN	COST OF BEING A WOMAN
WITH DISABILITIES	$ 8,360	$19,295	$10,935
WITHOUT DISABILITIES	$10,000	$21,000	$11,000
COST OF BEING DISABLED	$ 1,640	$ 1,705	$12,640

(SOURCE: Statistics Canada, 1986.)

What Is Discrimination and How Does it Cause Disadvantage in Employment?

In many ways, the job we hold defines who we are, becomes part of our identity, and shapes how we live in economic as well as social terms. Access to opportunities in employment therefore becomes central to our existence during our adult lives. We spend a large part of our daily lives in a working environment which, if it is inhospitable, can have devastating effects on our self esteem and personal efficacy. When access to employment, employment opportunities and a pleasant working environment are negatively affected by our sex, race, ethnicity, mental or physical ability, and are limited by this component of our identity, it is clear that discrimination is occurring. Discriminatory behaviour is complex and takes many forms. Discrimination may occur when power is used by dominant groups, or by individual members of such groups, in ways that support their positions of advantage, and at the same time deprive members of other groups of access to those same privileges and participation in the same opportunities. Discriminatory behaviour resulting in disadvantage may be intended, or unintended and built into the routine and traditional policies, practices, procedures, and patterns of decision making in the workplace.

Here are some examples of individual and organizational decision-making that discriminates in various ways against members of designated groups:

- a racial minority person doesn't get a job interview when the person screening the applications discards the application because the surname is characteristic of a particular national origin;
- a supervisor makes assumptions about a woman's family responsibilities and does not consider her for development and promotional opportunities;
- a manager decides not to employ a person who has a disability because of negative assumptions about the person's ability;
- a recruiter makes an assumption that an aboriginal person will not turn up for work on time;
- a human resources department does not respond to a request from an employee with a disability who requires an assistive device in order to apply for a promotion;
- a manager schedules weekly breakfast meetings at 7:00 a.m. to discuss important decisions, even though he has been told that the day care centre used by several staff members does not open until 7:30, and the workday begins at 8:00;
- men and women holding the same ranks have different pay levels;

- designated group members find themselves excluded from the informal decision-making that happens in social gatherings outside the work setting;
- racial minority managers find that they are not included in informal work groups or communication networks (Fernandez, 1988);
- access to a company car, expense account, or other "perks" is not distributed equitably (Alvarez, 1979);
- men and women doing essentially the same work have different job titles and therefore different ranks and compensation levels;
- safety boots and uniforms that are issued to all employees do not properly fit women working in skilled trades jobs, exposing them to hazards and discomfort;
- an employee for whom Saturday is a day for religious observance is told he must work on Saturdays or lose his job.

Some of these examples illustrate that discriminatory impacts may occur as a result of organizational practices that may appear "neutral," and that may even be applied in the same way to all employees. But such practices may result in inequitable outcomes for employees who are different from the white, culturally homogeneous, male, able-bodied population for whom these practices were designed. Employment equity involves identifying and changing organizational policies, procedures and practices that have been demonstrated to have discriminatory impacts, and that are not necessary to the organization's fulfillment of its mission.

Discrimination also occurs when the workplace environment is "poisoned" by harassment on the basis of group membership. Harassment has been defined as "a course of vexatious comment or conduct that is known or ought reasonably to be known to be unwelcome" (Ontario Human Rights Code, 1981, s. 9(f)). It can include verbal slurs, insults, jokes, unwelcome touching, physical assault, graffiti, as well as more subtle behaviours such as avoiding contact with someone from a designated group, refusing to be pleasant to them in a work setting, or under-valuing their contribution.

The issue of whether discriminatory behaviour is intentional or unintentional is far less important than the results of such behaviour. The purpose of employment equity is to provide remedies for the outcomes of discriminatory behaviour that has occurred in the past, and to prevent such discrimination — and the disadvantage that it causes — in the future. The primary purpose of an employment equity change strategy, then, is to eliminate behaviours which discriminate on the basis of sex, race or disability, and to foster the acceptance and accommodation of diversity in the workplace. In Chapters 4 and 5 we will examine some of the ways in which discrimination has been defined in Canadian law, policy and judicial decisions, and the implications for creating a more equitable workplace.

The impact of discrimination on members of the designated groups can create a crisis of confidence, a lack of self esteem, lowered expectations, and the perception that one has to be twice as good as a member of the dominant group to succeed. Abella (1984: 122) suggests that

> many more (target group members) who are qualifiable would undoubtedly apply for education, training or employment opportunities if they had greater confidence that they would not be rejected; if the workplace were more physically accommodating in both environmental and structural respects; if they had more personal support systems such as child care or a better transportation system in geographically remote areas; if the job requirements were more relevant to the job to be performed; or if there were more flexible work opportunities such as part-time work or varied hours.

Barriers to Equality in Employment

One interpretation of the fact of inequality in the workplace is to blame the victim by suggesting that factors such as "cultural deprivation, lack of delayed gratification, culture of poverty, and externalized locus of control" are responsible for inequality (Bowser, 1979: 175). This approach has been called "the new racism and neosexism" by Nasatir and Fernandez (1979: 271). In a system that was designed by and for the traditionally predominant white, male and able-bodied employee, it is not surprising to find those who regard differential employment outcomes for other groups as a product of the victims' shortcomings. Such a philosophy can be seen in the work of Block and Walker (1982: xvi), who suggest that there is "little truth in a basic presupposition of affirmative action; that in the absence of discrimination the various minorities — racial, sexual, ethnic — would have achieved earnings levels indistinguishable from the majority." Simplistic statements such as these show a lack of understanding of the research evidence, and of the barriers these groups face in the workplace and in the larger society, and of the effects of historical patterns of discrimination and inequality.

It is clear that, like poverty, the cycle of disadvantage and discrimination is hard to break. There is a cumulative effect that limits individuals' expectations, education, training and level of employment. The absence of role models and of decision makers in organizations who are members of designated groups, and the discouraging perception that the employment opportunities of women, minorities, aboriginal peoples and people with disabilities are narrowly restricted, perpetuates the cycle of disadvantage. It is the cumulative effect of this historical experience that perpetuates the disadvantage of the designated groups, and that requires remedies that are systemic and far reaching in their effects. As noted in Chapter 1, the Supreme Court's decision in *ATF* recognized the "cumulative effects of systemic discrimination" and the need for employment equity to address these effects.

Barriers to Access
Discrimination resulting in disadvantage on the basis of disability race, sex, and aboriginal ancestry is a complex phenomenon involving many kinds of barriers within the workplace and in the larger society. Although the focus of this book is on equity in employment, it is important to situate the workplace in its larger context in order to understand how disadvantage and discrimination operate at the level of the workplace. While employers are not directly responsible for changing factors outside their organizations, they are not justified in dismissing their responsibilities to address those disadvantages that do occur within their areas of influence.

Occupational Segregation and Barriers to Entry   Occupational segregation may be both cause and consequence of inequality of opportunity. Occupational segregation and unequal pay for similar work may be the result of unequal access to occupations and jobs, but, once in place, it tends to perpetuate itself. Sex-typed occupations or job ghettos such as clerical work, nursing or child care tend to reinforce sex segregation simply as a result of being labelled as "women's work." Occupational choices based on social custom may appear to be "free" choices, but they are based upon learned perceptions of what occupations are realistic and appropriate for one's own sex or ethnic group. Employers perpetuate the sex-typing of occupations in their hiring practices when they routinely assign the "appropriate" sex to a particular job (Peitchinis, 1989: 22-23; Reskin, 1984; Reskin and Hartmann, 1986).

An in-depth study of sex segregation, involving analysis of staffing patterns, personnel practices and job requirements in 266 establishments in California (1964-1979) found that over half of the establishments were *completely* segregated (*no* job title had members of both sexes assigned to it), and most of the others were almost completely segregated. Only 10% of the 61,000 workers in the study were in job titles to which both men and women were assigned (Bielby and Baron, 1987: 214). Using complex statistical analyses, the researchers found that decisions allocating men and women to specific jobs were not based on candidates' qualifications for the position. For example, jobs that were physically demanding excluded *all* women, and jobs that required finger dexterity excluded virtually all men. These are abilities that are quite easy for employers to assess for individuals, yet hiring was being done on the basis of stereotypes, not individual abilities.

Access to employment often operates informally through a network of contacts, for example, through word-of-mouth hiring and promotion practices. This tends to confirm the status quo and reproduces employment patterns, limiting opportunities for members of the designated groups by presenting barriers to their entry. Reitz, Calzavara and Dasko (1981) have suggested that protected labour markets that are controlled by white or "ethnic" gatekeepers are an important factor in examining levels of achievement in job status and income among ethnic groups.

Some types of jobs may be dominated by a particular ethnic or racial group as a result of a coping strategy of creating economic niches that provide easier access to employment opportunities for members of that community. For example, certain groups of Asian origin have found that operating convenience stores has provided them with an economic niche in Canada. This pattern of occupational concentration reinforces the assumption that members of

that group are identified with only a limited range of jobs, contributing to a cyclical and cumulative process of ghettoization.

Organized labour can also play a role in limiting access to
labour markets. Union practices that control entry, for example, to
construction trades, may make it difficult for those not in the union
to access employment (Abella, 1984). Joint union-management
collective agreements may limit transfer and promotion opportunities, and restrict access to jobs above the entry level to those within the bargaining unit.

Education and Training Systems The Abella Report (1984) listed several barriers to access to employment for the designated
groups, including insufficient or inappropriate education and training
facilities, inadequate information systems about training opportunities, and limited financial and personal support systems. Abella (1984:
175) concluded that "without the necessary education and training,
members of the designated groups cannot hope to join the economic
competition on an equitable basis. It is important to remember that
barriers to their access exist at this outer gate and that they are no less
formidable than the ones in the main employment arena." At the
same time, as we have seen, lower educational levels are not characteristic of all designated groups (for example, the racial minority population) or for all individuals within any of these groups. There are in
fact many qualified designated group members in the majority of
occupational groups in the labour market.

Accreditation Issues In 1987, the Ontario government commissioned a study to "identify entry requirements for the trades and
professions that appear as barriers for those trained outside of
Canada and that have a disproportionately negative impact on
members of minority and ethnic groups" (Abt Associates of
Canada, 1987: 13). A review of the requirements to enter a profession in Canada revealed:

- subjective and inconsistent decision making on academic
  qualifications and previous work experience attained outside
  Canada;
- language requirements not related to job requirements;
- limited access to retraining opportunities and internships.

In particular, it was suggested that their sex and country of training adversely affected women, and those from non-English speaking or racial minority populations. Inconsistent decision making and hiring conditions were also identified in the review of immigrant entry into trades. The *Access!* report of the Task Force on Access to Professions and Trades in Ontario, in October 1989, contained recommendations on how these barriers to access might be removed. These recommendations are now being considered by the provincial government.

Job Barriers in the Workplace

A barrier in the workplace exists when an organizational policy or practice limits the opportunities or experience of individuals because they are members of a designated group. Here we examine barriers in four areas: recruitment and selection practices; accommodation of diversity in the workplace; access to opportunities for career development and advancement; and the workplace climate. For example:

- access to jobs can be limited for aboriginal peoples when the educational requirements posted for the job are not required for the performance of the job;
- access to employment can be limited for people using a wheelchair when employers fail to accommodate needs for working surfaces at an accessible height;
- access to career development and advancement opportunities may be limited for women when the scheduling of working hours is inflexible and incompatible with family and childcare responsibilities;
- access to an hospitable workplace climate is limited for racial minorities when racial harassment, blatant or subtle, is present.

Recruitment and Selection   The recruitment, hiring and selection policies and practices of organizations can limit employment opportunities. Decisions related to screening, job descriptions, testing, interviewing, and job assignment all have the potential to unfairly exclude members of designated groups (Jain and Sloan, 1981; Muszynski and Reitz, 1982; Henry and Ginzberg, 1985; Collinson, Knights and Collinson, 1990).

In recruitment systems, reproduction of current workforce characteristics can occur when recruitment is done through word of mouth, and through inadequate and limited job posting both within and outside the organization (Braddock and McPartland, 1987). When recruitment is carried out only through employment agencies or "head hunters," accessibility may also be limited, as suggested in Box 2.10.

BOX 2.10
Discrimination in Recruitment

A survey of a representative sample of Canadian corporate personnel recruiters, hiring managers and agency recruiters conducted by the Canadian Recruiters Guild between 1985 and 1988 found:

- 97% of those surveyed reported that they had discriminated against job seekers on the basis of handicap, 95% on age, 94% on colour, 89% on offenses, and 81% on sex.
- Most corporate recruiters (87%) and all agency recruiters in this survey had received direct discriminatory requests from those they worked for, and most had complied with those biases.
- Only 13% of corporate recruiters followed any clear organizational guidelines for recruitment and selection standards and practices. The remainder of this group either had no such standards or if they did, they did not follow them (*The Human Resource, 1988:* 20).

• • • • • • •

In a 1991 study, the Canadian Civil Liberties Association contacted 15 Ontario employment agencies at random. Posing as employers, the researchers asked if the agencies would be willing to refer only white job applicants. Twelve indicated they would, despite the fact that their response was a violation of the law (*Globe and Mail,* Jan. 21, 1991).

• • • • • • •

In 1991 the Ontario Human Rights Commission investigated two Toronto-based employment agencies and found that their files contained notations about the race and ethnicity of applicants. As part of a settlement of the Commission's complaints, the agencies agreed to develop written policies on how to handle discriminatory requests from clients, and to train their employees about human rights, race relations and employment equity. The companies also agreed to establish three year employment equity plans to remove bias in recruiting, referral and placement (*Globe and Mail*, March 29, 1991).

The absence of members of a designated group from the organization's workforce can contribute to its lack of attraction to applicants from that group, and to its image as an inhospitable working environment.

Even when designated group applicants do apply, screening decisions may be made that exclude them from access either with discriminatory intent or unintentionally (Jain and Sloan, 1981). The assumptions behind the screening decisions may be unacknowledged and unrecognized by those who make them, and the repercussions for designated group members may not be recognized. For example, lack of acceptance of qualifications and experience obtained outside Canada can be a limiting factor in access to employment for racial minorities (Chandra, 1973). An assumption of disability, rather than an assumption of ability, can result in screening out persons with disabilities. Assumptions about clients' or customers' reactions to the designated group employee may result in the exclusion of racial minority or aboriginal applicants from positions that deal with the public, such as sales, retail banking, and supervising (Chandra, 1973).

Screening decisions made at various levels may limit access. For example, the person receiving applications at the reception desk may make the initial screening decision, or may encourage or discourage potential applicants on the basis of designated group status.

Job descriptions that demand qualifications that are not required to carry out the job are another source of systemic bias, as in credentialism — unnecessary requirements for educational levels that are not necessary to success in the job — (Jain and Sloan, 1981). Language requirements not necessary for the job can also exclude non-English or non-French speakers (Muszynski and Reitz, 1982).

Biased testing may also create a barrier to access (Arvey and Faley, 1988). Testing may be differentially applied, for example, language testing for only some candidates, or tests of mechanical aptitude for women candidates only. For example, one of the findings in the *ATF* complaint against CN Rail was that women were required to perform tests of ability, such as lifting an 80 pound brake shoe, while men were not. Yet, requiring both men and women to take the same test may also result in inequality if the test is not job-related. Such tests tend to screen out women. Examples are the mechanical aptitude tests used by CN. [*Action Travail des Femmes vs. C.N. Rail.* (1987), 40 D.L.R. (4th) 193 (S.C.C.)]

Interviews are particularly likely to be vehicles for discrimination against designated group members, but they continue to be used in hiring (Arvey and Campion, 1982). Discrimination may occur when inappropriate questions are asked (in spite of legislation to the contrary), and when subjective decisions are made about suitability or "fit" between an applicant and the employing organization. Failures in intercultural communication can pose problems for some racial minority and aboriginal candidates. Women and persons with disabilities are particularly vulnerable to assumptions made about their inability to carry out the job because of perceived limitations imposed by family commitments or their physical ability.

Although some of these human resource practices that exclude designated group applicants from access to employment are based on the exercise of discriminatory behaviour by individuals responsible for hiring, they become a corporate issue and a legal liability for the employer when the organization fails to control discriminatory actions and decisions by its employees. It is possible that employers and human resource decision makers are becoming more aware of how to identify and remove biases in recruitment and selection. A 1989 update of a 1984 study of racial discrimination by Toronto employers found encouraging improvement. In 1984, white job applicants received three job offers for every offer received by similarly qualified Black applicants. But in 1989, Blacks and whites received an equal number of job offers, although discrimination was reported in the interview setting (Economic Council of Canada, 1991: 118; Henry and Ginszberg, 1985).

Failure to Accommodate Special Needs   Paul Scott, Director of Equal Opportunity for Metro Toronto, has suggested that some of the cultural values that are predominant in Canadian workplaces are social homogeneity, upward mobility, separation of work and family, and physical limitations perceived as a personal flaw. He has argued that these values do not accommodate the needs of a diverse work force, and tend to exclude women, racial minorities, persons with disabilities and aboriginal people.

Workplaces are typically organized on the assumption that all employees are able-bodied, healthy, independent individuals who can work within a given time frame which suits the production needs of the workplace. Workers are expected to be flexible enough to cope with night shifts, overtime and last minute changes to the working timetable. As well, many human resource practices are based on the assumption of a homogeneous male, white, Anglo and Christian workforce. Few employers accommodate the diversity of needs found in the changing and more diverse Canadian work-force of the 1990s. For example, the building may not permit access to those who have some kinds of physical disability, and within the workplace lack of appropriate washroom facilities and equipment that can be used by someone with a disability may limit the employment opportunities of persons with disabilities. Lack of washroom facilities for women has been a contentious issue in male-dominated work sites. Lack of transportation may be a crucial barri-er for aboriginal people who live on reserves that are often located away from employment opportunities. Dress and grooming standards may not accommodate different religious observances. Perceived dif-ficulties about geographic mobility or travel as part of a job may be used as an excuse for not promoting women.

Barriers to Career Advancement and Personal Development   An employee has to take the right route within an organization to progress in a career. For a designated group employee, it may be difficult to find access to the right training and educational oppor-tunities, developmental job assignments, and appropriate career counselling. In addition, he or she has to conform to expectations rooted in the cultural norms and values of the majority, and of tra-ditionally powerful groups in the organization.

Designated group members may be excluded from advancement opportunities for a variety of reasons. Managers may assume that they are not suitable or interested, and designated group members them-selves sometimes lack confidence in seeking training or development opportunities. They become the victims of the employer's or their own limited expectations or aspirations, which may be realistic in view of past experiences of discrimination. Training programs may be biased to meet the perceived needs of white males, and be inappropriate in content, language and methodology for the diversity of the participants. For example, military and North American sport analogies as instructional devices may prove ineffective and alienating for some designated groups.

Inadequate career counselling based on discriminatory attitudes may mean that opportunities are blocked. Promotion policies and requirements may also set up systemic barriers for the designated groups by failing to allow some flexibility for meeting family needs, or for upgrading education or training (Avebury, 1986; Canadian Advisory Council on the Status of Women, 1987). When the number of hours worked is expected to increase with a promotion, or if travel requirements increase, women with family responsibilities can be at risk.

Opportunities for individuals may be blocked when inappropriate promotion patterns set designated group members up for failure, consciously or not. For example, individuals may find that they are promoted without sufficient exposure to or experience of other parts of the organization; such promotion deprives them of the necessary background to do the new job effectively. This can affect chances for future promotion. Promotion without the necessary qualifications can impair a person's credibility in a new job or limit further movement or salary levels within the position (Rosenbaum, 1979). On the other hand, sponsorship by senior people in the organization, mentoring and fast tracking processes may be denied to qualified designated group members, thereby limiting their opportunities for advancement (Braddock and McPartland, 1987). The absence of role models for members of the designated groups can also create a barrier to advancement.

Kanter (1979: 55) suggests that "sometimes institutional racism/sexism impacts on people's opportunity in a way that makes them appear to deserve their lack of mobility, but this is instead a function of limited situations." However, it is also true that the interplay between individual disadvantage created by past discrimination and current systemic barriers means that even when systems and structures are freed of bias, the individual can still be blocked from promotional opportunities because of individual disadvantage.

Bielby and Baron (1987), as well as Kanter (1977), have called attention to the power of the self-fulfilling prophecy. Influenced by stereotypes, employers may expect certain behaviours, such as high turnover from women, and assign them to dead-end, poorly paid jobs doing routine tasks. Turnover is indeed highest in such jobs, whether they are held by men or women. Women respond by leaving, thus reinforcing the stereotype — and the cycle continues.

Barriers in the Workplace Climate   Harassment on the basis of group membership is a misuse of power and a devastating experience for victims, who may respond in various ways (Thacker and Ferris, 1991). In some cases the employee who is harassed is not prepared to work in that environment and resigns from the job. Retention of good employees becomes an issue for organizations when members of the designated groups are lost as a result of harassment or an aversive environment. In other cases, there can be anger and a desire to fight back, resulting in an escalation of the conflict, poor interpersonal relationships, polarized work groups, low employee morale, and the possibility of legal action. Humiliation and damage to self esteem, as well as fears of reprisals if complaints are made, may result in an employee who is not able to work to potential either in terms of ability or full attendance. The Supreme Court of Canada has ruled that employers are liable for harassment occurring in their workplaces if they do not prevent or do not appropriately respond once they "know or ought reasonably to have known" it was occurring.

There are also more subtle issues in relation to the working environment for members of the designated groups. These may be shown in various ways, including patronizing and overprotective attitudes towards those with disabilities or women, the use of racially and sexually biassed language in policies and communication processes, or various avoidance behaviours that majority group members may not be aware of (Pettigrew and Martin, 1987). Subtle forms of discrimination create an environment that devalues and fails to validate the experiences of the diverse members of the work force. When other employees refuse to work or socialize with members of the designated groups, such groups may be isolated and marginalized within the workplace. The impact of such practices can be to reinforce organizational values that are hostile to diversity, as well as to make members of the designated groups feel as if they do not belong in that environment.

The organization can play a role in creating and sustaining prejudice, which in turn can create a discriminatory environment (Alvarez,

1979). The evidence presented by the Canadian Recruiters Guild suggested that individual decision makers discriminated on the basis of their own biases, but "often out of prejudices they perceived existed within their business environment" (*The Human Resource*, 1988: 20).

What Does Equity Mean?

The disadvantage and discrimination described in this chapter are the problems for which employment equity is a remedy. When we address the question of equity and what it means, we have to also consider whose definition of equality are we applying. The traditional approach has been to view equity as treating people equally. However, equality of treatment alone does not result in equality of outcomes. Abella (1984: 3) suggested that "sometimes equality means treating people the same, despite their differences, and sometimes it means treating them as equals by accommodating their differences."

BOX: 2.11
Union and Management Agree to Accommodate Diversity

"Bell (Canada) and the CWC introduced an Employment Equity Clause into the new collective agreement signed in October 1988. The clause, which recognizes that equal employment opportunity means more than treating everyone the same, endorses the principles of special measures and accommodation of differences as a means of providing equal employment opportunities to members of designated groups" (Bell, 1988:4).

If equity is defined as equality of outcomes, how do we know when we have achieved equity in employment? What will it look like? To some extent, equity is a moving target — organizational stakeholders negotiate what equity means to them, based on their experience over time. Employment equity is also the change process by which we get to "equity." It is a process that involves a constant interplay among the interests of the different stakeholder groups, each of which has its own perspective on what equity will look like, and its own agenda for change. In the following chapters we will address the crucial role of the different stakeholders in moving towards equity, and the ways in which employment equity can provide remedies for discrimination and disadvantage in the workplace.

Discrimination in employment reflects the exercise of power by one group over another, and the exclusion of some groups from decision making and power. Discrimination is a complex, cumulative and cyclical set of social behaviours and decision-making processes. Societal norms and values shape legal, governmental, educational and professional accreditation systems outside organizations, and influence decisions that impact upon people's work experience within organizations. These systems promote access to employment through a cumulative process of education, training, work experience, social background, the right moves at the right time, sponsorship in access to employment, and being the "right person" for the job. Designated group members can be deprived of these pathways to success by discrimination. Success in employment is usually facilitated by conformity to the norms and values of the organization, which result in systems designed for the "mainstream" employee.

The Challenge of Equity — How Do We Make it Happen?

In order to remove discrimination and disadvantage, we need a clear analysis of the many ways in which inequality occurs and an equally clear strategy for removing these sources of inequality. Employment equity programs that break down the barriers to access, accommodate the needs of a diverse workforce, open up opportunities for career development and advancement, and create a hospitable working environment are keys to the realization of equity for the designated groups within organizations. In the following chapters, we will examine employment equity as a strategy for organizational change designed to remove barriers to the full participation of designated group members, and to accommodate their special needs when necessary.

REFERENCES

Abella, Rosalie. *Equality in Employment: A Royal Commission Report.* Minister of Supply and Services, Ottawa, 1984.

Abt Associates of Canada. *Access to Trades and Professions in Ontario.* Prepared for Cabinet Commission on Race Relations. Government of Ontario, Toronto, 1987.

Alvarez, Rodolfo, Lutterman, Kenneth G, and Associates. *Discrimination in Organizations.* Jossey-Bass Inc. Publishers, San Francisco, 1979.

Arvey, Richard, and James Campion. "The Employment Interview: A Summary and Review of Recent Research. " *Personnel Psychology,* 35, 1982, 281-322.

Arvey, Richard, and Robert Faley. *Fairness in Selecting Employees.* New York: Addison-Wesley, 1988.

Avebury Research and Consulting Limited. *Decade of Promise.* Canadian Congress for Learning Opportunities for Women. Toronto, 1986.

Bagley, Christopher. "Lies, Damned Lies and Indian Ethnicity in the Canadian Census." *Ethnic and Racial Studies,* 1988, 11(2), 230-33.

Baron, James, and William Bielby. "The Organization of Work in a Segmented Economy." *American Sociological Review,* 1984, 49, 454-73.

Beaujot, R., K.G. Basavarajappa and R.B. Verma. Income of Immigrants in Canada: A Census Data Analysis." *Current Demographic Analysis,* Ottawa: Minister of Supply and Services, May 1988.

Bell, *Employment Equity Report,* Report Year 1988, Human Rights and Employment Equity.

Bielby, William, and James Baron. "Undoing Discrimination: Job Integration and Comparable Worth." In Christine Bose and Glenn Spitze (eds.), *Ingredients for Women's Employment Policy.* Albany: SUNY Press, 1987, 211-232.

Block E.E., and Walker, M.A., (eds.). *Discrimination, Affirmative Action, and Equal Opportunity.* The Fraser Institute, Vancouver, 1982.

Bowser, Benjamin P. "An Empirical Model for Measuring Racism in Large-Scale Organizations." In Alvarez, Rodolfo, Lutterman, Kenneth G., and Associates, (eds.). *Discrimination in Organizations.* Jossey-Bass Inc. Publishers, San Francisco, 1979.

Boyd, Monica. "Gender, Visible Minority and Immigrant Earnings Inequality: Reassessing an Employment Equity Premise." In Vic Satzewich (ed.), *Deconstructing a Nation: Immigration, Multiculturalism and Racism in the 1990s.* Toronto: Garamond Press, forthcoming 1992.

Braddock, Jomills Henry II and James M. McPartland. "How Minorities Continue to be Excluded From Equal Employment Opportunities:

Research on Labor Market and Institutional Barriers." *Journal of Social Issues*, 43(1), 1987, 5-39.

Canadian Advisory Council on the Status of Women. *Integration and Participation*. Ottawa, 1987.

Chandra, Kanur V. *Racial Discrimination in Canada: Asian Minorities*. San Francisco, California: R. & E. Associates, 1973.

Collinson, David, David Knights, and Margaret Collinson. *Managing to Discriminate*. London: Routledge, 1990.

Economic Council of Canada. *Economic and Social Impacts of Immigration*. Ottawa: Minister of Supply and Services, 1991.

Edwards, Richard, Michael Reich, and David Gordon. *Labor Market Segmentation*. Lexington, Mass.: D.C. Heath, 1975.

Fernandez, John P. *Racism and Sexism in Corporate Life*. Lexington, Mass.: D.C. Heath, 1988.

Gleik, James. "Why We Can't Count." *New York Times Magazine*, July 15, 1990.

Henry, Frances, and Ginzberg, Effie. *Who Gets the Work? A Test of Racial Discrimination in Employment*. Social Planning Council of Metropolitan Toronto and Urban Alliance on Race Relations. Toronto, 1985.

Jain, H.D., and Sloane, P.J. *Race, Sex and Minority Group Discrimination in the United States, Canada and Britain*. New York: Praeger, 1981.

Kanter, Rosabeth Moss. "Differential Access to Opportunity and Power." In Alvarez, Rodolofo, Lutterman, Kenneth G, and Associates, (eds.), *Discrimination in Organizations*. San Francisco: Jossey-Bass Inc. Publishers, 1979.

Kanter, Rosabeth Moss. *Men and Women of the Corporation*. New York: Basic Books, 1977.

Labour Canada (Women's Bureau). "Women in the Labour Force, 1990-91." Ottawa: Minister of Supply and Services Canada, 1990.

Labour Canada. "Occupational Safety and Health Concerns of Canadian Women: A Background Paper." Ottawa: Minister of Supply and Services, 1991.

Muszynski, L., and Reitz, J. *Racial and Ethnic Discrimination in Employment*. Working Paper No. 5, Social Planning Council of Metro Toronto, 1982.

Nasatir, David and Fernandez, John P. "Use of Log-Linear and Hierarchical Models to Study Ethnic Composition in a University." In Alvarez, Rodolofo, Lutterman, Kenneth G, and Associates, (eds.), *Discrimination in Organizations*. San Francisco: Jossey-Bass Inc. Publishers, 1979

OFL/TFO, Document 2, A Statement on Equal Action in Employment, 31st Annual Convention, November 23-27, 1987.

Osterman, Paul, (ed.). *Internal Labor Markets.* Cambridge, Mass.: MIT Press, 1984.

Peitchinis, Stephen. *Women at Work: Discrimination and Response.* Toronto: McClelland and Stewart, 1989.

Pettigrew, Thomas, and Joanne Martin. "Shaping the Organizational Context for Black American Inclusion." *Journal of Social Issues,* 43(1), 1987, 41-78.

Proceedings of "The Visible Minority Woman." Conference on Racism, Sexism and Work, September 30 - October 2, 1983.

Ramcharan, Subhas. "The Economic Adaptation of West Indians in Toronto." *Canadian Review of Sociology and Anthropology,* Vol. 17, No. 3, 1976.

Reitz, J, and L. Calzavara and D. Dasko. *Ethnic Inequality and Segregation in Jobs.* Research Paper No. 123, Toronto, Centre of Urban and Community Studies, University of Toronto, 1981.

Reskin, Barbara, (ed.). *Sex Segregation in the Workplace.* Washington, D.C.: National Academic Press, 1984.

Reskin, Barbara and Heidi Hartmann (eds.). *Women's Work, Men's Work.* Washington, D.C., 1986.

Rosenbaum, James E. "Career Paths and Advancement Opportunities." In Alvarez, Rodolfo, Lutterman, Kenneth G. and Associates, (eds.). *Discrimination in Organizations.* San Francisco: Jossey-Bass Inc. Publishers, 1979.

Shepard, William, and S.G. Levin. "Managerial Discrimination in Large Firms." *Review of Economics and Statistics,* Vol. 55, 1973.

Statistics Canada. *Dimensions: Profile of Ethnic Groups.* Ottawa: Minister of Supply and Services, 1989.

Thacker, Rebecca, and Gerald Ferris, "Understanding Sexual Harassment in the Workplace...," *Human Resource Management Review,* 1(1) 1991, 23-37.

Weinfeld, Morton. "The Development of Affirmative Action in Canada." *Canadian Ethnic Studies,* 13: 1981, 23-29.

Zureik, E., and Robert Hiscott. *The experience of visible minorities in the work world: the case of MBA graduates.* A report submitted to the Race Relations Division of the Ontario Human Rights Commission, March 1983.

3

Employment
Equity:
The Benefits for
Your Organization

I N THIS CHAPTER we will examine some of the
benefits and necessities of dealing with discrimination and disadvantage in the workplace, and
how employment equity can contribute to good human resource
management, the development of a skilled and responsive work-
force, better understanding of markets, as well as corporate responsibility for promoting fairness and equality. This chapter may help
you to develop the arguments you need to convince decision makers of the benefits of implementing employment equity in your
organization.

We discuss a number of changes that are having an impact on
the workplace as we move towards the year 2000, including:

- changes in the demographic characteristics of Canada's
  population
- a shortage of skilled workers

- the need for better and more productive uses of human resources
- a more diverse customer and client base
- a "rights seeking environment," supported by the legal system and stakeholder advocacy activity
- a larger regulatory role for government in the workplace.

Demographic Changes: The Impact on the Labour Market

Canada's population is changing and creating a labour market that is aging, growing less rapidly, and becoming more diverse.

Slower Growth Rates

Canada's population growth has been slowing down as fertility rates continue to fall, and population growth is now below 1% per year (Foot, 1988; Samuel, 1988). In order for the population to replace itself a fertility rate of 2.1% is needed, but by 1986 the fertility rate had fallen to 1.7% (Foot, 1988). There are some indications that the fertility rate has risen slightly in the early 1990s, but it continues to be below the replacement level, which means that the population growth rate is likely to continue to fall.

One way of increasing population levels is to increase immigration rates. However, Beaujot (1990) has suggested that "immigration levels that would maintain population growth in spite of low fertility over the period 2021–2036 would involve 60 immigrants per 100 births." This is far higher than the active rate of 35 immigrants per 100 births during 1971 – 1986. During the early 1980s immigration rates to Canada were historically low, and by the end of the decade the federal government was increasing the annual rates (Foot, 1988). However, even with current immigration rates, it is projected that Canada's population will begin to fall by the year 2025 (Beaujot, 1990).

Recent research about the impact of immigration on the labour force has suggested that the encouragement of immigration within certain age categories could supplement the falling rates that will occur as the baby boom generation ages (Foot, 1988; Beaujot, 1990). Historically, immigrants have had a major impact on labour force growth, and since the median age of immigrants is lower than the Canadian born population, there is also an impact on population age (Foot, 1988).

In the 1980s, slower population growth rates contributed to a corresponding slow down in the growth of the work force, from 3.1% per year between 1976 and 1981 to 1.1% per year between 1981 and 1986. Based on current projections it is expected that labour force growth rates will continue to drop during the 1990s (Foot, 1988). Slow growth and eventually an actual decline in the size of the work force may limit future increases in productivity and economic growth as labour becomes a less abundant resource.

Aging of the Population

Canada's population is also aging. The average age in 1971 was 26.2 years; in 1986 it was 31.6, and Beaujot (1990) suggests that projections for 2036 could be as high as 45 years. The aging process is reflected in the age profile of the labour force, and in addition lower fertility rates will continue to slow the entry of new workers into the workforce. This will accentuate an already established pattern of decline in the 15 to 24 age group in the labour force (Working Group on Employment Equity, 1989a). This decline will continue through the older cohorts, with the beginning of the decline marked by the aging of the baby boom cohort. The implications of an aging work force may include a reluctance by increasing numbers of workers to move from one regional labour market to another, as well as a reduced interest in retraining, which could lead to a less mobile and a less flexible work force. New ways to address mobility and retraining will become a priority for governments and employers.

Increasing Participation in the Labour Market by the Designated Groups

The composition of the labour market is also changing. The participation of the designated groups is projected to increase, while the traditional source of human resources in the paid labour force — white able-bodied males — is now declining.

Women Women are an increasingly important component of the work force as the number of women participating in the labour market grows. Between 1981 and 1986, women's participation contributed 94% of the total growth in employment in Canada (1986 census data cited in the *Globe and Mail*, March 2, 1988: 1). The growth of women's participation has occurred in all age groups. The Ontario government's Working Group on Employment Equity (1989b: 5) noted the rise in labour force participation rates of young women and women with children, and suggested that "new generations of women will be shaped by their mothers' patterns of labour market behaviour." Employment and Immigration Canada predicts that women's participation rate will reach 64% by the year 2000, while men's rate will continue to fall to 76%. Women will therefore be a basic source of future human resources in the workplace.

BOX 3.1
The Changing Family

In 1961, 65% of Canadian families were households consisting of two parents and children, with only the adult male working outside the home.

In 1985, only 16% of Canadian families with children had a male as sole earner.

(SOURCE: Statistics Canada, Survey of Consumer Finances, 1985.)

In a 1988-89 survey of 7,000 Canadian employees by the Conference Board of Canada, a third of respondents felt that their responsibilities for care of children, or elderly or disabled family members, have limited their career advancement. The primary issues were relocation (a problem for 72% of women and 49% of men), working overtime or long hours (difficult for 66% of women and 46% of men), and taking on extra tasks (a problem for 64% of women and 46% of men). Women were four times as likely as men to have left a previous job because of conflicts between family and work responsibilities. Survey respondents indicated that support from managers or supervisors is essential to them in balancing demands of work and family (*Globe and Mail*, Jan. 22, 1991: B2).

Racial Minorities   The ethnic and racial origin of Canada's population is also changing with clear implications for the growth of diversity in the work force. By 1986 about 16% of Canada's 25 million people were immigrants (about the same proportion as in 1951). Of the immigrant population, about a third had come from the Caribbean, Asia, Africa, South and Central America, and Oceana (Economic Council of Canada, 1991: 75).

The 1986 Census records the racial minority population of Canada as 6.3% of the total. The projections for the representation of this component of the population by the year 2001 range from 8.7% to 9.6% (Samuel, 1987). Canada's future workforce is therefore likely to include much higher proportions of racial minorities, particularly in some provinces. For example, between 1981 and 1986 Ontario attracted 45.9% of all immigrants to Canada, and it is projected that by the year 2011, 15% of Ontario's population will be racial minorities. The Multiculturalism and Race Relations Division of the Regional Municipality of Metropolitan Toronto estimates that racial minorities, now over 20% of the population, may reach about a third of Metro's population by the year 2000.

The age profile of the racial minority population is younger than the Canadian average, although this is not reflected as yet in the population of working age (Working Group on Employment Equity, 1989a). In 1986, 27% of the racial minority population was under age 15, compared to 21.5% of the Canadian population (Employment Equity Branch, Employment and Immigration Canada, 1991). The impact on Canada's ability to meet its future labour supply needs will be substantial if racial minority youth are limited in their access to employment opportunities.

People with Disabilities   According to the 1986 census, 7.3% of the population between the ages of 15 and 64 were "limited at work" on account of disabilities. There were slightly more women than men in this group. The age profile of the population with disabilities was older than the total population (Employment Equity Branch, Employment and Immigration Canada, 1991).

Aboriginal Peoples   Aboriginal peoples of Canada constituted 2.8% of the population in 1986, according to the census. As noted in Chapter 2, there are difficulties with these data since enumeration did not occur or was incomplete in some areas. The aboriginal population is therefore likely to be larger than recorded. Available data suggest that the age profile of the aboriginal population is also younger than the Canadian average: 57.7% are under 25 compared to 38.2% for the total population (Employment Equity Branch, Employment and Immigration Canada, 1991). Projections are for increased growth in the aboriginal population and above average growth in their labour force participation rates (Canada, 1980).

Implications of Demographic Change for Organizations
It is clear that the numbers and representation of women, racial minorities, aboriginal peoples and people with disabilities are growing in the labour market, and that the work force is increasingly characterized by diversity. In 1986, the members of the four designated groups represented over half of the Canadian work force (Box 3.2). Demographic projections propose that between now and the year 2000, 80 to 85% of new entrants to the labour force will be members of the designated groups, and by the year 2001 they will constitute 70% of the work force (Clarke, 1988). Given this change in the composition of the work force, in addition to slowing growth rates, no employer can afford to rely on the shrinking white able-bodied male segment of the labour market to meet the future need for skilled, competent and effective employees.

BOX 3.2
Representation of Employment Equity Groups in the Canadian Work Force, 1986

Designated group members as percent of population aged 15–64 who worked between 1981 and 1986:

Women	44%
Aboriginal peoples	2.1%
Visible minorities	6.3%
Persons with disabilities	5.4%

(SOURCE: Data Development and Systems Analysis, Employment Equity Branch, Employment and Immigration Canada, February 7, 1991.)

Demographic changes will also affect the ways in which workplaces operate and are managed. If workplaces continue to be managed so as to meet the needs of the traditionally dominant segment of the labour market — white able-bodied males, a projected 30% of the future work force — the clear implication is that the needs of 70% of the work force may not be met. For example, employers now confront the two-career family and the need of employees to balance work and family responsibilities as a preeminent concern. Cultural diversity in the workplace brings new value systems and priorities. Designated group members have the potential to provide "the best trained influx of new workers in Canadian history" (Phillips, 1985: 62). There is a heavy economic cost involved when the skills, expertise and potential of a majority of the work force is underutilized. A number of employers have publicly acknowledged the dangers of excluding the new majority of the work force from employment opportunities.

BOX 3.3
Employer Perspectives: Productivity and the Changing Work Force

CITY OF OTTAWA: If you're not using 100% of your human resource pool, then you're cheating the corporation, your employees and your citizens." MAYOR JAMES DURRELL

DUPONT CANADA INC.: We are committed to employment equity because it makes good sense... our business requires us to tap all of the talent that is available to us . . . there is a long range, bottom line reason for doing it. TED NEWALL, PRESIDENT AND CEO

(SOURCE: Ontario Women's Directorate, 1987.)

CITY OF TORONTO: Employees who are given equal opportunity to apply their skills and develop their career potential are motivated to perform their jobs well. A harmonious, fair, discrimination-free workplace improves employee morale, gains staff commitment, and reduced turnover. This, in turn, promotes organizational health and a heightened capacity for productivity. AN EMPLOYER'S HANDBOOK,
CITY OF TORONTO

WARNER LAMBERT: It is the right thing to do. It is the competitive thing to do. It is the only thing to do.
DON HENSON, V.P. HUMAN RESOURCES

(SOURCE: Address to the London Employment Equity Network, September 1989.)

How are organizations responding to evidence of demographic change impacting the workplace? Is the human resource function evolving to manage these changes? Are the human resource management decisions of line managers and functional specialists leading and supporting employment equity change?

In 1990-91, the international management consulting firm Towers Perrin and the Hudson Institute, a private policy research organization, conducted surveys on how American and Canadian companies are responding to demographic and labour force trends. The surveys attempted to gauge the level of concern about critical human resource issues, and assessed employers' response to the challenges of a changing work force. The study found that the response is not fast enough, and not yet broad enough, but it has begun (Towers Perrin, 1990:6; *Globe and Mail*, July 4, 1991: B1). The Canadian survey found that almost 30% of responding companies were not yet concerned about the needs of women in the work force, and half did not yet consider the need to respond to a diverse work force to be an issue. In the U.S., however, managing cultural diversity had become a paramount concern.

The Economic Imperative

Increased pressures to improve the productivity and competitive strength of Canadian organizations have heightened requirements for more technologically skilled workers, more effective human resource management, and an improved ability to respond to diverse markets and clientele. In 1989, a report by the Ontario Ministry of Citizenship analyzed the labour market environment and suggested that there was a strong "economic efficiency rationale" for employment equity. The implementation of employment equity for the designated groups can help meet the demands for an appropriately skilled and flexible work force, more productive use and management of human resources, and more responsive service to customers and clients in the private and public sectors. There is evidence that affirmative action may enhance productivity and efficiency in private sector organizations (Schotter and Weigelt, 1988), and that discriminatory practices can result in substantial cost to the organization, aside from legal liabilities (Dunnette and Motowidlo, 1982).

Need for Skilled Workers

In recent years, most employment growth in Canada occurred in the service sector which now accounts for about 70% of Canadian employment (Gower, 1988). In addition, the impact of technology in the workplace is redefining the types of labour that were required (Ginzberg, Noyelle and Stanback, 1986). By the late 1980s there were labour force shortages, particularly in highly skilled technical, professional and managerial fields, in nearly 60% of Canadian companies, according to the Towers Perrin Survey (*Globe and Mail*, July 4, 1991: B1). A 1988 study by the Ontario Ministry of Skills Development identified 159 occupational shortages in fields that required above-average skills, often as a result of technological change (Working Group on Employment Equity, 1989b). This study also pointed out that in the sectors of the economy where there were acute labour shortages, employment was male dominated. Women were under-represented in these fields (Working Group on Employment Equity, 1989a), as were people with disabilities and aboriginal peoples.

Technology can lessen the need for physical strength and muscle power in the workplace, and can move women and people with disabilities closer to parity with the undisadvantaged in their chances for employment (Patillio, 1988). In particular, computer technology has the potential to enhance the mobility and communication abilities of people with physical disabilities (Bloch, 1986). Patillio (1988: 48) concludes that "there is no reason why the physically disabled cannot effectively relate to these opportunities if given the training, the technological assistance, and the support necessary to make their participation a reality."

Changes in the demography of the labour market, as well as a growing demand for technologically skilled workers, together provide a clear rationale for employment equity implementation. There is a need for investment in human capital now in order to meet the future skills needs of the workplace. The designated groups who will increasingly come to dominate the labour market need to be the beneficiaries of that investment. Employment equity can thus contribute to reducing skills shortages and to "the overall social objectives of both equity and economic efficiency" (Working Group on Employment Equity, 1989a: 6).

Human Resource Management Needs

Employment equity can also result in improved human resource management outcomes. The current and projected decline in the growth of the labour force, together with the demand for skilled and technologically competent employees, will mean that human resources managements' strategic role will become critical to an organization's ability to meet its labour needs in an increasingly competitive labour market (Devanna, Fombrun and Tichy, 1981). Companies with innovative and effective human resource management policies and practices tend to do well in the market-place (Kanter, 1983; Newton, 1989: 42).

There is evidence that the need to use human capital more effectively will mean that human resources planning will be recognized as an integral part of corporate planning (Schuler, 1987). More sophisticated human resource planning capabilities will be required to implement employment equity strategies (Abella, 1984). In 1985, William McEwan of the National Association of Manufacturers confirmed that mandatory affirmative action programs in the U.S. "forced us to use all our human resources better" (*Globe and Mail*, editorial, April 25, 1988). Broadening opportunity, sharing power, and nurturing the talents and skills of all employees are interrelated aspects of the emerging direction of development in the field of human resources management as practiced by progressive employers.

BOX 3.4

Affirmative Action in the U.S.: News of Its Death Is Greatly Exaggerated . . .

Affirmative action is still alive and well in the U.S. despite recent Supreme Court decisions. The impact of these decisions has been to refine the meaning of affirmative action, but not to undermine its application. Affirmative action plans must be remedial in nature and based upon evidence of past discrimination, and employers must use job related hiring and promotion practices (Thacker, 1990).

Edwards (1991: 13) describes the current state of affirmative action in the U.S. as follows:

"There is now in the U.S. a kind of 'culture' of affirmative action which federal compliance requirements has no doubt helped to stimulate but which is by no means confined to federal contractors (nor to the private sector). Affirmative action (which in some of its manifestations in hiring practices and set-asides is indistinguishable from preferential treatment) is now commonplace practice. Considerable resources are devoted to it, there is a small industry of test validation, the costs of being found guilty of discrimination are high (because of class actions), a vast affirmative action apparatus has been constructed which will not easily be dismantled, and perhaps most surprising, large companies compete with one another to reach ever higher targets for minorities and women. Indeed, the main limitation to the effectiveness of employment affirmative action now is not the Supreme Court but the lack of availability of qualified minorities — to the extent that some companies head-hunt highly qualified blacks in order to reach self-imposed targets that go well beyond OFCCP targets. 'Good faith efforts' have been superceded by 'just do it'. . . .

The depressing side of all this is why it has come about. Ironically, and to the discomfiture of many proponents of affirmative action, it is the Supreme Court that holds the moral high ground on the issue. Whilst the court has arrived at most of its decisions within the context of remedial action for discrimination, the culture of affirmative action is being fuelled less by a concern about injustice or equality of opportunity than by the exigencies of demographic and labour market changes. If universities do not recruit more minority students, their student rolls will fall. If companies do not hire more minorities, they will be short of labour. . . . And as companies seek out new markets abroad, they want to demonstrate a diverse workforce. As one company manager told me, 'A diverse workforce is the only advantage we have over the Japanese'."

(SOURCE: John Edwards, "U.S. Affirmative Action Alive and Well Despite Supreme Court," *Equal Opportunities International*, Vol. 10, Number 1,1991, p.13.)

BOX 3.5

Benefits of Affirmative Action — Some U.S. Experiences......

- **Affirmative action can enlarge the talent pool in fast-growth industries:**
  "The computer industry is growing so fast that there are more opportunities than people. Minorities and women are enhancing our R&D workforce." SILVIA GERST, HEWLETT-PACKARD

- **Affirmative action can have business value in customer relations.** " Everyone is a potential customer of AT & T, and they look at us. Why would someone want to be a customer of an all-white male company?"   PEGGY SIEGHARDT, AT & T
- **Affirmative action may be cost-effective for the nation.** Estimates of the cost of implementing affimative action, and of its benefits to the U.S. economy, indicate that EEO may cost about $10 billion a year, but the value it adds to the economy is close to $15 billion a year — a 50% return on the national investment. Applying the same estimation procedure to a cost-benefit analysis of employment equity in the Canadian economy yields a benefit of $1.4 billion a year. (Townson, 1985: 3,9)

(SOURCE: Anne Fisher, "Hiring by the Numbers: Business vs. Reagan on Affirmative Action," *Fortune*, September 16, 1985, 16-21.)

The removal of discriminatory barriers for the designated groups within organizations can contribute to a healthy working environment with higher levels of employee morale and motivation, fewer grievances and employee complaints, lower rates of absenteeism, better retention of workers and therefore lower turnover rates, and increased productivity (Clarke, 1988; Allen, 1988). Once an appropriate level of designated group representation has been achieved, employment equity can mean that an organization can fill more of its promotional opportunities from within. Warner Lambert, which began to implement an affirmative action program for women in 1975, found that rewards for the company have included increased productivity and employee motivation, a decrease in employee turnover and absenteeism, and successful recruitment of women into non-traditional and managerial jobs.

Jain and Hackett (1989) found that among the organizations in their study that implemented employment equity, 100% did so in part because there were benefits for human resource management. Agócs' (1989) study of companies involved in the Federal Contractor's Program found that for those few companies that had programs before the FCP regulations took effect, the desire to use human resources more effectively was the most important influence on the decision to implement employment equity.

In a transitional period, there may be competition to hire and retain skilled designated group employees to meet employment equity goals. This means that designated group members will need to feel that they have opportunities within an organization in order to stay. Mobility and retention are clearly a challenge to human resource management and to those who shape the organization's public image. It is important to attract and retain employees from the designated groups, since they provide role models and incentives for other designated group members to see the organization as an attractive place to work.

Marketplace Needs

Markets both within and outside Canada are increasingly diverse, and within Canada, services are also delivered to an increasingly diverse population. It makes sense that the diversity of the marketplace and the client base should be reflected in the work force of an organization in order that the needs of both customers and clients are better understood and served. When the diversity of the marketplace is reflected in the employee base, a network of contacts between organizations and customers is easier to establish. Employees of differing ethnic and racial backgrounds can provide cross-cultural understanding, linguistic skills, and appropriate contacts with domestic and international markets that can improve an organization's ability to do business.

In particular, a broad spectrum of government services, including health care, welfare and social services, education, policing, and the correctional and justice systems, can all be perceived as more relevant and sensitive to the needs of a diverse population if their employees represent that diversity. Not only is access to service likely to be improved, but services can be offered that will be perceived as relevant to a more diverse client base. There is evidence that these benefits do not entail productivity losses (Lovrich et al., 1986).

Theorists of public administration use the concept of the "representative bureaucracy" to express the principle that the public service should be a "microcosm of the total society" in terms of such attributes as gender, racial and ethnic origin, social class background, and language (Kernaghan, 1978). It has been argued that a representative public service will be more responsive to the needs and interests of the taxpaying and client public. Since the public service at the federal and provincial levels generally does not reflect the diversity within the community, especially in its decision-making echelons, representativeness must be actively sought, and governments have undertaken employment equity measures and set goals to move toward a more representative bureaucracy. Such activity does not conflict with the merit principle that is central to the public service, but instead "illuminates and extends the principle of merit in its widest and most socially advantageous sense" (Wilson and Mullins, 1978: 534). The federal Public Service Commission has noted that the underrepresentation of women, aboriginal peoples, racial minorities and people with disabilities, as well as francophones, "may have the effect of reducing the sensitivity of the Public Service to the needs" of these groups in making policy and delivering services (Kernaghan, 1978).

Moving toward a more representative public service is also of symbolic and practical importance in making tangible to these groups — as citizens and taxpayers — their rights to relevant services and to career opportunities for themselves within public administration.

A Rights Seeking Environment

Within the Canadian workplace there is a changing political, social and legal climate in which more government intervention and increased stakeholder participation are having an impact on the way organizations operate. Piche (1986: 624) has suggested that employment equity needs to be seen as part of a "rights seeking environment." Others point out that it is not valid to view employment equity as a charitable thing to do: equity in employment is a basic human right (Allen, 1988). The various stakeholder groups have important and differing interests and investments in the organizational environment, as customers, shareholders, taxpayers, clients, and employees.

There is growing awareness that organizations benefit from maintaining a public image that is attractive to employees and to the public. Jain and Hackett (1989) suggested that 50% of the organizations in their study that were implementing employment equity felt that it improved public relations. Evidence that an employer is engaging in socially responsible practices promotes a positive public image. For example, Canadian National, whose corporate image was affected by a complaint that went before a Canadian Human Rights Tribunal, made a video, which is available to the public, and that seeks to show how CN has responded positively to the challenges of employment equity within its organization. (The case of *Action Travail des Femmes vs. CN Rail* will be more fully discussed in Chapter 4). The Canadian Auto Workers (1987: 9) suggested that General Motors was willing to negotiate with them on employment equity issues because of "the changing social and cultural climate, along with the company's desire to present a good corporate image."

Growth in Advocacy for Equity

Members of the designated groups are obviously among the most important stakeholders in the changing workplace. As the numbers of those in the work force from the designated groups increase, and their experience and perception of disadvantage continues, their attempts to lobby for better treatment and for equity will be stepped up. There are already clear indications that this is happening. Groups have become increasingly sophisticated in their advocacy methods and are demanding a voice in the development of policies and programs for equity. Organizations representing the needs of designated groups exist at the local, regional and national levels, and at the level of the workplace. In addition, associations representing the various designated groups are forming coalitions to strengthen their appeals for equity. There are also advocacy groups such as the Ontario Coalition for Better Child Care which, although not organized on a designated group basis, nevertheless work towards more equitable employment.

Associations that are active in promoting a rights seeking environment are pushing employers to take a more participatory approach to human resources management. As employers begin to consider the needs of the designated groups, they are becoming aware that knowledge and experience of diversity within the organization is limited — especially if members of these groups are absent from the workplace, or present in small numbers. One of their responses is to reach out to designated group associations for information and also for recruitment assistance. Such organizations can provide employers with valuable expertise, and can also play an advocacy role for the designated group within the organization.

The result may be that a variety of stakeholders come to work effectively together to meet mutual needs.

Stakeholder advocacy is not limited to associations representing the designated groups. Advocacy groups also include employment equity networks that have become a factor in the employment equity environment. These groups vary in their composition, but can include managers, human resource and employment equity practitioners, representatives of the labour movement, members of designated groups and public and voluntary sector agencies that promote the employment of the designated groups.

The role of the labour movement as a stakeholder in the employment equity process is crucial, especially in an environment of concerns about downsizing and its impact on job security. The Canadian Labour Congress and the Canadian Union of Public Employees have advocated mandatory affirmative action for many years. Many unions, including OPSEU, The National Union of Provincial Government Employees, the Canadian Auto Workers, and the Steelworkers, have employment equity policies and advocacy positions. In 1987, the Canadian Auto Workers (CAW) and General Motors of Canada jointly received an award from the Ontario Womens' Directorate for their work on employment equity issues. In 1988, the Labour Council of Metropolitan Toronto and York Region (fomerly the Toronto Trades Assembly) won an Employment Equity Award from the Government of Ontario. Representing approximately 40 union affiliates and more than 400 locals, the Council includes 181, 000 working people. Their employment equity initiatives included English in the workplace programs and a three-phase project to increase the awareness of equity within the Council and its member locals. The goal was to "initiate change so that union leadership will one day reflect the same percentage of women in its executive ranks as exist in the membership. The best way to ensure that womens' issues are treated as peoples' issues is for women to be fully represented at all decision-making levels ("This Year's Winners," Ontario Women's Directorate, 1988). The labour movement is recognizing that its growth and viability requires it to accommodate the diversity of the work force in its organizational structure, activities and mandate.

The legal system and human rights organizations are obviously influential stakeholders in a rights seeking environment. The Canadian

Bar Association, the Canadian Federation of Civil Liberties and Human Rights Associations, and the Canadian Civil Liberties Association have all expressed support for affirmative action concepts. Weinfeld (1981: 35) has suggested that the "legal community, as reflected in the briefs of the various legal and civil liberties associations, is unanimous in its support of the principle" of employment equity.

Designated group members, unions and employee associations, and advocacy organizations external to the workplace all help to create a rights-seeking environment to which organizations must respond. Being part of the solution, and therefore having some control over the outcomes, is a powerful inducement for the different stakeholders to become involved in an employment equity change process.

A More Regulatory Role for Government

Contemporary social values promoting a rights seeking environment have become embedded in legislation and policy. In the past two decades, as the economy became more complex, government intervention in the workplace has increased. Its scope has included regulation and or protection of employment standards, health and safety, and collective bargaining. In the face of evidence that employers are not voluntarily addressing issues of human rights and equity, these too have been subjects of legislation and regulation (Chapter 4 details the legislative and regulatory framework for employment equity). The increase in government regulation — especially in relation to equal opportunity — has been a major impetus to the expansion and growing sophistication of the human resources management function in organizations in recent years (Kochan and Cappelli, 1984: 146-47; see Box 3.6).

BOX 3.6
Government Equal Opportunity Regulations Have Contributed to the Growth and Influence of the Human Resource Management Function in the U.S.

In a 1977 Conference Board survey of personnel executives in the U.S., two thirds of respondents cited government regulations as "a major or primary influence for change in their company's personnel management over the past ten years." The most important of these regulations dealt with employment discrimination, and virtually all employers were affected. Of the firms surveyed, 97% had established an EEO unit, which was almost invariably attached to the personnel function.

Responding to government regulations, especially regarding affirmative action, required the human resource management function to become much more sophisticated. It was necessary to review employment systems, collect internal and external workforce data and track changes over time, and develop human resource plans involving the analysis of turnover, retirements, forecasts of human resource needs, and integration of human resource plans with business plans. These new skills and activities enhanced the influence of the human resource management function in the organization (Kochan and Cappelli, 1984: 146-148).

It is clear that employment equity legislation and regulation have precipitated a response by employers. Jain and Hackett (1989) found that government pressure was a factor for 96% of the organizations implementing employment equity in their study. Agócs (1989) found that 'for firms that were initiating programs in 1986–87, the Federal Contractors' Program regulations were the most important factor.'

Employers may also initiate employment equity with a view to avoiding litigation under current human rights law. (Andiappan et al., 1989). Top management is more likely to dedicate resources to equity if it is clear that the organization risks significant costs if systemic discrimination persists. Studies of the impacts of class action suits and contract compliance in the U.S. have shown that regulation and enforcement have prompted employers to act (O'Farrell and Harlan, 1984). The CAW suggested that General Motors Canada was receptive to employment equity initiatives in 1984 because it was aware of impending federal regulation and also concerned that in the United States, General Motors had paid a $42.5 million settlement arising out of a discrimination case (CAW/TCA Canada, 1987).

It is clear therefore that the rationale for employment equity to meet the needs of the designated groups goes far beyond the needs of individuals within these groups. Employment equity is necessary to meet the needs of the changing workplace in the Canadian society and economy, and for the following specific reasons:

- Demographics: members of the designated groups make up an increasing proportion of the Canadian work force;
- Economics: it makes sense to use the potential of the entire work force to meet the human capital needs of the economy and society;
- Marketplace and service demands: employment equity will help business and the public sector to understand and serve an increasingly diverse population;
- Productivity: employment equity is part of a progressive and strategic approach to the management of human resources;
- Social and legal responsibility: it is the socially responsible thing to do, and part of the legal environment within which employers must operate.

REFERENCES

Abella, Rosalie. *Equality in Employment: A Royal Commission Report.* Minister of Supply and Services, Ottawa, 1984.

Agócs, Carol. "Employment Equity Activity Among Federal Contractors in Ontario." *Industrial Relations Issues for the 1990s.* Proceedings of the 26th Conference of the Canadian Industrial Relations Association, Quebec, June, 1989.

Allen, Jane. *Employment Equity: How We Can Use It To Fight Workplace Racism.* Cross Cultural Communication Centre, Toronto, 1988.

Andiappan, P., M. Crestohl, and J. Singh. "Racial Discrimination in Employment in Canada." *Industrial Relations*, 44(4), 1989, 827-848.

Beaujot, Roderic. "Immigration and the Population of Canada." Employment and Immigration Canada, Research Abstract, March, 1990.

Bloch, Erich. "Preventing Obsolescence of Human Resources." *The Future of Work for Disabled People: Employment and the New Technology.* American Foundation for the Blind, New York, 1986, 81-87.

Canada, House of Commons. Task Force on Employment Opportunities for the '80s. *Work for Tomorrow: Employment Opportunities for the 80s.* Ottawa: Minister of Supply and Services, 1980.

CAW/TCA Canada. *Affirmative Action at Work, The Case of the Canadian Auto Workers and General Motors of Canada. Ontario Women's Directorate,* 1987.

City of Toronto. *An Employer's Handbook.*

Clarke, Marnie. "Milestones in Employment Equity." Paper delivered to Equinet, Toronto, June 29, 1988.

Devanna, Mary Ann, Charles Fombrun and Noel Tichy. "Human Resources Management: A Strategic Perspective." *Organizational Dynamics*, Winter, 1981, 51-67.

Dunnette, Marvin, and Stephan Motowidlo. "Estimating Benefits and Costs of Antisexist Training Programs in Organizations." In H. John Bernardin (ed.), *Women in the Work Force*. New York: Praeger, 1982, Ch. 7.

Economic Council of Canada. *Economic and Social Impacts of Immigration*. Ottawa: Minister of Supply and Services Canada, 1991.

Edwards, John. "U.S. Affirmative Action Alive and Well Despite Supreme Court." *Equal Opportunities International*, 10 (1), Sept. 1991, 9-13.

Foot, David. "Policy Implications of Demographic Change in Canada." Employment and Immigration Canada, Population Working Paper No. 10, 1988.

Ginzberg, Eli, Thierry J. Noyelle and Thomas M. Stanback Jr. *Technology and Employment*. Boulder and London: Westview Press, 1986.

Gower, David. "Labour Force Trends: Canada and the United States." Statistics Canada, *Canadian Social Trends*, Autumn 1988, 14-19.

Jain, Harish C., and Rick D. Hackett. "Measuring Effectiveness of Employment Equity Programs in Canada: Public Policy and a Survey." *Canadian Public Policy*, XV:2, 1989.

Kanter, Rosabeth Moss. *The Change Masters*. New York: Simon and Schuster Inc., 1983.

Kernaghan, Kenneth. "Representative Bureaucracy: The Canadian Perspective." *Canadian Public Administration*, 21, 1978, 489-512.

Kochan, Thomas, and Peter Cappelli. "The Transformation of the Industrial Relations and Personnel Function". In Paul Osterman (ed.), *Internal Labor Markets*. Cambridge, Mass.: MIT Press, 1984, ch. 5.

Lovrich, N., Brent Steel, and David Houd. "Equity versus Productivity: Affirmative Action and Municipal Police Service." *Public Productivity Review*, 39, 1986, 61-72.

O'Farrel, Brigid, and Sharon Harlan. "Job Integration Strategies, Today's Programs and Tomorrow's Needs." In Barabara Reskin (ed.), *Sex Segregation in the Workplace*. Washington, D.C.: National Academy Press, 1984, 267-291.

Ontario Women's Directorate. "Employment Equity Award Winners, 1987".

Newton, Keith. "Technological and Organizational Change in Canada." *New Technology, Work, and Employment*, 4(1), 1989, 42-47.

Patillo, Roger W. "Unlocking the Doors, An Examination of the Impact of Computer and High Technology on Employment Opportunities for the

Physically Disabled." Prepared for: Health and Welfare Canada, Assistance and VRDP Program, Social Services Program Branch, March, 1986.

Phillips, D. Rys. "Equity in the Labour Market: The Potential of Affirmative Action." In Rosalie Silberman Abella (ed.), *Research Studies of the Commission on Equality in Employment.* Ottawa: Supply and Services, 1985.

Piché, Louise. "Employment Equity: Managing in a Rights-seeking Environment." *Canadian Public Administration,* 29(4), Winter 1986, 624-29.

Samuel, T. John. "Third World Immigration, Multiculturalism and Ethnicity in Canada." Paper presented at the National Symposium on Demography of Immigrant, Racial and Ethnic Groups in Canada, August, 1988, Winnipeg.

Samuel, T. John. "Immigration and Visible Minorities in the Year 2001: A Projection." Ottawa, Centre for Immigration and Ethnocultural Studies, Carleton University, 1987.

Schotter, Andrew, and Keith Weigelt. "The Benefits of Equal Opportunity." *Business and Society Review,* 65, Spring 1988, 45-47,

Schuler, Randall. "Personnel and Human Resource Management Choices and Organization Strategy." In R. S. Schuler, S. A. Youngblood and V.L., Huber (eds.), *Readings in Personnel and Human Resource Management,* 3rd ed. St. Paul: West, 1987.

Thacker, Rebecca. "Affirmative Action After the Supreme Court's 1988-1989 Term: What Employers Need to Know." *Employment Relations Today,* 17 (2), Summer 1990, 139-144.

Towers Perrin and The Hudson Institute. *Workforce 2000,* 1990.

Townson, Monica. "The Costs of Employment Equity — Can We Afford Not to Implement It?" Paper presented to Second National Affirmative Action Practitioners' Workshop, Employment and Immigration Canada, Toronto, May 9, 1985.

Weinfeld, Morton. "The Development of Affirmative Action in Canada." *Canadian Ethnic Studies,* 13: 1981, 23-29.

Wilson, V.S. and W. A. Mullins. "Representative Bureaucracy: Linguistic/Ethnic Aspects in Canadian Public Policy." *Canadian Public Administration,* 21, 1978, 513-538.

Working Group on Employment Equity. *Status Report: Visible Minorities.* Ontario Ministry of Citizenship, Toronto, June, 1989 (a).

Working Group on Employment Equity. *Status Report: Women.* Ontario Ministry of Citizenship, Toronto, June, 1989 (b).

CHAPTER

4

The Legal
Framework of
Employment
Equity

THERE ARE SEVERAL REASONS why it is important for those concerned with employment equity in Canada to be familiar with its legal underpinnings. Some will use their knowledge of the legal framework to persuade and convince decision makers to commit the organization to change and to make resources available. Other practitioners need to know what compliance with human rights law, employment equity legislation, contract compliance regulations and other requirements will involve, and the standards against which their efforts will be measured. Some may consider the legal imperatives to be important, but not the key considerations in creating commitment to change, planning strategy and action plans, and measuring progress (see Box 4.1). Nevertheless, all practitioners need to understand in general terms the legal and policy context in which employment equity operates. Furthermore, and as discussed in depth in Chapter 5, understanding something of the logic behind the laws and how they are interpreted is helpful in developing a deeper understanding of the meaning of discrimination and disadvantage, how these meanings are evolving, and what responsibilities an employer has to provide remedies for them.

BOX 4.1

The Best Employment Equity Programs Are Undertaken by Employers in Their Own Interests and for Their Own Reasons.

Neil Gavigan, Director of the Federal Contractors Program, has said, "The best [FCP compliance] reviews — even those where we haven't agreed with everything that's been done — have been in companies where the employer has said, 'This is our program, not the government's. This is important to us internally. Therefore, we will establish an employment equity program that makes sense to this company and still fulfils the criteria.' Where that attitude has existed, the companies seem to be in very good shape and we've been generally happy with the plans. Where commitment exists, where work has started, even if not completed, it's a breath of fresh air."

(SOURCE: "Checking Out Compliance with the Federal Contractors Program," *The Equal Times*, October 1989, p.62.)

The Legal and Policy Structure for Employment Equity

Employment equity is firmly situated in the Canadian legal, regulatory and government policy frameworks. Its foundation can be clearly seen in the Charter, human rights law, employment equity legislation, regulation, and government policy at the federal and provincial levels. The paragraphs that follow provide an overview of the foundation of employment equity in the Charter, human rights law, specific legislation on employment equity at the federal and provincial levels, and regulations in various jurisdictions.

The Charter of Rights and Freedoms

Under Section 15(2) of the Charter, there is a clear constitutional mandate for employment equity that is as yet unchallenged at the Supreme Court level (see Box 4.2).

BOX 4.2

The Constitutional Mandate for Employment Equity

Section 15 of the Charter is often referred to as the "general equality clause," and section 15(2) as the "affirmative action" clause. They state:

15. (1) Every individual is equal before and under the law and has the right to equal protection and equal benefit of the law without discrimination and, in particular, without discrimination based on race, national or ethnic origin, colour, religion, sex, age or mental or physical disability.

(2) Subsection (1) does not preclude **any law, program or activity that has as its object the amelioration of conditions of disadvantaged individuals or groups** including those that are disadvantaged because of race, national or ethnic origin, colour, religion, sex, age or mental or physical disability. [emphasis added]

There are other equality clauses in the Charter:
• Section 25 - aboriginal rights
• Section 27 - multicultural diversity
• Section 28 - gender equality
• Section 29 - denominational schools

Several legal scholars have discussed the various interpretations the courts might give to Sections 15(1) and 15(2) in the future. According to Gwen Brodsky and Shelagh Day,

An interpretation of sections 15(1) and 15(2) that assumes they are contradictory also assumes that treating everyone the same is the norm of equality although special treatment may be justified in certain circumstances. On the other hand, reading sections 15(1) and 15(2) as a whole, assumes that equality is not merely or even primarily a matter of same treatment, but rather a matter of addressing and overcoming the disadvantage of historically oppressed and excluded groups. Because the latter interpretation can better address the reality of inequality, it is one that better fits the purpose of section 15 (Brodsky and Day, 1989:30).

The American experience with employment equity (or "affirmative action" as it is termed in the U.S.) is rife with legal debates and litigation about the validity of race and gender conscious decision-making. Affirmative action "quotas" for the hiring and promotion of minorities and women are at the centre of the controversy, which in part arises from the American value placed on individual equal treatment over group rights, and in part because neither U.S. anti-discrimination law (Title VII of the Civil Rights Act) nor the Constitution contain explicit provisions allowing employers to undertake preferential treatment of minorities and women. In Canada we have demonstrated a different conception of equality and of the remedies for disadvantage and discrimination. Judge Rosalie Abella has succinctly stated the distinctions between civil rights and human rights (Box 4.3). Section 15(2) of the Canadian Charter of Rights and Freedoms provides the constitutional foothold for progressive, strong employment equity initiatives in Canada, including preferential treatment.

BOX 4.3
Civil Rights and Human Rights

"Individual and group rights in Canada have not been either/or propositions. We acknowledge both. We respect a notion of equality that respects differences and we understand that there are different meanings to equality under each rights regime: the regime which gives primacy to the individual and the regime which gives primacy to the individual's group.

That is why it is important to appreciate the difference between civil liberties and human rights: otherwise, we will throw ourselves hopelessly into analytical anarchy over which approach applies when, especially under the Charter.

Civil liberties represents the theory of individual rights developed by Locke and refined by Mill, whose premise was that all individuals are equal in their right to be free from arbitrary state intervention. Every individual has the same presumptive right as every other individual to individual autonomy subject only to those limitations the state can justify as reasonable.

In human rights, on the other hand, we are talking of individuals in their capacity as members of groups which are disadvantaged for arbitrary reasons. It is about discrimination against individuals based on ascribed characteristics, because a whole group has been stereotyped as having those characteristics. Here the state is asked, indeed required, not to abstain but to intervene, to protect individuals from discrimination based on group affiliation. Equality here means not that everyone is the same, but that everyone has the same or an equal right to be free from discrimination, from arbitrary disadvantage caused by ignoring or inappropriately taking into account differences we attribute to individuals who are members of groups.

There is a difference between treating people equally as we do in civil liberties and treating people as equals as we do in human rights. For purposes of the former, we treat everyone the same; for purposes of the latter, we treat them according to their differences."

(SOURCE: Rosalie Silberman Abella, "Equality and Human Rights in Canada: Coping with the New Isms," *University Affairs*, June/July 1991, 22.)

Human Rights Legislation

When implementing employment equity, it is helpful to think of human rights laws in Canada as having two distinct purposes. First, they provide an interpretation of and remedy for discrimination by acting in a reactive fashion as anti-discrimination laws. Secondly, they provide employers and others with legal permission to proactively undertake "special programs" that take into consideration race, gender, disability and other distinctions. Both the reactive anti-discrimination and proactive special program elements of human rights law have practical importance for employment equity planning, analysis and monitoring.

For example, the implementation of an employment systems review requires an employer to identify the barriers the designated groups face in getting and keeping jobs, in training, development and progression, and in the environment in which they work. In carrying out an employment systems review we rely on the body of human rights case law to help us determine what is and is not considered to be discriminatory, and then devise the changes to employment policies and practices that are needed to remedy such barriers.

On the other hand, the special program provisions enable an employer to design and implement initiatives that go beyond non-discrimination and proactively improve the opportunities of the designated groups. Such measures may assist designated group members toward equality by strategically addressing sources and effects of the disadvantage and discrimination they face, have experienced in the past or are likely to in the future. Usually the special program provisions are used to assess and approve special measures, preferential treatment or exclusive opportunities for members of the designated groups. Later in the chapter, in the section entitled Human Rights Special Program Provisions, we discuss how these provisions may protect the employer from findings of reverse discrimination. We will now explore both the reactive and proactive aspects of human rights law.

Human Rights Anti-Discrimination Provisions International human rights laws have given impetus to the development of human rights and equality laws in Canada and other countries. The Universal Declaration of Human Rights of 1948 marked a global concern about issues of human rights. The Declaration was followed by a number of international covenants, among them the International Convention on the Elimination of All Forms of Racial Discrimination (1965) and the Convention on the Elimination of All Forms of Discrimination Against Women (1979). In 1976 all Canadian provinces and the federal government unanimously agreed to ratify the International Covenant on Civil and Political Rights. These declarations and conventions were, in general, legally binding on their signatories and internationally reviewed, but there were no enforcement provisions. There is evidence that international law has been used to interpret Canadian legislation on human rights matters, and Cohen (1988) has suggested that long-standing international agreements, such as the Declaration, "have acquired the force of international customary law."

Although Canada was a signatory to the Universal Declaration of Human Rights, it was three decades before the Canadian Government enacted federal human rights legislation (the Canadian Human Rights Act, 1978). Provincial action on human rights preceded federal initiatives, with Ontario the first, in 1962, to consolidate current anti-discrimination statutes into the Ontario Human Rights Code, and to establish a full-time Human Rights Commission with staff and Commissioners to enforce the act and undertake public education. Other provinces soon followed, for example: Nova Scotia (1963), Alberta (1966), New Brunswick (1967), Prince Edward Island (1968), Newfoundland (1969) and Manitoba (1970). It should be noted that some provinces had laws prohibiting certain kinds of discrimination prior to this, such as the 1944 Racial Discrimination Act in Ontario and the more comprehensive 1947 Saskatchewan Bill of Rights, followed by fair employment and fair accommodation practices legislation by many provinces beginning in the mid-1950s. However, comprehensive human rights statutes did not exist until the 1960s and 1970s (Tarnopolsky and Pentney, 1985: 30-31).

At the federal, provincial and territorial levels, the filing, investigation, and resolution of complaints of discrimination in employment rests with human rights commissions or their equivalent (such as the British Columbia Human Rights Council). There are differences among jurisdictions as to the grounds of discrimination for a complaint (see Box 4.4), the remedies which may apply, and procedures for complaint investigation and conciliation. In general, human rights commissions have powers to use education, persuasion and publicity to discourage and reduce discriminatory practices, as well as investigate and seek settlements to complaints brought by individuals, groups or third parties. Human rights commissions have the power to file complaints of discrimination on behalf of an individual victim of discrimination, or systemic discrimination complaints based upon statistical and other evidence about an employer's pattern of hiring and other employment practices.

Since 1988 the Canadian Human Rights Commission has used hiring, training and promotion data reported by federally regulated employers under the Employment Equity Act to assess whether there is reasonable cause to believe that discrimination in

BOX 4.4
Prohibited Grounds of Discrimination

Jurisdiction	Federal	Alberta	British Columbia	Manitoba	New Brunswick	Newfoundland	Nova Scotia	Ontario	Prince Edward Island	Quebec	Saskatchewan	Northwest Territories	Yukon Territory
Place of Origin		•	•		•			•	•		•	•	
Place of Residence												•	
Creed		•				•	•	•	•		•	•	•
Social Conditions										•			
Social Origin						•				•			
Source of Income				•									
Language										•			
Civil Status										•			
Harassment**	•				•	•		•		•			
Sexual Orientation				•				•		•			
Family Status	•			•				•				•	
Political Belief			•	•		•			•	•			
Ancestry		•	•		•			•			•	•	•
Physical Disability	•	•	•	•	•	•	•	•	•	•	•	•	•
Mental Disability	•	•	•	•	•	•	•	•	•	•	•	•	•
Criminal Conviction	•		•					•		•	•	•	•
Marital Status	•	•	•	•	•	•	•	•	•	•	•	•	•
Pregnancy/Childbirth*	•	•						•		•			
Sex	•	•	•	•	•	•	•	•	•	•	•	•	•
Age	•	• (18+)	• (45-65)	•	• (19+)	• (19-65)	• (40-65)	• (18-65)	•	•	• (18-65)	•	•
Religion	•	•	•	•	•	•	•	•	•	•	•	•	•
Nationality/Citizenship				•				•		•		•	
Colour	•	•	•	•	•	•	•	•	•	•	•	•	•
National/Ethnic Origin	•			•	•	•	•	•	•	•		•	
Race	•	•	•	•	•	•	•	•	•	•	•	•	•
Dependence on Alcohol/Drug	•												

*In Alberta discrimination on the basis of pregnancy is deemed to be discrimination on the basis of sex. In Ontario, Manitoba, and the Yukon, discrimination on the basis of pregnancy is included in discrimination on the basis of sex.
** Harassment is banned on all proscribed grounds of discrimination except in New Brunswick where it only refers to sexual harassment.

(SOURCE: *Canadian Master Labour Guide* 916, (March 20, 1990):245.)

employment practices and policies exists. However, rather than use its statutory powers to file and investigate a complaint against an employer, the Commission has "invited" targeted employers to jointly undertake an employment equity analysis. If the Commission's invitation to a voluntary joint review is declined by an employer, the Commission may then initiate a complaint. In the first year of this initiative, the Canadian Human Rights Commission entered into voluntary review agreements with seventeen major employers, including: Bank of Montreal, Bank of Nova Scotia, Royal Bank of Canada, Toronto Dominion Bank, Banque Nationale, Canadian Imperial Bank of Commerce, Canada Post, Canadian National Railways, Canadian Pacific Express and Transport, Denison Mines, Marine Atlantic, Saskatchewan Wheat Pool, Ministry of National Defence, Ministry of External Affairs, Ministry of Fisheries, Ministry of Revenue and Ministry of Transport. Two companies, Bell Canada and the Canadian Broadcasting Corporation, declined the review and the Commission initiated complaints (Canadian Human Rights Advocate, July, 1989:11). Box 4.5 explains the objectives of the Commission's approach to employment equity. Box 4.6 discusses an employment equity agreement signed in 1991 by the Royal Bank and the Canadian Human Rights Commission.

BOX 4.5
Canadian Human Rights Commission's Operational Procedures for Ensuring Compliance with Employment Equity

"The Canadian Human Rights Commission will use the information collected under terms of the Employment Equity Act and Treasury Board guidelines on employment equity to continue the work it started 10 years ago when the agency was established — that is, to ensure equality in employment as required by the Canadian Human Rights Act. (...)

The Commission's approach to employment equity has a two-fold purpose: To ensure employers change their employment systems and practices which have discriminated against these groups, so that discrimination does not continue in the future; and to ensure employers provide opportunities as quickly as possible for disadvantaged groups to remedy the effects of past discrimination.

> Because the Commission is committed to pursuing a co-operative approach with employers and to speeding up the implementation of employment equity, it will invite an employer with possible problems to undertake a joint review of its employment equity analysis with the Commission. The review, an alternative to initiating a complaint, will follow the same fact-gathering steps as a formal complaint. In both cases, the numbers resulting from a comparison of data will not constitute proof that an employer is discriminating but merely indicate where there may be problems.
>
> By 1994, when Parliament will undertake its second legislative review of the Employment Equity Act, the Commission intends to have conducted a voluntary review or investigation of all covered employers with problematic statistics. A summary of actions will be published in our Annual Report, including the number of complaints initiated, their scope and resolution, as well as similar data on voluntary reviews."
>
> (SOURCE: Canadian Human Rights Commission's Operational Procedures for Ensuring Compliance with Employment Equity, June 1, 1988, Introduction, pp.i-ii.)

If a complaint filed with a human rights commission cannot be settled by conciliation, an administrative tribunal may be appointed to hear the complaint and issue an order against an employer who is found to have discriminated. The order can specify that the discriminatory practice cease, that the victim(s) be hired or reinstated, and compensated for damages, loss of earnings, humiliation and mental suffering. Following the ATF decision (discussed in Chapters 1 and later in this chapter), administrative tribunals and the courts may also be able to order employers to implement employment equity measures, including quotas for hiring, training or promotion, where gross statistical disparities have been shown to exist between the employer's utilization of designated groups and their availability for such employment. Where the tribunal is presented with evidence of systemic discrimination, other preferential measures and assistance for groups discriminated against might also be ordered, as well as substantive and wide-ranging changes to employment policies and practices. Employment equity measures may also be undertaken voluntarily by employers as part of a settlement reached by conciliation prior to a tribunal hearing.

BOX 4.6
Pay Equity Article

Bank to move women up ladder, hopes to exceed native hiring target

The Royal Bank of Canada has become the first bank to sign an employment equity agreement with the Canadian Human Rights Commission, but a bank spokesman says the new deal is not far off the bank's existing programs.

The agreement follows a two-year commission review of the bank's policies and practices and sets targets and timetables for the hiring and promotion of native people, women and visible minorities. The commission will monitor the bank's progress over the next three years.

The goals set out in the agreement "in some cases are very close to what we already have [in the bank's employment equity plan]," said Lynda White, manager of employment equity for the Royal Bank.

"In the agreement that we have, I look at the goals for women executives and visible minorities and they reflect our own goals."

The bank has 37,943 full-time employees. The hiring targets in the agreement apply to full-time employees only.

The agreeement sets a goal of hiring 2.25 per cent native people a year in the clerical area, she said. "Last year we hired 2.2 per cent. Given that, I would think that we can do better" than the goal set in the agreement.

"I think there are things [in the agreement] that are additional," said human rights commissioner Max Yalden. "I think there are numbers that might increase more than they otherwise would have."

A statement from the commission indicated that promoting more women to senior ranks and an expanded support system for native employees were improvements made in the new agreement.

Canadian banks have been the target of criticism by women's groups, disabled groups and others for their failure to hire native people and promote women and visible minorities. One study showed that in 1988, women in banking made only 57 cents for every dollar earned by men, an increase of less than 1 per cent from 1987.

The Royal Bank's review did not arise from a specific complaint but was part of a commission effort to improve employment equity generally in the private sector, a commission offical said.

Ms. White said that in 1990, women made up 75 per cent of the Royal Bank's employees, about the same as in 1987. About 5 per cent were in upper management, she said, up from 1 per cent in 1987. In middle management, they were 49 per cent of the employee force.

Visible minorities constituted 11.6 per cent of the bank's employees in 1990, she said, up from 7.8 per cent in 1987. They also made up 49 per cent of middle management employees, she said. She gave no figure for visible minorities in upper management.

Native people made up 0.6 per cent of employees in 1990, up from 0.1 per cent in 1987, she said.

Statistics were not available for 1991.

Asked how fast those numbers would change and what goals the bank would strive to meet, Ms. White said that information is confidential. "Most of it is expanding on things that are already in place."

The commission is currently doing reviews with the Bank of Nova Scotia, the Toronto-Dominion Bank, the Bank of Montreal and the Canadian Imperial Bank of Commerce, a commission spokesman said.

(SOURCE: *The Globe and Mail*, Monday, June 17, 1991.)

The case of *ATF vs. CN Rail* (1987) has been of critical importance to the evolution of employment equity in Canada. As noted in Chapter 1, the *ATF* Supreme Court decision has helped to define the goals of employment equity (Box 1.6). It also illustrates how a broadly based systemic discrimination complaint can enhance the case law, and how extensive are the powers of a tribunal to order remedial and preventative employment equity initiatives and changes to employment systems.

In 1979 a Montreal advocacy organization, Action Travail des Femmes, filed a complaint of systemic discrimination against Canadian National Rail. Fourteen complaints had also been filed by individual women concerning their experience with discrimination in getting and keeping non-traditional blue collar jobs in the St. Lawrence region rail yards, and in response to the sexual harassment they faced in the workplace. Although the individual complaints were settled, the complaint by ATF on behalf of women could not be conciliated and the complaint was referred to a tribunal for decision.

In 1984, the tribunal found the complaint to be substantiated and ordered a wide ranging settlement. At the time of the complaint women held 0.7% of blue collar jobs in CNR's St. Lawrence region, and the tribunal found a pattern of discriminatory hiring practices that could not be justified as *bona fide* occupational requirements. The tribunal's order required the company to cease a number of past practices, such as the use of tests that were unrelated to job requirements and that had discriminatory impact on women, and to adopt new hiring and recruiting practices. The decision also required the company to hire women for 25 % of unskilled blue collar jobs in the St. Lawrence region until women hold 13% of such jobs, a target roughly equivalent to the proportion of women in the blue collar Canadian labour force.

The company appealed the decision and in 1985 the Federal Court of Appeal upheld two of the tribunal's three orders while striking down the quota hiring requirement on the grounds that the tribunal had exceeded its powers under the Canadian Human Rights Act. This decision was appealed to the Supreme Court which in 1987 unanimously reversed the finding of the Federal Court of Appeal and reinstituted the tribunal's hiring order. The Supreme Court held that the tribunal had acted within its powers since the hiring requirement was designed to break a cycle of systemic discrimination against women, thus ensuring that in the future, women applicants would not face these same barriers (CHRR, D/664). Chief Justice Brian Dickson gave the following opinion:

> When the theoretical roots of employment equity programmes are exposed, it is readily apparent that in attempting to combat systemic discrimination, it is essential to look to the past patterns of discrimination and to destroy those patterns in order to prevent the same type of discrimination in the future.

Employers have also been ordered to implement employment equity plans and to compensate employees under provincial human rights statutes. For example, Macmillan Bloedel was ordered to compensate two women employees for lost wages, and to implement an affirmative action plan, by a Saskatchewan board of inquiry (*Canadian HR Reporter* 3 [21]) (July 18, 1990) :3.

Human rights commissions vary widely in the resources at their disposal for implementing and enforcing human rights legislation. For example, Ontario's Commission, with about 180 employees, has a comparatively large staff dispersed throughout the province, while Saskatchewan's formerly strong Commission was weakened in the early 80s, and British Columbia disbanded its Commission in 1983 and now operates with a small council appointed by the Cabinet (*Globe and Mail*, Nov. 13, 1984, 22). Thus the impact of human rights legislation in reducing discrimination in employment depends not only upon legislative provisions, but also upon the resources available for monitoring discrimination and exercising the enforcement powers provided in the legislation, and upon the political context — notably the power and influence of the various stakeholders whose interests are affected by human rights legislation.

As we can see from the *ATF* decision, the case law that results from decisions and interpretations set out by human rights tribunals and courts is a significant factor in the impact of human rights legislation, and in the legislative context surrounding discrimination in employment and remedies for it. In the human rights field, both federally and provincially, a growing body of case law is defining what constitutes discrimination and appropriate remedies. For example, we see a slowly evolving body of legislation and interpretation that helps us to deal with matters of workplace harassment, the duty to accommodate, pregnancy, *bona fide* occupational requirements related to recruitment and selection, testing, and the importance of work environment and organizational culture to the successful integration of previously excluded or marginalized groups, and the relationship between "statistical disparities" of designated groups in an employer's work force and discriminatory employment systems.

There has also been a shift in the case law from a view that motives or intent must be demonstrated in order to prove discrimination, toward a view that focuses on results in identifying the existence of discrimination. In Chapter 5 we will discuss the distinctions between discrimination based on intent, and discrimination shown by results, and how to gather and analyze appropriate evidence related to each form of discrimination.

Human Rights Special Program Provisions   Federal, provincial and territorial human rights legislation provides statutory protection for employment equity under "special program" clauses. Although Alberta's Individual's Rights Protection Act (1972) does not contain an explicit special programs provision as found in other human rights statutes, a 1980 Supreme Court of Canada decision ruled that an affirmative action program to train and employ locally-based Native people in the Alsands Project for the development of the tar sands in northeastern Alberta was not in conflict with the Individual's Rights Protection Act. Mr. Justice Ritchie, in discussing the Alsands initiatives for Native peoples, addressed concerns about pursuing "a policy favouring any individual or group of individuals on the ground that in so doing other individuals would be discriminated against." This theory is characterized in the United States as "reverse discrimination." Mr. Justice Ritchie stated:

> In the present case what is involved is a proposal designed to improve the lot of the native peoples with a view to enabling them to compete as nearly as possible on equal terms with other members of the community who are seeking employment in the tar sands plant. With all respect, I can see no reason why the measures proposed by the "affirmative action" programs for the betterment of the lot of the native peoples in the area in question

should be construed as "discriminating against" other inhabitants. The purpose of the plan as I understand it is not to displace non-Indians from their employment, but rather to advance the lot of the Indians so that they may be in a competitive position to obtain employment without regard to the handicaps which their race has inherited (*Athabasca Tribal Council*, CHRR, 1980 D/437).

Special program provisions within the various jurisdictions both share certain characteristics and differ from each other in some ways. Professor Constance Backhouse, in the 1989 Ontario Board of Inquiry decision *Roberts vs. Ontario (Ministry of Health)* (CHRR, 1989 D/6353), compared and discussed these features with respect to the types of individuals or groups that can be assisted, the types of programs that can be devised, and the powers of the Commission with respect to such programs. The concept of affirmative action, the arguments for and against it, the legal status of affirmative action in the United States, the Canadian legislative response and the Charter are also discussed at length in *Roberts*.

The special programs provision of the Canadian Human Rights Act is representative of the proactive nature of such permissive clauses:

> s.15(1) It is not a discriminatory practice for a person to adopt or carry out a special program, plan or arrangement designed to prevent disadvantages that are likely to be suffered by, or to eliminate or reduce disadvantages that are suffered by, any group of individuals when those disadvantages would be or are based on or related to the race, national or ethnic origin, colour, religion, age, sex, marital status, family status or disability of members of that group, by improving opportunities respecting goods, services, facilities, accommodation or employment in relation to that group.

A few commissions, such as those in Saskatchewan and the federal jurisdiction, have issued criteria related to the development and implementation of special programs. Ontario has drafted "guidelines on special programs" and intends to enter into public consultations with a view to issuing final criteria in early 1992.

It is unlikely that an initiative undertaken by an employer as a "special program" would insulate that employer from a complaint of discrimination. However, the defense would be to demonstrate that the undertaking is consistent with the objectives of the special program provisions, and that the means taken to implement the special program can also be shown to be non-discriminatory.

The significance of legislative provisions allowing special programs is that under Canadian law, preferential treatment of groups historically subjected to discrimination in employment would not constitute "reverse discrimination." As we have seen, this principle is reiterated in section 15(2) of the Charter. Nevertheless, few employers have taken advantage of the special program permissions in human rights legislation. Many employers are aware of the legislative prohibitions against discrimination, but fewer know about and understand the permissive special program clauses. Furthermore, in our experience there is considerable misunderstanding and anxiety among employers about the legality of collecting work force data for the purpose of implementing a special program, or undertaking explicit outreach recruitment of all or some designated groups.

Another impediment to undertaking special programs is the perception that they constitute "reverse discrimination," giving special advantages to a particular group, or reflecting tokenism toward the less qualified. For example, the Chairman of the Toronto Transit Commission, in response to complaints by women's groups in 1987, cautioned that "the TTC would be running afoul of equal treatment under the law if it were to give special preference to women" (*Toronto Star*, April 8, 1987). The concept of special programs as a remedy for past discrimination and disadvantage, and as a short term initiative to "level the playing field" or create a critical mass of previously excluded groups, is not yet well understood.

Employment Equity Legislation

The special program provisions in human rights statutes are important because they may shelter the stronger forms of employment equity from findings of reverse discrimination. However, as we have noted above, such provisions are permissive, not mandatory. Employers are *allowed* to undertake special programs; they are *not required* to do so, unless ordered by a tribunal or court to remedy and prevent discrimination identified through the human rights complaint process. Thus, the special program provisions of human rights laws have essentially made the initiation of employment equity voluntary, not mandatory. Specific employment equity legislation or government contract compliance policy is required to move us from a voluntary to mandatory legal context in Canada.

As noted in Chapter 1 (Box 1.1), there is a federal law, The Employment Equity Act, the purpose of which is to

> achieve equality in the work place so that no person shall be denied employment opportunities or benefits for reasons unrelated to ability and, in the fulfillment of that goal, to correct the conditions of disadvantage in employment ... by giving effect to the principle that employment equity means more than treating people in the same way but also requires special measures and accommodation of differences.

Since 1987, the Act has required each federally regulated employer to submit annual statistical reports on standardized forms that show the representation of women, aboriginal peoples, racial minorities and people with disabilities in specific salary ranges and occupational groups in the organization. Annual counts of hirings, promotions and terminations by designated group status are also required. The Act also requires the employer to prepare and retain a plan setting out goals and timetables for employment equity implementation. However, there is no statutory requirement that this plan be submitted to the federal government or made public.

Hence, although there is an employment equity law applying to federally regulated industries such as those involved in banking, telecommunications, broadcasting and interprovincial transportation, as well as federal crown corporations, the statute requires mandatory reporting of work force statistics, not mandatory improvements in the employment opportunities of the designated groups. The law does not require employers to analyse their employment policies and practices, workplace environment and organizational culture in order to identify and remedy disadvantage and discrimination. Nor are employers required to take steps to ensure the integration and retention of designated group members that the organization hires and promotes. Goals and timetables — aids in planning for improvements in the representation and distribution of the designated groups — are not mandatory. Neither are employers required to seek the participation of the designated groups, unions and employees in employment equity planning, implementation, monitoring and assessment of progress. Consequently, it is difficult to envision how the legislative purpose of equality in employment can be fulfilled given the limited statutory requirements of the Act.

Nevertheless, the legislative framework for employment equity in Canada is likely to evolve considerably in the next few years. The review of the Employment Equity Act in 1991–1992, which is occurring under a provision of the Act, may result in a strengthening of the law and a broadening of its application, since as we have seen in Chapter 1, the legislation in its present form appears to be falling short of attaining its stated goals. In addition, there is likely to be further legislation at the provincial level. The government of Ontario plans to introduce mandatory employment equity legislation in 1992, and has stated that "a framework for discussion" about the proposed legislation is contained in a private members' bill introduced by Bob Rae in 1990, before he became Premier (*Globe and Mail,* June 22, 1991) (see Box 4.7 for a summary). The 1991 Police Services Act, which requires that all Ontario police departments and agencies must undertake employment equity, has initiated Ontario's response to the need for mandatory employment equity.

BOX 4.7
Summary of Bill 172(p), Employment Equity Act, 1990

> The Bill applies to employers with annual payrolls of more than $300,000 in both public and private sectors. Employers are required to develop, implement and monitor employment equity plans, specify positive practices to achieve equity, set targets for employment of designated group members at all levels, and file annual reports. There are fines for failure to comply. The designated groups are aboriginal peoples, women, people with disabilities, and racial minorities.
>
> In unionized workplaces plans are negotiated with trade unions, and seniority provisions are plant wide. In non-unionized firms employers are to consult with employees.
>
> (SOURCES: Ontario Legislative Digest Service, 2nd Session, 34th legislature, 1989-90, release 39, June 15, 1990; *Globe and Mail,* June 22, 1991.)

Employment Equity Regulations and Policies

Across the country, and at the provincial and municipal as well as the federal level, there is a web of regulations and policies that directly or indirectly address employment equity issues. Provincial regulations in a number of jurisdictions, notably those dealing with education, policing and health, are requiring employment equity implementation or encouraging it through the use of incentive funding. The most familiar of the regulatory measures is the Federal Contractors Program, which requires some employers who sell goods and services to the federal government to implement an eleven point employment equity program. (We discussed the FCP in Chapter 1 and Box 1.2.) In 1989 the Quebec government implemented a program for organizations with over 100 employees doing business worth $100,000 or more with the government. Suppliers are required to sign an agreement to report progress, and face penalties for non-compliance. Since 1990 the City of Toronto has required employers from whom it purchases goods and services to report employment equity data on their employees.

Quebec's and Toronto's programs, and the Federal Contractors Program, use the principle of contract compliance, which first became public policy in the United States during World War II when defense contractors were required to demonstrate that they employed Blacks in their work forces. Contract compliance is a mandatory form of employment equity whereby employers who contract to supply goods or services to government are required to prove that they are implementing employment equity regulations. In the case of failure to comply, contracts may be cancelled or contractors may be excluded from bidding on future contracts.

Governments at all levels have varied in the leadership they have displayed about implementing employment equity within their own workplaces. The federal government has undertaken a number of initiatives. The Bilingualism and Biculturalism Commission (1969) addressed the issues of equality for francophones, and as a result, Weinfeld (1981:28) has suggested that "the concerted effort to raise francophone proportions in the Public Service represents the first large-scale "affirmative action" program in Canada, though the specific legislative support for affirmative action was yet to be passed. Since the 1970s programs and initiatives have been undertaken for women, aboriginal peoples, people with disabilities, Blacks in Nova Scotia and subsequently all racial minority groups across the country in an effort to improve their representation in the federal public service.

Many provincial governments have initiated programs to improve employment opportunities in their own ministries and departments for various designated groups, particularly women. Saskatchewan, Manitoba, Ontario, Quebec and Nova Scotia have, at various times over the last two decades, been prominent and progressive in their initiatives, yet sustaining the momentum has often proved difficult when there has been a change of the party in power. Ontario initiated an affirmative action approach in its public service in 1974, and introduced numerical targets for women in 1980 (Welch, 1984). In 1985–86, there was an extensive review of the Ontario public service work force, as well as a work-force audit and review of recruitment and advancement practices. In June 1987 an employment equity program was announced, including francophones as well as women, aboriginal peoples, people with disabilities and racial minorities. Quebec also has mandatory legislation for provincial government ministries and agencies.

Local governments have varied widely in their responses to employment equity issues. Some, such as the cities of Toronto, Ottawa, and Saskatoon, and the Regional Municipality of Metropolitan Toronto, have been leaders in the field. Most have been silent. The Federation of Canadian Municipalities reported in 1989 that only 26 of the hundreds of municipalities across the country had undertaken measures to increase the representation of racial minorities in the civic work force.

Conclusion

Employment equity has a secure place within the evolution of human rights law and policy in Canada. Unlike our American counterparts, in Canada we have a clear constitutional and human rights statutory base for strong employment equity, including race, gender and disability conscious policies and programs. Employment equity is situated within both the reactive anti-discrimination and proactive special program objectives of the human rights legal framework. At a minimum, our legal structure requires non-discrimination in employment policies, practices and decision-making, workplaces and organizational culture. As well, it would appear that human rights laws may be used to address the statistical disparities found in the representation and distribution of the designated groups in workplaces.

Yet employment equity, as it has evolved in Canada, includes a recognition that non-discrimination alone does not define equality. Hence the special program provisions enable employers and unions to undertake progressive initiatives in order to remedy and prevent discrimination and disadvantage faced by the designated groups. Both the legal framework and decisions by the Supreme Court of Canada provide a supportive environment for stronger forms of employment equity such as special assistance for designated groups, preferential treatment and exclusive opportunities. It would appear that such measures are sheltered from findings of reverse discrimination so long as the legislative purpose of special programs is met.

Furthermore, and perhaps prompted by the growing advocacy of stakeholders for effective employment equity remedies, we are beginning to see human rights commissions address equity issues that affect classes of people, not just individuals. Commissions are focusing more resources on the review and investigation of the employment systems of large organizations, often using statistical work-force profiles as preliminary evidence of systemic discrimination. We also find human rights administrative tribunals and the courts ordering systemic and special program remedies for discrimination complaints involving groups and classes of complainants.

On the other hand, current statutory requirements for employment equity by federally regulated employers seem inadequate to the task of dealing with deeply entrenched patterns of discrimination in the workplace. The Employment Equity Act requires mandatory reporting of work-force statistical profiles, rather than mandatory improvements in the employment opportunities of the designated groups. Under current legislation, employment equity remains an essentially voluntary rather than mandatory instrument of change. However, given the current legislative review of the federal Employment Equity Act by the government, and the anticipated passage of an employment equity law in Ontario, the evolution of employment equity may begin to move away from an emphasis on bureaucratic procedures such as reporting work-force data towards evidence of action and change that will reduce inequality in the workplace.

At present, an employer's employment equity activities may be

- required under an employment equity statute,
- a result of contracting with a government agency to sell goods or services,

- an outcome of government policy and incentives,
- voluntarily agreed to as a settlement of a discrimination complaint,
- ordered by a tribunal or the courts, or
- voluntarily initiated by an employer and considered a legitimate special program.

All employment equity planning and implementation requires an understanding of what discrimination is and how to remedy it. In Chapter 5 we explore some of the evolving concepts of discrimination and then discuss how to analyse the barriers in employment systems and develop appropriate remedies.

REFERENCES

Brodsky, Gwen, and Shelagh Day. *Canadian Charter Equality Rights for Women: One Step Forward or Two Steps Back?* Ottawa: Canadian Advisory Council on the Status of Women, 1989.

Canada Act 1982, c. 11 (U.K.), Schedule B (The Constitution Act, 1982), Part I (Canadian Charter of Rights And Freedoms).

Cohen, Tannis. *Race Relations and the Law in Canada*. Toronto: Canadian Jewish Council, 1988.

Tarnopolsky, Walter S., and W. Pentney. *Discrimination and the Law in Canada*. Toronto: Richard De Boo, 1985.

CASES CITED

Action Travail des Femmes vs. CN Rail (1987), 40 D.L.R. (4th) 193 (S.C.C.).
Roberts vs. Ontario (1989), C.H.R.R. D/6353.

5

Legal Perspectives on Discrimination and Remedies

DISCRIMINATION IS AN EVOLVING CONCEPT. Legal experts as well as employers and other stakeholders must often work with less than precise definitions. Chief Justice Brian Dickson, referring in the 1987 *ATF* decision to the Abella Report, noted that while "Judge Abella chose not to offer a precise definition of systemic discrimination," the following passage from the Report contained "the essentials" of a definition:

> Discrimination ... means practices or attitudes that have, whether by design or impact, the effect of limiting an individual's or a group's right to the opportunities generally available because of attributed rather than actual characteristics... It is not a question of whether this discrimination is motivated by an intentional desire to obstruct someone's potential, or whether it is the accidental by-product of innocently motivated practices or systems. If the barrier is affecting certain groups in a disproportionately negative way, it is a signal that the practices that lead to this adverse impact may be discriminatory (Abella, 1984:2).

As noted in Chapter 4, human rights legislation prohibits discrimination against individuals, groups and classes of individuals defined by grounds such as sex, race, disability, age, marital status, and religion. However, the enumeration of grounds of discrimination in itself does not provide a definition and, for the most part, Canadian federal and provincial human rights laws do not define discrimination. Only the Quebec human rights legislation offers a definition: discrimination occurs where there is a distinction, exclusion, or preference based on one of the enumerated grounds with the effect of nullifying or impairing the human rights and freedoms of the person. In all other jurisdictions, the task of definition has been left to human rights commissions, administrative tribunals and the courts. Thus, we rely on the case law that has accumulated from human rights and other equality decisions for legal definitions and practical guidance in dealing with such questions as:

- What is discrimination?
- Must an intent to discriminate be proved?
- What steps is an employer required to take to accommodate diversity among employees?
- Is an employer liable for the sexual harassment of employees by a manager?
- Is discrimination because of pregnancy discrimination on the grounds of sex?

In this chapter we review how employment discrimination has been defined in Canada, contrasting this with American and British approaches. We note the confusion that has come to surround the definition and analysis of two forms of discrimination: adverse impact and lack of accommodation of diversity. In an attempt to clarify this confusion, we offer an analysis that deals with the lack of accommodation in human resource practices as a distinctly different form of discrimination from adverse impact discrimination, and therefore one that requires a very different kind of remedy. Within this context, we define systemic discrimination to include class-wide discrimination based on 1) unequal treatment 2) adverse impact, or 3) lack of accomodation.

One of the key components of any employment equity strategy is the review of employment systems. Employment systems are the organizational practices, policies and procedures — both formal and informal — surrounding recruitment and selection, training and development, promotion, compensation, terms and conditions of employment, termination, and any other human resources management decisions. The purpose of the review of employment systems is to identify any barriers contained in current practices that tend to impede the full participation of members of the designated groups in the work place, or that interfere unnecessarily with their career development, productivity and job satisfaction. Barriers that are identified through the review can then be replaced by other practices that are non-discriminatory, and that get the job done without unfairness to members of any particular group of employees or job applicants. Or, where appropriate, existing human resource management practices can be supplemented by arrangements that permit individual needs and social diversity to be accommodated in the workplace. It is important that these remedies — new practices designed to address inequalities — are consistent with the form of discrimination identified in the review of employment systems.

The chapter ends with a discussion of the implications of using human rights case law, and the conceptions of discrimination that underlie human rights decisions, as a framework for reviewing employment systems and developing remedies. We outline the kinds of analyses and remedies required when the employment systems review addresses any of the three forms of systemic discrimination: unequal treatment, adverse impact, and the lack of accommodation.

Supreme Court Interpretations of Discrimination

In recent years, in addressing these and a range of other issues, several decisions by the Supreme Court of Canada have helped us to understand both the meaning of discrimination in employment, and how to remedy it within the Canadian legal framework.

In a 1989 Supreme Court decision (*Turpin*), which dealt with Section 15 of the Charter and the appellants' right to equality before the law under the Criminal Code, Justice Bertha Wilson (now retired) referred to an earlier decision by Justice MacIntyre in *Andrews* (1989). Wilson noted that MacIntyre, acknowledging the deeper understanding of discrimination developed under the human rights codes, offered the following definition of discrimination:

> I would say then that discrimination may be described as a distinction, whether intentional or not but based on grounds relating to personal characteristics of the individual or group, which has the effect of imposing burdens, obligations, or disadvantages on such individual or group not imposed upon others, or which withholds or limits access to organizations, benefits, and advantages available to other members of society.

Justice Wilson provided a further interpretation:

> In determining whether there is discrimination on grounds relating to the personal characteristics of the individual or group, it is important to look not only at the impugned legislation which has created a distinction that violates the right to equality but also to the larger social, political and legal context. McIntyre J. emphasized in *Andrews*:
>
> > For as has been said, a bad law will not be saved merely because it operates equally upon those to whom it has application. Nor will a law necessarily be bad because it makes distinctions.
> >
> > Accordingly, **it is only by examining the larger context that a court can determine whether differential treatment results in inequality or whether, contrariwise, it would be identical treatment which would in the particular context result in inequality or foster disadvantage**. A finding that there is discrimination will, I think, in most but perhaps not all cases, necessarily entail a search for disadvantage that exists apart from and independent of the particular legal distinction being challenged (Wilson, *Turpin*, emphasis added).

As noted by the Supreme Court, the larger context, not just a particular employment policy or practice, needs to be examined in order to determine what is the appropriate means to achieve an equitable outcome. Later in this chapter we distinguish between intent and results types of discrimination, and then further differentiate between adverse impact and accommodation in the analysis and remedy of results based discrimination. We believe these concepts are useful to the practitioner who is attempting to identify practices that are discriminatory, and to design more equitable employment systems.

Several useful conclusions about the meaning and implications of discrimination within the Canadian context emerge from the case law. First, it is clear that the interpretation of the concept of discrimination is still evolving and developing. Even the Supreme Court is willing to reconsider and overturn its earlier decisions. Hence it is important that employment equity and human resource practitioners remain current on case law developments related to discrimination and equality in employment.

On some matters the case law provides clear answers. For example, evidence of intent to discriminate on the part of an employer is no longer required in order to conclude that discrimination exists in employment policies, practices or decision-making (*Bhinder*, 1985; *O'Malley* 1985). We also know that employers are liable for harassing behaviour and decisions of its managers and employees (*Robichaud* 1987; *Janzen* 1989). On the other hand, we do not yet have a clear definition of systemic discrimination nor judicial guidance on the role and use of work force statistics in making a case of discrimination under human rights law.

Second, if we compare the Canadian and American supreme court interpretations of discrimination over the last three decades, we find that prior to the mid-1980s, judgements of the U.S. Supreme Court were more progressive. U.S. decisions tended to expand the interpretation of discrimination from a standard of "evil motive" to the results-based concept of "adverse impact," and to support the principle of affirmative action, even in the absence of explicit statutory and constitutional mandates. However, the Reagan Administration appointments to the Supreme Court shifted the balance from broad decisions on discrimination and support for affirmative action, toward a far more narrow and restrictive interpretation. We need only look at recent American decisions that restrict findings of discrimination to situations that meet the requirements of a "similarly situated" test.

Since the late 1980s, then, decisions of the Supreme Court of Canada have been more liberal than those of the Supreme Court of the United States (Patmore, 1990: vii). The Canadian Supreme Court's judgements are enlarging the meaning of discrimination. One example is the difference between the U.S. and Canadian Supreme Courts in decisions on pregnancy discrimination. In the Manitoba case, *Brooks vs. Safeway* (1989), the Supreme Court of Canada made it clear that "distinctions or discrimination based on pregnancy" are to be regarded as discrimination based on sex, even though pregnancy based discrimination may not affect all women, that is, not all members of an "identified group" protected under human rights law. This decision departed from previous analyses by Canadian courts, and from current American decisions, which compared similarly situated women to men and concluded that unequal treatment based upon pregnancy was not sex discrimination. (We discuss the evidentiary process of making "similarly situated" comparisions later in this chapter.) The result of the *Brooks* decision was to provide Canadian women with legal protection under human rights laws for pregnancy related discrimination, while American women do not have such legal redress.

The broad interpretation of discrimination by Canadian courts in cases involving human rights legislation parallels their supportive decisions on special programs, as noted in Chapter 4. It may well be that the Canadian legal establishment is, in fact, responding to the challenge "to develop an indigenous rights-respecting jurisprudence that accommodates the Canadian experience" (Patmore, 1990: vii). To the extent that this is the case, Canadian policy and practice concerning equality in the workplace is different from the American experience, and potentially more effective in providing a framework for significant change.

Third, in Canada, unlike in the United States or Britain, there is explicit constitutional recognition of employment equity under Section 15(2) of the Charter. Supreme Court decisions regarding employment equity have been supportive of the concept, including preferential treatment of disadvantaged groups and explicit hiring quotas to remedy historical and current discrimination and prevent it in the future (e.g. *ATF*). Thus, we can anticipate continued judicial support of strong employment equity initiatives such as preferential treatment for the designated groups. At the same time, the courts can be expected to scrutinize the means by which employment equity measures are designed and implemented, as has been the case in affirmative action and reverse discrimination cases in the United States.

Finally, the practice of giving judicial deference to human rights commissions and administrative tribunals is likely to continue (Patmore, 1990: 78). Human rights law and its interpretation by these bodies could significantly and positively impact employment equity initiatives in the future if human rights commissions begin to give greater attention to building a body of human rights case law that addresses systemic discrimination and employment equity remedies. Unfortunately, although the opportunity exists for this to occur, commissions have not widely used their statutory powers to address systemic discrimination, and to seek employment equity remedies, focusing instead on individual complaints and redress. Even the Canadian Human Rights Commission's initiatives discussed in Box 4.5 fail to build the human rights case law that employers and other equality seekers rely upon to understand and implement the non-discrimination and proactive elements of human rights statutes.

Systemic Discrimination: Clarifying the Confusions

Human rights laws lack a clear, fixed and comprehensive set of definitions of discrimination. Words applied to discrimination are used in a variety of ways, and this vagueness results in considerable confusion and perhaps even in inappropriate and misguided analyses of discrimination in employment. It is difficult to design appropriate remedies for discrimination and to plan employment equity initiatives that will conform to legal understandings if there is confusion about the basic concepts with which practitioners must work.

It is likely that a large part of the confusion that has developed over the past two decades arises from the importation and rather haphazard blending of terminology and concepts from American and British contexts. Their application is not always appropriate to the Canadian legal and policy framework, and they have been drawn upon in an eclectic fashion by human rights commissions, tribunals, the courts, policy makers and practitioners. The result has been a mixture that has created a unique — but muddy —

Canadian approach to defining and designing remedies for employment discrimination, particularly systemic discrimination.

In the late 1970s and early 1980s there was a good deal of attention by the Affirmative Action Branch of the Canada Employment and Immigration Commission to the evolution of American concepts of discrimination, with emphasis on the notion of systemic discrimination. In U.S. legal usage, three categories of discrimination have developed: "evil motive", "disparate treatment" and "adverse impact" (Blumrosen, 1972). The concept of adverse impact became synonymous with the term "systemic discrimination." British equality policy and legislation tends to distinguish between "direct" and "indirect" discrimination. The Canadian human rights expert Walter Tarnopolsky, in *Discrimination and the Law* (1985), defined direct as intended discrimination, and indirect as unintended discrimination. With the passage of time, the overlay of the American distinction among three categories of discrimination, on top of the British distinction between direct and indirect discrimination, has resulted in considerable conceptual confusion in Canadian interpretations.

Unfortunately, in our view, much of the case law — especially concerning systemic and adverse impact discrimination — is analytically confusing. Some of this confusion has developed duing the 80s as a result of using an adverse impact analysis when accommodation issues have been challenged through the human rights complaints process. For example, in each of the following Supreme Court decisions, the problem was identified as the adverse impact of employer policies — yet the appropriate remedy was an accommodation of an individual's special needs:

- wearing turbans rather than hard hats (*Bhinder*),
- the scheduling of Sabbath keepers for work on Friday evening and Saturday (*O'Malley*) and on religious holidays (*Central Alberta Dairy Pool*).

If an adverse impact analysis is used in cases involving an accommodation issue, there is an inconsistency between the diagnosis and the remedy. An appropriate remedy for adverse impact is to discontinue the discriminatory policy and replace it with one that is not discriminatory — for example, replacing a height and weight requirement with a strength requirement. However, when an employer accommodates a special need, the organization-wide policy is left intact and supplemented with the needed accommodation. For example, the employer may retain the requirement to wear a hat as part of a company uniform while allowing those who wear a turban as part of their religious practices to replace the hat with a turban. We consider these distinctions further in the discussion that follows (see also Box 5.2).

In an attempt to clarify this confusion, we offer the following ways to think about discrimination and construct appropriate remedies. We believe that this formulation may be helpful to the practitioner, and hope that those concerned with policy and legal analysis may also find it beneficial. We suggest that discrimination may be viewed as consisting of two distinct types: intent and results based discrimination. Each is associated with different evidentiary and analytical procedures:

1) Intent based discrimination:
   a) direct evidence of discriminatory motive
   b) comparative evidence of discriminatory motive
2) Results discrimination identified by its outcomes:
   a) discrimination shown by evidence of differential adverse impact
   b) discrimination arising from lack of accommodation.

BOX 5.1
Intent and Results Based Discrimination

TYPES OF DISCRIMINATION:	FORMS OF DISCRIMINATION:	EVIDENCE:
Intent based discrimination	Unequal treatment	• Direct ("overt") evidence of discriminatory motive: -statements -physical evidence.
		• Comparative ("covert") evidence of discriminatory motive.

TYPES OF DISCRIMINATION:	FORMS OF DISCRIMINATION:	EVIDENCE:
Results based discrimination	Adverse impact	A specific employment requirement or qualification that has an adverse and disproportionate impact on a protected group, and cannot be justified as a *bona fide* occupational requirement or a business necessity.
	Lack of accommodation	Steps are not taken by the employer to seek an accommodation of a known need or special requirement of a protected group, short of undue hardship, even where a rational connection to job performance is shown.

We now turn to an examination of these concepts, with examples and references to the relevant legislation and case law.

Intent Based Discrimination

The largest settlement for racial discrimination and harassment in Canadian history is a classic example of intent based discrimination. In 1989 five former employees of the electronic equipment retailer Majestic Electronics Inc. received nearly $300,000 for the threats and harassment they experienced after they refused to carry out orders from the company's president that they considered racist and sexist. The investigation by the Ontario Human Rights Commission, following complaints by the five who resigned, found that the president made "bigoted and racist remarks, and when the occasion arose, insisted that they fire minorities and women they had hired despite his threats." Four of the five former employees who initiated the complaint in 1987 were white males holding senior positions at Majestic, including the vice-president of finance and the personnel director. The latter said that the president used racist slurs to refer to members of racial minorities (*Globe and Mail*, January 7, 1989:A1-2).

There are two kinds of evidence of intentional discrimination — direct and comparative evidence.

Direct Evidence of Discriminatory Motive   In the past this kind of discrimination was often called "overt" discrimination. Statements and physical evidence are used to prove intentional, direct, and overt discrimination on the basis of gender, race, disability, or other prohibited grounds.

Examples of direct evidence would be racist statements such as those cited in the Majestic case. Other examples might include comments like the following:

- We do not hire women as truck drivers.
- People who are blind cannot do this kind of work.
- Your accent will not be acceptable to our customers, so we can't hire you in sales.
- We can't expect our other employees to change their work habits and job duties to accommodate your religious practices [or disability].

Direct evidence might also consist of physical evidence such as:

- pink application forms for women and blue forms for men.
- annotations on files or application forms identifying men and women, or different races.
- notes or letters with statements related to employment decisions that differentiate adversely on the basis of gender, race or disability.

Comparative Evidence of Discriminatory Motive   This kind of discrimination may be more hidden, and in the past was often called "covert" discrimination. Yet it still relates to differential treatment of individuals, groups, or classes of people based on gender, race, disability and other prohibited grounds of discrimination. Sometimes the only difference between direct and comparative discrimination is that for comparative or covert discrimination there are no witnesses, and no physical evidence or explicit statements by a "perpetrator" that can be used as evidence, as in the Majestic case. Consequently people often ask how one "proves" covert discrimination.

Comparative evidence is sometimes called "similar fact evidence" since it attempts to replicate what happens or might have happened to two similarly situated individuals who differ only in their gender, race, or disability status. For example, evidence compares what happened to the victim — a woman — with what happened to a similarly situated man. The analysis can be applied to groups or classes of people as well as to individuals.

Some examples might include:

- A case where the qualifications required, the application process, and the selection decision process are all reproduced and compared for all the women and all the men who applied for a job. Differences are found in the procedures used for women as compared with men, resulting in proportionately fewer women being hired.
- The treatment of the victim of discrimination — a woman — is compared to that of equivalent or parallel male employees in the same workplace. The analysis focuses on whether, on a balance of probabilities, the woman was subject to different treatment than the men were. The treatment of other women may also be considered in assessing the evidence.

Conservative U.S. Supreme Court decisions have given increasing emphasis to narrowly interpreted "similarly situated" evidence in making a case of discrimination, while our Supreme Court is broadening both what is considered similarly situated and how discrimination may be defined by the results of decisions, as well as treatment, in the management of human resources.

In the last decade workplace harassment emerged as one of the most significant "treatment" issues, drawing attention to what managers and co-workers say and do, and the decisions they make. Both sexual and racial harassment have gained prominence as matters to which employers must give serious, prompt and appropriate attention, both in their prevention and remedy. In the future there is likely to be greater attention to issues of disability harassment. For example, the reluctance and refusal of managers, human resource practitioners, union officials and co-workers to take the steps to accommodate persons with disabilities may create a "poisoned" work environment for those seeking accommodation.

Supreme Court of Canada decisions have confirmed that work place harassment places a significant legal liability on corporations and public sector organizations, as well as some individuals. "Persons with authority," whether managers, supervisors, union officials or others in organizations, have a legal responsibility both to prevent work place harassment and to deal well with it once it occurs. Those who create, contribute to or ignore an harassing environment at work are now legally accountable.

Results Based Discrimination

Unlike intent based discrimination, results based discrimination gives no consideration to the motive of the employer. The intent or mental state of those who may have discriminated is irrelevant: their actions may be well-intentioned, benign, involve conscious or unconscious bias, or be malicious or paternalistic. What is examined is the *result* of using a particular rule, requirement or standard for the employment opportunities of classes of people protected by human rights laws.

We will use two familiar examples to illustrate results based discrimination: height selection standards, and company uniform and grooming requirements. In analysing such practices to identify discrimination and in compiling evidence for legal remedies, we are not required to discover whether the motive or intent of the employer was biased against women, people with disabilities or racial minorities. Instead, our analysis focuses on the result or outcome of the employer's use of "standard operating procedures" in making human resource decisions.

Evidence of results based discrimination is more complex than evidence considered under the intent approach described above. For example, in examining height standards, we consider a statistical analysis of those included and excluded by the use of a height cut-off, such as a minimum height of 5 feet 10 inches, to screen applicants. In examining a company uniform and grooming rule, our analysis moves us through a problem-solving exercise which first requires us to clearly understand the need for an alternative to the rule. There appear to be two distinct kinds of analyses one can apply: impact and accommodation.

Adverse Impact Discrimination   This kind of discrimination has been called "adverse effect," "adverse results," or "adverse impact" discrimination, and it is often equated with "systemic discrimination." We understand systemic discrimination to be a broader, more inclusive concept than this, such as the definition offered in the "Thesaurus of Human Rights Terms" of the Canadian Human Rights Reporter: "systemic discrimination means practices entrenched in systems which operate to limit a group's right to opportunities or to exclude a group from participating in an activity." Whatever terminology one chooses, the analysis of "impact" requires four steps, as follows:

Step 1: Identify a specific employment rule, qualification, standard, or requirement (a standard operating procedure).

For example, a requirement for selecting police officers is a minimum height of 5'10".

Step 2: Show evidence, preferably statistical rather than impressionistic, that this requirement acts to select out— that is, leads to the rejection of— a significantly greater proportion of a protected class (such as women) than of others (men).

For example, a 5' 10" height requirement that appears to be neutral, and that is applied equally to women and to men, is shown to have a differential and adverse impact (result) on women as a group when applied to female applicants, than when it is applied to male applicants.

In this example, as in many adverse impact situations, there are two potential ways to assemble the impact evidence: 1) population or labour market data, and 2) flow data specific to the employer's applicant, hiring or promotion pools. In the example above, the flow data would consist of the applicants for the job. Often flow data are not available, or may be tainted by other factors such as a chilled applicant pool. This means that individuals from protected groups do not apply because of repeated rejection or past discrimination (actual or perceived) against members of their group by that employer, or in that type of occupation.

To continue our example: women who are less than 5'10" in height, and who are aware of the height requirement, do not apply. Hence the women in the applicant pool are taller than most women in the labour market, and many otherwise qualified women do not apply because of the requirement.

This kind of analysis is easiest to carry out with two large and comparable groups such as women and men. It is significantly more difficult when dealing with issues of race and disability.

For example, if the requirement is a minimum height of 5'10" and the concern is the impact on racial minorities, then an analysis must identify whether the concern is with all racial minorities or selected racial minorities, and if so, which ones. For example, will Blacks be included in the analysis? All Asians, or only certain groups of Asian origin? All aboriginal peoples, or only certain groups? Since average heights of women and men vary regardless of race, it must also be clear whether the analysis will only address racial impacts, or a combination of race and gender impacts.

For all groups there is a problem of accessing appropriate statistical data in order to determine whether there is a disparity; such data may not be available.

Let us consider another example. If the concern is about a "word of mouth" recruitment practice, then we must decide whether we can gather and assess statistical evidence regarding who is in the employer's work force, who knows about and refers applicants, to whom these employees pass on information about the availability of jobs, and who submits applications. Perhaps the evidence that is available is impressionistic or anecdotal rather than statistical.

Step 3. Let us assume that there is evidence of a job requirement that appears neutral (*Step 1*), and that requirement is shown to have a differential, adverse, and disproportionate impact on a protected group (*Step 2*). The analysis then focuses on whether the employer can show that the requirement is nevertheless a *bona fide* occupational requirement or qualification, or a business necessity.

A 1979 Canadian case involved the Ottawa Police Department's height and weight requirements for police applicants. These requirements were shown to have a disproportionate and adverse impact on women, and a valid link between the selection standard and job performance as a police officer could not be demonstrated. The height requirement, then, was not a *bona fide* occupational qualification or a business necessity.

Step 4. Perhaps the employer can establish that the requirement is a *bona fide* occupational requirement or a business necessity. But it is still possible that those challenging the requirement can show that an equally valid alternative that has no adverse impact, or a lesser adverse impact, could be used in place of the original requirement.

For example, in some instances height requirements might be replaced by strength requirements.

As we have seen, an "impact analysis" of an employment policy or practice can be a complex analytical exercise. Yet such an analysis can help employers and other stakeholders to examine the validity of policies and practices in the workplace in order to determine whether they may result in illegal discrimination. As well, a well documented analysis will lead to clarification of the appropriate remedy.

Discrimination Based on Lack of Accommodation

Accommodation — or failure of the employer to accommodate diversity — may occur for individuals, groups, or classes of individuals, or all three. Although the concept of accommodation is currently used most frequently to discuss the needs of people with disabilities, its application developed in the first instance with reference to the special needs of minority religious groups whose religious practices, dress, and observances necessitated arrangements that differed from the norm of most employment policies and practices. For example, there may be a need for time off to be granted for observance of religious holidays or Sabbath, or allowances for different forms of dress and grooming.

Accommodation raises one of the fundamental confusions about equality: how can different treatment mean equality? Don't we have to treat people the same in order to ensure equality? Judge Abella addressed this issue in her discussion of the implications of employment equity for industrial relations (see Box 5.2).

BOX 5.2
Remedies for Discriminatory Employment Systems Based on Employment Equity Includes Respecting and Accommodating Diversity

"Sometimes equality means treating people the same, despite their differences, and sometimes it means treating them as equals by accommodating their differences.

Formerly, we thought that equality only meant sameness and that treating persons as equals meant treating everyone the same. We now know that to treat everyone the same may be to offend the notion of equality. Ignoring differences may mean ignoring legitimate needs. It is not fair to use the differences between people as an excuse to exclude them arbitrarily from equitable participation. Equality means nothing if it does not mean that we are of equal worth regardless of differences in gender, race, ethnicity or disability...

Ignoring differences and refusing to accommodate them is a denial of equal access and opportunity. It is discrimination. To reduce discrimination, we must create and maintain barrier-free environments so that individuals can have genuine access free from arbitrary obstructions to demonstrate and exercise fully their potential. This may mean treating some people differently by removing the obstacles to equality of opportunity they alone face for no demonstrably justifiable reason...

To create equality of opportunity, we have to do different things for different people. We have to systematically eradicate the impediments ... according to the actual needs of the different groups, not according to what we think their needs should be..."

(SOURCE: Excerpt from Rosalie Silberman Abella, "Employment Equity — Implications for Industrial Relations", Industrial Relations Centre, Queen's University, 1987, pp. 2-3.)

The first step in addressing issues of accommodation is to become aware of a need for accommodation. The need may be brought to the attention of the employer by an individual seeking accommodation or by an advocate who raises the issue. As in the case of workplace harassment, there may be an onus on the employer to take steps to accommodate if the employer "ought reasonably to have known" of the need for accommodation. For example, the employer ought to know, without specifically being told, that wheelchair users require accessibility to the place of employment in order to work there. It has also been suggested that an employer ought to know that various dietary requirements are associated with different religions. Therefore there ought to be standard arrangements to provide suitable meals or allow for notification of special dietary needs as a normal part of conference planning.

On the other hand, the onus to make the need for an accommodation known might legitimately be placed first on the individual or group if their need is "invisible" or not normally expected. For example, the need for regular rather than *ad hoc* meal and snack (coffee) breaks for an employee with diabetes controlled by diet is probably not visible and obvious to the employer. The need for time off for religious observances might also not be known by the employer, thus shifting the onus to the employee to make the need for accommodation known.

Once the need for accommodation is understood, the employer is required to show that the employment practice in question is rationally connected to the performance of the job *and* that the employer has made efforts to accommodate the employee's (or applicant's) need up to the point of undue hardship. The elements of undue hardship may include financial cost, safety and practicality.

Accommodation — more than any other type of discrimination or equality issue — requires a problem-solving and cooperative approach involving all stakeholders. Often the best accommodations arise through the joint efforts of both the employer and the employee. When the issues affecting designated groups are systemic in nature, employers may find it beneficial to involve internal and external representatives of these groups in order to identify accommodation problems and potential solutions. On some matters, such as barrier-free design for people with disabilities, it may be helpful to seek the advice of subject matter experts.

Unfortunately, accommodation is an issue about which there is a great deal of confusion in policy and the case law. It has often been assumed by human rights commissions, tribunals, and the courts — including the Supreme Court of Canada — that accommodation and impact are the same kind of issue, involving the same approaches to analysis and remedies. Often we will see an impact analysis, involving some of the steps we have discussed earlier, to assess situations having to do with accommodation. Yet as we have seen, accommodation is a distinctly different matter requiring different kinds of evidence and remedies. Box 5.3 discusses and illustrates these differences.

BOX 5.3
Treatment, Impact and Accommodation:
What Stays, What Goes, and What Is Added on?

In assessing employment systems there are three underlying questions a line manager, human resources staff member or employment equity practitioner may ask regarding employment policies and practices:
1. What needs to be changed? Why? What ought to replace existing practice?
2. What can remain the same?
3. What needs to be added on?

Understanding the distinctively different remedies to three generic types of discrimination — treatment, impact and accommodation — can help you to assess existing practices, understand the type of analysis you may need to undertake, and know what evidence is required in order to carry out an employment systems review. The following may help you to organize your analysis and search for appropriate remedies. In the examples, A, B, C and D stand for formal or informal employment policies and practices.

REMEDY FOR UNEQUAL TREATMENT

If A applies to the majority and B to the minority, *then stop B and use A for everyone.*

Example: The problem is that different and discriminatory questions about family, children, and child care are asked of women applicants at a job interview. Men are not asked these questions. The remedy is to stop asking these questions, and use job related questions for all job applicants.

REMEDY FOR ADVERSE IMPACT

If A applies to everyone, yet is shown to adversely impact on the minority, *then stop using A, replacing it with C for everyone.*

Example: The problem is that a 5'10" height requirement for selecting police officers selects out disproportionately more women and certain racial minority groups. The remedy is to discontinue the use of a height requirement, replacing it with a valid, job related selection requirement, such as strength or physical fitness.

REMEDY FOR ACCOMMODATION

If A applies to everyone, yet is shown to not provide accommodation to the minority, *then continue to use A but add on D as the accommodation.*

Example: A requirement to wear a hat as part of the employee's uniform is broadened to permit the wearing of a turban.

Human Rights Case Law: Implications for Analysis of Work-Force Data and Employment Systems Review

Any policy, practice or procedure which is *not* legal, consistent, without adverse impact, valid, job-related, necessary for safe and efficient operation of the business and documented in neutral language, is likely to present an employment barrier to designated group members. (Ontario Government, "Employment Systems Review: Technical Assistance Package" (draft), 1991:3)

This is the direction given to Ontario Government ministries by their central human resources policy makers. As illustrated in Box 5.3, the impact of the human rights case law on employment equity implementation and the practice of human resources management is significant — and confusing. We conclude this chapter by linking the legal framework with the practice of equity in developing and reviewing employment systems — the organization's arrangements for recruiting, selecting, hiring, training and developing, promoting, compensating and terminating employees.

As mentioned in Chapter 1 and Box 1.7, the collection and analysis of data is a fundamental element of implementing an employment equity strategy. Government regulations require or suggest both an analysis of data about an employer's work force, and a review of employment systems in order to identify and remove barriers. When employment equity is implemented within the context of an organizational change process involving the key stakeholders, the analysis and review of work-force data and employment systems will be done with their participation, and it will be ongoing rather than something that is done only once and "completed."

Regardless of the choice of organizational change strategy, it is necessary that employment equity and human resource practitioners understand relevant aspects of the human rights case law regarding non-discrimination and special programs. This body of case law can offer guidance in identifying discrimination, designing appropriate remedies, and dealing with historical and future disadvantage.

Unfortunately, most of the human rights case law addresses discrimination faced by individuals. Thus we have little assistance and advice on the proper use of work force statistical data and how to analyse it to determine whether discrimination exists based on statistical evidence alone. It is this kind of analysis that may permit us to draw conclusions about disparities between the representation and participation of designated groups in a workplace, and their labour market availability — an important part of the justification for taking employment equity measures. Like CN Rail in the *ATF* case, many work forces will demonstrate gross statistical disparities, a finding that makes it much easier to argue the need for proactive measures to increase and improve the hiring, training and promotion of the designated groups. (We discuss this further in Chapter 12 and 13.)

When we look to the human rights case law for help in conducting an employment systems review, again we find that most human rights complaints have focused on specific decisions, policies or practices rather than dealing with employment systems or with the aggregate impacts of employment decision-making on designated groups over time. Consequently, the case law provides little direction on how to assess whether discrimination exists within systems. It doesn't tell us how to undertake a comprehensive employment systems review and how to analyse the cumulative effect of an array of employment policies and practices — formal and informal — which result in decisions and activities affecting the job and career opportunities of the designated groups. For example, we rarely see a complaint that examines all of the recruitment, selection, hiring, promotion and development policies and practices ("systems") of an employer. Even the notable exception, *ATF*, only examined some of these systems for women, but not for the other designated groups, and only regarding entry into blue-collar jobs in the St. Lawrence region.

In Canada, human rights case law is oriented to the analysis of specific, discrete decisions, rules, requirements and practices. Remedies are oriented to making the victim of discrimination, usually identified as an individual, "whole." Thus, compensatory damages, back pay, job offers and apologies are typical remedies. Increasingly, remedies require the employer to remove or discontinue specific employment policies or practices, yet it is rare that a remedy specifies what the replacement policy or practice is to be. For example, a human rights settlement or tribunal order might stop the use of a 5'10" height requirement, a specific aptitude test, or a requirement that applicants have Canadian work experience, yet we seldom see a statement of what the employer *is* to use as a requirement or qualification. Nevertheless, we know that something will be used to fill the gap.

Limited as it is, human rights law provides only rudimentary guidance regarding work-force analysis and the review of employment systems. Thus, most employment equity and human resources practitioners may be familiar with such concepts as bona fide occupational requirements or qualifications, validity, accommodation short of undue hardship, adverse impact, business necessity and so on — all of which are derived from the human rights case law — but find it difficult to apply these concepts to the employment systems review process. Given these gaps in the case law it is not surprising that the review of employment systems is often a narrow bureaucratic and technical process reflecting the jargon of human rights law, and lacking a foundation in basic principles and a sense of the purpose to be achieved.

The examples given in Box 5.4 highlight this difficulty. It seems that just as the analysis of quantitative workforce and availability data has become a technical operation, and an end in itself rather than a tool for change, so too has the conventional employment equity approach attempted to make the assessment of employment systems a technical exercise, even though such policies and practices are qualitative rather than numerical. There is a tendency to lose sight of the reasons why these procedures are important, and how data analysis and the results of the systems review can be an essential part of an organizational change process. This issue is discussed more fully in Chapter 6.

BOX 5.4

Employment Systems Reviews: Guides from the Ontario Government and Canada Employment and Immigration Commission

FOR ONTARIO GOVERNMENT MINISTRIES:

In evaluating your employment systems, the bottom line is whether or not a policy, practice or procedure undermines or promotes an equitable work environment and the full participation of all employees. All policies, practices and procedures must be evaluated using the following equity criteria:

Legality	Does the policy or practice conform to existing human rights legislation?
Consistency	Is the policy or practice applied in the same way for everyone — except where the specific needs of designated group members are met through accommodation of special needs?
Adverse Impact	Does the policy or practice have a greater negative impact on designated group members?
Validity	Is the policy or practice objective and predictive — does it measure what it sets out to measure?
Job-Relatedness	Is the policy or practice (i.e. stated job qualifications) directly linked to the effective performance of the essential job requirements?
Business Necessity	Is the policy or practice essential to the safe and efficient operation of the organization — have all realistic alternatives to the practice causing adverse impact been explored — will the removal or modification of the policy or practice impose hardship on the organization?
Neutral Language	Is the policy or procedure documented in non-sexist language and in language that does not promote racial, ethnic or other stereotypes?

(SOURCE: Ontario Government, Human Resources Secretariat, Workforce Planning and Employment Equity Branch, "Employment Systems Review: Technical Assistance Package," (draft), 1991:2-3.)

For Employers Covered by LEEP or FCP:

The usual test for systemic discrimination involves assessing the policy, practice or system by the following criteria:
- Is it job related?
- Is it valid? Does the test, or required qualification, have a direct relationship to job performance?
- Is it consistently applied?
- Does it have adverse impact? (i.e., affect members of designated groups more than those in dominant groups)?
- Is it a business necessity?
- Does it conform to human rights and employment standards legislation?

Each of these questions needs to be asked of every employment practice. The answers will allow employers to tailor their employment equity planning to their organization, industry, and legal environment.

In a large organization with complex systems, an experienced team will be required to carry out the analysis. In a smaller organization, one or two informed persons can undertake a fairly comprehensive review.

(SOURCE: Employment and Immigration Canada, "Employment Equity: A Guide for Employers," 1989:24.)

The concern many people have is not about the need to identify discrimination and disadvantage but that much of the advice about how to do this appears mysterious, impractical or lacking in concrete details. There is no road map that provides direction about how to review employment systems in order to identify various types of discrimination.

We cannot offer a fool-proof method for conducting the utilization analysis nor the employment systems review — topics requiring more than a part of one chapter. However, building on our earlier discussion of intent and results based discrimination, we try to direct the practitioner who is analyzing organizational systems and data, and who wants to devise appropriate and realistic remedies. In Chapter 12 and 13, we suggest a way to organize how one thinks about discrimination and disadvantage in organizations, and present a stakeholder process for the diagnosis of discrimination.

Box 5.3 summarizes a way to conceptualize discrimination and appropriate remedies in employment systems by thinking about the distinctions between unequal treatment, adverse impact and the lack of accommodation. Below, we suggest a way of thinking about discrimination in relation to an organization's "standard operating procedures" (SOP) in human resource decision making regarding recruitment, selection, hiring, training and development, promotion, and termination of employees.

Remedies for Unequal Treatment Discrimination

To provide a remedy for unequal treatment discrimination it is necessary that the "standard operating procedure" (SOP) applicable to the majority be consistently and equally applied to all groups, minority and majority alike. Therefore differential treatment accorded the minority must be stopped and replaced by the generally accepted practice in the organization. If the SOP is to ask certain specific questions of white, male able bodied applicants of the cultural majority group, then additional or different questions must not be asked of racial minority, female, disabled and ethnic candidates.

The *ATF* tribunal and subsequent Supreme Court decisions recognized this when they ordered that "CN shall immediately modify its system of interviewing candidates; in particular, it shall ensure that those responsible for conducting such interviews are given strict instructions to treat all candidates in the same way, regardless of their sex." A further example from *ATF* is: "CN shall immediately discontinue all practices pursued by foremen or others in which female candidates undergo physical tests not required of male candidates, mainly the test which consists of lifting a brakeshoe with one arm." (By the way, a brakeshoe weighs approximately 80 pounds!)

Remedies for Adverse Impact Discrimination

A remedy for discrimination involving adverse impact requires that the SOP applied equally to everyone must cease and be replaced by a new SOP having no differential and adverse impact on the minority group. If this is not possible, it must be replaced by an SOP with a lesser adverse impact.

The classic example from a U.S. Supreme Court decision, often cited in Canada, was the requirement by the Duke Power Company in North Carolina that an applicant or employee have a high school diploma in order to be hired, transferred, or promoted into departments other than the Labor Department. The Supreme Court found that this requirement disproportionately selected out Blacks, and was not a business necessity. The diploma requirement was dropped.

Let us look at a more contentious example. Is "word of mouth" recruitment a SOP with an adverse impact? Perhaps — but maybe not. Clearly it is a neutral practice, and equally applicable to everyone — or so it would seem on the surface. However, the analysis must focus on to whom this informal information about available jobs and the application and selection process is circulated. If men are the only persons in the information networks (the familiar "old boys' network"), and if the news does not reach women, then this apparently nuetral practice may well be discriminatory. But what if women and minorities are part of the network? What if the men working in the company tell their female family members, relatives, neighbours, friends, and colleagues? Then it is likely that this SOP is not discriminatory, at least not against women. But it may still have an adverse impact on racial minorities, people with disabilities and aboriginal peoples. Often word of mouth practices are all viewed as potentially discriminatory. Yet we know that one of the most effective outreach recruitment techniques is to build on the power of informal information networks among members of the designated groups by spreading knowledge about jobs and hiring practices through current employees, the community, and special interest and advocacy groups. So, word of mouth practices may either hinder or help the employment equity process — we need to examine the specific case.

Remedies for a Lack of Accommodation

To develop a remedy for discrimination involving a failure to accommodate requires that an accommodation be added to the SOP in order to address the particular needs of the group or individual needing accommodation. An example of a systemic accommodation may be the implementation of special complaint and counselling measures to deal with workplace harassment. Even companies with elaborate collective agreements whose provisions set forth the steps of the grievance procedure, or non-union firms with employee complaint procedures, may need to establish a special process for filing, investigating, and resolving harassment complaints. Such an accommodation recognizes that while the regular complaint process may work well for most problems in the work place, there are special needs to be addressed when dealing with issues of harassment because of race, gender or disability. Thus the regular grievance or complaint mechanisms remain in place and are supplemented by a process designed to respond to the special needs and requirements of the designated groups, as well as of managers and co-workers, when harassment issues arise.

A 1977 unreported Ontario human rights board of inquiry (*Singh vs. Security and Investigative Services Ltd.*) dealt with the uniform requirements of security guards when a conflict about dress and grooming requirements became apparent. The SOP was the use of a company uniform including a hat, and grooming standards requiring guards to be clean-shaven and with conventionally cut hair. The remedy was an accommodation permitting orthodox Sikhs to retain their beards and wear the regular uniform with the cap replaced by a turban on which the identification badge was pinned.

An accommodation may be required by both the employer and the employee. The 1990 Supreme Court decision *Central Alberta Dairy Pool* involved the employer's onus to show it made efforts to accommodate the employee's religious beliefs up to the point of undue hardship, while at the same time noting the need for adequate notice of the employee's requirements to the employer, and an effort by the employee to accommodate the employer without compromising his religious beliefs. The Board of Inquiry found that the employee's attempts and efforts to accommodate his employer were adequate and "other alternatives could have been explored if this employer had been open to such a discussion."

Jim Christie worked for the Dairy in the production operations of their milk processing plant in Wetaskiwin, Alberta. As a member of the World Wide Church of God he was expected to not work on the Saturday Sabbath and specific holy days. His request to not work on Easter Monday was refused for reasons of plant operating needs since Mondays of every week are especially busy milk canning and shipping days in order to prevent spoilage of the weekend milk. He did not report for work and was dismissed. The Supreme Court found that the Dairy could have accommodated Mr. Christie, but failed to do so. Mr. Christie's complaint of discrimination was upheld.

In our experience, making a distinction among treatment, impact and accommodation as forms of discrimination helps us analyse whether there is evidence of discrimination, and then devise a remedy that deals with the problem. However, on occasion what may appear to be a relatively easy human rights or employment systems issue poses a challenging puzzle for analysis and remedy. For example, what ought a company to do about toilet and change room facilities for females when they begin to work in jobs that have been exclusively held by males? Box 5.5 challenges you to consider the problem and the remedy from the viewpoint of all three kinds of systemic discrimination: treatment, impact and accommodation.

BOX 5.5
Are Washroom and Change Room Facilities for Women Issues of Treatment, Impact, or Accommodation?

An oil refinery has always hired men as process operators in the plant. Although there are women's washrooms in the office section, in the plant itself only men's washrooms have been provided. The men also have changing rooms and lockers available for their use. The refinery is about to hire its first women operators. What is the analysis?

When confronted with this problem solving exercise, people assess it in different ways.

1. Some see it simply as unequal treatment. If men have washrooms exclusively for their use, then the same should be provided for women. Thus, construct the same facilities for the women.

2. Some people see the provision of male only facilities as a practice having an adverse impact on women. In their view, it's not that the firm wants to keep women out, it has simply been a traditional — and practical — practice. The suggested solution is to discontinue the practice and build new facilities for women, or retro-fit the current facilities.

3. Others see that the recent employment of women in these positions creates a new and special need. With women employees there is a need to provide additional facilities. Their suggestion is to "add" facilities for women, leaving the men's facilities as they currently exist.

4. Some assess the situation as not discriminatory, claiming that the female operators can use the office facilities already in place.

Our analysis is to consider this as a matter of equal treatment. Washroom and change room facilities are provided for male employees, thus the solution is to **make facilities of equal use available to female employees**. The office washrooms do not provide equal treatment because they are not close by, and were not designed to serve as change rooms. To provide equal use facilities may not mean the construction of identical facilities, something that may be unreasonably costly or impossible if new construction or retro-fitting is required.

Thus the array of equal treatment solutions include, but are not limited to:

- construction of equal facilities for women,
- provision of temporary (but equally usable) facilities for women,
- joint use of the same facilities, especially if there are few employees, with attention to the need for privacy by locks on doors, use of an "occupied" sign, or different schedules for changing and wash-up by men and women at the end of a shift.

All of these "women's washroom" solutions have been used with success by work groups. Why not ask them what might work best for them?

Conclusion

This chapter briefly considers the the various meanings and interpretations of employment discrimination that have evolved in Canada. The importance to employment equity practitioners of understanding and keeping informed about the human rights case law is emphasized. In our view, there is confusion surrounding definitions of discrimination in current use. In particular, the tendency to apply an adverse impact analysis to accommodation issues presents a major problem in current thinking about how to identify and remedy systemic discrimination. An inappropriate analysis neither fits the issues involved, nor leads to remedies that appropriately address discriminatory practices.

We suggest that discrimination be viewed as either intent based or results based. First, direct and comparative evidence of discriminatory intent, or motive, is discussed, and examples of intent based discrimination are given to illustrate "unequal treatment." We then consider discrimination based on results, which may take one of two forms: adverse impact discrimination or a lack of accommodation. The process of analysis for each is examined and examples given. Practitioners are advised to consider the distinctly different remedies that are appropriate to each of the three forms of discrimination: unequal treatment, adverse impact, and a lack of accommodation.

Finally, we link our definitions, analyses and remedies of discrimination to the employment equity practices of analysing workforce and availability data, and reviewing employment systems. Gaps in the human rights case law regarding systemic discrimination and employment systems are noted. Examples of advice from the Ontario and federal governments concerning the implementation of an employment systems review are used to highlight the difficulties practitioners and equity seekers encounter in trying to examine employment policies and practices for barriers, and then design practical remedies. Suggestions are made, building on the intent and results based definitions of discrimination, to help employment equity and human resource practitioners to conceptualize the review of employment policies and practices. Chapters 12 and 13 will expand upon this discussion of how to diagnose and remedy discrimination and disadvantage.

REFERENCES

Abella, Rosalie. *Equality in Employment: A Royal Commission Report*. Minister of Supply and Services, Ottawa, 1984.

Blumrosen, Alfred. "Strangers in Paradise: *Griggs vs. Duke Power Co.* and the Concept of Employment Discrimination," (1972) 71 *Michigan Law Review* 59.

Patmore, Glen A. *An Inquiry into the Norm of Non-Discrimination in Canada*. Kingston, Ont.: Industrial Relations Centre, Queen's University, 1990.

Tarnopolsky, Walter S., and W. Pentney. *Discrimination and the Law in Canada*. Toronto: Richard De Boo, 1985.

CASES CITED

Alberta Human Rights Commission vs. Central Alberta Dairy Pool (1990) 2 S.C.R. 489.

Andrews vs. Law Society of British Columbia [1989] 1 S.C.R. 143.

Bhinder vs. CN Rail (S.C.C.) 7 C.H.R.R. D/3093.

Brooks vs. Canada Safeway Ltd. (S.C.C.) 10 C.H.R.R. D/6183.

Janzen vs. Platy Enterprises Ltd. (S.C.C.) 10 C.H.R.R. D/6205.

Law Society of British Columbia vs. Andrews (1989) 56 D.L.R. (4th) 1 (S.C.C.).

O'Malley vs. Simpson- Sears Ltd. (S.C.C.) 8 C.H.R.R. D/4326.

Robichaud vs. Canada (Treasury Board) C.H.R.R. 1987 D/4326.

Singh vs. Security and Investigative Services Ltd. 1977 (Ontario, unreported).

Turpin vs. R., unreported, May 4, 1989, S.C.C.

6

Organizational Change: How It Works

O N THE SHOP FLOOR in a large automobile assembly plant there is a poster showing a desperate and very determined man aiming a pistol straight at you, the viewer. He is snarling, "go ahead, make one more change!" The poster reflects the frustration of workers who are coping with the introduction of new technology, employment equity, and new management styles that push responsibility downward, all at the same time. It is also a message of resistance to management, who have been imposing these changes from the top down.

Employment equity is only one of many types of planned organizational and technological change that are transforming the workplace today, and most organizations are engaged in one or more ongoing change initiatives. Because the environment in which we do business and serve the public is changing rapidly and often unpredictably, we are forced to adapt by changing our work organizations and operating procedures. Some of the new approaches to organizing and managing reflect paradigm shifts —

alternative ways of seeing and thinking about peoples' behaviour in the workplace— that emerge in response to the failure of traditional approaches to management to deal effectively with the impacts of changes in the environment (Imershein, 1977).

Two of these fundamental types of change in organizational structures and cultures have been objects of extensive attention and controversy in recent years. One type includes change strategies designed to improve productivity, job satisfaction and efficiency by peeling away layers of management and pushing power and decision-making responsibility downward within the organization. Examples include various forms of participative management, workplace democracy or employee involvement(Cohen - Rosenthal, 1983). The second broad category of changes — employment equity — is aimed at accommodating and valuing diversity in the workplace, removing discriminatory barriers, and correcting inequities built into the way in which our organizations have traditionally functioned. Examples of organizational responses to these needs include pay equity, policies and procedures to deal with workplace harassment, training about cultural diversity, preferential hiring and promotion, improving accessibility, making assistive devices available, and arrangements to permit people to balance work and family care responsibilities.

The integration of change strategies for sharing power with those whose goals are equity and human rights implies a fundamental social restructuring of the workplace. It is important to recognize that these two broad types of change are conceptually linked, and they should also be viewed as interrelated in practice. From the research and theoretical literature, and from our experience as practitioners, we have learned that changes intended to lead to equity in the workplace are most effectively implemented through a process of sharing power.

Employment equity can be viewed as a strategy for planned organizational change aimed at broadening opportunity for groups that have historically been disadvantaged in the workplace. As we saw in Chapter 3, employers and unions are getting involved in employment equity because they are confronted by challenges from a changing environment, notably an increasingly diverse labour and client marketplace, and a regulatory context that reflects governments' responses to that diversity. Employment equity is a large-scale and complex change strategy in that it has impacts across the entire spectrum of human resource management decisions, from job design and evaluation, recruitment, and selection to termination, and it has the potential to affect each of these kinds of decisions profoundly. Employment equity involves basic changes in the organization's relationship both to its own members— individually and collectively— and to the community at large. In this sense, employment equity complements the emerging strategic, proactive, professional, and value oriented profile of the human resource management function as we approach the twenty-first century.

The complexity involved in implementing an employment equity change program designed to benefit four very different groups suggests the need for a carefully planned strategy for change. However, even change programs that are thoughtfully planned often have disappointing results. They may become stalled or bogged down, stopping short of their intended objectives, or have unanticipated consequences and not produce the results that were intended. And we have all heard of change programs that ended in disaster because of the disillusionment and resistance they mobilized.

Why are some programs of change more successful than others in attaining their objectives? Obviously, because of the complexity of organizations and their environments, there are no rules or fail-safe approaches to implementing change that guarantee success. Although every situation is different, there is a body of theoretical and research literature upon which employment equity practitioners can draw in planning and implementing a process of change within their own work environment. In this chapter we suggest that it is important to focus on the *process of implementing change,* and that it is helpful to look at any kind of complex organizational change process from the perspective of generic models of how change occurs. Practitioners can use these change models, which are based upon theory, research, and practice in a variety of applications, as resources in planning and implementing a process of employment equity change in their organizations.

Why Worry About the Change Process? Isn't It the Results that Count?

The choices we make about who will be involved in change, and how they will be involved, fundamentally affect the outcomes of a change process. The means we use are important in themselves, since the experience of involvement in change will shape participants' views of its outcomes. It is not enough to set sound policies and procedures: there must be a strategy for following through in order to make sure that change will occur and that new patterns are firmly established. The change process may be especially important for employment equity, since this is an example of an intervention whose goals or outcomes are in most cases impossible to define very clearly, or to evaluate in relation to some generally accepted standard of adequacy.

It is typically assumed that the goal of employment equity is to improve the representation of designated group members, within the limits set by their availability in relevant labour markets. It is less often recognized that the goals of retaining those who are hired, and improving the quality of their working lives, are equally important. Yet none of these equity goals lend themselves to unequivocal judgements about the adequacy of outcomes.

What is equity? How much progress is sufficient for us to claim that our change program is successful? And what kinds of change efforts are to be given priority? Such issues are likely to be highly controversial in organizations involved in employment equity because of differences and conflicts among the priorities of various internal and external constituencies, and tensions between government requirements and organizational objectives.

In such cases, **procedural justice**, which refers to perceptions of the fairness of the decision making process itself in resolving controversial issues, may be as important as **distributive justice**, which is concerned with judgements about the adequacy and fairness of outcomes (Lerner and Whitehead, 1980). In other words, in implementing employment equity, **how we do it** can be as important as the **results** we get. Moreover, both the results and peoples' perceptions of the outcomes will be affected by their experience of the change process. Employees at all levels are more likely to be willing to support, or at least not resist, a change process that they see as fair, and in which they have had a voice, than one that they feel has been imposed upon them without their consent.

Theory and research, as well as our experience as practitioners, suggest that a change program that is implemented by means of a participatory process is likely to produce less resistance and more movement along the road toward equity over the long term. This approach in essence involves broadening opportunity through a process of sharing power and responsibility in the workplace.

Models of Change? What Good Are They?

Kurt Lewin, one of the early and most influential theorists of organizational change, claimed that "nothing is so practical as a good theory" (Lewin, 1951). It is also worth noting that basing a program of change on a misguided or inappropriate theory can waste resources and mobilize resistance. Unfortunately the practitioner cannot dodge the issue by avoiding theoretical commitments altogether since there will always be a framework of assumptions about human behaviour and organizational change underlying any program of change. But too often, those assumptions are not acknowledged and examined, and therefore do not reflect conscious choice.

Organizations cannot avoid changing because change is pervasive in the environments in which they must survive. The question is not *whether* to be involved in change, but *how*. Will the change process be planned and managed, or unplanned and out of control? Most of us would prefer to plan and make choices about the kinds of change in which we participate, to the extent possible, rather than being the passive objects or victims of unplanned change. It follows, then, that we are better off examining the assumptions, value premises and concepts in which our planning is rooted, rather than operating on the basis of hidden and unexamined assumptions.

The pictures in our minds of organizations, of how they change, and of the role of the change agent, are important because they shape our expectations about what can be achieved and about how people will respond to a change program. The assumptions and theoretical models to which we subscribe also guide our action and inform our behaviour as practitioners, and as a consequence they may become self-fulfilling prophecies. For example, if managers perceive that trade unions are troublemakers rather than legitimate partners in decision making, those managers may deal with the unions in such a way as to make that perception a reality.

Three Models of Organizational Change

In this chapter we examine three generic approaches to organizational change that will be familiar to readers who have observed recent change experiments in private and public sector organizations. The first is a model of top-down change rooted in the traditional management styles and assumptions associated with scientific management and classical organization and management theory. The second is a cultural change model that grows out of the theory and practice of OD (organization development). The third approach is a political model based on stakeholder participation within the framework of the strategic analysis of power relationships and interests.

Our objective in this discussion is to examine some of the underlying assumptions and values reflected in these three approaches to implementing change, and to explore some of their practical implications. We are concerned here with the change *process* in the workplace— with how we move toward the equity goals we have in mind. We suggest that there are important lessons and insights for the employment equity practitioner contained in each of the three models of implementation. Each approach has strengths in that certain elements of the change process are singled out for emphasis, yet each has shortcomings and blind spots that the practitioner would be well advised to consider.

All three models are applicable, and can be seen in practice today, in a variety of change contexts: in this sense they are generic approaches. For example, each model might be used as a basis for implementing new technology (eg. Hirschheim, 1985; Tapscott, 1982), or an employee involvement program, or an employment equity program. Our summaries of the three approaches are exaggerations in the sense that they present rather extreme statements of each model for purposes of analysis. Any actual program of change may tend to resemble one of our "ideal types" but will probably not contain all of its elements, and may include some aspects of one or two of the other models.

In our view, the stakeholder participation model provides the most useful basis upon which to build an effective employment equity change strategy. This emerging paradigm incorporates some elements of the first two models which preceded it in the development of organizational theory, and adds other insights that we believe reflect the realities of organizational life. Unfortunately, however, our observations suggest that the first two models we discuss, particularly the traditional top-down approach, are much more familiar to practitioners and more widely applied than the participatory model. An understanding of these flawed change strategies, and of the liabilities they carry, will help the practitioner to diagnose problems and failures in the change process, and may account for why a carefully planned and well-intentioned program of change has disappointing results.

Organizational Change from the Top Down

From the early twentieth century we have inherited a concept of the large or medium sized organization as a bureaucracy. The bureaucracy is a pyramid-shaped organization with a formal structure of authority that is hierarchical and highly centralized and that operates according to a set of rules. The power to make and enforce rules is concentrated at the pyramid's peak and carefully delegated downward to managers at successive levels, with elaborate control arrangements to ensure that the limits of the authority assigned to each position in the structure are not exceeded.

The assumption that underlies the bureaucratic concept of the organization is that people are rational actors. If they are told what the rules are, and understand that there are penalties for infractions and rewards for compliance, and providing there are procedures for checking to ensure that the rules are being followed, people will act in predictable ways and the organization will function efficiently. The organization is seen as machine-like, with management at the controls.

The management ideology that typically accompanies this vision of the organization is rooted in Frederick Taylor's doctrine of scientific management. It is a perspective that Alan Fox has called a "unitary frame of reference" (Fox, 1966) — an image of organizational actors as a team or family with shared goals and values and a centralized authority structure. Management operates as an unelected captain or *paterfamilias*, the only legitimate source of leadership and decision making authority. Management assumes that it acts in the best interests of the organization as a whole, rather than primarily in its own interest. This assumption underlies a managerial ideology that rationalizes and legitimates management's right to unilateral control of the work process. Employee participation in decision-making, if any, is not a right but a favour bestowed and withdrawn by management at its discretion.

The process of organizational change is seen as strategically planned and orchestrated by top management, which issues orders, perhaps attractively packaged in a "vision" through which the chief executive projects "leadership." Once this is put forth, everyone at lower ranks in the hierarchy works busily to realize the plan. The long and frustrating process of moving from strategic plan, to action, to concrete results — the implementation process— is ignored. It is as if this movement were automatic once the CEO throws the switch that starts the organizational machine in a new direction. The fact that there is often a very obvious gap between the policy enunciated at the top, and the results we see in peoples' actions, tends to be overlooked from the perspective of this model.

Until quite recently, managerial practice and theory have been largely based upon this top-down, bureaucratic vision of the organization and the prerogatives of management. Although the top-down model is now widely criticized as being unsuited to the contemporary environment and contrary to democratic values, a great many of the operating procedures followed in organizations, as well as the ways in which jobs are designed and grouped and authority is assigned, reflect this traditional concept of the organization even today. It seems to be easier to find fault with the nature of organizations as they are than it is to devise practical ways to eliminate bureaucratic forms and move towards new organizational visions.

Even when the stated goal is to introduce more participation in decision making, "employee involvement" is usually imposed unilaterally or brought to the bargaining table by management, and tends to involve little real sharing of power to make decisions (Clegg, 1983:9; Newton, 1989; Spector, 1985). The Canadian Auto Workers have taken a position against collaborating with employers on work teams or Quality of Work Life programs on the grounds that such initiatives are being used to erode workers' rights (*Globe and Mail*, Oct. 23, 1989).

Many elements of the top-down model are implied in the regulations of the Federal Contractors Program (FCP) and in the provisions of the Employment Equity Act, and reflected in guides for implementing programs that are available from various government agencies. The FCP regulations are quite specific as to the chief executive's responsibility to personally commit the organization to employment equity, to inform employees, review policies and practices, set numerical goals and timetables, and develop special measures to assist in their attainment (Box 1.2). Both the FCP and the Employment Equity Act require employers to collect workforce data, which can be used as a basis for a review that could result in sanctions against the organization, unfavourable media attention, or both. The Canadian Employment and Immigration Commission's booklet, "Employment Equity: A Guide for Employers" (1987), appears to reflect a top-down model of implementing change with its definition of "consultation":

> a full and sufficient opportunity and sufficient information are provided by the employer to employee representatives or, in a unionized setting, to bargaining agents, so that they may have a reasonable opportunity to ask questions and submit advice (Glossary, p. 2).

Information circulated by government agencies and consultants, and workshops and publications addressed to practitioners, typically emphasize that change must begin with "senior level commitment" (e.g. Ontario Women's Directorate, 1990; Greiner and Schein, 1988). This commitment is to take the form of a policy formulated and publically announced by the chief executive, stating the organization's adherence to the principles of employment equity and the executive's assurance that managers will be held accountable for their attainment. An effective approach to implementation also involves the commitment by the top executive of appropriate resources to the change effort, beginning with the appointment of an employment equity officer.

All of these are important and necessary features of the regulatory framework for employment equity which, if anything, need to be strengthened to ensure that employers take their responsibilities seriously. The top-down model of change acknowledges the relationship between the employer and government, which has the power to regulate and to hold the chief executive accountable for compliance. The assertion that a program of change such as employment equity must "begin at the top" also reflects a basic truth about the nature of power, control and resource allocation in bureaucratic organizations that cannot be ignored. (See Kent [1989] for a discussion of senior management's role in implementing organizational change.)

A comprehensive review of evaluations of the effects of organization development (OD) change programs notes,

> the importance and effect of top management support and involvement is evident... While top management involvement probably is not, in general, sufficient to produce effective organizational change, it does seem to be one necessary condition for the achievement of such change (Frohman, Sashkin and Kavanagh, 1976: 157).

In reporting on its survey of human resource issues in U.S. and Canadian companies, Towers Perrin and the Hudson Institute noted,

> What is clear is the importance of top management support in dealing with any of the issues. Both the prevalence of programs aimed at effective work force management— and the willingness to strike out in more innovative ways— rises significantly when top management is interested and involved. While support from the top often can ensure a bigger budget, that may not be the sole, or even chief, reason for differences in how companies approach these problems. Top-down support may also send a signal that the company wants and needs creative, professional, well-thought-out approaches to human resource management (Towers Perrin, 1990: 18).

However, employment equity legislation, regulations and guides have little to say about what is involved in bringing about the complex behavioural and attitudinal changes that are required if the workplace is to become a more equitable environment. In the absence of a broad strategic perspective on the change process, employment equity remains management's program. It is something the top orders the middle to do in the name of the bottom, to paraphrase Rosabeth Moss Kanter (1983: 244).

Research on organizational change, including evaluations of efforts to push decision making down the hierarchy, has often noted that a top-down approach is likely to result in strain and resistance to the process itself, regardless of the nature of the change proposed (Nightingale, 1982; Beer and Driscoll, 1977; Beer, 1980:59). The top executive's decision to embark is a necessary but not sufficient condition for arrival at the destination of an organizational change journey. The engine of change will stall outside the door of the executive suite if the people who must carry out all the complex operations required to make the program run cannot be induced to climb aboard, or if they resist or even sabotage the process.

Furthermore, the view that an employment equity program is successful if it produces the workforce data the government requires, and on time, may be like designing an elaborate train schedule on the assumption that this will ensure that the train gets to its destination when it is expected. Even the most successful data collection effort is not likely to be what women, racial minorities, persons with disabilities and aboriginal people have in mind when they think of equity in employment. Making data an end in itself, while neglecting to plan the implementation process, is symptomatic of a disease that is chronic in bureaucratic organizations: the confusion of means with ends. In a 1985 speech to employment equity practitioners, Shelagh Day reminded us that "data is the tail and equality is the dog," and that "you can have a beautiful tail on a sick dog" (Day, 1985). If we don't want the tail to wag the dog, and we are sincerely committed to getting results, we will find it necessary to go far beyond compliance with government requirements, and to invest considerable time and resources in the implementation of a change process that is systemic and long-term.

There are clear implications for the practitioner's role as change agent in the top-down change model. It is usually understood that the change agent is the individual who was assigned technical responsibility for employment equity by the chief executive. This person's position in the organization's hierarchy, his or her reporting relationship and other duties are matters of critical importance to the effectiveness of the change program in getting results, as we discuss more fully in Chapter 10. In the ideal situation the employment equity practitioner is assigned full time to the employment equity function, rather than adding it on to a variety of other duties, and reports to the highest level executive responsible for human resource management, or directly to the chief executive, rather than to a junior personnel manager. But even under ideal conditions, the top-down change model operates as a constraint on the employment equity practitioner's ability to act effectively to mobilize change.

Within the framework of the top-down model, the employment equity practitioner's primary tasks are technical, and include completing the census, developing a data base, analyzing and reporting the data to government, and setting quantitative goals and timetables for increasing the representation of the four designated groups based upon availability data. It is unreasonable to expect that these activities *in themselves* will lead to change which will move the organization toward equity, although they are essential components of a larger employment equity strategy. There is little evidence that gathering and reporting data, as an isolated activity apart from direct action initiatives, will produce changes in behaviour (Frohman, Saskin and Kavanagh, 1976:144). There is also no reason to expect that organizational decision makers and designated group members will take goals seriously that are a product of a technical exercise performed by the employment equity officer acting alone.

Yet very few Canadian organizations appear to have progressed very far beyond these data collection and goal setting activities in implementing employment equity. If the data collection exercise does not exhaust organizational energy and resources, the logic of the top-down model is that the role of the employment equity practitioner will shift from technical expert to enforcer. It becomes the employment equity practitioner's task to see that the quantitative targets are attained, just as managers of other corporate functions are responsible for achieving numerical goals for market share, sales or production. However, "the equalizer" has far less control over the means of achieving these targets than colleagues in marketing or production are likely to have. Moreover, even if there are efforts to improve the recruitment and hiring of underrepresented groups, and these measures are successful, it is unlikely that net gains in representation will occur unless the climate in the workplace changes so as to encourage them to stay and develop careers.

Given the employment equity practitioner's relative powerlessness in the face of the task, and the role ambiguity inherent in the position, we should not be surprised if stress, burnout and turnover are common among people in this role. The true nature of their task as change agents has not been recognized or supported. The top-down model of change does not acknowledge the realities of interests, power, and resistance to change in organizations. It does not recognize that the employment equity practitioner will not be able to help the organization move toward equity if his or her role is viewed as narrowly technical.

Organizational Change as Cultural Change

Our second change model is rooted in a challenge to the classical views of the organization as a bureaucracy managed from the top according to scientific management principles. It is a theoretical tradition whose North American roots can be traced to the Hawthorne studies of informal social relations in the workplace, and later, the human relations theories of management and organizational behaviour (e.g. Likert, 1961; McGregor, 1960; Maslow, 1954; Mayo, 1933; Roethlisberger and Dickson, 1939). The applied field of organization development originated in Kurt Lewin's work in group dynamics, and was influenced by British socio-technical systems theory (Pettigrew, 1985; Burke, 1987:Ch. 3). Organization development (OD) applies theories and concepts from the behavioural sciences to the management of organizational change.

OD practitioners act as consultants and facilitators in various change contexts, and OD has become recognized as one of the most influential bodies of theoretical and applied knowledge at the disposal of the change agent. In fact, OD is sometimes confused with the practice of organizational change itself, or assumed to be the only body of theory and practice available to the change agent.

The OD model of organizational change is also a top-down model since it is top managers who hire the external consultant to come in and solve a problem important to them (Pettigrew, 1985; Greiner and Schein, 1988). Most OD texts assume a scenario in which an external consultant is engaged by senior managers, and is informed about the goals of the consulting contract by them; hence the "client" is in fact senior management (e.g. Greiner and Schein, 1988; Burke, 1987). Especially in the U.S., OD interventions, along with various types of employee participation programs, have frequently been used by management as part of a "union substitution" strategy (Berman, 1986). Kochan and Cappelli (1984:150) note that these approaches "seek to bypass or substitute for the union and establish direct communications between management and workers." The trade union movement has naturally been suspicious of these types of interventions in the workplace.

In diagnosing the issue that has been identified by top management, and in planning a strategy for change, the OD practitioner frequently focuses on making explicit the culture of the organization. Organizational change is assumed to occur primarily through changes in culture— in members' norms, values and attitudes, perceptions, communication patterns, leadership and management styles, and ways of dealing with interpersonal conflict (Burke, 1987: 16-17). Hence most actual OD interventions occur at the micro-level and involve attempts to change individuals and small groups, for example by using team building and group problem solving and conflict resolution approaches (Hage and Finsterbusch, 1989: 34).

Structural changes have increasingly been included in OD's area of concern in recent years, but OD practitioners tend to be "fairly naive about and reluctant to deal with power and politics in organizations" (Burke, 1987:17). Burke observes that "very little `new OD' has been created during the latter half of the 1970s and the 1980s. Team building no doubt still remains as the most common practice of OD consultants, which currently takes the form of `facilitating an off-site meeting'" (Burke, 1987: 164).

Underlying the OD model is the assumption that the change process begins with personal self-awareness and attitude change at the level of the individual, and that organizational change really means bringing individual goals into alignment with organizational goals (Burke, 1987:11). To make the change "stick," however, it is also necessary to establish new patterns at the level of the work group, in order that change in individuals will be reinforced and supported.

While the top-down model channels the process of managing change through organizational rules, the formal structure of authority and compliance, and symbols of legitimacy conferred by top management, the OD cultural change model works primarily through influencing the informal, interpersonal and attitudinal aspects of organizational life. The role of the change agent is to assist organizational members in becoming conscious of their collective attitudes, values and patterns of behaviour and to consider alternative possibilities, much as a therapist might facilitate the individual's growth toward self-awareness and new behaviours based upon that insight.

By now it may have occurred to the reader that this way of thinking about organizational change has little obvious relevance to the practical goal of moving more women, minorities and people with disabilities into desirable jobs. How important is it that employees begin with favourable attitudes toward having a woman as their supervisor, for example? Are we confronting another case of goal displacement — a confusion of means with ends?

Research in intergroup relations has suggested that the relationship between attitudes and behaviour is multi-faceted and highly contingent upon context, and that attitudes frequently conform to experience (e.g. Newman, 1973:Ch.5).Pettigrew and Martin (1987: 65) note that "in contrast to the traditional view that racial behaviour will change only after racial attitudes change, modern social psychology emphasizes that altered behaviour is more often the precursor of altered attitudes, and behaviour is shaped in important ways by the situation in which it occurs." This observation is also true of attitudes and behaviours in relations between the sexes. In practice, employees may not welcome a woman as their supervisor at first, but if the appointment is an appropriate one and the position is properly defined and empowered so that the new manager is able to succeed, acceptance is likely to follow.

Of course it would be fallacious to argue that an employment equity program can succeed without any effort to help people to change their attitudes. Measures to raise awareness, challenge traditional stereotypes and attitudes, reinforce new values, and build a foundation for the acceptance of new patterns of behaviour are an important element of an overall change strategy. Training experiences and simulations designed to sensitize organizational members to the existence of cultural differences, stereotypes, and discrimination, or to introduce new patterns of behaviour, might be seen as OD applications within an employment equity context.

For example, Metro Toronto has developed a significant capability in human rights, equal opportunity and race relations training. Metro's Kingswood Management Training Program, a five day experiential learning exercise on managing racial, inter-cultural and gender issues, was initiated in 1984 and has been completed by a majority of the corporation's managers. Metro Toronto also provides training for staff in working with a multicultural clientele, dealing with workplace harassment and human rights complaints, AIDs information, career management, and accommodating employees with disabilities (Metropolitan Toronto, 1989: 8-9).

Cultural change initiatives such as the Kingswood exercise may help to develop and maintain a working environment that is hospitable to designated group members so that they will remain within the organization and be successfully integrated once they gain access to employment. For example, attitude change programs may assist employees at all levels to see why language that labels, stereotypes or excludes women and minorities tends to reinforce patterns of inequality.

There is also a need for training to develop an information base, skills, and insight, as we will discuss further in Chapter 11. Managers involved in hiring, developing and promoting employees need to be given an opportunity to understand their accountability for equal treatment and accommodation of difference, and given tools that help them to be effective in fulfilling these responsibilities and in dealing effectively with intergroup tensions or discriminatory behaviour by subordinates. Union leaders need to be informed about what their members may gain from employment equity, and given assistance in supporting their members as they adapt to change.

The OD model emphasizes the development of awareness, understanding, and problem solving capabilities based upon empirical analysis of how organizational members perceive their reality. OD practitioners sometimes use a social science technique known as action research, which involves collecting information from organizational members and feeding it back to them as a basis for planning a change strategy, or for "taking the pulse" of the organization. We will examine the action research approach more fully in

Chapter 8 when we discuss strategies for planning and implementing employment equity.

Interventions reflecting an OD emphasis on change in organizational culture and interpersonal communication clearly contribute to an effective employment equity strategy. But these alone are not enough. For example, training to sensitize employees to avoid engaging in racial or gender harassment needs to complement the establishment of structures and systems to ensure that the organization will deal decisively and effectively with harassment when it does occur. Moves to improve peoples' knowledge base, and work to change attitudes and values, do not come to grips with the interests and entrenched privileges embodied in the organization's structure and culture, and that have excluded women, minorities, people with disabilities, and aboriginal peoples from access to the opportunity and power structures of the workplace. And inviting designated group members to participate in meetings, discussions, or training sessions in itself does not result in the removal of discrimatory barriers that block their advancement.

Organizational Change Through Stakeholder Participation

The third model rests on a complex image of the organization in an open system, involved in continual transactions with other organizations and influenced by technological developments, market conditions, government policy and numerous other factors in its changing environment. The organization itself consists of people interacting within a structure of authority, rules, and informal codes of behaviour that they collectively create and modify. People as individuals and as members of groups have distinct perspectives and interests that are linked to their positions in the hierarchy and to their unique responsibilities, identities as members of professions or trades, and various other sources of meaning in their working lives. Some groups with which employees affiliate, such as unions, professional associations or advocacy groups, extend beyond the organization's boundaries.

The coming together of a variety of interests, loyalties, values and views of the world that are constantly changing and may at times be at odds with each other means that the organization is a political arena (Nightingale, 1982, Pettigrew, 1985, Tushman, 1977). Getting things done, and in particular making change, involves identifying the various stakeholder groups that have an interest in the outcomes, providing means for them to articulate their interests, and then moving toward shared objectives through bargaining, negotiation, collaboration, and conflict. The distribution of power and opportunity within the organization is a fundamental reality that limits the possibilities for action and affects how people behave and experience their work environment, define their interests, and react to change (Kanter, 1977).

In any particular program of organizational change there are a variety of stakeholder groups, each of which has a direct and vital interest in the change process and its outcomes. Some of these stakeholder groups are within the workplace and some are part of the community or the larger society. For example, stakeholders with an interest in the implementation of an employment equity program in a manufacturing firm might include top management, line managers at all levels, the human resources staff, other departments in the organization, trade union officers and members, members of designated groups working at the firm, advocacy associations in the community that would like the company to hire more of the people they represent, and government officials responsible for the implementation of employment equity regulations.

Chapter 7 discusses the stakeholder groups involved in employment equity in various types of settings in some detail. For the present, we need to be aware that these various groups may bring diverse and often conflicting interests to the change process, and it is not always obvious how a particular group will perceive the program's impacts in areas of concern to it. However, it is important that insofar as possible, stakeholders are involved in the change and in a position to work toward at least some goals important to them through participating in the change process. In practice, as change unfolds in day to day action, the outcomes of the change process are not defined exclusively by senior management: they are only one of the stakeholders, although a critical one.

However, because power and opportunity are distributed unequally in the workplace, some stakeholder groups have the ability to set the agenda for change, while others are powerless and unable to influence the process unless special effort is made to empower them. This is true of women, minorities, aboriginal people and people with disabilities — the intended beneficiaries of employment equity. It is precisely because these groups are underrepresented in the organization, and in decision-making roles within it, that employment equity programs are needed. Therefore if the change initiative is to be relevant to their needs, arrangements must be made to involve them in planning and implementation.

There are some fairly clear implications in the stakeholder model for the practitioner responsible for implementing a change program such as employment equity. While the practitioner must be thoroughly familiar with governmental requirements and with the jargon and techniques associated with employment equity implementation, his or her role is not primarily a technical one. The change agent's role is political, in that it centers on the mobilization of support and participation within and external to the organization. Even with top management support, the employment equity practitioner cannot successfully initiate and sustain a complex program of organizational change alone. His or her task is to bring together a variety of interests and constituencies in common actions — small and big — directed toward change.

As we will discuss further in Chapter 10, the change agent works not just with individuals, but with groups, and with individuals as representatives of the interests of groups, on all aspects of program planning and implementation. He or she spends a great deal of time and energy communicating, listening, negotiating and bargaining to clarify each group's stake in the program and deal with sources of resistance. The change agent clearly has an advocacy role in relation to the designated groups, and a responsibility to ensure that their concerns are addressed and that they have appropriate opportunities to influence the direction and content of the change program.

The employment equity initiative is not the employment equity practitioner's program: it is the organization's program. It belongs to all the various groups that make up the organization. If there is to be change, these groups together will make it happen.

While it is likely that the change process will be formally launched at the top of the organizational hierarchy, the stakeholder model acknowledges that the impetus for change can arise anywhere in the organization. At times the change agent will become aware that internal critics and external pressure groups can be valued allies in moving things forward. The participation of community-based advocacy groups can be essential when the organization has few members of the designated groups in its current work force, and therefore little insight into barriers to their entry and how to overcome them.

However, it is important to realize that stakeholder participation in a political process of change is not simply an end in itself. If that participation does not lead to demonstrated results—to real change —it is likely to end in the frustration and sense of betrayal that can result from unmet expectations. This is likely to occur if the key stakeholders — the designated groups — lack the power to influence the change process, and participation turns out to mean cooptation.

Change Models and Employment Equity

Bolman and Deal (1991) examine "frames" or paradigms in organizational theory that are useful in understanding the value premises, assumptions, and strategic decisions that underlie various approaches to organizational change. They suggest that the practitioner will benefit from drawing upon each of these frames — the structural or top-down model, the human resource or OD model, and the political or stakeholder model — since each spotlights a different dimension of the organization, in that each provides the viewer with a different window on behaviour in the workplace.

Tichy's analysis of change management (1983) presents three organizational models. The classical/mechanistic model is derived from classical organization theory, viewing the organization as a structure whose essence is rules and a hierarchy of authority. From the perspective of this model, change is a technical exercise of moving the organization toward some "objective" standard through the use of such technologies as time and motion studies; job analysis and evaluation; revision of policies, procedures and control systems; and change in the organizational chart. Change is planned and executed by technocrats with the impetus and legitimacy for the change process coming from top management (Tichy, 1983: 42-43).

The human resources/organic model is derived from human relations theories of organizational behaviour and OD, and is aimed at "unfreezing" and changing the mechanistic culture and moving toward a more organic organizational culture that is open, democratic, flexible, and people-oriented.The political model assumes that politics, the use of power, and the building of coalitions are fundamental processes in organizations, and that making change involves negotiation and bargaining among interest groups. Like Bolman and Deal, Tichy suggests that each model, in isolation, leaves out critical considerations, and that an effective organizational change strategy will be informed by all three (Tichy, 1983: 49). Tichy's analysis emphasizes the importance of aligning the technical, political, and cultural components of the organization, and the behaviour of groups and individuals within it, in implementing change.

In thinking about how these suggestions might be useful to the employment equity practitioner, it is clear that the top-down, cultural change (OD), and stakeholder models all have something to contribute to an effective change strategy. The top-down model emphasizes the importance of leadership and allocation of resources by the top executive, and of arrangements to ensure that managers are accountable for the attainment of employment equity goals. The top-down model also points to the key role of government regulation and enforcement in securing senior management commitment. The cultural change (OD) model shows the need for training and learning experiences to create a receptive climate for the integration of designated group members by building awareness and understanding of the need for change. It shows how education can assist in developing relevant skills to assure the competencies required to implement change. The stakeholder model accommodates these elements within a strategic change process that proceeds by mobilizing participation of groups throughout the organization, as well as external stakeholders. It acknowledges that the change process is decentralized, and may be top-down, bottom up or lateral at different stages. Planning and implementation are viewed as flowing into each other. They are parts of the same whole, not separate functions, with planning done at "the top" and implementation of "their" plan delegated to "subordinates."

If a complex change process such as employment equity is to be effective it must spread outward from its origin and involve many people and groups throughout the organization. If the employment equity effort is to result in changes in customary ways of doing things, people must be enticed rather than coerced to join. Mobilizing and organizing broad participation is a complex task of strategic management that involves elements borrowed from the top-down and cultural change models, within the framework of a participatory approach. In Chapters 7 and 8 we discuss in greater detail the "why" and "how" of stakeholder participation, and examine strategic issues in implementing change using a participatory process.

If implemented through stakeholder participation, employment equity brings together key elements of major currents of change in the workplace today, including trends toward equality of opportunity for previously excluded groups, democratization of decision making, protection of human rights, and enhanced quality of working life for all members of the organization. It also implies a fundamental reorientation of the organization's relationship to the larger community. Given the emerging demographic composition of labour markets and of the workplace, as well as the democratic values that are being articulated by people around the world, these changes are long overdue.

REFERENCES

Beer, Michael. *Organization Change and Development: A Systems View.* Glenview, Ill.: Scott, Foresman, 1980.

Beer, Michael, and James Driscoll. "Strategies for Change." Ch. 7 in J. Richard Hackman and J. Lloyd Suttle (eds.), *Improving Life at Work: Behavioral Science Approaches to Organizational Change.* Santa Monica, Cal.: Goodyear, 1977.

Berman, Melissa. "More Say Versus More Pay." *Across the Board* (Conference Board), 23, June 1986, 70-71.

Bolman, Lee, and Terrence Deal. *Reframing Organizations: Artistry, Choice and Leadership.* San Francisco: Jossey Bass, 1991.

Burke, W. Warner. *Organization Development, A Normative View.* Reading, Mass.: Addison-Wesley, 1987.

Clegg, Stewart. "Power and Participation,." In Colin Crouch and Frank Heller (eds.), *Organizational Democracy and Political Processes.* Vol.1, New York: John Wiley, 1983, 3-32.

Cohen - Rosental, Edwards. "Worker Participation in Management: A Guide for the Perplexed." In Daniel Skrovan (ed.). *Quality of Work Life: Perspectives for Business and the Public Sector*, Reading, Mass.: Addison - Wesley, 1983, Ch. 14.

Day, Shelagh. "Affirmative Action Update, 1983-1985." Employment and Immigration Canada, 2nd National Practitioners' Workshop, Toronto, May 8-10, 1985.

Fox, Alan. "Industrial Sociology and Industrial Relations." Research Paper 3, Royal Commission on Trade Unions and Employers' Associations, London: Her Majesty's Stationary Office, 1966.

Frohman, Mark, Marshall Sashkin and Michael Kavanagh. "Action Research as Applied to Organization Development." In L. Spray (ed.), *Organizational Effectiveness: Theory-Research-Utilization*. Kent, Ohio: Kent State University Press, 1976, 129-161.

Greiner, Larry, and Virginia Schein. *Power and Organization Development: Mobilizing Power to Implement Change*. Reading, Mass.: Addison-Wesley, 1988.

Hage, Jerald, and Kurt Finsterbusch. "Three Strategies of Organizational Change: Organizational Development, Organizational Theory and Organizational Design." *International Review of Administrative Sciences*, 55, 1989, 29-57.

Hirschheim, R.A. *Office Automation Concepts, Technologies and Issues*. New York: Addison-Wesley, 1985.

Imershein, Allen. "Organizational Change as Paradigm Shift." *Sociological Quarterly*, 18, 1977, 33-43.

Kanter, Rosabeth Moss. *Men and Women of the Corporation*. New York: Basic Books, 1977.

Kanter, Rosabeth Moss. *The Change Masters*. New York: Simon and Schuster, 1983.

Kent, Robert. *Installing Change: An Executive Guide for Implementing and Maintaining Organizational Change*. Winnipeg: Pragma Press, 1989.

Kochan, Thomas, and Peter Cappelli. "The Transformation of the Industrial Relations and Personnel Function." Ch. 5 in Paul Osterman (ed.), *Internal Labor Markets*. Cambridge: MIT Press, 1984.

Lerner, Melvin, and Linda Whitehead. "Procedural Justice Viewed in the Context of Justice Motive Theory." In Gerold Milula (ed.). *Justice and Social Interaction*. New York: Springer-Verlag, 1980, 219 - 256.

Lewin, Kurt. *Field Theory in Social Science*. New York: Harper, 1951.

Likert, R. *New Patterns of Management*. New York: McGraw Hill, 1961.

McGregor, D. *The Human Side of Enterprise*. New York: McGraw Hill, 1960.

Maslow, Abraham. *Motivation and Personality*. New York: Harper and Brothers, 1954.

Mayo, Elton. *The Human Problems of an Industrial Civilization.* Boston: Harvard University Graduate School of Business, 1933.

Metropolitan Toronto. Equal Employment Opportunity Division. "Equal Employment Opportunity Division - *A Strategy for the 90's*", July 1989.

Newman, William. *American Pluralism: A Study of Minority Groups and Social Theory.* New York: Harper and Row, 1973.

Newton, Keith. "Technological Change and Organizational Change in Canada." *New Technology, Work and Employment,* 4(1), 1989, 42-47.

Nightingale, Donald. *Workplace Democracy.* Toronto: University of Toronto Press, 1982.

Ontario Women's Directorate. "Organizational Change and Organizational Impact." Queen's Park: Government of Ontario, 1990.

Pettigrew, Andrew. *The Awakening Giant: Continuity and Change in ICI.* Oxford: Basil Blackwell, 1985.

Pettigrew, Thomas, and Joanne Martin. "Shaping the Organizational Context for Black American Inclusion." *Journal of Social Issues,* 43(1), 1987, 41 -78.

Roethlisberger, F.J., and W.J. Dickson. *Management and the Worker: An Account of the Research Program Conducted by the Western Electric Company.* Cambridge: Harvard University Press, 1939.

Spector, Bert. "From Protest to Partnership: The Dilemma of Managing Change in the Democratic Union Organization." In Richard Walton and Paul Laurence (eds.), *Human Resource Management Trends and Challenges.* Cambridge: Harvard Business School Press, 1985, Ch. 7.

Tapscott, Don. *Office Automatation: A User-Driven Method.* New York: Plenum, 1982.

Tichy, Noel. *Managing Strategic Change.* New York: John Wiley, 1983.

Tushman, Michael. "A Political Approach to Organizations: A Review and Rationale." *Academy of Management Review,* 2, 1977, 206-216.

Towers Perrin and The Hudson Institute. *Work force 2000,* 1990.

7

Stakeholder
Participation

I F WE THINK OF EMPLOYMENT EQUITY as a process
of organizational change in which stakeholders
play central roles, it is obvious that the stakes
for members of the designated groups inside the organization are
high. It is also clear, as we discussed in Chapter 1, that the
employment equity process is unlikely to be seen as successful if
there has not been progress toward the goals and priorities of the
designated groups who have a stake in the organization. The
importance of top management's participation as a stakeholder in
any large-scale change process is also generally understood and
accepted. It may be less obvious that the involvement of a number
of other stakeholders is also critical to the success of the employment equity process.

If you were asked to think of an organization that fits the classical model of the bureaucracy, in which authority is centralized,
action is directed from the top, and there is a rule for almost everything, you might think first of the armed forces or a police service.
A police service may also come to mind when one thinks of a
closed system — an organization with a relatively impenetrable
barrier that insulates it from public scrutiny and influence. One

might think that in such an organization the implementation of a change program would be a fairly straightforward matter: the chief of police would issue orders and they would be carried out throughout the ranks, with few questions asked.

However, recent events in Canada have shown that police services and other parts of the criminal justice system have had to become open and responsive to the critical scrutiny and involvement of a variety of external and internal stakeholders. Community advocacy groups, police associations, local and provincial politicians, social agencies, academics, provincial government bureaucracies, human rights commissions, and a variety of other stakeholder groups are successfully seeking to influence the nature of police work and the composition of police services. Even in these relatively centralized and closed organizational systems, change involves responding to, and working with and through, a diversity of interests. Change is anything but a simple and straightforward process.

External stakeholder groups have been very effective in influencing police organizations to become more accountable to the public, and in mobilizing political power, which translates into legislation and regulation. The Donald Marshall inquiry in Nova Scotia, the attacks on Native people by the Sûreté du Québec at Kanasetake and Kanawake, the criticism of Metro Toronto's police by organizations representing racial minorities, and the aboriginal justice inquiry in Manitoba are recent examples of the nation-wide scope of the issue. The Montreal Urban Community Police Service has undertaken a employment equity program in response to a 1988 Québec Human Rights Commission report on relations between police and visible minority communities. Under the plan, women are to make up 33%, visible minorities 6% and aboriginal peoples 1% of the 4,300 member force by the year 2000 (*Globe and Mail*, July 19, 1991: A4). In Ontario, regulations under the Police Services Act (1990) require police services to submit hiring goals by 1992 that reflect the makeup of the communities they serve, along with plans for training and promoting designated group members, and for undertaking a variety of employment equity measures to improve the representation of members of racial minorities, women, persons with disabilities and aboriginal peoples (Box 7.1).

Box 7.1
Selected Employment Equity Regulations, Police Services Act, Ontario, 1990

POLICE SERVICES ARE REQUIRED TO:

- set goals and timetables for the representation of racial minorities, persons with disabilities, aboriginal persons, and women, that are equivalent to the representation levels of those groups in the population of working age within sixty kilometers of the area served by the police force;
- submit an employment equity plan for July 1, 1992 - December 31, 1993 to the Solicitor General by May 1, 1992. The plan will contain work force, hiring and promotion goals for the representation of designated group members in the police force, by level and occupational group, by the end of the plan period. It will also set out the steps that will be taken to attain these goals and to monitor progress.
- conduct a voluntary employment equity census of their employees and maintain this information
- establish measures to eliminate systemic barrriers in recruitment, selection, promotion and retention of designated group members. These include training on race relations, diversity and human rights, as well as policies to deal with workplace harassment, stereotyping and biased language use, family care, and accommodation of persons with disabilities.
- establish positive measures for outreach recruitment, assistance to applicants, internships, bridging positions, accelerated promotion, direct entry of designated group members to administrative postions, lateral entry, and designation of positions for designated group members. The regulations do not require the hiring or promotion of persons to positions for which they are not qualified.
- evaluate senior officers and managers on progress toward implementation of the plan, and apply rewards or sanctions accordingly.

- provide documentation of consultation with police associations, unions and community groups.

(SOURCE: "Regulation Made Under the Police Services Act, 1990, Employment Equity Plans.")

Critics point out that there are too few members of the designated groups in policing, and very few in command positions. For example, in 1991, only 6.4% of police officers in Canada were women, according to Statistics Canada. There is considerable research evidence, as well as allegations from community representatives, suggesting that the traditional culture of the police force tends to be unfriendly toward diversity and defined by conservative white able-bodied male values and norms of behaviour. Police services have been described as lacking in appropriate skills for dealing with a community that is both pluralistic and caught up in rapid transformation (e.g. Manning, 1977; Van Maanen, 1975).

Police services in many municipalities and provinces, as well as the RCMP, have been working to change these realities of organizational structure and culture. Their efforts are having some success: for example, the Ontario Provincial Police force, which has an active employment equity program, has 89 members who are racial minorities and 77 who are aboriginal. In contrast the Sûreté du Québec, which is preparing to start its first employment equity program, is estimated to have three members who are racial minorities (Globe and Mail, July 19, 1991: A4). In implementing their employment equity strategies, change agents in the larger police organizations may find that, while it is critical to have commitment at the top, it is not effective to introduce change from the top only, and to depend exclusively on formal authority structures and rules to establish new patterns. Nor can external stakeholder groups be excluded from the change process. One might expect that those responsible for implementing the employment equity provisions of Ontario's Police Services Act will find it necessary to move toward a participatory approach to change in order to attain the results required. Box 7.2 identifies some of the potential stakeholders in employment equity in police services, and lists examples of some of their concerns or interests in the change process.

BOX 7.2

Potential Stakeholders in Employment Equity in Policing, and Some of Their Interests

STAKEHOLDERS:	INTERESTS OR CONCERNS:
Individual members of designated groups	1) Access to employment and career development opportunities, 2) responsiveness of police services to group needs 3) supportive work environment in which their contribution is valued
Board of Commissioners	Public image of service, efficient and effective use of resources
Chief of Police and other senior officers	Meeting public expectations and government requirements, performance and morale of officers, efficiency and productivity
Civilian employees	Job satisfaction, career development opportunities, compensation, working conditions
Uniformed middle and first line managers (superintendents, inspectors, sergeants)	Career development opportunities, work load and requirements, morale
Uniformed officers	Job security, personal safety, job satisfaction, compensation and benefits, recognition
Solicitor General or other provincial authority	Compliance with legislation and regulations, responsiveness of police services to citizens

Police association	Staffing levels, compensation, bargaining and collective agreement, working conditions
Taxpaying public	Level and responsiveness of services to community needs
Other police and protective services (e.g. fire, ambulance, corrections)	Resource levels
Community advocacy organizations	Responsiveness of police services to constituency (e.g. victims of family violence, racial minority youth, aboriginal communities); police workforce that reflects the racial and ethnic diversity of the community

Police services have been involving external stakeholder groups in their change efforts. For example, the police service in London, Ontario, sends representatives to meetings of the London Urban Alliance on Race Relations, and has been working with the Alliance on race relations issues, recruitment, and training (*London Free Press*, Oct. 13, 1990). In Montreal, the police department has worked with the Black Coalition of Quebec over the past two years to improve police/community relations (*Globe and Mail*, July 19, 1991: A4).

Why might it be important to involve internal stakeholders at all levels in the implementation of employment equity in policing? The goal of improving the representation of women and minorities in senior positions, for example, cannot be attained by simply placing individual members of the designated groups in such jobs and ordering their subordinates to obey them. No matter how capable they are as individuals, or how well disciplined their subordinates are, the new senior officers will confront conditions that may seriously undermine their ability to function. They may not be able to succeed in their new positions in the absence of a broad range of measures to change the prevailing culture and to remove structural barriers that have impeded their ability to function in the past, and to enter and move up in the organization. In other words, it is necessary to make a variety of changes in those patterns that have hindered the advancement and acceptance of women and minorities as equals in police services — otherwise there would be no need for employment equity!

In changing the structure and culture of the organization, groups within the police service need to be involved — for example police associations, as well as superintendents, inspectors, sergeants, and persons in other uniform and civilian positions who will be interacting as peers or subordinates with newly recruited women and minorities. It will be critical to involve these stakeholders on issues affecting their vital interests, as when revered and widely accepted values need to be scrutinized and perhaps redefined and then institutionalized in a new form. For example, the traditional mode of promotion from within appears to be challenged under the employment equity regulations in Ontario's Police Services Act by the need to develop positive measures such as lateral entry, as well as direct entry, to administrative positions by members of designated groups.

Cultural change involving stakeholder participation will also need to occur in order to create a climate in which diversity, and a broader concept of the professional image of the officer, are accepted. A woman cannot perform effectively in policing if she is a victim of sexual harassment, or if peers exclude her from collegial social interaction, or if superior officers are paternalistic and do not assign her to certain functions or provide informative performance evaluations.

It is evident that a great deal of work must be done with and through groups and individuals at various levels of the organization and within the surrounding community to ensure that employment equity initiatives will succeed. In Chapter 6 we sketched three models of organizational change, and suggested that the stakeholder participation model is particularly useful when the kind of change required is far-reaching, complex, and long term, as is the case for employment equity. In this chapter we discuss this change model more fully in relation to employment equity implementation at the level of the workplace. After examining circumstances in which stakeholder involvement is especially important in implementing organizational change, we identify some of the principal stakeholders in employment equity, and their stakes in the process. We examine ways in which they may attempt to influence the change process, whether through cooperation or resistance. Finally, some of the difficulties of working with stakeholders in the employment equity change process are considered. In this chapter we examine the "why," "who," "what" and "when" of organizational change through stakeholder participation. In Chapter 8 we move on to look at *how* stakeholders can be involved in the strategic process of planning and implementing employment equity change.

BOX 7.3

Blacks and Whites, and Men and Women, May See the Organizational World Very Differently . . .

- A study of 164 U.S. executives found that of individuals with leadership qualities, 2% of men and 67% of women said that executive women are subject to hostility from their superiors; 75% of men and 33% of women agreed that their firms actively encourage women's career development.
- In a U.S. corporation, a survey of 2000 managers, of which 150 were Black, found substantial differences of opinion between white and Black managers regarding race relations in the organization. Generally, whites held more favourable views, and saw decisions as linked to qualities of individuals. Blacks saw evidence of racism that whites did not perceive, and saw decisions about individuals as stemming from organizational factors rather them individual qualities. Both groups felt that their own racial group was at a disadvantage in comparison with the other group. For example, a comparison of white and Black male managers' responses to selected questionnaire items showed the following percentages in agreement:
- Race relations within the company are good: 89% of whites, 45% of Blacks
- Good one-to-one black-white relationships are common in the company: 74% of whites, 40% of Blacks
- Blacks are almost never evaluated fairly by white supervisors: 12% of whites, 60% of Blacks
- White managers share vital growth and career-related information with Black managers: 89% of whites, 42% of Blacks

- Qualified whites are promoted more rapidly than equally qualified blacks: 9% of whites, 95% of Blacks
- Qualified blacks are promoted more rapidly than equally qualified whites: 82% of whites, 14% of Blacks.

(SOURCES: L.R. Gallese."Why Women Aren't Making it to the Top." Across the Board [Conference Board], 28 (4). April 1991, 18-22.)

(Clayton Alderfer, Charleen Alderfer, Leota Tucker and Robert Tucker. "Diagnosing Race Relations in Management." *Journal of Applied Behavioural Science.* 27, 1980, 135-166.)

The Stakeholder Participation Model: Groups, Politics, Power, and Interests

The stakeholder participation model envisions the organization as a political entity within a complex and changing external environment upon which it depends for survival. The organization is comprised of groups and individuals who come together, each with its own perspective (see Box 7.3) and its own loyalties and interests to protect and advance. Action, and in particular the implementation of change, occurs through conflict, cooperation, and accommodation among diverse and changing interests over time (Nightingale, 1982; Pettigrew, 1985; Tushman, 1977; Bolman and Deal, 1984: Ch.7)

Traditional views of organizations held that organizations have, or ought to have, clear, consistent goals that are established at the senior executive level and communicated to all members of the organization. In contrast, the stakeholder/political model assumes that there are a variety of often conflicting goals within the organization, and that these are overt as well as covert. Different stakeholders have different goals that correspond to their distinctive needs and interests, on the basis of which they make claims on scarce resources.

Some organizational actors —"authorities" — are entitled to make decisions about the use of organizational resources, but these top-down actors are under pressure from "partisans" who exercise various forms of power in an attempt to influence those decisions and their outcomes from the bottom up (Bolman and Deal, 1984: 114-116; 134). This is an ongoing process, not one that ends or is resolved once key decisions are made.

Organizational change, then, is not just a matter of having a good idea or a sound objective and convincing others of its value. Change is an outcome of the exercise of power, and may involve shifts in the balance of power in organizations. Bolman and Deal (1984: 133) observe.

> The political frame says to a change agent: In order to make things different you need power and you need to be prepared for conflicts as a part of the process. The degree, intensity, and form of the conflict will vary with the issues at stake and with the forms of power that you mobilize.

This view suggests that the central dynamic of organizational life is the successful act of influencing others to do what you have in mind. Objectives of using influence may include affecting outcomes of events; benefitting from resource allocation decisions; defining the problems to be addressed; or creating, sustaining, or changing power or opportunity structures so as to benefit you or your group.

Contemporary analyses of how power works in organizations emphasize that power is relational, rather than an attribute of individuals (Kanter, 1977, 1979). You can only influence another person or group if they acquiesce. That may happen if you have the legitimate power to coerce their cooperation, but coercion is a poor basis for a sound working relationship for the future. You are more likely to be effective in influencing others if they, as well as you, have something to gain by cooperating. In everyday life at work, most of us, no matter where we are in the organization, are involved in ongoing relationships with others. Even if we were in a position to coerce others this would not be a wise or useful strategy, since we will need to depend upon these working relationships in the future (Fisher and Ury, 1981). It is also true that legislation, legal precedent, the need for a positive corporate image, corporate policies, and collective agreements — as well as the ethical codes of individuals, professions and organizations — limit the scope for using coercion to influence the behaviour of others. Since power is relational, then, the political processes of bargaining, negotiation, coalition-building and deal-making are central to the making and implementation of decisions in organizations.

Bargaining occurs and deals are made with respect to interests — matters that bear directly on the wellbeing or identity of organizational participants. The stakeholder participation model of the change process highlights the central role played by groups that coalesce around common interests, especially where those groups have something to gain or lose by participating in a program of change. In applying the model it is important to identify the stakeholder groups that have an interest in a particular issue, and to be clear about what their interest is, and what they may have to contribute to a change process. These suggestions are illustrated in Box 7.4 and will be discussed later in this chapter. But first we will consider some of the reasons why stakeholders should be involved in organizational change, and in particular, in employment equity.

Why and When to Involve Stakeholders in Change?

There is a large scholarly literature that discusses theories about how organizational change can be effectively implemented, as well as evidence from many studies about what contributes to success and what accounts for failure in organizational change experiments. The literature on the theory and practice of organizational change examines different kinds of change in various settings, including the introduction of new technology in the office or factory, employee involvement programs such as quality circles, programs to improve service to the client or customer, and organizational restructuring to move toward team-based or matrix management. Oddly enough, only a few contributions to the published literature — notably those of Rosabeth Moss Kanter — recognize that affirmative action or employment equity is a kind of organizational change that might be best understood in terms of a broader perspective on organizational change and how it works (e.g. Kanter, 1977; 1980; also Chertos, 1983).

Employment equity has several features in common with other forms of organizational change; therefore we can apply insights and findings from the generic literature on organizational change as we design a strategy for employment equity implementation. This literature suggests that under certain conditions, the change process is more likely to attain the results we intend — rather than being derailed, stalled or sabotaged by resistance — if the key stakeholder groups are involved throughout the process.

The conditions under which stakeholder participation in implementing organizational change is likely to be most effective are summarized in the paragraphs that follow, which attempt to explain *why* and *when* stakeholder involvement may be an appropriate strategy.

1. Involve stakeholders when the change project is broad, complex, and long term.

Stakeholder participation is particularly important in large-scale projects. A recent survey of 312 cases of large-scale organizational change found "a significant positive relationship between the extent of employee involvement in program activities and program success".

> ...programs in which all levels of employees participated in program activities were rated as significantly more successful than programs in which only top managers participated... These results are consistent with years of research on the impact of participative management on decision acceptance... and performance on ill-structured, uncertain tasks (Covin and Kilmann, 1988:67).

2. Involve stakeholders when expert or specialized knowledge about a broad range of topics is needed.

Employment equity involves critical examination of existing policies and practices in order to identify those that may constitute barriers to the access or full participation of the designated groups in the workplace. As we will discuss more fully in Chapter 12, it is valuable to begin the employment equity diagnosis by involving members of the designated groups in a review of their experiences in seeking and maintaining employment in the organization. Each designated group brings unique perspectives and needs to the workplace, so the review of systems to identify barriers, and the design of outreach recruitment initiatives and special measures for women, aboriginal people, minorities and people with disabilities, requires that the organization learn from the life experience and the expert knowledge of representatives of those groups. This knowledge may be accessed in formal ways, or through informal consultation. Examples of formal ways of involving designated group members in the change process include:

- representation on committees or task forces, whether these groups operate in an advisory or decision-making capacity, and whether they are *ad hoc* and temporary or standing;
- participation in mentoring programs in which new employees who are designated group members receive mentoring, and they are also consulted about how the organization can improve its outreach recruitment and selection practices, or its service to clients or customers who are designated group members;
- systematic feedback through use of focus groups, employee surveys, exit interviews, and other data collection activities;
- designated group networks or action groups to provide mutual support as well as taking an advocacy or information-sharing role within the organization or union or both;
- staff positions dedicated to problem-solving, education and training, and dealing with harassment complaints and with concerns of members of a designated group (e.g. a Race Relations Officer, Vice President for the Status of Women, Accommodation Coordinator). Suggestions for developing structures to facilitate communication, participation and decision making involving designated groups will be further developed in Chapter 8.

Following the systems review and identification of barriers it is necessary to propose new policies and practices that are practical as well as equitable: after all, the job must still get done, and standards of efficiency must be met. Clearly the design of alternative practices requires detailed and specific knowledge of work operations and the competencies that are necessary to perform them. This knowledge usually resides in those people who are responsible for jobs on a daily basis. The knowledge of employees, line managers, and designated group representatives who are familiar with the workplace capabilities and requirements of their members, could contribute significantly to the development of workable alternatives for accommodation, recruitment and selection, and other equity issues.

Technical skills such as those needed to design a data base to support employment equity planning and monitoring, or to design an effective communications and public relations package, are also required in employment equity implementation. There is clearly a need to draw upon knowledge in many specialized areas in order to develop effective employment equity measures. This knowledge can best be tapped by means of a participatory strategy that can draw in a broad spectrum of organizational functions and levels.

3. Involve stakeholders when strong or long-term resistance is anticipated.

Resistance to change is always to be expected, but is likely to be exacerbated when people perceive both the process and the substance of change as threatening. People are less likely to resist a change process in which they have a voice, than one that they feel is imposed upon them without their consent.

Rogers and Shoemaker (1971: 36-37; 296-97; 213-13) suggest that change in organizational behaviour might occur through three types of decisions: authority, collective, or contingent decisions. Authority decisions that commit an organization to change are forced on individuals by persons of higher rank, regardless of those individuals' attitudes toward the change; they are ordered to comply. These kinds of decisions might result in the fastest rate of adoption of the change by some individuals in the organization, but such decisions are more likely to be circumvented and resisted in the long run, and continued compliance is unlikely without surveillance and sanctions. In contrast, collective decisions are those that organization members agree to, and which apply to all individuals once they are made. Acceptance of such decisions is related to the degree to which organization members participate in the decision.

Contingent decisions are those that individuals make about whether to adopt an innovation that has already been decided upon by the organization. For example, an organizational decision to adopt a workplace harassment policy can be an authority or a collective decision: individuals can then decide whether or not to make use of that policy, or to accept its influence upon their personal behaviour in the workplace.

The distinction between these three types of decisions highlights two potential points at which support or resistance can be mobilized: the organization's decision to initiate change, and the individual's decision about whether or not to be affected by that change. Establishing vehicles that involve organizational members in the change process can affect both of these decision points.

Contingent decisions made by individuals might be particularly influenced by their interpersonal communications with other organizational members.

Research on organizational communication suggests the importance of informal networks, especially those that connect individuals who are socially similar, in spreading accurate information and awareness of a change program and in persuading people to support change (Rogers and Shoemaker, 1971: 24, 225, 226). Informal opinion leaders in various management functions, among work colleagues, in the unions, and among members of designated groups, may play a critical role in mobilizing support for change and in legitimating the process, provided that they are consulted and their views are heeded.

Participation should entail authentic involvement in decision making, not merely "pseudo-participation" that "leaves the structure of power intact but enables management to obtain the collaboration of workers in making changes" (Pateman, 1983: 110-111). Arnstein (1969) discusses eight levels of participation: manipulation, therapy, informing, consultation, placation, partnership, delegated power, and citizen control. Only the top three rungs of Arnstein's "ladder of participation" involve some redistribution of power and real influence in decision making by traditionally powerless groups. Stakeholder participation, then, goes beyond engineering support, educating, or listening, while authority to decide is reserved for traditional power-holders.

Creating planning committees with no real authority to decide, no budget or resources, or no real links to stakeholder groups, does not provide for participation, as is clear from research findings on reasons why quality circles and other employee involvement schemes frequently have disappointing results (e.g. Lawler, 1986). If stakeholders perceive that their involvement is only for appearances, this in itself can result in resistance to the change process, regardless of the objectives of that process. So-called participation may be a waste of employees' time and energy if the opportunity to participate is a "gift" by management that keeps the giver in control, rather than a right, or a means to accomplish a task that needs to be completed (Kanter, 1983: 245).

4. Involve stakeholders when a diversity of interests are affected and when many levels and sectors of the organization need to be involved in carrying out the change program.
Support can be expected only if stakeholders see payoffs for themselves, or for the organization with which they identify, as a result of the change program. Participation of key stakeholders in program planning and implementation enhances the likelihood that each will share in the benefits of the program in some way. This in turn increases the level of support for change. Ideally, this support would take the form of willingness to devote time and energy to the change effort, since a change program of the scope of employment equity cannot succeed if it must depend upon the energy of only a few people. In Chapter 8 we will discuss ways in which structures can be created and strategies developed that permit stakeholder groups to work on employment equity projects relevant to their specific interests.

5. Involve stakeholders when the experience of participation in itself helps to develop needed competencies and understandings, and to support the change effort.
For women, minorities, aboriginal peoples and people with disabilities, the act of participation itself contributes to their emergence from disadvantage and subordination. Their involvement in the change process addresses the linkage between the low status these groups occupy in the organizational hierarchy, and lack of opportunity for them to participate in decision making. Moreover, participation has a cumulative impact, strengthening the skills, political experience, and self assurrance of those involved, thus contributing to their ability to succeed as employees (Patemen, 1983: 50-51).

Individual employees may benefit from participation by becoming more promotable or more competitive on the job market. But the organization may also benefit from the growth in skills and job satisfaction of employees at lower levels, with payoffs including more competent and promotable employees, and greater commitment on the part of designated group members to remaining in the organization. Involving employees who are members of designated groups on employment equity and other committees and task forces both makes appropriate use of their experience and expertise, and contributes to their development as individuals and as members of the organization.

However, it is important not to overburden members of designated groups when there are few such persons in the organization, by asking them to sit on numerous committees as "representatives" of their group. It is also unfair to coerce designated group members or other employees to participate in working on employment equity projects in which they have no interest: they should be invited to participate, not told that it is part of their job.

For participants who are not members of the designated groups, working with women, minorities, persons with disabilities or aboriginal people will contribute to the spread of awareness and understanding of the need for change. This in turn will strengthen the organization's capacity for learning and change.

6. Involve stakeholders when goals are vague or conflicting, and when outcomes are hard to define clearly and to get agreement on. Participation in the change process is particularly important when there are a variety of perspectives on what constitutes "results" or "success." As discussed in Chapter 6, this is true of employment equity. In such cases stakeholders may feel they can support a program of change on a continuing basis only if they have an opportunity to influence the program as it develops. Not all stakeholders can be satisfied at a single point in time, but stakeholders whose support is important may be willing to participate if they feel their needs or interests will be addressed in the long term. Employment equity goals and strategies for the attainment of these needs or interests may be in direct conflict with traditional management goals. For example the need to fill a key vacancy quickly, in the interests of efficiency, may conflict with the need to undertake a thorough search in order to identify qualified applicants from unrepresented groups. Such goal conflicts need to be managed by involving stakeholders that can ensure that employment equity remains a priority in managerial decision making.

In complex change initiatives such as employment equity, given resource limitations, the most pressing needs must be identified and priorities for change must be set. For strategic reasons, the establishment of priorities may depend in part on the strength and location of resistance and support within the organization. If all the important stakeholders are involved in decision-making, there is a greater likelihood that these tasks will be done effectively and that decisions will be politically acceptable to key constituencies.

7. Involve stakeholders when change programs must be tailored to the particular requirements of a local environment.
An employment equity strategy that might be appropriate for a manufacturing firm will not work in a hospital, and one that would meet the needs of a resource company operating in Alberta would not be appropriate in Newfoundland. Employment equity is a kind of change program that is highly site-specific. For this reason, employment equity practitioners are forming inter-organizational networks within their own sector so that they can share information about solutions that work in that environment. For example, employment equity officers in post-secondary educational institutions have a network in Ontario, and one in the western provinces. Approaches to reviewing employment systems, collecting and reporting work-force data, or goal-setting that work in private sector companies tend not to be transferable to universities and colleges.

The development of special programs and the accomodation of diversity are activities that are particularly shaped by the organizational context. Through stakeholder involvement, there is a greater chance that program elements will be relevant to the conditions within a particular workplace, and that they will therefore win wider acceptance and support, as well as being effective solutions to employment equity problems.

8. Involve stakeholders when change agents have low organizational power relative to those likely to resist the change (Kotter and Schlesinger. 1979: 112).
As will be discussed in Chapters 9 and 10, the employment equity change agent is unlikely to have a great deal of formal authority in an organization, and probably lacks the power to unilaterally implement a broad strategy of organizational change. There will be considerable resistance to change from some individuals in positions of authority and power. It is probable that individuals and groups at middle and lower organizational levels will also "devise a

host of creative and maddening ways to resist, divert, undermine, or ignore change efforts" (Bolman and Deal. 1984: 140). It is therefore essential to the effectivenesss of the change process that the employment equity practitioner work with a coalition of informal opinion leaders, decision makers, and a broad constituency that favours employment equity change, and that these stakeholders be involved throughout the change process.

Child (1984: 282; 285) cautions, however, that where there is inflexible and very strong opposition to a change process that is rooted in basic differences of interests and goals, participation is likely to be used as an opportunity for obstructing change. In Child's words, "participation is a way of confronting the political issues in change, not a means of avoiding or smoothing over them. If there is a deep-seated conflict of interest between the parties involved in a proposed change, participation will probably not turn up a mutually acceptable solution."

Who Are the Stakeholders in Employment Equity?

A stakeholder is a group or a person that has a direct, vital, and perhaps material interest in decisions that are made in an organization. The interests of stakeholders may be linked to their positions in the hierarchy, to their unique functions and responsibilities in the organization, to values or beliefs, or to various dimensions of their lives outside the workplace, among other concerns. Stakeholder groups may extend beyond the organization's boundaries, as in the case of unions, professional or community associations, or they may be confined within the organization, such as departments or union locals. Some stakeholder groups may be formally constituted while others are informal networks or "collective identities" based on friendship, similar values or interests. Some stakeholder groups are likely to accept or partake in management leadership while others are counter-cultures defined in opposition to structures of authority (Renaud, 1983). Any of these stakeholder groups or micro-communities may go through various stages of formation and dissolution, and they may be quiescent on some issues, while mobilizing for action on others. Box 7.4 lists some of the possible stakeholder groups in employment equity implementation, with suggestions regarding concerns that may be central for each. The discussion that follows suggests considerations that may be involved in employment equity from the perspective of some, but not all, of the potential stakeholders — top and line management, unions, and designated groups.

Top Management

Top management is only one of the stakeholders in employment equity, and not necessarily one of the most important participants in the change process. Yet there is still a strong tendency for theorists of organizational change, even those who acknowledge the importance of understanding and using power effectively, to focus their attention on influencing top management to act in support of their organizational development strategy — while ignoring all the other stakeholders whose participation can make or break a program of change. For example, Greiner and Schein (1988) emphasize the importance to the change agent of building a power base, primarily through influencing "key powerholders," but give little attention to the need to assist powerless stakeholders to influence events. In implementing employment equity this is a serious omission, since it is impossible for this kind of change effort to succeed if the designated groups oppose it, or if it does not meet their needs because they have not had an opportunity to influence it.

However, as discussed in Chapter 6, it is important to recognize that a large body of research evidence documents the crucial importance of top management commitment and ongoing support to the survival and effectiveness of organizational change (e.g. Mirvis and Berg, 1977). For example, in a study of affirmative action officers' judgements of the effectiveness of university programs, top administrators' commitment was the strongest of 13 predictors of program effectiveness, "receptive attitude on the part of key university personel" was second, and "resources provided for affirmative action" was very important (Hitt and Keats, 1984: 215).

Top management stands to realize some benefits from making a commitment to employment equity implementation, as Box 7.4 suggests, and as discussed in Chapter 3. Yet research examining the early stages of employment equity implementation by Canadian organizations suggests that the commitment of top corporate decision makers rarely occurs without government requirements that are enforced (e.g., Jain and Hackett, 1989).

BOX 7.4
Employment Equity Stakeholders and Examples of Their Potential Concerns and Interests

STAKEHOLDERS	EXAMPLES OF INTERESTS AND CONCERNS
Racial minorities	Access to employment and career development; recognition of credentials obtained in other countries; freedom from racial harassment
People with disabilities	Access to employment and career development; accommodation of special needs in order to do work they are capable of; acceptance as equals
Aboriginal peoples	Access to employment and career development near the home community; opportunity to learn marketable skills; freedom from harassment; friendly and supportive work environment
Women	Access to employment and career development opportunities; fair compensation; creation of a workplace climate where women are accepted as equals; day care
Top management	Productivity of managers and employees; decreased turnover; positive corporate image; profit
Human resources management	Organizational reputation as a progressive employer; higher profile of the HR function in the organization; more harmonious employee relations
Line management	Increased productivity; lower absenteeism and turnover; fewer grievances; higher morale; visibility in the organization

Officers of union local	Member satisfaction and support; recognition for representing members effectively; increased membership; employer's viability and financial performance
Non unionized employees	Fair and equitable treatment; access to career development opportunities; fair compensation
Government agencies	Effective program implementation; public support; adequate employment equity resources; favourable political climate
Community or special interest groups	Well-being of constituencies; participation in and influence on decisions affecting their constituencies

Prior to the introduction of employment equity regulation, employers rarely undertook this form of change voluntarily, despite the potential benefits in terms of employee satisfaction and productivity and corporate image that had been publicized in management-oriented commentaries on the U.S. experience with affirmative action. The evidence is strong that external triggers for change are of key importance in gaining the support and commitment of top management, as we will discuss further in Chapter 9.

In today's results-oriented business and service environment, top management may perceive a stake in a participatory employment equity change process as an extension of other current management concepts such as closeness to customers, total quality, employee responsibility for effectiveness and efficiency, and market-driven systems. Involving all stakeholder groups in a goal-oriented change process that may lead to higher levels of morale and job satisfaction, a better trained and motivated work force, and better relations with emerging client and customer segments, as well as compliance with government requirements, may make sense to top managers as part of a broader management strategy.

BOX 7.5
Good Management Means Responsibility to Stakeholders

"My research program, at the Centre for Corporate Social Performance and Ethics in the University of Toronto's Faculty of Management, has evaluated the social performance of more than 60 large Canadian corporations over the past eight years. This research shows clearly that those companies that emphasize profit maximization and the bottom line at the expense of their responsibilities to other stakeholders [other than shareholders] are less profitable than their competitors. Those companies that balance their responsibilities toward all their stakeholders are more profitable over an extended period of time. Profit is maximized over the longer term only when all significant stakeholders continue to be reasonably satisfied."

(SOURCE: Max Clarkson, "In Praise of the Stakeholder Concept," *Globe and Mail*, Dec. 28, 1990.)

Line Management

Covin and Kilmann (1988) found that line managers, especially middle managers — rather than external consultants — are typically the "key figures" in large scale change efforts. Employment equity is an example of a change strategy that is implemented through the everyday actions of both staff and line managers, union leaders, members of the designated groups, and employees at all levels. In particular, line managers are responsible for many of the kinds of decisions that are within the domain of an employment equity process. Line managers are really the pivotal group in translating policy and top management's general statements of commitment into visible results in the form of improved rates of designated group representation and retention. Because of their central role in hiring, task allocation, performance appraisal, resource allocation, and creation of a workplace climate, line managers are in a position to make the difference between success and failure in implementing employment equity. It simply does not make sense to initiate the kinds of changes employment equity requires without their involvement, to the extent this is possible to obtain.

Line managers therefore need to be consulted and involved throughout the process. Without their participation, a change program may appear to surprised managers (and trade unionists) "as an unwelcome white rabbit pulled out of a centrally located top hat" (Pettigrew, 1985:91).

Unions

In a unionized workplace it is obviously important to involve union officers at the beginning of a change process (Spector, 1985). Their opposition is likely to sink the program, while their support can win its acceptance by many union members. Because of their detailed knowledge of the task environment and the everyday life of the workplace, union leaders and members who are interested in employment equity are in a position to contribute valuable information that can make a change program relevant to its locale.

Moreover, their role as official elected representatives of their membership gives union officers a legitimate and vital interest in developments, such as an employment equity program, that have an impact on their members' well-being. There are a number of reasons why employment equity has significant impacts on unions and their leaders. Obviously many of the discriminatory barriers identified in a systems review, and many of the needs for accommodation, will involve matters covered in provisions of the collective agreement that management and the union have both endorsed. Changes in policies and practices, in many instances, will need to be bargained or in some way agreed to jointly by management and the union, either through collective bargaining or through a joint committee process. In the evolving human rights and employment equity environment, unions are also aware that they may face legal liabilities in connection with the duty of fair representation of members who are also members of designated groups, as well as members who may be accused of harassment by co-workers, and fellow union members who are members of designated groups. Not to recognize these complex and varied interests by involving unions at an early stage in planning and implementing employment equity would understandably provoke their resistance to the change process, and would fail to make use of a resource critical to success.

It is not necessarily true that the union will wish to participate in a direct or public way in the sponsorship or decision-making surrounding an organizational change program. Because of a legacy of mistrust in many workplaces as a result of the union's sense that management has manipulated change projects such as quality circles, quality of work life, and employee involvement programs in its own interests, union officers may prefer to stand back from direct involvement in paternalistic management-initiated projects that are billed as part of a "progressive" approach to human resources management (e.g. Jain and Giles, 1985; Newton, 1989; Spector, 1985). In such cases, consultation on what union officers would consider to be appropriate forms of involvement in employment equity, and good faith efforts by management to build trust, would need to precede closer forms of cooperation.

However, it should be recognized that employees who are not members of the bargaining unit may have distinct interests, and need to be recognized as stakeholders in their own right. The union may be unable or unwilling to represent all employee groups that have a stake in employment equity, or to give the change effort whole-hearted support. If the union is a white, able-bodied male organization whose membership does not include a significant number of members of the designated groups, the union cannot be depended upon to represent these stakeholders. Unlike corporations, unions are formally democratic organizations in which leaders are elected by a majority of the membership. If the majority reject change it is difficult for union leaders to move in new directions and still retain the support they require from their members. Union leaders may support change if their environment or membership changes, or if management initiates the process from a position of mutual trust, and undertakes a joint union/management educational process for the membership, as well as joint decision making. These initiatives require an investment of time.

Employment equity initiatives designed to benefit members of the union may not address the needs of other employee groups, such as clerical workers. For example, the award-winning joint employment equity program of the Canadian Auto Workers and General Motors (Sugiman, 1989) focuses on increasing the representation of women in automobile production and skilled trades jobs, but offers little to the other three designated groups, and nothing to the non-union office staff.

In an organization in which union locals are predominantly white male groups, oriented toward the traditional concerns for job security and terms and conditions of employment, it would be important to reassure union members of the organization's continued commitment to addressing these concerns even in a time of change. Beyond this, there are interests that this kind of stakeholder group may bring to the employment equity process that can be effectively addressed, given some trust and authentic consultation. For example, union members may benefit from initiatives, such as training, to help them to cope with the new and perhaps uncomfortable experience of working side by side with people with disabilities, women and minorities. As well, employment equity initiatives designed to benefit people with disabilities might include measures that address the union's concerns about an aging membership, or about an increase in the numbers of members whose lessened physical condition requires accommodation.

BOX 7.6
Negotiating Employment Equity

"An employment equity program must be designed, implemented, monitored and assessed through a joint union-employer structure....Because an Employment Equity Program represents a fundamental review and revision of workplace processes it will define a series of measures and link them together... For example, changes to recruitment processes will depend on the identification of under-representation of specific groups of employees, which will depend on the willingness of group members to cooperate in a self-identification survey, which, in turn, depends on the quality of the initial education program for employees. It is critical that the union be involved at each of these program stages... Responsibility for the Employment Equity Program is thus very much an all-or-nothing proposition. A union cannot be expected to take responsibility for the implementation stage of a Program if the union has been excluded from the design stage. Nor can it be expected to provide a positive public assessment of the Program if it has not shared in the implementation or monitoring of the Program... The collective involvement of leadership — union and employer — will give each

side the assurance that the other is fully committed to the success of
an Employment Equity Program, and it will signal both management
and employees that, at the highest organizational levels, there is a
serious project under way."

(SOURCE: National Union of Provincial Government Employees, "Negotiating
Employment Equity, A Policy Paper," June 1990, pp. 8-9.)

Designated Groups

The representation of the interests of the designated groups is
not a simple matter in organizations where they are poorly represented. Even where such stakeholders are more numerous, the
issue arises of who speaks for them, or how to make appropriate
arrangements for the representation of their interests. For example, women working for the organization may be divided among
themselves by rank, type of job, and level of support for feminist
ideals. Somehow priorities must be set that address the spectrum
of interests within the group, from access to promotion to senior
management, to access to skilled trades, to arrangements that
help employees to balance work and family needs, to ridding the
workplace of biased language and sexist jokes. A broad process of
consultation would be needed to encompass the range of issues of
concern to women. A parallel argument could be made concerning each of the designated groups, since all are heterogeneous.
Furthermore, there is the issue of securing support for special
projects that are needed to deal with disadvantage that has been
identified, but that will benefit one specific designated group
rather than all groups.

In workplaces where designated group members are few, it may
be important to arrange for the participation of representatives
external to the organization, in order to ensure that employment
equity initiatives designed to benefit these groups are credible, relevant and effective. Advocacy or community organizations, or government agencies whose mandate is to serve the designated groups,
may be good sources of advice. Here again the issue of who speaks
for the designated group may arise, as well as the concern that some
designated group interests may not be addressed. For example, the
elected officers of an all-male band council may not be the best
sources of advice about recruiting First Nations women.

Members of designated groups within the organization may have a wide variety of interests related to their position within the organization. The interests of designated group members in their various roles as applicants or potential employees, decision-makers, customers or clients, or equality seekers may or may not coincide. Change agents need to avoid stereotyping or over-generalizing about designated group members' interests.

Identifying and Working With Stakeholder Interests in Employment Equity

The various stakeholders in employment equity implementation may bring a broad spectrum of interests to the process, and those interests may change over time as the work force ages, or as turnover, changing social values, or legislative and policy changes bring new expectations and requirements to the workplace. Employment equity practitioners will therefore need to analyze the roles and concerns of the various stakeholders strategically on a continuing basis. The purposes of this analysis are:

1. to identify the most important stakeholders, in terms of the centrality of their interest in change, the nature and sources of their power or influence, and their ability to contribute to the success or failure of the change process;
2. to identify the primary interests and concerns of these stakeholders in the short and long term, including the enduring values that guide their behaviour in relation to this form of change, and their priorities for change;
3. to identify potential issues around which conflict or cooperation may develop, or coalitions may form;
4. to identify those stakeholders that might be most immediately supportive, and the resources and sources of power they might command, in order to involve them at an early stage and benefit from their energy and commitment;
5. to identify stakeholders that are likely to consistently resist the change program as a whole, and whose cooperation is not crucial, in order not to waste energy on "hopeless cases."

A stakeholder analysis can start with a simple mapping exercise to identify stakeholders with an interest in a particular issue, together with their interests, level of concern, alignment, potential contribution to the change process and rewards for participating, and tendency toward support or resistance (Freeman, 1984). Box 7.7 provides a schematic diagram for this kind of analysis.

While such an exercise in analysis may be of value to the employment equity practitioner, it is important to remember that it can only provide a snapshot. The actors, their perspectives and interests are constantly changing, and today's sources of resistance may be tomorrow's supporters. It should also be recognized that these same stakeholders may align themselves very differently on another employment equity issue. For example, practitioners may find that a stakeholder is very supportive of efforts to redress disadvantage for one of the designated groups, people with disabilities perhaps, but quite unsympathetic, or even hostile, to initiatives for another group, such as women. The equality seeker will need to continually reassess the configuration and alignment of stakeholders on each issue as it develops.

Box 7.8 illustrates a stakeholder map for a real example of an employment equity issue — getting support for a proposal to develop a special initiative to improve the representation of aboriginal persons in administrative staff and unionized jobs in a university. In this example, the "trigger for change" was a work-force audit which disclosed that only a dozen of the university's 6100 employees identified themselves as Native, although there are three reserves within commuting distance of the university, as well as a sizable aboriginal population within the municipality. The President's Standing Committee for Employment Equity responded by coordinating the development of two proposals for special initiatives. One project was designed to bring more aboriginal people into existing positions for which they are qualified (see the example shown in Box 7.8). The other project was aimed at increasing the size of the labour market of Native people having credentials and skills sought by the university and other employers, by means of educational initiatives to assist aboriginal persons to enter and complete undergraduate and graduate programs of study. The proposals for both projects were put together by working groups composed of stakeholders from within the university and knowledgeable members of the aboriginal communities.

BOX 7.7
Schematic Stakeholder Map for an Employment Equity Issue or Project

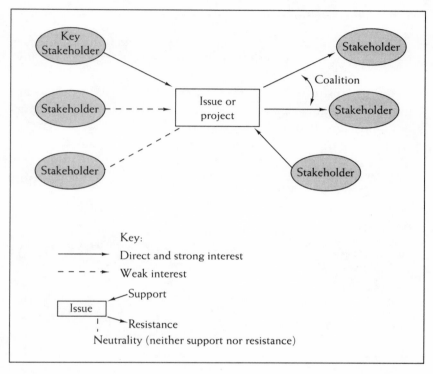

The working group for the employment project consisted of members of the Employment Equity Committee, the Human Resources Department, and two aboriginal persons who were working as professional liaison officers among employers, higher educational institutions, and aboriginal communities. The working group also consulted with aboriginal organizations providing educational and employment services to the local aboriginal population. The proposal contained a package of initiatives including outreach recruitment and consultation in reserve and urban aboriginal communities, voluntary applicant self-identification, designation of specific positions for advertisement to Native communities only, Native representation on the selection interview panel, coaching for Native applicants and mentoring for those who are hired, awareness training for supervisors and co-workers of new Native employees, and evaluation of the project.

BOX 7.8
Stakeholder Map: Pilot Project to Increase Native Employment in University Staff Positions

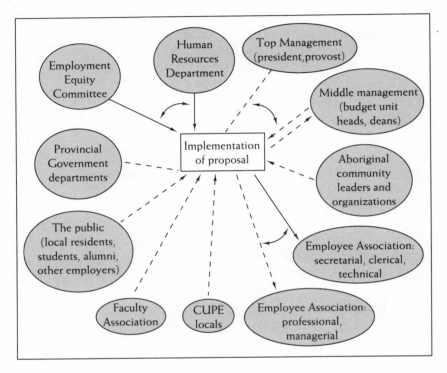

The stakeholder map in Box 7.8 shows the alignment of stakeholders when the proposal was first circulated for broader consultation, after it had been developed by the working group. The map identifies the stakeholders whose support is essential to the success of the project at this stage in its development, and of those, the stakeholders whose support is uncertain or missing. It is clear that the change agents, in this case the university's Employment Equity Officer, the Chair of the Employment Equity Committee, the consultant working with the Committee, and the project's champion in the Human Resources Department, need to focus their efforts on those stakeholders by ensuring that they are fully informed and consulted, that their interests are known and addressed, and that they stand to gain something important to them through participating, or at least by not resisting, the project. At this stage, these key stakeholders include the two employee associations and the union locals, and key people in the aboriginal community. It is not a priority at this time to work with top or middle management or the Faculty Association, although these stakeholders may be important at a later stage of the project's development.

Very briefly, the key stakeholders in the Native employment project, and their interests at this stage, are as follows:

- Officers and Employment Equity Committee representatives of the employee associations and union locals:

These stakeholders are committed to the principle of employment equity and to the idea of addressing disadvantage and under-representation of Native people in the university's work force. But they are responsive to their members' anxieties about lay-offs because of budget cuts that will continue over three years. Members are losing their jobs, and continuing employees are seeing fewer opportunities to move upward or laterally, and are feeling boxed in. The jobs that would be available as part of the employment project are in the bargaining groups represented by the associations and union locals. The proposal for the project will probably be acceptable to the members except for one provision — the designation of certain positions for Native applicants only. This is considered a key element of the proposal, since without it, it will be difficult to ensure real gains in the representation of Native people, or to avoid a ghettoization effect if only entry level positions are targeted. If this provision were pushed through without the associations' consent, the successful implementation of the project might be undermined by backlash from co-workers who resent the hiring of new employees under a special program. Another underlying issue is that the Human Resources Department has taken ownership of the project since it would be the primary agency for implementing it. There is a history of a certain amount of antagonism between some members of the associations and the Department, which has little empathy for the associations' concerns regarding this proposal.

- Directors of key community organizations representing and serving aboriginal people, and socioeconomic officers of the local bands:

These stakeholders are supportive of the concept of the proposal, but are inclined to be skeptical as to whether the university will really deliver, since it has not been responsive to the educational or employment needs of aboriginal people in the past. It is essential to the success of the outreach recruitment and consultation aspects of the proposal that these stakeholders be partners in its implementation. They may also play a role in funding, because of recently announced provincial funding opportunities for Native post–secondary education, which will be administered through local Native decision-making committees. While the employment proposal can be implemented without external funding, it would be advantageous for the university to hire a full time outreach recruitment and liaison person to work in the local Native communities on both the employment and educational projects. This position would have to be funded in part from external sources. The primary stakeholder with an interest in this possibility is the Employment Equity Committee, which would like both projects to be successful.

The stakeholder analysis suggests that at this stage, time and attention must be devoted to assisting the leaders of the employee associations in assessing the proposal's impact on their members. These stakeholders need an opportunity to influence the implementation of the proposal, and to make suggestions regarding trade–offs that would be advantageous to them. The key representatives of the Native communities must also have a chance to influence the project and to identify the role they would like to play in its development. These are the two priorities upon which the change agents must focus at this stage.

The interest of a stakeholder in a particular issue, as illustrated by this example, may lead to support for a proposed initiative, opposition to it, or a combination of support for some aspects of the change process and resistance to others. Because of the complexity of the mix of potential stakeholder responses, it is often difficult to predict how a stakeholder will perceive an initiative. **It is important not to make assumptions about stakeholder interests, but to identify them through a consultative or participatory process.**

As an example, management in a manufacturing company decided to implement a proposal for an employment equity project they knew the union would support. Yet the union grieved the decision, not because they did not favour the initiative, but because it was introduced unilaterally by management rather than bargained or jointly agreed to.

In some instances there may be ambiguity about stakeholder interests. The executive of a union local, for example, may either welcome or resist the proposal that a special complaint procedure be established to deal with workplace harassment that involves union members as potential victims or harassers, or both. On the one hand, the union may have found that the standards of evidentiary proof for substantiating harassment complaints are complex, as are the substantive issues, and current grievance procedures under the collective agreement may not entirely meet the need. On the other hand, unions may resist the establishment of multiple avenues of redress for employee complaints, either because they distrust a management-centered process, or because they wish to protect the union's turf as the representative of employee interests.

The interest of a stakeholder in an issue may be broad or narrow and specialized, and the salience of a particular proposal may be high or low, depending upon its perceived centrality to their interests, and the importance of those interests to the stakeholder. For example, line managers and supervisors may be interested in participating in goal-setting only insofar as it affects the filling of vacancies in their own units in the short run or intermediate term. They may have little stake in goal-setting at the corporate level, or in other work units. Another example is that a designated group may or may not perceive a stake for itself in special measures related to the other three designated groups. Initiatives for child care, barrier-free access, race relations training, or English in the workplace may each be of interest to a different set of stakeholders. However, a comprehensive policy, complaints process, and training program to deal with workplace harassment affecting all designated groups may be of broad interest to line management, unions, human resources staff, community advocacy groups, and government agencies as well as all four designated groups.

The need for constant feedback on how proposals are perceived is one reason why it is important for key stakeholders to be involved in a continuing process of consultation as a change process unfolds. The most convenient and consistent way for this to occur may be through a formal structure, such as a committee or task force, established for this purpose, supplemented by informal consultation as issues arise, and as other key stakeholders emerge.

How Do Stakeholders Use Power?

On the basis of interest, stakeholders will be likely to attempt to influence the outcomes of decision making, or the process of implementing decisions, on matters they deem important. In exercising influence, stakeholders may rely on a variety of power bases, including information and expertise, access to political decision makers, ability to mobilize a constituency in the organization or the community, formal authority, control over resources others want, or access to the media.

Since the exercise of influence occurs within a power structure — an organizational framework in which the power to successfully influence outcomes is unequally distributed — different stakeholders have access to different power bases. This reality must be recognized and addressed.

For example, in most workplaces, both power and opportunity are unequally distributed on the basis of gender, as was clear in the dual labour market model discussed in Chapter 2. Women, if they are present at all, tend to be concentrated in lower ranks, in non-unionized sectors, in a narrow range of specialties, and in jobs that are on truncated career ladders and that have low levels of compensation. Because they are virtually absent from senior levels of management or union leadership they have little formal influence on decisions, and little access to formal means to advance their interests. In many workplaces men and women inhabit separate and unequal worlds, and women's arena for the exercise of influence is severely restricted.

Women, racial minorities, aboriginal people and people with disabilities are among the key stakeholders in employment equity who are likely to lack access to mechanisms through which to influence decision making and program implementation. This does not mean, however, that these groups, or others who occupy positions at the lower ranks of organizations, are without power. It does mean that a change strategy must

1) take into account the complex variety of interests and ways of exercising influence among various stakeholders; and

2) provide for ways in which stakeholders that lack access to the traditional ways of influencing decisions can make their voices heard. After all, a major purpose of employment equity is precisely to improve their access to the exercise of power.

The methods of influence a stakeholder may use may be direct and overt, through formal or officially recognized or sanctioned channels. The use of direct, formal mechanisms for the exercise of influence is the prerogative of stakeholders who have "position power," or formal positions in the structure of authority in the organization. Stakeholders that lack this power base may adopt more covert, indirect means of influencing decisions and their implementation. For example, stakeholders at lower levels who feel the need for the organization to change, or who are inclined to resist a change program, may influence events by complaining, by failing to carry out responsibilities, or by more militant collective action such as "blue flu" or wildcat strikes, or by using the media to raise their concerns. Of course, stakeholders who have formal position power may have access to the entire spectrum of means of influencing decisions and events, including informal as well as formal methods.

Stakeholders who have historically been absent from or seriously underrepresented in a workplace may nonetheless have some means of influencing organizational decision making. For example, associations representing aboriginal peoples, including band councils, have been effective in putting forth their constituents' requirements for opportunities to work in resource-based industries near aboriginal communities. Power bases underlying successful claims to these opportunities may include control over land on which resources, strategic communication links or other infrastructural elements are located, or requirements that corporations comply with government employment equity regulations, or corporate concerns about their public image. Advocacy groups representing stakeholder interests, and operating externally to the organization, may be in a position to exercise considerable influence on corporate policies and practices. This was clear in the example of the role of advocacy groups representing racial minorities and aboriginal peoples in challenging bias in policing and the criminal justice systems, mentioned at the beginning of this chapter, and in the case of *Action Travail des Femmes vs. CN Rail*, discussed in Chapter 4. Advocacy organizations representing people with disabilities have kept the issue of underrepresentation of their constituency in companies covered by the Employment Equity Act in the public eye, and have successfully applied pressure to improve the validity of employers' work-force statistics on people with disabilities.

These examples provide evidence that organizational change can start at the bottom of the organization, or even in the community beyond its boundaries. The power to make decisions that influence the course of events in the organization does not reside exclusively in top management, or indeed in management as a whole. A variety of stakeholder groups may participate in a collaborative process of organizational change to move toward equity in the workplace.

Employment equity begins with a shared vision of the need for change, and of the benefits of change to the organization and its various stakeholders, as discussed more fully in Chapter 8. Given this orienting value framework, the identification of overlapping interests and shared underlying values might provide a useful basis for planning a program of change. For example, top management, line managers, human resource managers, union officers, and members of the designated groups all share an interest in good human resource management practices whereby employees are treated fairly and consistently. They all share an interest, too, in improving productivity in the workplace so that the organization maintains a strong competitive position in the market, and in improving job satisfaction at all levels so as to ensure a consistent and highly competent population of employees and union members.

Fisher and Ury (1983) argue that especially when there are several interested parties to a negotiation, a focus on underlying interests stands a far greater chance of "getting to yes" than a focus on positions. Interests are the multiple concerns, needs, wants and fears that motivate behaviour and that lie behind positions people take on issues (Fisher and Ury, 1983: 42). Focussing on interests opens up the bargaining process to increase the number of alternative solutions to problems, since there are usually several positions or alternatives that could satisfy an interest. The objective of negotiation or joint decision making, then, is to identify an alternative that addresses an important interest of all of the participants, or even one that addresses the common interest of all.

Chapters 10 and 11 discuss in detail the ways in which stakeholders can use negotiation, bargaining and collaboration to facilitate the change process and deal with resistance.

Some Cautionary Notes On Working With Stakeholders

We do not mean to give the misleading impression that basing a program of change on a stakeholder participation strategy is the path to success, or that the process will be easy and without complications. Far from it! There are several obvious problems or pitfalls inherent in this approach. A careful evaluation of conditions in your organization in the light of these considerations may lead you to conclude that the stakeholder participation model is not for you. Let us consider some of the problems:

1. Insufficient time:

Participation is time consuming, and is not possible under conditions of severe time constraint (Kanter, 1983:122). Perhaps your organization has been selected for a compliance review by the Federal Contractors Program, or you must staff one or more positions immediately, or the manager to whom you report is obsessed with deadlines. In such cases you may not have the scope or latitude to "do it right." This is unfortunate for all concerned, since developing approaches that get results in terms of employment equity goals takes time.

Another crucial issue related to time is organizational arrangements for freeing employees from their usual duties to spend time participating in the change process. Hourly employees cannot be expected to sit on committees or attend training sessions on their own time. Nor will they be able to participate effectively if their supervisors resent the time they spend on employment equity, or if participation is an add-on to an already overburdened manager's list of responsibilities. One of the most tangible signs of top management commitment to the success of a change program is the establishment of arrangements whereby employees can dedicate time to participation, and be recognized rather than penalized for their contribution to the organization. For example, the joint General Motors/Canadian Auto Workers affirmative action clause provided for the company to pay affirmative action committee representatives for up to twelve hours a week of time off from production work to perform affirmative action duties (Sugiman, 1987: 16).

Another time-related issue is the need to assure some continuity so that people who have developed knowledge, mutual trust and effective communication linkages can continue to work on projects.

2. Inadequate resources, especially for training:

Organizations that have been involved over a period of time in change programs designed to broaden opportunity or decentralize power typically find that stakeholder participation is a crucial component of such programs. But people have to be given the tools they need in order to participate effectively. The most important tool is a shared base of knowledge of what employment equity involves, and common understanding of why it is needed. Developing this knowledge base that is the prerequisite to sound debate and decision-making requires access to training and educational programs. These may be provided in-house, as discussed in Chapter 11, or externally, through attendence at specialized seminars, workshops and courses offered by government agencies, consultants, unions, colleges, professional associations, or other sources. Without an adequate knowledge base, people may avoid participating in the change program, or may not make the contribution that is expected of them, or may resist the effort because of misinformation.

3. Stakeholder suspicion or mistrust:

Stakeholders may choose not to participate in employment equity if they mistrust the process, the management auspices under which it is initiated, or the purpose of the participatory strategy. This is especially likely in organizations where there is a history of mistrust and conflict between management and designated groups, or management and unions. It may also occur when management or other stakeholder groups use employment or pay equity as a "trojan horse" to bring about other changes they desire, such as instituting cutbacks or productivity programs. In such cases the change process may benefit from the critical perspective and stimulus to change that independent stakeholders who choose to remain outsiders, or watchdogs, are able to provide. External critics can make a valuable contribution to change by raising issues and applying pressure on top management and other decision makers who may not be responsive to the internal change agent's influence. Stakeholder resistance to co-optation, then, may prove to be a blessing to the committed agent of change.

On the other hand, it can be highly demoralizing and discouraging to change agents working toward equity when advocacy groups adopt a consistently critical stance toward change initiatives that are informed by genuine efforts to secure their participation. It is also inappropriate for stakeholders to use employment equity as an engine to which to hitch a variety of other, unrelated issues, such as perceived unfairness in employment practices not directly related to employment equity, or management dissatisfaction with the costs and administrative burdens associated with an increase in government regulation. Change agents are well advised to attempt to create other structures or mechanisms for dealing with issues that are not directly tied to employment equity.

4. Unwillingness to play fair:
The stakeholder participation approach to change rests on the assumption that participants will be able to agree to and follow a set of guidelines about how the process will work. This implies that participants will not violate the trust that is necessary for negotiation and decision making to be effective, and that they will attempt to strengthen and to make use of the organization's internal mechanisms for addressing inequity. A program of change based on participation cannot succeed if management undermines trust by reneging on promises, or abusing its power, or failing to recognize the legitimacy of interests other than its own. Likewise, the process cannot succeed if designated group members seek redress through external sources, including the media, without first using internal mechanisms that have been established to deal with issues. Trust is delicate; it is easily violated and difficult to restore if it has been damaged.

5. Participation is difficult to bring about because it is alien to the organization's culture and reward systems.
A strategy for making change in an organization must be at least to some degree compatible with existing modes of decision making if it is to have credibility. Participatory structures and ways of operating should build upon and extend practices that are currently acceptable. If they depart too radically from established practice it may be difficult to attract participants who have credibility in the organization, or to gain acceptance of decisions.

Creating a framework for effective participation in organizational change presupposes an organizational culture in which participation is possible: not just accepted, but encouraged and supported. This is a questionable assumption in a majority of workplaces, despite widespread lip service to greater employee involvment in decision making. For example, in a study of technological and organizational change in 1000 private sector firms in Canada, Newton (1989) found that change projects rarely entail real shifts in the scope or locus of decision making, and generally leave existing structures of power and authority intact. Very few organizations were involved in innovations characterized by even limited employee participation in decision making, such as semi-autonomous work groups or quality circles. Most organizations continue to operate on the assumption that management controls the workplace, and the union acts as a countervailing power in a very restricted domain.

In Argyris' (1964) terms, too often organizations continue to treat employees in such a way as to create and reward dependence, submissiveness to authority, and powerlessness, rather than to encourage and reward responsible behaviour. Under such circumstances it is likely to be difficult to create a participatory process involving all stakeholders that will produce real change. However, the creation of a participatory change process for employment equity may help to change the organization's culture, if it is supported by a broader strategy designed to move toward developing a more participatory organizational culture. It is also possible that the employment equity process could serve as a demonstration project for the benefits of a participatory approach to other kinds of change in the organization.

6. Some key stakeholders are not interested in participating in a change process:

Some employees who are members of the designated groups may prefer not to cooperate with employment equity initiatives. For example, women or minorities who have attained job security or higher level positions may not wish to have the rules change for those who come after them. Some may not fully understand — or may feel their fellow employees do not understand — that employment equity does not involve a "lowering" of standards or the provision of opportunities that are not fully deserved. Some designated group members may not acknowledge the existence of discrimination, either direct or subtle. Others may feel that supporting a program of change will entail risks for them that they are unprepared to accept.

Some members of designated groups, trade unionists, and others may choose not to participate directly in an organizational change process on priniciple. Adamson, Briskin and McPhail (1988: Ch.5) suggest that there are two basic strategic alternatives for feminists and others who are critical of existing institutions and interested in making changes: mainstreaming, and disengagement. The politics of mainstreaming begins with the daily experience of a disadvantaged group and attempts to involve members of that group in changing specific and immediate conditions in the workplace, government, or elsewhere, so that these institutions are more responsive and less oppressive to members of that group. Mainstreaming responds directly to the political, social, economic and ideological circumstances and institutions in which designated group members find themselves, and works within these frameworks to achieve change through collective action.

The politics of disengagement is rooted in a fundamental critique of existing institutions, and a vision of replacing them with new structures. This orientation toward change might involve promoting that division by establishing alternative and separate organizations or collectivities, outside of existing organizations, and perhaps in opposition to them.

Stakeholders in employment equity may adopt either of these strategic alternatives. Stakeholders inclined to a mainstreaming strategy may wish to participate directly in some aspects of the organization's change process and to be involved in the committees and other structures that carry that process forward. Stakeholders who subscribe to a strategy of disengagement may also play an active and very valuable, but very different, role in the organization's change process by providing another view — perhaps a more detached perspective; by monitoring and evaluating results; and by applying pressure to organizational decision makers who might otherwise be inclined to give employment equity change a low priority.

Perhaps most important, those who practice the politics of disengagement may develop and substain an alternative vision of what is desirable and possible that can help all those working for change to clarify the goals toward which they are striving, and to distinguish real progress from compromises that undermine the spirit of their efforts. Without a vision of institutional transformation and a substantive critique of existing structures, equality seekers can end up simply working within the confines of what exists, failing to challenge the limitations of that framework. In working out of the politics of mainstreaming alone, it is too easy to lose sight of the struggle that is involved in change, and to allow political issues to be watered down into technical exercises.

Change agents should be prepared to work collaboratively with all stakeholders, whether they opt to practice the politics of mainstreaming or the politics of disengagement. Persons with disabilities, aboriginal persons, women and racial minorities will differ among themselves in their perspectives on change, and in their assessments of the organizational climate, especially in a large organization in which conditions may vary greatly from one department or job function to another. This diversity of perception and experience must be acknowledged and accommodated in working toward the priorities of those designated group members who do perceive a need for change.

7. Lack of balance between process and outcomes:

Some of the research literature on organizational change suggests that change initiatives may lose support if the process of participation becomes an end in itself, and a focus on results is lost. At the same time, the process is important in itself since it entails substantial time and effort on the part of participants. There should thus be some rewards inherent in the experience of participating, as well as concrete achievements in which participants can take pride.

Conclusion

A former director of the Federal Contractor's Program observed that: "Experience has proven that those contractors who have sought the collaboration of their employees, either through unions, associations, or special employment equity committees, have had a far better track record than those who have not done so. In the long term, union participation is likely to prove critical to program success" (Cullen, 1988).

A strategic analysis of interests, power bases, and relationships among stakeholders should provide a guide for identifying issues and initiatives that offer the possibility of collaboration among stakeholders for their mutual benefit. This kind of analysis is grounded in a local workplace environment and is oriented toward a change process that occurs over time through the experience of participating, negotiating, listening and learning. It is not a process aimed at carrying out a preconceived blueprint or grand design for change, or a plan formulated by an external expert. In the next chapter we will discuss strategic issues in working toward employment equity through stakeholder participation.

REFERENCES

Argyris, Chris. *Integrating the Individual and the Organization*. New York: Wiley, 1964.

Arnstein, Sherry. "A Ladder of Citizen Participation." *AIP Journal*, July 1969, 216-224.

Bolman, Lee, and Terrence Deal. *Modern Approaches to Understanding and Managing Organizations*. San Francisco: Jossey-Buss, 1984.

Chertos, Cynthia. "Hard Truths for Strategic Change: Dilemmas of Implementing Affirmative Action." *Women's Studies International Forum*. 6(2), 1983, 231-241.

Child, John. *Organization: A Guide to Problems and Practice*. London: Harper and Row. 1984.

Covin, Teresa Joyce, and Ralph Kilmann. "Critical Issues in Large-Scale Change." *Journal of Organizational Change Management*, 1 (2), 1988, 59-72.

Cullen, Nicole. *"Federal Contractors Program."* Paper presented at Employment Equity Seminar. Queen's University, June 8, 1988.

Fisher, Roger, and William Ury. *Getting to Yes: Negotiating Agreement Without Giving In*. New York: Penguin, 1983.

Freeman, R. Edward. *Strategic Management, A Stakeholder Approach*. Marshfield, Mass.: Pitman, 1984.

Greiner, Larry, and Virginia Schein. *Power and Organization Development: Mobilizing Power to Implement Change*. Reading, Mass.: Addison Wesley, 1988.

Hitt, Michael, and Barbara Keats. "Empirical Identification of the Criteria for Effective Affirmative Action Programs." *Journal of Applied Behavioral Science,* 20(3), 1984, 203-222.

Jain, Harish, and Rick Hackett. "Measuring Effectiveness of Employment Equity Programs in Canada: Public Policy and a Survey." *Canadian Public Policy,* 15(2) 1989, 189-204.

Jain, Hem, and Anthony Giles. "Workers' Participation in Western Europe: Implications for North America." *Industrial Relations,* 40(4), 1985, 747-772.

Kanter, Rosabeth Moss. *Men and Women of the Corporation.* New York: Basic Books, 1977.

Kanter, Rosabeth Moss. "Power Failure in Management Circuits." *Harvard Business Review,* 57 (4), 1979, 65-75.

Kanter, Rosabeth Moss. "The Impact of Organization Structure: Models and Methods for Change." In Ronnie S. Ratner (ed), *Equal Employment Policy for Women.* Philadelphia: Temple University Press, 1980.

Lawler, Edward. *High Involvement Management.* San Francisco: Jossey Bass, 1986.

Manning, Peter. *Police Work.* Cambridge: MIT Press, 1977.

Mirvis, P., and D. Berg (eds.). *Failures in Organizational Development and Change.* New York: John Wiley, 1977.

Newton, Keith. "Technological and Organizational Change in Canada." *New Technology, Work and Employment,* 4 (1), 1989, 40-45.

Nightingale, Donald. *Workplace Democracy.* Toronto: Univ. of Toronto Press, 1982.

Pateman, Carole. *Participation and Democratic Theory.* London: Cambridge Univ. Press, 1970.

Pettigrew, Andrew. *The Awakening Giant: Continuity and Change in ICI.* Oxford: Basil Blackwell, 1985.

Reynaud, Emmanuelle. "Change in Collective Identities." In Colin Crouch and Frank A. Heller (eds.), *Organizational Democracy and Political Processes,* vol. I, New York: John Wiley, 1983, 249-64.

Rogers, Everett, and F. Floyd Shoemaker. *Communication of Innovation.* New York: Free Press, 1971.

Spector, Bert. "From Protest to Partnership: The Dilemmas of Managing Change in the Democratic Union Organization." In Richard Walton and Paul Lawrence (eds.), *Human Resource Management Trends and Challenges.* Cambridge: Harvard Business School Press, 1985, Ch. 7.

Sugiman, Pamela. "Affirmative Action at Work: The Case of the Canadian Auto Workers and General Motors of Canada." Queen's Park: Ontario Women's Directorate, Change Agent Project, 1987.

Tushman, Michael. "A Political Approach to Organizations: A Review and Rationale." *Academy of Management Review,* 2, 1977, 206-216.

Van Maanen, John. "Police Socialization: A Longitudinal Examination of Job Attitudes in an Urban Police Department." *Administrative Science Quarterly.* 20, 1975, 207-228.

8

The Process
of Strategic
Change

MICHELLE RAMONE MOVES ALONG THE
HALL toward her office, her guide dog
Heidi confidently leading the way.
Michelle is considering saying a polite "no" to the request that she
sit on her employer's Employment Equity Committee. Michelle has
the chance of gaining greater responsibility in her position as pur-
chasing officer for a provincial government department over the
next couple of months, and she knows that she would have a credible excuse to decline the appointment.

But the fact is, it's the prospect of frustration, of spinning her
wheels on such a committee, that Michelle has little patience for.
She is also apprehensive that the other members of the committee
will assume that she knows everything there is to know about people with disabilities. She thinks back to a couple of years ago when
she joined the department, and remembers the isolation she felt
because people didn't include her at coffee breaks and when they
went for lunch. She thinks of other committees she has been on,
and of the meetings in which she was given piles of worthless

THE PROCESS OF STRATEGIC CHANGE

printed material at the last minute. And at breaks, there's always the need to be patient in making people aware that Heidi is a working dog and not to be patted and fussed over when she is in harness.

And then there's the care she must take in requesting any kind of accommodation, in case her boss, co-workers or colleagues translate accommodation into some kind of special treatment, or into doubts about her ability to perform. She's beginning to be convinced that the real workplace harassment disabled people face is not being treated like children, but being regarded as threats to the gods of consistency. Any request for accommodation is seen as a problem, not problem-solving, with the person making the request the biggest problem of all!

Michelle checks her voice mail. There's a message to confirm her attendance at the first meeting of the Employment Equity Committee. If she agrees, how can she be part of something that brings about real change?

Michelle's dilemma raises many of the strategic issues involved in implementing employment equity from the standpoint of the individual stakeholder. In essence, Michelle's concern is about whether the organization will recognize the need to change, identify the kinds of changes that are needed, and move ahead toward those goals by setting in motion a process that will get results. There is the concern that one's efforts will be in vain, and furthermore, that participating will be a painful experience. To the individual who is a member of a designated group, these issues are intensely personal — they relate directly to daily experience in the workplace and to one's personal future. The stakes are very high.

A strategic approach to change, whether taken by an organization or an individual, involves asking these questions:

1. *Why* should the organization change?
2. *How* should the change process be managed?
3. *Who* should be involved in planning and implementing change?
4. *What kinds of changes* are needed?
5. How can the *information* be acquired that is needed as a basis for setting goals and planning?

6. What *resources*, in the form of money, time, talent and skill, will be required?
7. How can the *effectiveness* of the change process be evaluated?
8. How can the changes we are achieving be *sustained*?

The question of *why* the organization should change was addressed in Chapters 2 and 3. As we discuss in more detail in Chapter 9, in thinking about employment equity as a strategically planned and managed process, it is important to develop answers to this question that fit the conditions and challenges that are present within a specific workplace. People cannot be expected to become part of a change process if they do not understand why it is necessary for them, in their organization.

The broad issue of *how* change should be managed was addressed in Chapter 6, in our discussion of three models or paradigms of change. We have suggested that a participatory approach, based upon a blend of top-down and bottom-up involvement, might offer an effective guide to the change process. The question of *who* should be involved in change was discussed in Chapter 7, in which we examined how to identify the various stakeholders in employment equity and their potential interests in participating in change.

In this chapter we consider the implementation of change from a strategic perspective, beginning with a discussion of why employment equity involves strategic thinking, and what that really means. To say that employment equity implementation is a strategic process of organizational change means that it is planned, that it is based upon careful analysis, and that it is data-driven. We discuss a model of the implementation process that builds upon an analytical and data-based approach to change known as action research. This discussion provides a framework for thinking about how we get the information we need as a basis for planning, how we plan through a participatory process, and how we can identify the resources needed for change. In this chapter, then, we are concerned with the "how" of change as a goal-oriented process. In Chapters 9 through 14 we focus on a number of specific dimensions and techniques that comprise parts of the change process.

How Does Strategically Managed Change Happen?

To say that the employment equity process must be strategically planned is not to suggest that it can be managed by drawing up and following a blueprint for action. The notion of strategic planning is often associated with rational analytical schemes concocted around a polished table in a boardroom far above the noise and struggle of organizational politics. This image could not be farther from the truth.

In fact, this view of the strategic planning of change is not supported by research on how organizational change really happens. For example, an in-depth longitudinal study of cultural and structural change in five associated British chemical companies through the sixties and seventies found "little evidence ... of change occurring as a result of a rational linear process of calculatedly forming a strategy and then sequentially proceeding to implement it through controlled and programmatic planning" (Pettigrew, 1985: 457). On the contrary, strategic change in these five companies was a long, slow process in which planning and the gathering and analysis of information occurred within a political context. Successful implementation of change depended upon exploiting opportunities presented by environmental trends and events, building on existing sources of support for change, forming coalitions and mobilizing new sources of support based upon mutual interests, and developing awareness of the need for change throughout the organization. The agents of change began as small and often rather isolated groups with a new sense of what the organization could be. Their task was to communicate that vision and how it could be played out, using all the patience, commitment, and analytical skills at their disposal.

The British research found, furthermore, that the change process could not be described as a smooth flow of activity or a cumulative building of momentum over time. Change proceeded erratically: "patterns of strategic change at the level of the firm may be understood in terms of long periods of continuity, learning, and incremental adjustment interspersed with hiatuses or revolutions featuring abnormally high levels of change activity" (Pettigrew, 1985: 440; also Mintzberg, 1978: 943; Quinn, 1982). It was a process that

resembled paradigm change in science as described by Thomas
Kuhn in *The Structure of Scientific Revolutions* (1962).

BOX 8.1
On the Art of Managing Change

The art and architecture of change works through a different
medium than the management of the ongoing, routinized side of an
organization's affairs. Most of the rational, analytic tools *measure what
already is* (or make forecasts as a logical extrapolation from data on
what is). But change efforts have to *mobilize people around what is not yet
known*, not yet experienced. They require a leap of imagination that
cannot be replaced by reference to all the 'architect's sketches,'
'planner's blueprints' or examples of similar buildings that can be
mustered. They require a leap of faith that cannot be eliminated by
presentation of all the forecasts, figures, and advance guarantees
that can be accumulated...

   In short, the tools of change masters are creative and interactive;
they have an intellectual, a conceptual, and a cultural aspect. Change
masters deal in symbols and visions and shared understandings as well
as the techniques and trappings of their own specialites. Thus, those
of us interested in promoting change should be wary of excessively
logical 'how-to' approaches, whether in the form of strategic-planning
models or that of other one-two-three guides... Instead of a formal
model of change, then, or a step-by-step rational guide, an outline of
patterns is more appropriate and realistic, a set of guiding principles
that can help people understand not how it *should* be done but how to
understand what might fit the situation they are in.

(SOURCE: Rosabeth Moss Kanter, *The Change Masters*, New York: Simon and Schuster,
1983, 304-306.)

Strategic Change Is Value-Driven

Like change in scientific institutions and paradigms, organizational
change entails a process of legitimating a new interpretation of
reality and a new set of principles to guide action — in essence a
new ideology for the organization. It is the establishment and
eventual legitimacy of a new ideology to guide the perceptions and

behaviour of organizational participants that makes the change "stick." This is the institutionalization of change — the final stage in Kurt Lewin's well-known formulation of the change process.

BOX 8.2
Kurt Lewin's Three Steps in Change

1. **Unfreezing** present behaviour patterns
2. **Movement** toward desired new patterns
3. **Refreezing** to establish and reinforce the new patterns

(SOURCE: Kurt Lewin, *Field Theory in Social Science*, New York: Harper and Row, 1951.)

In reference to employment equity, the legitimation of a new ideology means the widespread acceptance of values that assert the worth of women, minorities, aboriginal peoples and persons with disabilities as members of the organization and contributors to its work in all sectors and at all levels, and enshrine their right to fair treatment. It means principles of decision making based upon new and more inclusive understandings of fairness and equity in human resource management and in daily interpersonal behaviour. And it means pride in the organization's image and performance as a workplace where diversity is valued and accomodated, and where individuals are respected for their uniqueness.

Like other forms of strategic organizational change, employment equity is focused around fundamental values. Successful implementation of employment equity means attaining widespread commitment to these values throughout the organization. This does not mean that everyone must endorse or become part of the change process, or fully accept the new values. Support for change will grow over time, largely on the basis of perceptions that gains are to be made, and interests advanced, through participation. But ultimately the prevailing value system in the organization needs to support, rather than undermine, the goals of employment equity as an institutionalized collective pattern of behaviour. Systems of accountability, rewards and sanctions within the organization must come to reflect these goals and the new values on which they rest.

Strategic management of the employment equity change process means, in essence, bringing organizational systems and patterns of behaviour into harmony with these new values. The analysis of the values that are reflected in traditional and emerging patterns of behaviour in the organization entails the ability to see the difference between "intended" but unrealized strategy, and "realized" strategy (Mintzberg, 1978). In other words, we need to be able to recognize the difference between intentions and lip service to the values that underlie employment equity, and actual behaviour and decision outcomes. Employment equity as a process of organizational change means reducing that gap between behaviour and values.

The tendency toward inertia in organizational life is strong, especially since those with the power to influence decisions stand to benefit from continuing the practices that have served them so well. It is a truism that most organizations were created by white able-bodied males, and the rules by which organizations operate reflect the interests and values of their creators. To move toward policies, practices and modes of interpersonal behaviour that do not privilege able-bodied white males, but that are fair to everyone, involves overcoming resistance that is deeply entrenched and founded upon established interests. Changing this reality involves far more than getting people to express adherence to a value system in which men and women, white people and racial minorities, people who are able-bodied and those with disabilities, and people of all cultural backgrounds, are accepted for who they are, as equals. Employment equity means establishing an organizational framework that encourages and rewards members for acting on this value system every day.

The Process of Strategic Change: A Model

Box 8.3 shows a model of the change process for employment equity. While this model suggests that the stages are sequential, in fact these elements may occur more or less concurrently, and some elements may continue to be present or develop throughout the change process. For example, top management commitment, education, and the identification and management of support and resistance, are necessary from the beginning and on a continuing basis. The various steps in the change process shown in the model may occur in a different sequence, depending on the organizational context.

BOX 8.3
The Process of Organizational Change for Employment Equity

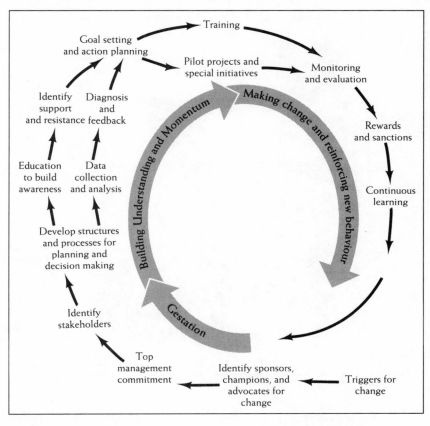

(SOURCE: Adapted from Joyce M. Young, "Affirmative Action Strategies," in *The Human Resources*, Aug./Sept. 1985.)

In this chapter on strategy, we single out for special attention the elements of the change model that involve strategic thinking and choice, and that are not addressed in other chapters. These elements include:

- the development of structures and processes through which stakeholders can participate in planning and decision making;

223

BOX 8.4
Relating Employment Equity Tasks to Organizational Processes

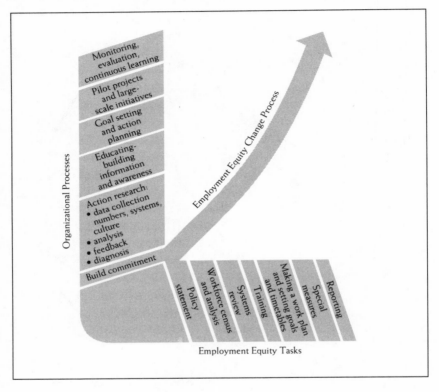

the action research approach to data collection, analysis, and feedback; and

goal setting and action planning, which involves stakeholder participation in specifying what would constitute a successful change process, in identifying priorities for action, and in outlining and getting support for an implementation plan which specifies accountabilities for results.

Box 8.4 shows how the typical employment equity implementation tasks relate to the components of the change process in the organization. As mentioned in Chapter 1, the change strategy we present includes all of the traditional elements of an employment equity program, but places them within an organizational change context. We now turn to a discussion of three strategic components of the change process: creating structures that provide for stakeholder participation in employment equity planning and implementation; using an action research strategy to collect, analyze and interpret organizational information about equity; and developing employment equity goals and an action plan for attaining them.

Creating Structures for Planning and Decision Making by Stakeholders

An early step in the change process is to identify key stakeholders and their interests in change. It is then possible to establish a structure, such as a committee or task force, on which these stakeholders are represented as participants in the planning of an implementation strategy. The stakeholder participation model suggests that this should be a vehicle for producing a strategy that is both realistic and acceptable to the key constituencies that have a stake in employment equity. Other committees, task forces or working groups might then be spun off to manage change at the sub-unit level, or in specific issue areas. The flexible, *ad hoc* nature of this kind of structure is well suited to the requirements of a change process in a complex and changing domain such as employment equity.

Research in the management of change has pointed to the value of creating "organic" and parallel structures that can operate outside the constraints of the functional specialization and hierarchy that so often limit innovation in large organizations. Equity issues often span departmental and functional boundaries, and levels of authority. It is useful to have broadly based task force or committee structures empowered to recommend appropriate remedies for dealing with problems of this nature. On the other hand, some equity issues are quite specific to particular work units or types of jobs, and problem-solving mechanisms to address this level of specificity are required in such cases. It may also be beneficial to have a network or support group for members of each designated group within the organization. Such groups can be important resources for women, people with disabilities, aboriginal peoples and racial minorities, as well as providing a voice for these stake-holders and a means of empowering them.

It is likely that in a medium to large organization, several kinds of structures will be needed to focus energies and resources on the identification and solution of equity problems. Some structures may endure for a considerable time, while others may be transitory. To be effective, employment equity committees or task forces require direct access to top decision makers, a mandate, influential members or decision making authority, and appropriate resources (Morrison and Von Glinow, 1990: 205).

Rosabeth Moss Kanter (1983: 200-205) speaks of the "parallel participative organization" as a tool for innovation in organiza-tions. The parallel organization is a change-oriented structure that is embedded within the hierarchical, bureaucratic organization. Its task is "the continued re-examination of routines; exploration of new options; and development of new tools, procedures, and approaches. It seeks to institutionalize change. As their utility is demonstrated, the new routines can be transferred into the bureau-cratic organization for maintenance and integration" (Stein and Kanter, 1980: 384).

The structure of the parallel participative organization is a network of *ad hoc* action groups that bring together stakeholders from various departments, and various positions in the hierarchy, who have interests and expertise related to specific issues or projects. These action groups usually have no difficulty in recruiting volunteers, since they appeal to stakeholders who are pleased to have an opportunity to devote energy, skills and knowledge to a change project they care about. Such work-ing groups, if facilitated skillfully, given a mandate to accomplish a meaningful task, resources, organizational time in which to work, and recognition for what they have contributed, typically develop a high level of morale and produce results. In Kanter's words, "it appears that when it is in the interests of the people involved, and they are given genuine opportunity and power, they can be committed to finding the time to contribute to solving organizational problems ... In the compa-nies I have observed, projects involving grass-roots participation have not suffered from a lack of willing volunteers who find or make slack time for their involvement " (1983: 203).

Box 8.5 illustrates how one organization — a university — established a policy committee to gather and assess information,

BOX 8.5
Example of a Stakeholder-Based Employment Equity Planning and Implementation Structure at a University

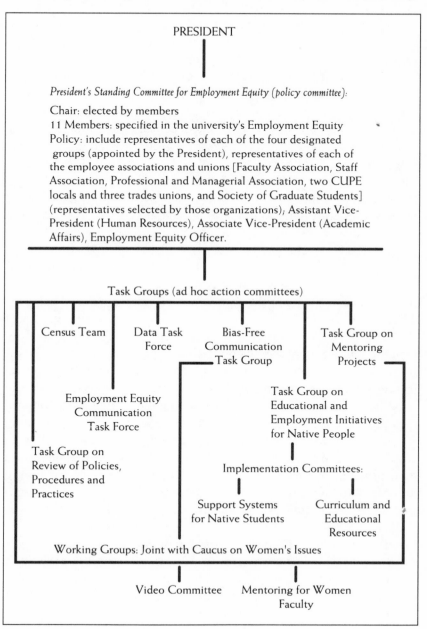

PRESIDENT

President's Standing Committee for Employment Equity (policy committee):

Chair: elected by members
11 Members: specified in the university's Employment Equity
Policy: include representatives of each of the four designated
groups (appointed by the President), representatives of each of
the employee associations and unions [Faculty Association, Staff
Association, Professional and Managerial Association, two CUPE
locals and three trades unions, and Society of Graduate Students]
(representatives selected by those organizations); Assistant Vice-
President (Human Resources), Associate Vice-President (Academic
Affairs), Employment Equity Officer.

Task Groups (ad hoc action committees)

Census Team   Data Task   Bias-Free   Task Group on
               Force   Communication   Mentoring
                             Task Group   Projects

               Employment Equity   Task Group on
               Communication   Educational and
               Task Force   Employment Initiatives
                                        for Native People

Task Group on
Review of Policies,   Implementation Committees:
Procedures and
Practices   Support Systems   Curriculum and
                         for Native Students   Educational
                                               Resources

Working Groups: Joint with Caucus on Women's Issues

               Video Committee   Mentoring for Women
                                   Faculty

plan, and make recommendations at the strategic level. As this committee set priorities for action to work toward solving employment equity problems it identified, it spun off *ad hoc* working groups to implement specific projects. These working groups brought their reports and recommendations to the policy committee for discussion and approval. Their members included members of the policy committee, working together with other members of faculty, the staff associations and unions, and the administration, as well as experts from outside the organization as needed. Some of the working groups were jointly struck by the Employment Equity Committee and an independent advocacy organization of women faculty and staff on campus. A working group existed until the task it was set up to perform was completed, and then it disbanded, or the parent committee redefined its mandate. This structure permitted a flexible, innovative implementation process to operate while maintaining continuity and a strategic, goal-oriented focus, within an essentially conservative organizational structure whose culture was unfriendly to change.

It also provided an outlet for the energies and commitment to change of stakeholders within the organization who previously had no structure or mandate through which to work on equity projects. These projects included the voluntary employment equity census of the work force, systems review involving assessment of all documents covering employment policies and practices to identify systemic barriers, a communication strategy and lecture series to inform the university community about employment equity and the need for it, a policy and guidelines to encourage equity in communication, an educational video and training manual about the subtle forms of discrimination that victimize women faculty and staff, employment and educational projects for aboriginal people, and a mentoring pilot project for women faculty. These projects were identified and approved by the committee on the basis of information from designated group stakeholders about their concerns, as well as in response to requirements of the Federal Contractors Program and the findings of the employment equity census.

In workplaces where there are unions or employee associations, there should be formal procedures for involving these organizations in planning and decision making for employment equity. Participation might occur through existing arrangements, in particular the collective bargaining process, through which agreements might be reached either on substantive issues relating to employment equity outcomes, or on a process for joint planning and decision making. Or, given the complexity and continuous evolution of employment equity implementation, it might be preferable to establish more flexible structures, such as a joint union-management commitee, to provide for ongoing dialogue and decision making on employment equity matters. The particular structure and process through which employee associations or unions participate in joint decision making would depend upon the history and current relationship of labour and management in the workplace.

In Canada and the U.S., joint committees emerged in the seventies as supplementary mechanisms to collective bargaining — not substitutes for it. Joint committees may be better equipped to deal with complex issues related to the quality of the working environment (Kochan and Dyer, 1976). About half of Canadian collective agreements provide for labour management committees, and recent experience with joint committees devoted to occupational health and safety matters provides an interesting example of a structure and process that might be adaptable to employment equity applications (Riddell, 1986: 11-12).

Regardless of the kind of structure that is jointly selected, it is important that employee associations and unions participate in employment equity decision-making from a position of power, and that their participation is accepted as a legitimate right (Kochan and Dyer, 1976). Their commitment and influence on the change process is indispensible to working through some of the most vexing problems of employment equity implementation. For example, there is little hope of effectively addressing the relationship between seniority provisions in the collective agreement, and special measures to improve the access and promotion opportunities of designated group members, unless unions or employee associations work collaboratively with management. The union will need to make proposals for resolving the issue, participate with management in deciding upon a workable approach, and ideally, take some responsibility for implementing the solution and making it work.

At present it is unclear what the responsibility of unions is, under the doctrine of the duty of fair representation, for working toward workplace equity for its members who are also members of designated groups. In the future, legislation, regulations, or case law may shed some light on this issue, and provide some guidance as to the kinds of structures and processes that might support joint union-management planning and decision-making for employment equity.

In addition to ensuring union participation, in some communities or workplaces it may be useful to create a broadly based community development approach to employment equity. This would involve going beyond simply consulting with external stakeholders in order to gain access to resources that the employer lacks, such as expertise or linkages to the designated group labour markets. In a community where designated group members constitute a majority or a sizable minority of the population, an employer may wish to participate with community representatives in a broader process of consultation and decision making regarding the long term development of the labour market and the economy of the community (Lockhart, 1987; Painter, Lockhart and Spalding, 1984).

This kind of approach might be relevant where there is a substantial aboriginal or racial minority population. Concerns in the community about access to educational and employment opportunities, and about success in establishing self government and economic self-determination, may be complemented by the employer's concern about having a local workforce that will meet future educational and skill requirements. Or a band council may wish to undertake joint ventures with external groups interested in establishing a business in the community or investing in an existing or proposed business (McCallum, 1989). In such cases it might be appropriate to set up a planning committee on which employers, community organizations, band and municipal politicians and administrators, and trade unions are represented. This committee could use an action research process to develop an employment equity strategy for the community, or for a sector of the local economy (Trist, 1976). Canadian precedents for this kind of community-based planning for local economic development have occurred in Cape Breton, Sudbury, and St. Catharines, among other places, and in the U.S., in a famous experiment in Jamestown, New York. Box 8.6 illustrates a setting in which a community-based approach to employment equity planning might be especially useful, and is being attempted.

BOX 8.6
Community-Based Employment Equity Planning: Inuit in the Northwest Territories (a 1985 Snapshot)

Many Inuit are worried that benefits achieved through the settlement of land claims and the creation of Nunavut, which is the concept to divide the Northwest Territories into two territories — one in the east and one in the west — may be undermined by a shortage of Inuit with the skills necessary to assume positions as managers, professionals and technicians. Without a skilled Inuit manpower base, it is almost certain that the rate of importation of skilled southeners would increase. Unemployment among Inuit is increasing now as more young Inuit look to the wage economy for a living rather than to the traditional economic activities.

Systemic discrimination has become the unfortunate consequence of government and private sector development in Inuit homelands. At present, although Inuit represent 84% of the labour force age group within Nunavut ..., they hold only 45% of the jobs with the largest employer there, which is the Government of the Northwest Territories. Furthermore, their jobs are clustered at the lowest end of the job spectrum. There is only one Inuk at a senior management level in the Goverment of the Northwest Territories. These are pretty appalling statistics.

At the same time, the unemployment rate among Inuit is far above the national average. In 1984, the GNWT Bureau of Statistics reported an unemployment rate among Inuit of 28%, compared with 7% for non-natives. However, this is based upon a participation rate of 52%, meaning that almost half of the population is considered to be out of the labour force because they are either involved in subsistence activities or not actively seeking work. A survey undertaken by hamlet councils away from government centres, commissioned by Nunasi Corporation, consistently estimated unemployment to be around the 75% level. Although this survey was carried out only in communities within Nunavut, similar social and economic conditions characterize the lives of Inuit in northern Quebec and Labrador.

It is therefore clearly evident that Inuit are presently in the midst of a serious crisis requiring drastic measures in order to bring about lasting changes. Furthermore, it is also a crisis that can be expected to become more serious if action is not immediately taken. For example, the latest federal census reported that 56% of the Inuit population in Canada were under 20 years of age, compared to 32% of the Canadian population as a whole. As the Inuit population ages, the number of people looking for employment will increase dramatically. A number of Inuit organizations are working to ensure that all necessary steps are taken to bring about improvements. They have taken the initiative in forming a coalition called the Task Force on Inuit Management Development.

Beginning in November 1984, the task force has a mandate to examine all Inuit management training programs and develop an overall strategy for training the managers who will be needed to implement our land claim settlement and the division of the Northwest Territories, should the present territory be divided. Task force membership includes Inuit Tapirisat of Canada, the Inuit Broadcasting Corporation, Nunasi Corporation, the Tungavik Federation, the Arctic Cooperatives, the Department of Education of the Government of the Northwest Territories, and the Canada Employment and Immigration Commission.

Given the membership of the task force, it is ideally suited to dealing not only with specific training issues but also with the political and cultural factors that underlie many of the current difficulties Inuit face. Yet the task force has had very little success in having its recommendations acted on by various levels of government. Inuit want to be partners in the process of policy development and program implementation. Such an arrangement would not only benefit Inuit in general but also governments that lack sufficient knowledge of those they are attempting to assist. Without a co-ordinated approach under Inuit direction, policies and programs will continue to address the symptoms of the problem, often in a piecemeal fashion, and never the basic underlying causes. Therefore, I think over the past few decades Inuit have had to adapt to the situations of institutions in the north, rather than the institutions adapting themselves to the Inuit.

(SOURCE: Rosemarie Kuptana, President, Inuit Broadcasting Corporation, minutes of testimony before the House of Commons on Bill C-62, An Act Respecting Employment Equity, December 10, 1985, Issue no. 4, p. 45-46.)

In some situations, external community based advocacy organizations may choose to establish their own structures and processes for putting pressure on local employers who have been resistant to implementing employment equity change. Saul Alinsky, a community organizer in the U.S. in the 1960s and 70s, developed a strategy for coalition-building among local community organizations, based upon their interests (Peabody, 1976). By joining together to work for change, community organizations in Rochester, New York, and other cities gained the power to successfully pressure employers such as Eastman Kodak to provide access to jobs for unemployed Blacks. Such community organizations, if successful in challenging the employer to act, may subsequently choose to engage in collaborative planning and decision making with employers to develop an approach to employment equity that responds to the community's and the employer's needs. Internal advocacy organizations composed of employees who are frustrated by an employer's failure to act, perhaps working with external groups, might also form coalitions or use strategies similar to Alinsky's to press for employment equity action.

In considering what kind of structure to establish to work toward employment equity, the critical considerations are the stakeholders' objectives, the strategy for change that they wish to pursue, and the particular local conditions of organizational and community structure, culture and history that form the context for change. There is no single appropriate model for a structure to provide for stakeholder participation in change. However, no matter what structural arrangements are selected, they should be perceived as effective and credible by the various stakeholders who need to participate in the employment equity change process.

An Action Research Approach to Data Collection and Analysis

After a committee or other coordinating structure for involving stakeholders in employment equity is created, one of its early tasks is to gather information that can serve as the basis for diagnosing change issues, measuring change with reference to a baseline, and planning remedies. Some of the tools that can be used to provide an information base include a census or survey, results of reviews of policies and practices bearing on all kinds of human resource management decisions, public meetings and discussions, consultations with informed persons, focus groups, and briefs from groups or individuals. The analysis of quantitative and qualitative information about the status of the designated groups in the workplace can serve as the basis for diagnosing equity problems and developing an action plan that identifies the areas where change is possible and needed, in order of priority. In Chapters 12 and 13 we discuss this diagnostic process in detail.

Action research is a methodology that is intended to provide an empirical and analytical foundation for a program of organizational change. It was developed primarily by organization development (OD) theorists and is identified with the OD tradition (Frohman, Sashkin and Kavanagh, 1976: 142). Action research involves the use of behavioural science knowledge and research techniques to assist organizational decision makers in solving problems. It has the potential to generate valid and relevant data that can serve as a basis for diagnosing problems, providing accurate information to all members of the organization about the need for change, planning relevant change strategies, and monitoring change over time to identify gaps between goals and results of the change program.

A stakeholder-based action research process might proceed through the following stages, which represent a modified version of the conventional OD model of action research:

1) after consulting stakeholders about what kinds of information are needed, change agents gather data from employees and other stakeholders to support the diagnosis of problems and the planning of relevant remedies and organizational responses;
2) change agents prepare a preliminary analysis and interpretation of what the data show;
3) change agents feed the preliminary findings back to other stakeholders;
4) stakeholders review and discuss the findings and their interpretation, providing supplementary or contradictory perspectives;
5) stakeholders attempt to arrive at a common diagnosis of what the critical problems are;
6) change agents and other stakeholders discuss alternative actions and measures that would remedy or allieviate the problems they have identified;

7) stakeholders agree on an action plan consisting of measures to remedy the problems;

8) stakeholders continue to review information about the change process and its outcomes as part of an ongoing monitoring and evaluation process as the action plan is implemented. The plan is modified as needed in order to adapt to changing conditions and to feedback concerning results of initiatives.

Action research may be useful in employment equity applications as a guiding framework for:

- gathering and analyzing information,
- setting objectives for change,
- planning and prioritizing specific change initiatives
- identifying resource needs,
- identifying roles, responsibilities and accountabilities for action to attain objectives, and
- evaluating the results of the change process.

Action research presupposes involvement of stakeholders from a cross-section of organizational functions, and a vertical slice of the hierarchy. It also assumes the creation of structures — such as committees, focus groups, or task forces — within which participation in data-gathering and analysis, planning, and decision making can occur.

One of the most valuable elements of the action research approach for employment equity is the feeding back of data to stakeholders by means of a process that offers them an opportunity to verify the findings, discuss their implications, and participate in the planning of change initiatives that address areas of concern identified in the data. Discussion meetings in committees, or at the level of the work unit, often serve as the vehicles for this purpose.

Participation in the data collection, feedback and planning processes in itself raises the level of awareness and information throughout the organization about the problems and the need for change, and may elicit relevant and practical suggestions for elements of a change program. Participation in the collection and analysis of data, and in action planning, increases the probability that the means used to collect data will produce a valid and relevant diagnosis, that the action plan will address the issues of concern, and that there will be a high level of voluntary response to the employment equity census. Participation in the action research process may also promote stakeholders' sense of ownership of the change project, and their identification with its objectives (Child, 1984: 289).

Employment equity is a data-based approach to change, in that data collection and reporting are required by government, and are indispensable to the planning and implementation of an effective change program. While data collection and reporting in themselves may make little if any direct contribution to change in the representation or working environment of the designated groups, the participation of stakeholders in the action research process may contribute to the "unfreezing" stage of change by clarifying the nature and scope of inequities in the distribution, compensation, and working conditions of women, minorities, aboriginal people and persons with disabilities.

Because of legal and regulatory requirements, almost every workplace involved in employment equity undertakes a census of its work force, and all employment equity practitioners are accustomed to the tasks of conducting the census, creating a database composed of census results and an extract from the human resources data system, analyzing and reporting statistical information. Harvey (1988) and Harvey, Severn and Blakely (1990), and free publications from Employment and Immigration Canada and other government agencies provide comprehensive discussions of the considerations involved in conducting an employment equity census, creating and updating the data base, and using various analytical procedures for reporting work-force data.

There is less recognition of the importance of qualitative data from members of designated groups about their experience, and from managers, employees, union officers, and people from the community who know about the barriers faced by outsiders who attempt to gain access to employment. The uses of this kind of information in employment equity diagnosis are discussed in Chapters 12 and 13. A stakeholder based action research process is well positioned to gather and make good use of information about the experience of designated group members, and about how organizational policies are actually implemented and decisions are made. This kind of information will be essential to the development of an action plan that identifies and addresses the real equity issues in an organization.

BOX 8.7

Types and Potential Sources of Data for Employment Equity Diagnosis, Planning, Goal Setting and Monitoring

A. DESCRIPTIVE AND EXPERIENTIAL INFORMATION:

From:

- employees who are members of designated groups
- members of the community who have worked or attempted to obtain employment in the organization, or members of organizations or agencies familiar with this type of experience
- union officers, legal counsellor, employee relations staff, and others whose responsibilities include dealing with employee complaints
- line managers and human resources staff involved in hiring, promoting, evaluating performance

Collected by means of:

- surveys of employees or open-ended questions on the employment equity census
- testimony or other submissions, in person or in writing, to the employment equity committee or task force
- interviews or focus groups conducted and summarized by members of the committee or by the employment equity practitioner
- documentation regarding complaints or grievances, if access is not foreclosed by confidentiality procedures
- open meetings or discussions in the workplace, or in departments or other sub-units

B. FINDINGS OF FORMAL REVIEWS OF EMPLOYMENT POLICIES AND PRACTICES (SYSTEMS):

From:

- report prepared by the task force, committee, human resources or employment equity staff, or other group or persons responsible for systems review

C. EMPLOYMENT EQUITY CENSUS DATA:

From:

- voluntary survey of all employees regarding their designated group status, updated as employees enter and leave the organization

D. PERSONNEL DATA:

From:

- human resources data system, which may include information on each employee's job title, rank, organizational unit, educational level, other qualifications, salary, start date, probable retirement date, and career history

E. APPLICANT DATA:

From:

- voluntary self identification of designated group status as part of the application procedure

F. EXTERNAL AVAILABILITY DATA (COUNTS OF QUALIFIED MEMBERS OF DESIGNATED GROUPS):

From:

- Census of Canada
- Health and Activity Limitation Survey
- local and provincial data from surveys or records
- associations of professions, trades, and other occupational groups
- designated group associations
- band offices on reserves

Setting Goals and Developing an Action Plan

The setting of goals for change is a fundamental part of a strategically managed employment equity process. There is evidence from the U.S. experience with affirmative action that setting goals and timetables promotes improvements in the representation of women and minorities in firms subject to compliance reviews: "the establishments that promise to employ more do actually employ more" (Leonard, 1985: 18).

Goals serve three important purposes:

- setting out the standards by which the success of the employment equity process will be defined and measured;
- setting priorities for action, and for the investment of limited resources of time, energy and money to achieve maximum impact;
- motivating action toward change, both at the corporate level and in sub-units within the organization.

Chapters 12, 13 and 14 discuss the kinds of information that may play a part in setting goals and monitoring progress, and how that information might be used as part of an evaluation process. Here, we are concerned with the kinds of goals that might be set, how goal-setting relates to other organizational processes, and ways in which stakeholders might be involved in setting goals and developing implementation plans.

BOX 8.8
Employment Equity Goals Are Like Other Business Goals...

> Business sets goals and timetables for every aspect of its operations
> — profits, capital investment, productivity increases. Setting goals
> and timetables for minority and female participation is simply a way
> of measuring progress.
> William S. McEwen
> National Association of Manufacturers
>
> (SOURCE: Anne Fisher, "Hiring by the Numbers: Business vs. Reagan on Affirmative
> Action," *Fortune*, Sept. 16, 1985, p. 19.)

At the start, it is important to be aware of some of the assumptions that may guide the setting of goals, whether these assumptions are recognized or hidden. We have discussed organizational change as a value-driven process: this is particularly true of the goal-setting component of employment equity. For example, the benchmark or standard of comparison to be used by the organization in setting numerical goals for the future representation of designated groups is not merely a technical exercise, although it is often presented this way. What kinds of information are to be used as a basis for goal setting? For a municipal government administration, for example, should goals for designated group representation be set with reference to their proportion of the city's population? What sector of the population — people of working (and taxpaying) age, or total population, or school-age population? Or should goals reflect the availability of designated group members in the local labour market who are qualified to work in the fields included in the city's work force? Now, or projected for the future? Is a national or provincial labour market a more appropriate reference group? Or the population of municipal workers in the province or the nation? Or should goals be based on graduates in fields of study from which the city hires?

Selecting one of these reference populations as a benchmark for goal-setting reflects this organization's perception of itself, and of whom it perceives to be its primary stakeholders. As well, the choice sets a standard that may be very conservative, relatively moderate, or more progressive and forward-looking, given variations in demographic characteristics among these reference populations. The nature of the assumptions that underlie the goal-setting process reveal the values that inform the choices involved. Depending upon those values and assumptions, goal-setting may be just a paper exercise intended to fulfill the government's requirements at a minimal level, or a statement of commitment to move the organization toward equity.

There are several types of decisions that need to be made in relation to the goal-setting process. These decisions include:

1. **The designated groups to be included in the goal setting process**
While government requirements, such as those under the Federal Contractors Program, include goal setting for all four groups, some employment equity programs begin with the intention of increasing the representation of one group first, and adding the others in later. This approach certainly does not address the interests of all the stakeholders in employment equity.

2. **The standard of comparison**
There are a number of choices that must be made regarding the representation of the designated groups within a specific geographic area, at a particular time, in a population defined in terms of qualifications, availability for work, client or taxpayer status, or other criteria, as discussed above.

3. **The time span over which change is to be measured**
Goals could be set as of a year from now, three years, five years, or for a longer term, or a combination of short, medium and long terms. Specific aspects of the organization's context or environment may influence this choice. For example, it may make sense

for employment equity goal setting to be integrated with the organization's strategic planning or budgeting cycle, or its human resource or succession planning arrangements. Or there may be key events that are important to stakeholders and provide a meaningful definition of a planning term, for example, the company's twenty-fifth anniversary year.

4. The ways in which the goals will be used by change agents and other stakeholders

Will goals be viewed as guides to decision making? Quotas that must be filled? Ceilings? Benchmarks in a long term process of assessment? Will they be viewed in ways similar to other organizational planning tools, such as sales or market share goals, which are tied to systems of rewards and penalties?

5. The span for goal setting and the process for generating goals

It is highly likely that there will be goals for the organization as a whole, but how will they be set? By means of a centralized process whereby a decision is made at the top to establish organization-wide goals? Will they apply equally to every department or other sub-unit in the organization? Or will each sub-unit set its own goals, in a variant of a management-by-objectives process that relates organization-wide goals to local conditions, including turnover projections, availability of qualified workers in relevant fields who are members of designated groups, and plans for internal changes such as expansion or cut-backs? A decentralized goal-setting process offers the possibility of involving stakeholders at the level of the sub-unit, thus creating local commitment to goal attainment, and increasing the probability that goals are attainable and realistic.

6. Type of goals

Discussions of goal-setting typically imply that goals are always numerical, referring to counts of members of the four designated groups in various job classes over time. Quantitative goals are essential, but insufficient, as noted in the discussion of data collection. It is equally important to set goals that identify changes that will be sought in the quality of the workplace environment experienced by the members of the designated groups. As will be discussed in detail in Chapter 13, we suggest that goals be set in three broad areas:

- **numerical representation**: objectives for representation of designated group members by level or rank;
- **employment systems**: objectives for the nature and quality of decision making on specified human resource management matters (eg. hiring and selection, retention, training and development, promotion, compensation, terms and conditions of employment, due process for employees who have experienced harassment, accountability of managers for employment equity results);
- **organizational culture**: objectives for improving the quality of experience of designated groups in the workplace, including job satisfaction, freedom from harassment and biased language, social and professional support systems.

These three goal-setting domains are interrelated in practice, since failure to make progress on one will impede movement in the others. For example, without changing human resource management systems and preventing harassment, there is unlikely to be long term improvement in designated group representation, since members will not gain access to the organization, or if they do, they may leave. On the other hand, without improvements in designated group representation it will be difficult to change organizational culture and systems, given the dynamics of tokenism and stereotyping discussed in Chapter 2.

The employment equity planning committee or other responsible body will need to develop an action plan that identifies and prioritizes the elements of the implementation program that need to be undertaken in order to attain the goals. The diagnosis of equity issues based upon the analysis of organizational information, and the assessment of sources of support and resistance and their strength, will serve as the basis of the action plan. It is crucial that the plan be endorsed by the top decision makers in the organization, that resources are made available for implementation, and that accountabilities for results are established.

BOX 8.9
Some Components of an Employment Equity Work Plan

For: planning unit: Industrial Products   Date: Jan. 1992

PART 1. NUMERICAL REPRESENTATION

A. Status and Goals:

	Racial minorities	Persons with disabilities	Aboriginal persons	Women	Total employees
Current rep.					
#					
%					
Rep. in external labour market (%):					
Anticipated turnover:					
# retirements:					
# new positions:					
# positions cut:					
Net vacancies:					
Goals for:					
Jan. 1993					
Jan. 1996					
Jan. 2000					

B. Actions:
   Racial minorities
   Persons with disabilities
   Aboriginal persons
   Women

C. Accountabilities:

D. Resources required:
   employee time
   expert/technical support
   materials, etc.
   space

E. Key stakeholders and arrangements for their participation:

PART 2 EMPLOYMENT SYSTEMS:

	Racial minorities	Persons with disabilities	Aboriginal persons	Women

A. Current status:

B. Goals
   Jan. 1993
   Jan. 1996
   Jan. 2000

C. Actions:

D. Accountabilities:

E. Resources required:

F. Key stakeholders and arrangements for their participation:

PART 3. WORKPLACE CULTURE:

	Racial minorities	Persons with disabilities	Aboriginal persons	Women

A. Current status:

B. Goals
   Jan. 1993
   Jan. 1996
   Jan. 2000

C. Actions:

D. Accountabilities:

E. Resources required:

F. Key stakeholders and arrangements for their participation:

A comprehensive educational strategy is an important component of the action plan for cultural change, initially to ensure a high response rate for the employment equity census and other data collection activities, and later to build support for and involvement in the implementation of action plans. It is important to inform all employees why the change is happening, what is involved, what choices need to be made and by whom, and what the costs and benefits are likely to be. All employees need an opportunity to be informed, to ask questions, and to talk about how they will be affected.

Pilot projects and special initiatives are also important parts of the action plan for all three goal-setting domains. Pilot projects can provide opportunities to test program ideas on a small scale without the commitment of substantial resources or the risk of damaging failure. Special initiatives to accomodate the needs of target groups will assist them in becoming equal and fully productive members of the organization.

The evaluation of the entire change process, especially a review of progress made against baseline indicators, will help to provide a basis for the next round of the action planning process. As we will discuss in Chapter 14, evaluation will identify needs for modifying program elements to improve future effectiveness.

The Strategic Context of Change

We now turn to a discussion of the strategic context within which change is managed. We will move through the change model, looking at some strategic dimensions of its three principle stages: gestation, building understanding and momentum, and making change.

The Gestation Stage

During the gestation or "unfreezing" phase of the change process, a sense emerges and spreads among decision-makers that change is needed, usually as a result of pressures from the environment, such as legislation, regulation, competition, or other changes. This sense may begin among a small group or even with an individual champion of change whose commitment becomes widely shared through a sustained and effective effort to communicate concern that things are not as they should be. This concern, perhaps initially a vague discontent in relation to a rather ill-defined bundle of issues, is articulated and labelled as a problem that requires serious attention, perhaps in relationship to another problem that already has a profile as a "front-burner" issue in the organization. Or it may be that a change in the top management, or several new employees, or an influential consultant, can bring a fresh perspective that attracts support. In Chapter 9 we elaborate on some of the specific triggers for change associated with the identification and sponsorship of employment equity as an issue of concern to a critical mass of people, including top management, who are in positions to influence opinion and decision making.

The gestation period is a politically sensitive one in which problem identification and diagnosis needs time to develop, and understanding of the issues gradually deepens through discussion and debate. It is important not to rush precipitously into actions for which adequate preparation has not been made. Appropriate action proposals are most likely to emerge from an exploration of alternative diagnoses and responses and their implications, within the context of a felt need for change. For example, an announcement of an affirmative action goal or quota for filling job vacancies with women may precipitate a great deal of resistance if there is not yet a clear understanding across the organization of the problem for which this particular remedy is legitimate. If an action proposal such as this is to succeed, the political will required to make it happen must be present. This would likely arise from strongly held values and convictions on the part of key decision makers that the proposal should be implemented, or from an external force such as a decision of a court or human rights tribunal, or a legal requirement or regulation.

On the basis of a study of a complex program of organizational change over two decades, Andrew Pettigrew cautions that the gestation period may be very long, especially in a large organization. In the companies he studied, it took a great deal of time to "move beyond the phase of philosophical debate, of developing concern that all was not well and acknowledging and understanding some of the problems that eventually caught a critical mass of management attention, towards the phase of concrete planning and action for change" (Pettigrew, 1986: 463).

Building Understanding and Momentum
When the forces of inertia are entrenched, it takes time and persistence to discredit the dominant ideology that supports current arrangements and shift the balance of power toward new ideas.

From a strategic perspective, change agents attempting to build understanding and momentum in order to create a climate of acceptance of employment equity might consider several suggestions that emerge from the research literature on organizational change, and from experience of practitioners.

The integration of responsibility for managing employment equity into the human resource management function can be advantageous. As staff, human resource managers often have the opportunity to interact with line managers throughout the organization and to influence their perspectives on the solution of every-day staffing and personnel management problems. In particular, it is valuable to be able to influence the staffing process, not only to place the hiring, promotion, and development of designated group members on the agenda, but also to orient new management appointees to employment equity as an issue of corporate concern. Ultimately, the aim of an employment equity program is to inte-grate equity approaches into all aspects of human resource man-agement in the organization.

In the early stages of the change process it may be useful to bring people from various parts of the organization together for a conference, presentation by a speaker, or informal meeting to talk about equity issues and action alternatives that have not been overtly raised before. Such events are useful in increasing the flow of information that effectively discredits the acceptability of maintaining the status quo. Getting people, especially line man-agers, involved in gathering information and hearing about the concerns of designated group members, and considering evidence of disadvantage, will contribute to understanding and momentum for change.

One of the most challenging strategic issues facing those in the vanguard of making change is developing an effective relationship with the organization, so that they can champion new ideas with-out becoming isolated and marginalized. It is crucial that the change agents and the program be firmly rooted in their local envi-ronment, since they cannot be effective political actors if they are alienated from the organization's culture and structures and cut off from access to information and support. After all, "to change the World one must live with it" (Wilson, 1973: 167, quoted in Pettigrew, 1986: 505).

On the other hand, agents of change cannot be seen as co-opted by those who benefit from the status quo, and unwilling to issue challenges. They need to represent new values, advocate change, and take the risk of "thinking the unthinkable" and presenting a vision of an alternative future. The trick is to find the right balance between advocacy of new ideas and ability to understand and com-municate with people in the organization as it is.

In a study of innovating groups, Pettigrew found that this balance is a very difficult one to maintain. The initial supporters of change often cultivate the image that they have a superior mission that gives them the right to attack the status quo. Their conviction is an important source of the high energy and commitment that is required to make an impact on bureaucratic inertia. But change agents risk losing their legitimacy and power to influence action if they attract a high level of resistance at an early stage of the change process, or alienate key stakeholders who might otherwise be inclined to contribute their energy and ideas to the change process.

Resistance to change often takes the form of "shooting the messenger" who presents new ideas. Labelling and stereotyping, stigmatizing, and devaluing change agents is a common tactic used to discredit the change process. The creativity of those threatened by change can sometimes be surprising, and all too effective in isolating and marginalizing innovators. The deviant and marginal roles of the innovators may be exaggerated. They may be labelled as oblivious to business necessities, as militant or radical, as dreamers out of touch with the way things really work, as radical feminists, or as hyper-sensitive people with no sense of humour. Such tactics are often used, as well, to silence members of designated groups who speak out about discrimination they or their colleagues have experienced.

A destructive cycle can set in if advocates of change engage in the natural tendency to protect themselves by erecting a protective boundary between their small group and the rest of the organization. By becoming exclusive, developing an esoteric sub-culture and strong in-group ties and a distinctive social identity, they create a support system for themselves, but at the cost of cutting themselves off from the sources of support and bureaucratic legitimacy they will need if they are to be effective agents of change. Self doubt, disillusionment and self-destructive factional conflicts may follow if the tendency toward exclusivity becomes entrenched (Pettigrew, 1986: 510, 479-80).

It is obviously necessary for innovators to strategically manage their own domestic and foreign relations in order to be effective. Marginalization may be especially likely if advocates of change have no real mandate to act, or if they are closely identified with an unpopular top-down change initiative for which there is no clear need, especially if the top management sponsor moves on. Change programs identified with external consultants run the risk of being marginalized, as do initiatives championed by organizational members who are perceived as weak or peripheral in their normal roles.

It is helpful to the change initiative if its sponsors are respected, and core rather than peripheral members of the organization; it is strategically important to involve strong line managers in the process at an early stage. Those leading the change need to retain a secure place within the organization's structure and to build upon their networks. In creating a structure to support and carry the change process, it may be useful to emulate the model of a decentralized movement, a loose network of small groups linked by common membership or joint activities, and some common objectives. This kind of structure may help supporters of change to survive in an unreceptive or hostile environment without attracting strong resistance, since they may be able to support each other and attain a variety of limited objectives while remaining integrated within their local environments. Over time, evidence of accomplishment and commitment will help credibility to grow.

As the change effort acquires legitimacy and momentum, new supporters will join and the movement for change will become more inclusive, avoiding the dangers of exclusiveness and marginality.

Making Change and Reinforcing New Behaviour

The general awareness of the issue of employment inequity within the organization and of the need for change, developed during the gestation and momentum-building phases, needs to be reframed as an interrelated collection of manageable chunks that can be acted upon within the context of the organization's structures for management and decision making. It is helpful if these chunks, or actionable issues, can be seen as contributing solutions to other current organizational problems. For example, changes in human resource management policies and practices that may be required for reasons of equity may address other problems that have already been identified, such as poor morale, turnover, or difficulties in recruiting people with needed skills.

Timing is of critical strategic importance in identifying projects in response to actionable issues. It is useful to be able to time and order initiatives so that their impacts are mutually reinforcing and amplifying. It may be possible to pull several *ad hoc* or piecemeal activities together around a central focus, thus making more effective use of resources. Experience with complex and long term efforts to change organizations suggests that the process is most effective if it is incremental, gradual, and composed of a heaping up of small scale initiatives, since a monolithic and large scale restructuring program is likely to provoke a great deal of resistance. In Charles Lindblom's terms, the policy making and implementation process involves "muddling," or adaptive planning, rather than redesigning the organization from the ground up. But the "muddling" must be informed by persistent, continuous and value-driven advocacy of change.

In conclusion, we return to some suggestions contained in Chapter 1, where we indicated that our vision of employment equity is a change process that is:

- strategic: planned, goal oriented, and based on clearly articulated values;
- participatory: implemented through structures and processes that empower stakeholders to put their concerns forward and influence the change process;
- open and accountable: visible to all who are affected, so that decision makers view employment equity as a priority for themselves;
- based on sound analysis of how organizational change happens, how and why it is resisted, and how resistance can be managed;
- based on a sound diagnosis and action plan focused on the employment equity issues of concern to members of the designated groups, and
- informed by understanding of the nature of discrimination and disadvantage.

An employment equity change process is not likely to be a grand strategy set forth by the generals and carried out by the troops, but a process created gradually over time through hundreds of discussions and decisions, small and large, throughout the organization.

REFERENCES

Child, John. *Organization: A Guide to Problems and Practice.* London: Harper and Row, 1984.

Harvey, Edward. *Information Systems for Employment Equity: An Employer Guide.* Don Mills: CCH Canadian, 1988.

Harvey, Edward, Eric Severn, and John Blakely. *Computing for Equity: Computer Applications for Employment Equity.* Don Mills: CCH Canadian, 1990.

Kanter, Rosabeth Moss. *The Change Masters.* New York: Simon and Schuster, 1983.

Kochan, Thomas, and Lee Dyer. "A Model of Organizational Change in the Context of Union-Management Relations." *Journal of Applied Behavioural Science,* 12 (1), 1976, 59-78.

Kuhn, Thomas. *The Structure of Scientific Revolutions.* Chicago: The University of Chicago Press, 1962.

Leonard, Jonathan. "What Promises Are Worth: The Impact of Affirmative Action Goals." *The Journal of Human Resources,* 20 (1), 1985, 3-20.

Lockhart, Alexander. "Community-Based Development and Conventional Economics in the Canadian North." In Edward Bennett (ed.), *Social Intervention: Theory and Practice.* Lewiston, Ontario: Edwin Mellen Press, 1987, Ch. 14.

McCallum, Larry. "Breaking Out: Many Native Indian Bands Want to Kick the Passive Wait-for-a-Handout-from-Ottawa Syndrome." *BC Business,* 17 (9), 1989, 21 ff.

Mintzberg, Henry. "Patterns in Strategy Formation." *Management Science,* 24(9) 1978, 934-48.

Morrison, Ann, and Mary Ann Von Glinow. "Women and Minorities in Management." *American Psychologist,* Feb. 1990, 200-208.

Painter, Bert, Alexander Lockhart, and Jon Spalding. "Joint Development of Community and Work Life." In J.B. Cunningham and T.H. White (eds.), *Quality of Working Life: Contemporary Cases.* Ottawa: Labour Canada, 1984, 329-50.

Peabody, George. "Power, Alinsky, and Other Thoughts." In G. Zollschan and W. Hirsch (eds.), *Social Change.* New York: Wiley, 1976, Ch. 34.

Pettigrew, Andrew. *The Awakening Giant: Continuity and Change in Imperial Chemical Industries.* Oxford: Basil Blackwell, 1985.

Quinn, James Brian. "Managing Strategies Incrementally." *Omega: The International Journal of Management Science,* 10 (6), 613-627.

Riddell, W. Craig. "Labour-Management Cooperation in Canada: An Overview." In Riddell (ed.), *Labour-Management Cooperation in Canada*. Toronto: University of Toronto Press, 1986, Ch. 1.

Stein, Barry, and Rosabeth Moss Kanter. "Building the Parallel Organization: Creating Mechanisms for Permanent Quality of Work Life." *Journal of Applied Behavioural Science*, 16 (3), 1980, 371-388.

Trist, Eric. "Engaging With Large-Scale Systems." In Alfred W. Clark (ed.), *Experimenting with Organizational Life*. New York: Plenum, 1976, Ch. 4.

9

Getting Started:
Triggers
for Change

Inertia: Property of matter by which it continues in its existing state of rest or uniform motion in straight line, unless that state is changed by external force.

(The Concise Oxford Dictionary, 1982)

"MORE WINDOW DRESSING," Victoria Johnson thought as she skimmed through her morning newspaper. An article on recent employment equity reports submitted to the federal government examined the initiatives and progress of employers. However, when you looked at the fine print, "progress" boiled down to a *decrease* of one aboriginal upper level manager — the only aboriginal woman — from 1987 to 1989 in almost 400 companies reporting under the Employment Equity Act. The overall picture of aboriginal representation in decision-making roles was even more discouraging: only 12 aboriginal senior managers out of 4,465 in 1987, and 11 out of 5,426 in 1989!

Another article praised a natural resources company and its union for actively implementing an employment equity program to assist northern Native people. It was a good initiative, Victoria thought, but the focus was obviously on Native men. She didn't have a problem with accommodations by companies for hunting and trapping activities of Native male employees, but she'd be a lot happier if the company also gave attention to the domestic and child-care responsibilities Native and non-Native women face while they try to make it in non-traditional jobs.

Picking up the telephone, Victoria called her co-chair of the Employment Equity Coalition, a community group formed over the last year to lobby for more effective employment equity for racial minorities, aboriginal peoples, women and people with disabilities. "Issa, I'm glad to reach you. Have you seen the papers? Discouraging and encouraging at the same time isn't it? Guess we should add these news articles to our agenda for the Coalition next week. Do you think we could get someone from the government to come and talk about this? O.K., you make some calls and I'll draft a brief. We'll go over it later this week."

Victoria poured another cup of tea and looked out her kitchen window. Another fall almost over, she thought to herself, as the autumn leaves blew across the yard. Another year past, another set of employment equity reports but so little change. Will there never be true equality of opportunity in the workplace? Will her children also have to form community groups to pressure government and employers to eliminate discrimination and disadvantage? Another employment equity progress report and another brief to government. Is there any way we can make them listen — and act?

As an advocate of change, Victoria is frustrated with the slow progress companies are achieving under the Employment Equity Act, and with interpretations of the data that cloud a balanced assessment of what is really happening. She recognizes the influence that cooperative community advocacy may have on bureaucracies and the media; thus she has joined forces with other equity seekers to form a coalition to press for change. Nevertheless, she still searches for a way to capture the commitment of those who can effect real change in organizations: people of influence and decision-making power who can make employment equity happen.

Like Victoria Johnson, most people seeking results know that the critical consideration in getting employment equity or any other change process started — and then maintained — is how to get "buy in" from key stakeholders. Sufficient commitment of power, information and resources is required to initiate and sustain any large-scale organizational change. What are the footholds we need to find or create as we try to move an organization forward? How and from whom do we get the spark that will trigger change? What convinces key decision makers or the dominant coalition of decision makers and power brokers to sponsor change? Who does the persuading? What leads to commitment? What strategies and information can be used to demonstrate connections between employment equity and the organization's needs so that the power structure is receptive to change? What roles might the various stakeholders play in creating an environment for change, and moving beyond inertia?

Overcoming the Inertia

Despite the natural tendency to inertia, we have evidence that within the last decade companies, bureaucracies and the general public have changed their practices, attitudes and behaviour in ways previous generations would never have anticipated. Consider, for example, the changes in practices, behaviour and attitudes regarding drinking and driving, smoking, and conservation. Although profit may be a priority, we find that even costly conservation and pollution reduction activities have become a matter of regular business practice in many firms. Pressure to reduce pollution has prompted some firms to seek new ways to recycle waste material and by-products, in some instances helping the company to decrease costs or generate revenues. "Reduce, reuse and recycle" has become a common marketing and public relations theme.

Other examples encourage our optimism that the entrenched behaviour patterns of individuals and organizations can be changed. Consider the "revolution" in fitness, exercise and nutrition in North America. On a global scale we see an increase in democratic values, with people demanding a greater voice in the social, economic and political decisions affecting their lives. Thus we know that substantive change — whether individual, organizational or national — is possible.

How then might employment equity change be triggered? This chapter examines how potential change agents might mobilize information, pressure and the forces for change; provide a rationale that speaks to the interests of the organization or its key decision-makers; and create buy-in and a "felt need" to change, leading to a search for ways to deal with the threat or opportunity that change presents. All of this provides a basis for the commitment needed to commence and maintain a large-scale organizational change process like employment equity.

We noted in Chapters 6 and 7 that top management support is necessary but not sufficient to make employment equity a reality. We also believe that mandatory legislation is a necessary but by itself an insufficient precondition for effective employment equity progress. A comprehensive and substantive regulatory framework may help to motivate key decision makers to take employment equity seriously and make it happen, as discussed in Chapter 1. Yet, whether or not the legal framework of employment equity prompts change, there are those who say the real work only begins once legislation or regulations are introduced or the courts have ordered remedies. Many employment equity practitioners have told us that even with legislation requiring the filing of employment equity reports, and even if there is an internal policy commitment to employment equity, there has not necessarily been real buy-in — real commitment to change. Their experience suggests that while the legalities may trigger the support of top management, you have to get many other stakeholders "on board": line managers, supervisors, human resources staff and union officials, all of whom can make or break an effective change effort. Experience also shows that only an employment equity initiative will be deemed "successful" only if the designated groups themselves define it so.

The process of gaining commitment — "buy-in" — leads to a consideration of the interests of the various employment equity stakeholders. For example, senior management commitment is not likely to be perceived by other stakeholders as adequate if sufficient financial and human resources are not dedicated to the employment equity planning, implementation and monitoring process. If there is talk of employment equity, but budgets and work priorities do not take equity initiatives into consideration, a realistic assessment is that commitment is lacking. Employment equity is marginalized, and people are left to do what they can based on their own motivation when all the other work is done, and in such a way as to "work around" the status quo rather than to confront it directly. Similarly, if union negotiating teams treat equity issues as mere proposals, but never as significant issues for hard bargaining, then these issues will come to play a role as trade-off items in collective bargaining, not as serious matters for action by the union and management. A contentious issue of commitment for many employment equity advocates and practitioners is the degree of integration of employment equity into human resources management practices and structures. Some see integration as assimilation, with employment equity becoming lost in the process. For others, the only way to effect change over the long run is to make employment equity a part of how the organization manages people, not a separate process of decision making, activity and assessment.

In this chapter we examine the complementary roles of three types of change agents — sponsors, champions and advocates — and consider how change agents create and gain an awareness of the need for change. This "felt need" may relate to one of four basic reasons for organizational change: success, survival, strategy and self-interest. The final outcome of a strategically and successfully managed triggering process is "buy-in": a new or continuing interest or commitment to change as the organization searches for strategies to take advantage of the opportunities that change presents, or cope with threats to the status quo. The steps in developing an organizational commitment to change are shown in Box 9.3 and are discussed later in this chapter. First, we look at the roles change agents play in effecting organizational change.

Creating Momentum: Roles of Sponsors, Champions and Advocates

Agents of change may include sponsors, champions or advocates. There is a common denominator to all three change agents: each in its own way supports the employment equity change process. It is equally true to say that while all change agents are key stakeholders or members of key stakeholder groups, not all stakeholders will act as change agents. Box 9.1 suggests examples of employment equity change agents.

BOX 9.1
Examples of Stakeholders Who
May Act as Change Agents

CHANGE AGENTS:	STAKEHOLDERS:
Advocates	Community/special interest groups of or for disabled people, racial minorities, women, aboriginal peoples; Employees, ex-employees or applicants external avenues of complaint, redress or education; National and regional union officials, labour councils and organizations; sometimes union locals if they see themselves "outside" the organizational structure; The media, journalists, investigative reporters; Government and administrative agencies (e.g. human rights commissions, the Employment and Immigration Commission); Academics, researchers, educators; Consultants in employment equity, human resources management, organizational effectiveness and change; Lawyers; Family, friends or peers of a champion or sponsor.
Champions	Employment equity practitioners, committees and task forces working for the employer; Human resource practitioners; Senior, middle and line managers; Legal counsel within the organization; Employees using internal avenues of complaint, redress or education; Union officials of the organization's bargaining units, or officials of employee associations if they perceive they can work effectively from within the organization.

Sponsors	Board of directors or elected officials;
	Chief executive or administrative officer;
	Senior management: individual or group;
	The manager or supervisor of a unit or
	work group aiming at employment equity
	change within that unit;
	The top human resource manager if he or she
	has organizational clout;
	Leaders of unions or employee associations
	if they can mobilize power, information and
	resources to effect change and commit the
	union or association to action.

The roles of sponsor, champion and advocate of change are not mutually exclusive: sometimes an individual or group may act in two or all three capacities, either on different issues or interests, in respect to different organizations, or over time. Government, for example, may act as the **sponsor** of employment equity change within its own departments and ministries. It may **champion** change within the broader public sector of education, health and local government. Or, it may act as an external **advocate**, pressing for change by the private sector. For most organizations, champions and advocates of change already exist, but sponsors usually need to be created. How to create sponsors of employment equity change is a key concern of this chapter. Box 9.2 highlights distinctions among sponsors, champions and advocates. The discussions that follow further explain and illustrate these three kinds of change agents.

BOX 9.2
Change Agents: Distinctions Between Sponsors, Champions and Advocates

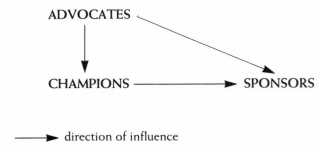

259

SPONSORS:

- The role of the sponsor is to take ownership of the change project and commit the organization, or an organizational unit, to action.
- They use their power, information and resources to support an organizational change process if they perceive an organizational or personal benefit. They are the only ones who can say "Go!" and thereby trigger implementation.
- Sponsors need internal champions of change to follow through with the implementation process once support and resources have been committed.
- Usually, sponsors need champions of change to inform them of the need for change.

CHAMPIONS:

- Champions are like advocates, but operate from within the organization.
- They have a dual role: 1) to identify the need for change, and 2) to follow through on implementation.
- The need for change is often brought to the attention of potential sponsors by an internal champion who interprets the external signs and pressures for change, or who acts as the conduit between external advocates and the potential sponsor.
- Champions do not have the power or resources to unilaterally approve the implementation of a change process.
- Their strength often lies in their understanding of the organization and its environment.

ADVOCATES:

- Advocates operate from outside the organization.
- Often they "spark" an awareness of the need for change in an organization by voicing support for employment equity goals and the implementation of employment equity activities, or lobbying for results.

Sponsors, such as top management, have power, information and resources. They will lend their support for the change process only if they reap some benefit from it for their organization or themselves. The stakeholder participation model suggests that the impetus for change to begin is unlikely to result from a rational strategic decision by the chief executive. Kniskern and Coll (1988) refer to "the catalytic value of crisis" in precipitating a decision to act on a problem that is big, messy (in the sense that several functions or departments are involved), long-standing, and expensive to solve. In such cases, experts and top management in the area of concern (the potential sponsors for change) may consider alternatives and even make recommendations as to preferred solutions, but nothing is decided until a crisis occurs — perhaps at the instigation of a manager or other actor (internal champion or external advocate) who feels the problem has festered long enough. Then a decision to act is taken on more or less intuitive grounds. As Kniskern and Coll (1988) put it, "Somebody has to take a deep breath and say 'Go!' — triggering implementation. This typically is where decision theory leaves off and management leadership begins." In reference to employment equity, the crisis that pushes top management or another sponsor to decide to act may be the prospect of a compliance audit, a human rights complaint, or media exposure of the organization's equity position.

Whatever the precipitating event, program implementation typically begins when top management takes ownership of the problem and commits the organization to action. The commitment is institutionalized in a policy, resources are allocated for implementation, structures are created for problem solving and action, and measures are adopted to make decision makers accountable for results. Measures to ensure accountability include a procedure for setting goals, reviewing the contribution each decision maker has made to reaching them, and arrangements for appropriate rewards and sanctions. Without accountability, change is unlikely to be taken seriously.

Change needs a sponsor, yet a sponsor needs an internal champion to implement the change and to identify the need for change or interpret in organizational terms the signals coming from advocates or from the external environment. Champions help the sponsor and other organizational stakeholders to understand their environment and cope with change occurring within it. A characteristic of effective champions is their understanding of their organization and its environment, what is changing, why and how. They also have a good sense of the advocates, or potential advocates, their hopes and expectations, who or what they are targeting for change, and how advocates may measure the organization's success or failure in bringing about change. Champions may come to understand and appreciate the range of strategies advocates may use to bargain for change and the compromises they may be willing to make. Advocates may be equally astute in coming to know the champion, his or her organizational environment and the negotiation strategies available to them.

Champions and advocates share many characteristics and frustrations. Both often have little power and few resources, at least not the kind that can say "yes" on behalf of the organization to the initiation of a large change process like employment equity. Yet both usually have far greater information sources and competencies than the sponsor. Information is their source of power and strength as change agents. Both champions and advocates will support the need for a change and argue in its favour, using information to provide a rationale for change. The main distinction is that champions operate from within the organization, while advocates bring their influence to bear on the organization from its external environment.

Employment equity practitioners are, by definition, champions of change. So might be the director of personnel who is assigned responsibility under the Federal Contractors Program for the implementation of an employment equity program that ensures the continued contractor bidding status of the company. A production supervisor interested in hiring people with disabilities into shop floor jobs may champion an outreach recruitment initiative, prepare co-workers to accept the new employees through awareness and training sessions, and seek the assistance of lead hands and the union shop stewards in integrating new workers into the work unit. A salesperson who sees a need for more minorities in sales and marketing may research and document his or her concern as a "business proposition" for the sales manager, opening the door for discussion and action.

Government policy makers and compliance officers are advocates of change with public and private sector employers, as are community groups and organizations of and for the employment equity designated groups. Indeed, the latter often call themselves advocacy groups. Union executives may play either a champion or advocacy role, depending on how closely they align themselves with the organization and its management. Within the union decision-making structure, union leaders will need to act as the sponsors of organizational change if internal action on employment equity is to gain a foothold with labour.

Champions benefit from the activities of outside advocates because it is often they who spark an awareness of the need for change, or who maintain a fine balance of uncertainty and support in order to sustain the change effort. Similarly, advocates need champions on the inside who can strategically identify, communicate with and influence sponsors to bring about the change objectives, processes, activities and outcomes they want. Sometimes an advocate may have direct access to a potential change sponsor. However, this is rare, and even when it occurs, unless the sponsor creates internal champions to nurture the desired changes, the organizational change process may wither and die since external advocates do not have the internal influence or resources required to motivate and sustain change.

All three change agents — sponsors, champions and advocates — have important roles to play in dealing with change. These roles may also change over time. Today's champion may be tomorrow's sponsor. A sponsor may then become a champion of the same or a different change initiative. For example, a manager sponsoring an employment equity training, awareness and goal setting process in her department may champion the development of a company-wide mentoring program designed to facilitate the integration and retention of women in supervisory and management roles. She may champion this company initiative by starting, under her sponsorship, a pilot project in her own area in order to demonstrate why this undertaking is of benefit and how to implement it. A small-scale "success story" in one pocket of the organization may trigger corporate buy-in from senior management, the interest of other middle managers, and pressure from junior women managers for expansion of the pilot. Kanter (1983: Chapter 7) illustrates this process with an example of pilot action groups that analyzed and devised new solutions for production problems at an assembly plant of a leading U.S. computer manufacturer.

Change agents may develop very close and complex working relationships among themselves. Their interfaces with other key stakeholders are equally important and will continue to develop as a change process evolves. The following experience of an employment equity officer working in a municipality illustrates the web of relationships among the different change agents and their complementary roles. The employment equity officer championed the building of an on-site day-care centre because, when asking community activists on women's issues what their measure of success was for the city's employment equity program, she was told that the start-up of a day-care centre at city hall was their goal: it would benefit working women as well as show support for workplace day-care. For these advocates, the visibility of a city hall work place day-care would be a positive model for other local employers, and encourage the city to negotiate on-site day-care in development applications for commercial and industrial building projects. Having been alerted to these concerns of community advocates, the employment equity officer knew she needed to cultivate internal sponsors for such a large-scale initiative. In particular, support was needed from influential members of city council who could mobilize a sufficient number of their political colleagues to vote the funds. Support was also needed from key senior administrators: including the personnel commissioner (her immediate supervisor); the commissioner of urban planning, through whom day-care might be included in development agreements; and senior public health and social service administrators who controlled many of the community day-care authorizations. The support of union officials who represent local government employees and bargain for the benefits available to such workers was also important. Thus, the employment equity officer needed to work collaboratively with a variety of community advocates and internal sponsors, and to secure support of other key stakeholders.

Triggering Organizational Change

Change may begin in many ways, as a result of any number of influences. The remainder of this chapter suggests a way to think about how large-scale change is triggered in organizations. We have conceptualized it as a process — one that appears linear and rational — so that change agents, especially the internal champions and external advocates of change, will be able to think through how they might "make a case" for change, or take advantage of "the catalytic value of crisis" in order to generate the support and leadership they require from change sponsors to institutionalize commitment for employment equity implementation. The four steps in this triggering process, leading to a commitment to organizational change, are outlined in Box 9.3.

BOX 9.3
The Triggering Process

REASONS FOR CHANGE: ORGANIZATIONAL STRESS
  Stress impacts on organizational:
              survival
              strategy
              success
          sponsor's self-interest

INTERPRETING THE TRIGGERING INFORMATION
  Sponsors and/or Champions interpret
  stresses on the organization using:
        historical comparisons
        planning comparisons
  extraorganizational comparisons
      expectations of stakeholders

BUY-IN: "FELT NEED"
      A "felt need" to change
          is perceived as
    a **Threat** and/or an **Opportunity**

TAKING ACTION
        A search for strategies to
          cope with the threat
                and/or
        maximize the opportunity

COMMITMENT
          The beginning of
        Commitment to Change

Change Needs a Reason

How often have you heard it said:

- "But they've just got to wake up and change. They can't continue to ignore what is happening."
- "I don't see how they can hold out any longer. Sometimes I can't believe such dinosaurs exist."
- "They'll have to change."

The truth is that no person or organization has to change. If change were mandatory in the face of "turbulence" then we would not have to dismiss someone for poor performance, and organizations would not go bankrupt because they failed to adjust to changing markets. The unfortunate reality is that people and organizations usually prefer not to change and may resist it even in the face of the threat of losing everything. Unplanned change may happen to the organization, but embarking on a planned change process is a choice that may or may not be made.

How then might change agents mobilize commitment to planned change? Sponsors need to be convinced that organizational success or survival is at stake, that current strategies to improve organizational performance will be hindered, or the sponsor's self-interest will be affected. Champions and advocates of change may find that their efforts spark a positive response from potential sponsors who are key decision makers when they explicitly link the power structure's awareness of the need for change with a stress — a source of uncertainty — in the environment. Such stress suggests to the potential sponsors that the status quo may not continue to fulfill their personal self-interest, their organization's definition of success, or their strategic plan — or that basic survival is threatened. Tichy refers to the impact of this uncertainty and stress as the "felt need" for change. Box 9.4 illustrates some of the events or activities that can create uncertainty or stress for an organization so that sponsors' commitment to employment equity change begins or is sustained.

BOX 9.4
Examples of Some Employment Equity Stresses on Organizations

SUCCESS

At a large public utility, line managers and human resource officers are beginning to witness a change in their applicant pool for semi-skilled, manual, clerical, technical and administrative jobs: more women and minorities are applying. Some of the line managers and supervisors are saying: "I've never hired a woman as a labourer. It's heavy, dirty work. Will she be strong enough?" "It's a real change for the guys to work with a woman, especially as their boss." "How do I assess foreign credentials?" "What if the public won't accept a Native women as a customer service rep?" The human resources department realizes that managers need education, guidance and problem-solving assistance if they are to carry out their selection and hiring responsibilities in a fair, legal and valid fashion. And if this doesn't happen soon, there's little doubt a manager will ask discriminatory interview questions and the company will get hit with a human rights complaint. Already human resource officers are finding managers making hiring decisions based on questionable — if not illegal — grounds.

SURVIVAL

A human services organization finds that its "mainstream" family counselling services are under criticism for displaying a lack of understanding of minority racial and cultural groups. Already two "ethno specific" community organizations, the Chinese Information and Interpreter Centre and the Indian Friendship Centre, have initiated family counselling services. The mainstream organization is concerned that its client base — and funding allocations — may be seriously affected in the future if this trend expands to other groups.

STRATEGY

Mandatory employment equity regulations under the Police Services Act are passed, requiring all Ontario police departments to implement an employment equity program. The initial plans are due in a year, and must include action plans as well as goals and timetables.

SELF-INTEREST

The deputy minister of a government department finds that appraisal of his job performance now includes successfully attaining a "diverse workforce" and ensuring the smooth implementation of employment equity goals.

SURVIVAL/STRATEGY

The customer base of the hospitality industry has shifted: now, more women, racial minorities and people with disabilities are travelling for business and pleasure. A hotel and restaurant chain has begun to hear voices of dissatisfaction from these groups regarding the services they are — or are not — receiving. The company is concerned that unless it moves quickly to prevent and deal with these complaints, it will lose business to competitors and suffer significant damage to its corporate image.

SUCCESS/STRATEGY

Retention rates of women who are customer service representatives at a national bank are dropping, particularly those who are 20 to 35 years of age with young families. Given the financial cost and time involved in recruitment, hiring, orientation and training, this high turnover is hindering the bank's ability to keep personnel costs within budget, and is therefore pulling down its profit indicators.

SUCCESS/STRATEGY

Fewer junior and middle management staff are prepared to transfer from one region to another unless career relocation assistance is provided to spouses. If this issue is not addressed, the company's management development and promotion plans will be undermined.

SUCCESS/SURVIVAL

Racial minority job candidates have been "chilled out" by newspaper stories that management and the unions have ignored incidents of racial harassment on the production line. Community activists are stepping up the media campaign and are considering a boycott of the company's products.

STRATEGY

A senior manager makes public comments about "the unqualified people we're being forced to hire because of employment equity." Minorities and women working in the company react by filing complaints of discrimination detailing the harassment and unequal treatment they have encountered.

SUCCESS

A national transportation company is proud of its demonstrated commitment to employment equity and the results it has achieved to date in eliminating barriers in its employment systems. Considerable time and resources have also been spent on management and employee awareness and education. Joint union-management problem-solving teams have been established, and the integration of members of the designated groups into work units is carefully implemented and monitored. However, the company is downsizing its operations, resulting in lay-offs, and infrequent hirings and promotions. Consequently, reports to government under the Employment Equity Act show little if any change in the representation of designated groups, whose participation is significantly below availability. On the basis of these reports, the Canadian Human Rights Commission issues an "invitation" to the company for an employment equity review — a process that will take considerable time, effort and resources of the company.

The impetus for creating or voicing a "felt need" for employment equity change appears to be grounded in four organizational "stresses": success, survival, strategy and self-interest. Understanding these four basic reasons for change helps champions and advocates of change to conceptualize how potential sponsors may decide whether to support the status quo, or to participate in a change process. The decision to support change may be triggered by information about some event, activity or perception that creates "uncertainty." It is then fed by a champion, advocate or advocate/ champion partnership until it grows into a "felt need" requiring a decision to undertake change. A crisis may speed up the process considerably! If a company is informed by the Federal Contractors Program that within thirty days they will commence an audit of the company's compliance with the eleven FCP criteria, then there may be immediate action on those items that, to date, have not received attention. Of course, some of the FCP criteria, such as the census, goal setting and the development of a workplan, cannot be done "over night." Nevertheless, the audit may act as sufficient stress for key sponsors, prompting the organizational commitment that has been lacking.

While *success*, like beauty, may well be in the eye of the beholder, we can think of it as the favourable outcome of an undertaking that results in attaining or accomplishing what we aimed for. Gaining commitment for working toward employment equity begins by defining what employment equity success might be for your organization or the organization you want to influence, as well as identifying the benchmarks of success the organization as a whole is aiming at, given its reason for existence. For example, the public utility wants to hire applicants who can perform effectively on the job. The ability of line managers to competently — and legally — assess candidates helps the com-pany achieve the productive work force it requires.

In contrast, organizational *survival* means to get through turbulence or crisis still intact as a viable organization. If a human services organization is unable to meet the needs of a more diverse community and client base, then it will not only be the focus of public criticism, but it will begin to lose large segments of its client base — and potentially its funding — to other organizations that are able to meet the needs of these clients.

An organization's *strategy* focuses on how to get from the present state or status quo to a desired organizational goal using routes, methods or processes preferred by the organization. The new mandatory employment equity regulations for police agencies in Ontario present such a challenge.

The example of the hotel and restaurant chain blends the survival and strategy stresses: its vision and corporate goal of excellent customer service will not be achieved and its business viability may be in jeopardy if the company is unable to adjust to changing markets.

Finally, one's own interests, whether professional or personal, are the *self-interest* footholds. The deputy minister, like any manager whose performance evaluation rests on the demonstration of results, has a clear interest in lending support to his ministry's employment equity initiatives.

Triggering Information

The dominant coalition — the potential sponsors of change — will use one or more of the following sources of information to determine whether there is sufficient uncertainty for them to consider changing the status quo: comparisons with the past, with the future, or with other organizations; or consideration of the expectations of key stakeholders (Tichy, 1983:152). The paragraphs that follow briefly describe and illustrate each type of triggering information.

- A **historical comparison** describes the difference between current performance and past performance. Only if relative performance gets worse over time will change be considered. For example, an airline's reputation as a good corporate citizen is shattered when allegations of sexist and racist hiring and promotion policies are substantiated. Or, a federal contractor's second audit by FCP shows a substantial decrease in the number of people with disabilities, indicating problems with retention and hiring.

- A **planning comparison** is the opposite; rather than comparing current performance with the past, it compares it with the future. Future projections must show that a change commenced today will maximize tomorrow's performance and outcomes. The Canadian Armed Forces identifies that, given the changing population and labour force demographics, they will need to employ more women in order to remain at full strength in the years to come.

- Unlike historical and planning comparisons, which use information internal to the organization, an **extra-organizational comparison** contrasts the performance of the organization with that of competitors — other organizations, usually within the same sector. Relative rather than absolute performance triggers consideration of changing from the status quo. For example, a board of education may not position itself as an employment equity leader, yet neither does it wish to be assessed as the least progressive board within that part of the province. As noted in Chapter 4, human rights commissions may use sector comparisons to initiate systemic complaints or review processes.

- Finally, the **expectations of key stakeholders** may prompt sponsors to undertake a change effort. Of particular relevance for employment equity change are people's expectations of equity, fairness and organizational responsibility for ensuring equality of opportunity. The early CAW/GM employment equity initiatives illustrate this. A GM worker, a woman, wrote a letter to the President of GM criticizing the company for "the blatantly sexist culture within its plants." The company and union then began talks on this issue, subsequently setting up a joint committee to study it (Sugiman, 1987: 1-2).

Stakeholder expectations may include the sponsor's own career self-interest: a large-scale change will create visibility, an asset for those who are seeking senior management status or peer recognition. For example, the CEO of a major auto parts manufacturer profiles himself and his company as an outspoken supporter of employment equity for people with disabilities. Tichy contends that managers often start change projects based on what they envision will be positive outcomes of the change for their own careers (Tichy, 1983: 152).

Sometimes sponsors do not stay around long enough to see the change through, especially if it is long-term. If this is the case, there may be little or no long-term commitment unless the early change processes yield positive results of benefit to the sponsor's career or reputation. A fire chief, scheduled to retire within the year, took a special interest in the hiring of the department's first woman firefighter. Yet he would make no commitment to support a comprehensive outreach recruitment strategy, review of selection criteria, validation of the physical testing used to assess firefighter applicants, or a cooperative planning process involving the firefighters' union. Because these initiatives would not result in change within the fire chief's tenure, it was not in his self-interest to support them.

Opportunity or Threat: A Matter of Perception

The relationships of change agents and the interpretation of triggering information may be complex in some environments. But the outcome may simply be a sponsor's perception of a threat, an opportunity or a combination of threat and opportunity, as well as a perceived need to respond in a timely and effective manner. It is not unusual for the same triggering information to be interpreted differently by different change agents. What is perceived as a threat by one is an opportunity for another. In written Chinese, "change" is represented as twin symbols: "danger" and "hidden opportunity." Mandatory employment equity legislation or regulations illustrates this dual perception. A regulatory requirement to submit work-force data and action plans, and the threat of government intervention, may be seen by a sponsor as a danger to "free enterprise" and a burden without benefit to the organization. For another sponsor, the same requirement may act as an opportunity to provide top management commitment, priority and budget for the development of an employment equity change strategy — one that will positively impact on the organization's productivity, human resources practices, and public image.

The Employment Equity Act may be perceived as a "danger" by some potential sponsors since it imposes requirements on the employer and no longer allows them to undertake employment equity on a voluntary basis. The sponsor's company must report to a government agency; open up information on its employment practices to the media and community activists; potentially submit to a review of its data and employment practices by one or more government bodies; and it may face a voluntary review and potential compliance action by a human rights commission (as discussed in Box 4.5). By contrast, employment equity laws may be perceived by a different sponsor as an opportunity to undertake the human resources programs and measures he or she may have wanted to enter into but was unable to gain organizational commitment to initiate until legislation made them mandatory. Some progressive human resources practitioners see mandatory employment equity as a means to elevate the strategic role and status of their function in the corporate hierarchy.

On the other hand, an advocate of employment equity change may see the same regulatory requirement as an ineffective government policy instrument: a "toothless tiger." Most advocates of the designated employment equity groups welcome legislation, as an opportunity for change, although some see "weak" legislation as a danger, appearing to bring about change in the work force, yet bogging down real movement toward equity in endless red-tape, volumes of complicated statistical reports, backlogged government agencies and compliance provisions which require reports and the filling in of forms, but little fundamental change. Hence, what is perceived positively by some advocates is a threat to equity for others.

Similarly, notice of an audit by the Federal Contractors Program may be secretly or openly welcomed by the organization's employment equity practitioners as an opportunity to "finally get things underway," to get the attention, priority, information and resources the program needs to effect change. On the other hand, such an audit may threaten and hinder some of the early change processes if the government agency emphasizes the collection of data and production of lengthy reports at a time when sensitive negotiations are underway by the employment equity practitioner with line management and the unions on goal setting.

As Rosabeth Moss Kanter (1983: 64) has stated:

> Change can be either friend or foe, depending on the resources available to cope with it and master it by innovating. It is disturbing when it is done to us, exhilerating when it is done **by** us. It is considered positive when we are active contributors to bring about

something that we desire, or at least to making something valuable out of what is inevitable — lemonade from the economy's lemons.

Staying ahead of change means anticipating the new actions that external events will eventually require and taking them early, before others, before being forced, while there is still time to exercise choice about how and when and what — and time to influence, shape or redirect the external events themselves.

Conclusion

To initiate and continue a large-scale organizational change process such as employment equity requires a commitment from key stake-holders. The commitment of power, information and resources to change requires three elements: change agents, a reason, and a search for strategies. Advocates or champions of change may begin the process by identifying a reason to move away from the status quo because some event or activity causes stress on the organization. This uncertainty is interpreted by the potential sponsor in relation to self-interest, an organization's need for survival, or a need for alignment with organizational strategy and success. The sponsor, perceiving the felt need as a threat, an opportunity or both, reacts by searching for strategies to cope with or take advantage of the need for change.

In attempting to move the organization towards buy-in we search for strategies to address the needs of designated groups and meet the employment equity goals of organizations. Once this search for strategies begins we have taken a major step toward securing organizational commitment to change. The change process has begun.

REFERENCES

Kanter, Rosabeth Moss. *The Change Masters*. New York: Simon and Schuster, 1983.

Kniskern, Hank and Joan Coll. "Decision Making, A Monday Morning View." Paper presented at the 1988 Annual Conference of Human Resource Management and Organizational Behaviour, Los Angeles, October 1988.

Sugiman, Pamela. "Affirmative Action at Work: The Case of the Canadian Auto Workers and General Motors of Canada," Queen's Park: Ontario's Woman's Directorate, Change Agent Project, 1987.

Tichy, Noel. *Managing Strategic Change: Technical, Political and Cultural Dynamics*. Toronto: John Wiley, 1983.

10

Practical and Strategic Issues for the Employment Equity Practitioner

ORGANIZATIONS EMBARKING upon employment equity often assign specific responsibility to someone within the organization. In our experience, such individuals often find themselves faced with what seems like an overwhelming task. This chapter is directed primarily towards practitioners who have been given responsibility for employment equity initiatives for particular organizations. If you are in such a position you may have already faced some of the challenges of making employment equity happen in your workplace, and realized that various stakeholders have different and sometimes contradictory expectations and perceptions of your role. In this chapter we offer some practical and strategic solutions that will help you to succeed as employment equity practitioner.

If you are an employer considering the selection of employment equity practitioners in your organization, you may find the information in this chapter useful in developing selection criteria and defining realistic expectations for these positions. We will also discuss the need for appropriate support for employment equity practitioners.

Profile of the Employment Equity Practitioner Role in Organizations

Typically, an organization advertises for, interviews and hires an employment equity "officer" or "co-ordinator" who is charged with the responsibility of implementing employment equity for the organization. The following advertisement appeared in the *Toronto Star* in January, 1991. The advertisement's apparent confusion of pay equity and employment equity, its emphasis on rules, enforcement and legislation, as well as the implication that a six month contract position is appropriate for an employment equity co-ordinator position, all signal a lack of understanding of the employment equity process. If the organization does not provide an effective framework for employment equity implementation, the chances for success are not great, however skilled or effective an individual practioner may be.

BOX 10.1
Advertisement for an Employment Equity Co-Ordinator

MAKING SURE EVERYBODY PAYS BY THE SAME RULES
That's why you're here. Here being XYZ, a progressive organization committed to enforcing employment equity right across the board. You'll be a key player in the game, and in fact, you'll help design it — co-ordinating the XYZ's Employment Equity Program under the direction of the Personnel Manager.

It's a challenge that'll fill every day of this **6-month contract position**. One that will test your knowledge of Employment Equity Legislation to the maximum. You're also an ideas person and a persuasive communicator — two traits you'll rely on to develop innovative proposals and make recommendations. As an experienced HR professional, you're familiar with Pay Equity legislation and the Employment Standards Act. And you're more at home in front of a word processor than a manual typewriter.

> Finally, you're a champion of equal justice - a firm believer that when you pay fair, everybody wins. In return, you can expect our full support, and of course, generous (but fair) compensation. Make the first move by sending a resume to ....., Personnel Department.
>
> (SOURCE: *Toronto Star*, Jan. 26, 1991.)

In some cases, the new employment equity appointee may have no human resource management experience, and perhaps only a scanty knowledge of what employment equity is all about. Sometimes a person already in the organization, usually in the human resources department, is given employment equity responsibilities in addition to those that she or he already holds. This person also may have little or no knowledge or understanding of employment equity issues. Sometimes an organization reassigns an employee who is not needed elsewhere to the employment equity position.

However, in the last few years the number of individuals with some knowledge and experience of employment equity has clearly grown and there is more general awareness of employment equity as an issue. Some organizations are also becoming knowledgeable about what constitutes a more accurate description of a practitioner's position.

BOX 10.2
The Employment Equity Practitioner's Job Description

> Each organization will need to decide what should be included in an employment equity practitioner job posting, depending on the organization's approach to employment equity implementation. The following suggestions may help to you to identify what is appropriate for your organization.
>
> JOB DESCRIPTION:
> * the organization's commitment to employment equity (with concrete examples);
> * reporting relationship and location in the organization
> * organizational support for the position, including resources
> * major functions/responsibilities of the role
> * expectations about interaction between the incumbent and other stakeholders

- expectations of the organization about outcomes
- term and compensation levels

In describing the desired qualifications of the applicant for the job, Box 10.8 may be useful.

What's Expected of the Employment Equity Practitioner?

Whatever the process used to select a person designated to take on employment equity responsibilities, there may be differing expectations of the role on the part of senior management, the other stakeholders that we have identified in Chapter 7, and not least, by the newly designated employment equity practitioner.

The Perspective of the Employment Equity Applicant

What attracts someone to apply for an employment equity position? The person may be socially concerned, with an interest in human rights issues and in working towards organizational change to bring about social justice. A strong commitment to the issues involved in employment equity is an important prerequisite for an applicant, and one which will help to sustain the employment equity practitioner through the challenging process of implementation in the face of resistance. However, the employment equity practitioner needs to understand how to move from a concern for social justice and fair play to a comprehension of what it means to be a change agent in an organization. This means that a practitioner needs to be able to think strategically, and to understand and work with the political process within the organization. Experience in advocacy work with the designated groups can also be invaluable.

An inexperienced employment equity practitioner may enter a new position with some misconceptions or unfounded assumptions. For example, a neophyte may assume that he or she is responsible for the success or failure of the employment equity initiatives, that the CEO's commitment means organizational commitment, and that resources are available. At the same time, she or he is probably aware that resistance to change will be encountered, and may have a somewhat negative view of union involvement, seeing labour representatives as potential adversaries rather than allies.

Top Management Expectations

Senior management may expect that the employment equity practitioner will be a trouble-shooter for the organization on employment equity issues who can keep the organization out of trouble with government and other external stakeholders. There may be an assumption that the practitioner will protect the organization against human rights complaints and charges; this involves policing organizational policies and practices to ensure that they comply with human rights codes. Human rights complaints within the organization may get routed to the employment equity practitioner — the only person who is expected to know how to deal with them. Furthermore, the employment equity practitioner may be seen as a buffer against the concerns and complaints of community or advocacy groups within and outside the organization. The employment equity practitioner's role may be questioned by those who wonder why he or she is being paid to make trouble. Or the practitioner may be expected to make the organization look good on employment equity issues. If the organization is involved in employment equity under government regulations or legislation, the role of the practitioner may be seen as that of a number cruncher, record keeper and reporter whose primary task is to comply with government requirements.

The practitioner may be expected to act as administrative liaison with all parts of the organization and to be the chief co-ordinator on employment equity issues. The practitioner's responsibilities may include writing an employment equity policy, managing corporate communications on employment equity, and developing training on these issues. The organization may also cast the practitioner in the role of "cultural interpreter" of the concerns and needs of the designated groups, or broker between the designated groups and the organization. Finally, the employer may expect the ultimate responsibility for employment equity outcomes to lie with the practitioner, with implications for a role in monitoring, policing and evaluation on an ongoing basis.

Expectations of the Human Resource Department

The human resources department may expect the practitioner to be a technical expert in every facet of human resources management, and lack of knowledge and expertise in these areas may undermine her or his credibility. At the same time, the employment equity practitioner may be seen as a trouble maker who wants to change systems that have been developed within the department over the years and to which there is a great deal of attachment. The practitioner may be seen as invading the human resources department's turf, and as an extra drain on its budget and time.

On the positive side, the human resources department may appreciate the practitioner as a source of needed expertise for the department, as well as a signal that the department is seen as a progressive and growing function within the organization.

Community/Advocacy Group Expectations

Sometimes the practitioner will be expected to act as advocate for the designated groups — a role that may be incompatible with some of senior management's expectations as outlined above. Designated group stakeholders may have various views of the role of the practitioner, depending on whether they are inside or outside the organization. Some external stakeholders see the practitioner as a representative of management's interests, or as a number cruncher and paper pusher who is out of touch with community issues and needs; such stakeholders may have an essentially suspicious and negative viewpoint. On the other hand, some members of designated groups within the organization may see the employment equity practitioner as the guardian of their interests, who advocates on their behalf and polices the organization on its progress towards equity outcomes.

Labour Expectations

Expectations may differ among various trade union or employee organizations inside and outside the organization. Some may see the practitioner as a mouthpiece for management, a spokesperson for "personnel," or a threat to the gains made through collective bargaining. Others may see the employment equity practitioner as an advocate for labour interests, who works through and with the union or employee association from the beginning of the process.

Clearly there may be a wide range of expectations and assumptions about the employment equity position. The appointee is typically expected to play multiple roles, only one of which is that of facilitator of change for the organization, and some of the roles may be in conflict with each other. Box 10.3 provides a list of the spectrum of possible roles. The key point here is that the level and nature of organizational commitment to employment equity is demonstrated by the expectations that the organization has of the employment equity practitioner.

BOX 10.3

Organizational Expectations
of the Employment Equity Practitioner

Change Agent
Enforcer
Advocate
Cultural Interpreter
Technician/Number Cruncher
Organizational Administrator/Coordinator
Personnel Expert and Administrator
Buffer/Broker
Trouble Shooter
Information Source

Reality Shock

The expectations of the employment equity practitioner and those of other stakeholders may not reflect the realities of the organization or of what it takes to implement employment equity. The clash between a new employee's expectations of a job and his or her actual experience after entering the organization can result in "reality shock" (Hall, 1976). Reality shock can arise from the organization's failure to use the abilities of a new recruit, from an absence of feedback on how she or he is doing, or from unrealistic hopes or expectations about the job's responsibilities, about the authority attached to the position, or about what can be accomplished. Regardless of the causes, the result can be the demoralization of the employment equity practitioner, and the possibility of ineffectual job performance or turnover in the position. An accurate and clear job description, and a realistic orientation to the organization, can help to minimize reality shock.

The Employment Equity Practitioner — Building a Strategy for Effectiveness

If we are to avoid the problems arising from unrealistic expectations of the employment equity practitioner's role, the role must be carefully analyzed. An examination of the employment equity practitioner's position, its place in the organization and the opportunities and constraints faced by the practitioner, will provide a basis for developing a strategic approach to the role and a clear understanding of how to perform it effectively.

The Employment Equity Practitioner's Placement in the Organization

We need to begin with a realistic assessment of the place of the employment equity practitioner in the organization, in terms of access to power, resources and expertise. For a variety of reasons, the employment equity practitioner is likely to occupy a relatively powerless position in the organization. If the position is new, or its term is limited, or the salary and authority attached to the position are low, it may carry little clout. Access to the power networks within the organization may be initially lacking, and the newcomer has yet to learn the explicit and implicit norms of behaviour and organizational culture. Defining the employment equity position as a specialist staff role may mean that it carries little decision-making authority — it may be only advisory. The position may carry responsibility but no real authority to act.

In a majority of organizations, the employment equity position is part of the human resources management team. This location has important implications for the practitioner's access to the power needed to bring about change. Traditionally, human resource management has been a relatively powerless function in the organization, playing a subordinate service role in support of the major thrust, which is to deliver goods or services (Sept, Westmacott, Agócs and Suttie, 1989: McDonough, 1986). Although the influence of the human resource function has increased in recent years, in many organizations its role may be perceived as dealing primarily with payroll and benefits, staffing and labour relations. The strategic role of the human resource department, and its long range contribution to planning for productivity, may not be recognized (Devanna, Fombrun and

Tichy, 1981; McDonough, 1986; Kanter, 1983; Burack, 1985). There has also been a lack of confidence among human resource professionals in moving beyond traditional service and support functions (McDonough, 1986: Sept, Westmacott, Agócs and Suttie, 1989). Yet we have seen that a strategic planning approach to employment equity is essential.

When the employment equity position is set within the human resources department, difficulties may arise when the practitioner needs to criticize from within. After all, employment equity involves scrutinizing and changing a wide range of traditional human resource management practices and policies. Employees who wish to complain about discrimination in the organization may find the physical location of the employment equity office in the human resources department somewhat problematic and be concerned about the confidentiality of their concerns. There may also be barriers to the employment equity practitioner's effectiveness inherent in human resource management systems. For example, the confidentiality of personnel records may mean that employment equity information about the work force is not available to stakeholders in the organization who are interested in influencing the process. In addition, the baggage of past experience in the relationship between labour and management, especially if this has been adversarial, is likely to have an impact on the role of the employment equity practitioner situated in the human resource department. If organizational change projects such as employment equity are to be effective in getting results, the defensive stance of some human resource departments toward unions and employee associations needs to be replaced by a cooperative approach that recognizes their right to be partners in the change process, and the legitimacy of their interests.

Nevertheless, the importance of the human resources management function to the implementation of employment equity change cannot be denied, and in organizations where human resources departments take effective responsibility for employment equity leadership and initiatives, the potential for success can be enhanced. In addition, there is growing recognition of the contribution that human resources management makes to the successful operation of organizations. To the extent that this is so, the human resources department may provide the equity practitioner with access to corporate decision makers, and to the exercise of influence within the organization. So despite some difficulties, the location of the employment equity position in the human resources department may be effective, since it will be essential to get support from the human resources department. It is imperative that the practitioner make a realistic assessment of both the assets and the liabilities associated with the position's location in the organization.

The Employment Equity Practitioner's Contract and Reporting Relationships

If the employment equity practitioner is not to be hindered by unrealistic expectations about the job to be done, all parties involved in defining and filling the position should be fully informed and consulted. It is also important to carefully negotiate the characteristics of the position including its placement in the organization, its term, compensation, and reporting relationship. These features of the position will provide the employment equity applicant with the information he or she needs to make an initial assessment of the extent of the organization's commitment to employment equity change.

If a contract has already been entered into, and it is clear that the employment equity practitioner and those to whom the position reports do not share the same expectations about the role, then it is important to start by analyzing the position as it is currently described and perceived, and to see what can be done. One option would be to renegotiate a more realistic contract. If that cannot be done, the personal costs attached to the position need to be assessed and the would-be employment equity practitioner may need to make decisions about whether it is advisable to continue in the position. Box 10.4 provides some suggestions about how the employment equity practitioner can clarify his or her role.

BOX 10.4

Clarifying the Role of the Employment Equity Practitioner

> "If the employment equity officer were operating in an optimally effective way, what would she be doing?"
> Clarifying role expectations and obligations may be critical for the short and long-term effectiveness of the employment equity

practitioner. How might this be done, given the often sensitive nature of the role, and the variety of stakeholders affected by the employment equity process?

An organizational development (OD) activity called **role analysis technique** may help the practitioner clarify her or his role. It aims to eliminate the ambiguity, confusion and conflict often associated with specialized roles. In a structured series of steps, the employment equity practitioner — in conjunction with key employment equity stakeholders, internal or external to the organization — defines and delineates the requirements of the role.

STEP 1: The employment equity practitioner examines her role, its place in the organization, the rationale for its existence, and its place in achieving overall organizational goals, along with the specific duties of the position.

Specific duties and behaviours are listed on flip charts, and discussed by the employment equity practitioner and the group of stakeholder representatives. Behaviours, responsibilities and duties are added and deleted until the group and the practitioner are satisfied that they have defined the role completely.

STEP 2: The next step examines the employment equity practitioner's expectations of the key stakeholders. She lists her expectations of the other roles that most affect her own role performance. These expectations are discussed by the group, modifying and supplementing the list until agreement is reached.

STEP 3: The third step examines others' expectations and desired behaviours of the employment equity practitioner's role: the key stakeholders describe what they want from and expect from the employment equity practitioner. Again, these expectations are discussed, modified and agreed upon.

STEP 4: A written summary is prepared by the employment equity practitioner of the role as it has been defined in steps 1 through 3. This role profile consists of:

-the prescribed and discretionary elements of the role,
-the obligation of the role to each other role in the group of key stakeholders, and
-the other key stakeholders' expectations of this role.

STEP 5: If the group wishes to analyze the other roles in the group, then the written role profile of the employment equity practitioner is first briefly reviewed before another role is analyzed.

For an employment equity practitioner seeking to work effectively with, for example, the other specialized roles in the Human Resources Department, this role analysis technique may help to clarify the mutual demands, expectations and obligations of interdependent stakeholders. Similarly, members of an employment equity committee may find it helpful to go through a role analysis process.

(Adapted from Wendell French, and Cecil Bell, Jr. *Organizational Development.* Englewoood Cliffs, N.J.: Prentice-Hall, 1984, 146-148.)

The authority and compensation attached to a position, and its term and arrangements for funding it, are critical to the employment equity practitioner's effectiveness. The location of the employment equity position in the hierarchy of the organization requires careful consideration. What is the source of the position's authority, and to whom will the incumbent report? Clearly, the employment equity practitioner needs support from senior management throughout the implementation process — support which includes highly visible commitment to the concept of employment equity as well as the allocation of necessary resources including funds, people, time, and access to organizational decision makers. This support is essential to validating the role of the employment equity practitioner as a change agent, and to giving it the necessary profile with all parts of the organization. Many experienced employment equity practitioners feel that the position should report to the highest level possible in the organizational structure in order to be effective. While this reporting arrangement may be a source of power, it also has its limitations. For example, the employment equity initiative may be identified too closely with senior management, and not receive commitment from the rest of the organization, including labour and designated group members.

One of the difficulties inherent in the employment equity role has been the way in which the position has been funded. In the public sector in particular, employment equity positions have been funded partly through government grants, for a one, two or three year period. Short term funding has led to short term approaches to implementation, and to a sense that the employment equity practitioner's role is a temporary add-on. The position is further weakened when experienced incumbents move on to more secure jobs, leaving yet another newcomer to start again. If the position is part-time, or if it is seen as temporary, there is little power or authority vested in it, and planning tends to be short term. One result has been a tendency for employment equity practitioners to focus upon implementing small discrete initiatives with high visibility, such as educational programs directed toward women that are intended to raise their consciousness of promotion opportunities, or to teach self-protection. While these projects may have their place in an employment equity process, they are not a substitute for an integrated, goal-oriented and strategic approach to implementation.

In order to be successful, an employment equity incumbent therefore needs to bargain for a position with an appropriate status in the organization. This will mean that the position should be a full time and if possible, a permanent rather than limited term contract position, and remuneration should be sufficient to give the job some credibility.

It will also be necessary to negotiate the resources necessary to support the work. A budget will be needed with some discretionary control over expenditures. Some of the major headings for budget items include support for the following needs:

BOX 10.5
Budget Requirements for Employment Equity

- administrative/clerical support
- adequate office space, which provides privacy for those with complaints of discrimination
- access to legal advice (general and specific to employment equity and human rights law)
- access to internal and external technical assistance for work-force census, statistical analysis, and database management
- training and development of staff
- specialized consultative assistance, for example, for policy development
- expert advice, for example, on barrier free design
- stakeholder consultations

We have mentioned the importance of investing the position with power and authority from the top of the organization. It is also important to look at the linkages between the position and the rest of the organization and the various internal and external stakeholders in the employment equity process. If a committee structure is already in place to deal with employment equity issues, it will be necessary to examine its role and composition. If there is no such structure, there will probably be a need to establish some kind of committee, as discussed in Chapter 8 and later in this chapter.

An employment equity policy and a realistic job description will define the mandate of the employment equity practitioner within the organization, and can be used to validate the effectiveness of the role. On a practical level, the practitioner will need to examine the differing expectations and responsibilities we have discussed above, and decide which of these can be delegated, which should be retained, and which should be eliminated. Decisions will have to be made on which expectations to meet at different times in the process, and this again emphasizes the need for strategic planning.

BOX 10.6

Key Elements in a Contract for an Employment Equity Practitioner Position

- reporting to a level in the organization that can deliver support and resources
- status of position, as defined by conditions of appointment (full time, permanent) and salary that confirms importance of position
- access to budget with some discretionary control
- recognized importance of stakeholder linkages and consultation
- authority to impact on human resource management and get support from human resources department
- access to corporate decision making and communication channels
- realistic job description, supported by employment equity policy framework

Building for Success

Essentially, the role of an employment equity practitioner should be that of a change agent, so we need to examine how the practitioner can play that role effectively. In the following pages we will look at how the practitioner can acquire information, expertise, resources and support to gain the organizational power necessary to be an effective change agent.

BOX 10.7

Strategies for Change Agents

* identify power tools
* mobilize information and build expertise
* mobilize resources
* mobilize support

Identifying Power Tools

Because the ability to effect change requires organizational power, the change agent needs to be able to access and exercise power in order to be effective. Kanter (1979: 61) suggests that "power is the capacity to mobilize resources, human or material," and that it can be used to "influence or shape organizational goals, policies and decisions," as well as to mobilize these resources to accomplish organizational tasks. As we have seen, change agents with employment equity responsibilities often have very limited capacity to exercise power within an organization. It is essential therefore that the employment equity practitioner address this issue by identifying accessible elements of power within the organization.

Organizational power tools include: "**information** (data, technical knowledge, political intelligence, expertise); **resources** (funds, materials, space, time); and **support** (endorsement, backing, approval, legitimacy)" (Kanter 1983: 159). How can the employment equity practitioner mobilize information, resources and support? In order to develop and build credibility in the organization the employment equity practitioner needs *information* in the form of expertise on employment equity issues, and on the organizational change process. Access to *resources* can be maximized by developing bargaining and negotiating skills, which are necessary in influencing the description of the employment equity position, the budget, the reporting relationship and the staff support. *Support* systems build on a network of people committed to employment equity. Developing support requires the employment equity practitioner to play a facilitative role, gaining allies by assisting stakeholders in attaining their goals.

Mobilizing Information and Building Expertise

In a strategic analysis of the employment equity role a high priority needs to be put on the information needs of the employment equity practitioner. Depending on the knowledge, skills and expertise that a practitioner brings to the job, various forms of information and skills development may be required. The knowledge, expertise and skills needed by the practitioner must be assessed, and a judgement made about what is a prerequisite for the position, and what can be learned.

BOX 10.8
Employment Equity Practitioner Profile

REQUIRED AREAS OF KNOWLEDGE
- employment equity issues, policies, and applications
- organizational change theory and practice
- familiarity with the business of the particular organization or sector in which the position is located
- human resource management (general knowledge)
- discrimination and disadvantage, and its manifestations for each of the designated groups
- human rights and employment equity legislation, regulations, and case law

REQUIRED EXPERTISE AND EXPERIENCE
- strategic planning
- understanding of organizational politics
- consultancy experience
- work with unions
- advocacy
- team building

PERSONAL ABILITIES AND SKILLS
- interpersonal skills
- negotiation, consensus building skills
- communication skills
- leadership abilities
- problem solving skills
- presentation skills
- ability to communicate commitment to human rights and equity principles

If the person is new to employment equity, it is essential that he or she has the opportunity to become educated and informed about the complexities of the issues and strategies for implementation. An employment equity practitioner needs access to formal training on employment equity through conferences, courses, seminars, workshops, audio visual and written materials. This process is also useful as a means to identify good training resources including learning materials, expert trainers, and consultants, which can be used later for educating the organization on the issues as well. Funding for training for the incumbent needs to be assigned as soon as the employment equity practitioner's position is created.

Employment equity networks recently established in cities across the country provide opportunities for practitioners to build professional expertise and to find support from others who are involved in the employment equity process. Free consultation on employment equity is also available through regional offices of the Canada Employment and Immigration Commission, and from some provincial agencies and human rights commissions.

On an informal level, the employment equity practitioner needs to find out about the political and strategic priorities of the organization, how planning occurs, which individuals have the power to influence decision making, and the impact of organizational culture on how the organization operates. The practitioner will also need to identify where to get needed expertise that is lacking, such as legal and technical advice (see Box 10.4). While some of this expertise can be found within the organization, some may have to be brought in from external sources.

Mobilizing Resources

As discussed earlier in this chapter, negotiating the responsibilities of the position and a reporting arrangement to the highest level possible in the organization, as well as a budget, staff support, and suitable office space, are critical aspects of mobilizing resources. It is also important to ensure that accountability for the success of the employment equity initiatives will not reside exclusively with the employment equity practitioner, but be integrated into the existing accountability structure, performance appraisal process and reward systems of the organization. For example, the employment equity practitioner may need to negotiate with senior management to ensure line management accountability for employment equity performance and progress within their responsibility areas.

Mobilizing Support

The employment equity practitioner's role should be seen as that of facilitator of change rather than the person who will single-handedly make the program happen. No single individual can be responsible for such a major organizational change process alone, without involving other stakeholders who can assist by providing expertise, knowledge, skills, and support for implementation of plans. The negotiation of a job description that stresses the facilitative and enabling role of the employment equity practitioner is therefore essential.

How the Employment Equity Practitioner Works: Developing a Collaborative and Strategic Approach

Throughout this book we have stressed the importance of a strategic approach to employment equity, and of stakeholder involvement. In order to be effective within this framework, the employment equity practitioner needs to:

- take a strategic planning approach that integrates employment equity into the way the organization does business and manages human resources;
- identify stakeholder interests in employment equity, and build on these to develop collaboration and support systems;

- develop knowledge, expertise and skills necessary for implementing organizational change designed to attain employment equity objectives.

1. Taking a strategic planning approach that integrates employment equity into the way the organization does business and manages human resources.

The employment equity practitioner should avoid getting sidelined into implementing an assortment of discrete and unrelated initiatives. It is important to develop and maintain a broad overview of the desired outcomes of an employment equity process. This involves setting specific initiatives within a context, and planning strategically so that initiatives complement and augment each other. An essential first step is to develop an integrated strategic planning approach. Such an approach involves identifying organizational needs for information, skills, and resources in order to implement employment equity, and arranging for the participation of all the stakeholder groups, as discussed in Chapters 7 and 8. In developing a strategic approach, the employment equity change agent will find ways of relating employment equity implementation to the business and human resource management priorities of the organization. As long as employment equity strategies remain separate from, and additional to, other systems in the organization, they will be ineffective in really making a difference, and in times of cutbacks and shifting priorities they will be competing for scarce organizational resources from a position of weakness. Employment equity needs to be seen as an integral part of the long term strategic vision of the way the organization does business, and employment equity measures need to be integrated into the organization's management of its human resources.

BOX 10.9
3M Canada — Strategic Planning

At 3M Canada, representatives from payroll, staffing, corporate information systems, benefits and other departments were invited to get together to consider a strategic planning approach to the management of human resource information over the next twenty years. The information that was needed obviously included data for

> employment equity purposes, which could also support decision making in relation to other human resource management issues such as training and human resource planning
>
> (SOURCE: 3M Canada presentation to the London Employment Equity Network).

For example, a company in the financial services industry wishes to develop new products directed towards members of the designated groups — market segments it has not traditionally served. An employment equity strategy linking the recruitment and development of a sales force and management group representative of the diversity of the population, to a broader corporate employment equity strategy, clearly makes sense. For a public sector employer such as a municipality or a school board, the importance of developing appropriate services for a changing population provides an impetus to recruit and promote members of the designated groups.

The employment equity coordinator's understanding of the needs of the organization in relation to its market or clientele can support a claim that employment equity should be an essential component in the long term business and strategic planning process of the organization.

2. Identifying stakeholder interests in employment equity, and building on these to develop collaboration and support systems.

Developing effective working relationships with stakeholders is a key strategic approach for employment equity practitioners. In Chapter 7, we identified stakeholders and examined examples of their interests in relation to employment equity issues. As we have seen, stakeholders have differing interests or stakes and these are not always compatible. How can the employment equity practitioner develop strategies that accommodate these different interests and needs, and which relate these interests to the process of implementing employment equity? Different stakeholders may need to be involved at different stages in the process, and in different ways, depending on their stake in a particular issue (see Box 10.10).

BOX 10.10
Stakeholder Consultation

Three examples of ways in which stakeholder involvement is essential to the success of employment equity implementation:
- diagnosis of the organizational climate for the designated groups includes consultation with members of the designated groups within the organization
- development of outreach recruitment strategies to improve representation of aboriginal peoples in the organization involves consultation and cooperative initiatives with representatives of the aboriginal communities outside the organization
- development of a more physically accessible workplace involves consultation with the physical plant department, as well as with internal or external representatives of people with physical disabilities, and experts who understand accessibility

3. Developing knowledge, expertise and skills necessary for implementing organizational change designed to attain employment equity objectives.

As suggested in Chapter 7, widespread participation in program implementation by those who know most about task requirements, stakeholder priorities and target group needs is essential to the success of an employment equity program. Therefore, involvement of stakeholders has to go beyond the creation of an employment equity committee.

Involving the Stakeholders — Creating an Employment Equity Committee

Involvement of the stakeholders in a cooperative and participatory approach can happen in many ways. One of the most visible ways of doing this is by establishing an employment equity committee on which the key stakeholder groups are represented. Committee members can become change agents within their own stakeholder groups, promoting the involvement of all sections of the organization in employment equity implementation. It is important that the committee be structured and integrated in ways that are consistent with and appropriate to the organizational culture. If committee work is seen as negative within the organization, then the usefulness of establishing such a committee needs to be examined. Other methods of involving stakeholders, such as task forces or planning sessions, may be more appropriate.

Setting up a committee of stakeholders has to be done skilfully so that it can be effective. For example, an employment equity committee may lack credibility if its membership consists of "acceptable" designated group representatives handpicked by the employer, or if it is closely identified with the personnel department. The committee's effectiveness may also be hampered if it is headed by an employment equity manager, or by a highly visible but token representative of one of the designated groups who has not been given the mandate or resources to be effective.

Some designated group members who are employees may not wish to act as change agents by sitting on an employment equity committee. They may not want to risk being identified with their "group" issues if the climate is not supportive of employment equity implementation. Or they may not be interested in the issues or not see themselves as representatives of a designated group. The committee's work may also be hindered by a lack of meaningful input from designated group members outside the organization. If the committee is isolated from potential allies both inside and external to the organization, it may be incapable of mounting a large scale program of change. In developing liaisons and cooperative ventures with representatives of designated groups, the practitioner needs to consider these possibilities.

Having set up a committee, it is important to give it the power, resources, mandate and information it requires to do its work effectively. It is likely that one of the primary needs of members of the committee is knowledge and understanding of the issues; hence resources for training will be required to develop the expertise of the committee members. In addition, the committee, in order to be effective, needs to develop some sense of mission. The mandate of the committee should be clearly defined, and realistic assumptions made about its role. For example, it is unlikely that an employment equity manager working with a small committee would have the expertise or time to deal with the task of redesigning job specifications in a variety of task areas, or to plan and implement a comprehensive accessibility strategy. However, the committee may play a key role in setting priorities for specific components of the employment equity program, in identifying issues for action, and in monitoring the success of the employment equity outcomes. The role of the committee may change over time depending on the stage in the implementation of the program.

Creating Task Forces

Another way of involving stakeholders is by establishing task groups that are responsible for various components of employment equity. Task forces are often used as vehicles for getting employees involved and participating in the change processes (Kotter and Schlesinger, 1979). This approach can minimize resistance and build commitment to employment equity initiatives (Somerset, 1989). For example, a task force might be set up to develop a plan for job sharing, or an organizational response to issues of sexual and racial harassment. However, as mentioned in Chapter 8, it is important that these tasks be seen within an overall strategic framework for employment equity implementation, and that linkages are provided between the overall vision, as defined and promoted by the employment equity coordinator and committee, and the work of the different task forces.

Developing Cooperative Approaches

Less formal means can also be used to involve stakeholder groups in various components of the employment equity process. For example, employment equity implementation involves data collection and maintenance, both at the beginning of the process and on an ongoing basis. Those responsible for employment equity will need to work with data experts in the organization, and to develop cooperative ways to communicate their data needs and to arrive at common understandings of terminology (Harvey, 1988). Employment equity coordinators and human resource professionals may need to work at increasing their level of comfort with data collection, analysis and reporting in order to take advantage of the strategic planning tools which employment equity data provide.

Conclusion

The role of the employment equity coordinator is an extremely challenging one, and failure may be built into the role if expectations of the position are unrealistic and structural arrangements are inappropriate. Burn-out is an occupational hazard, and a practitioner needs to know how to assess the chances of success, and how to make tough decisions about personal survival when it is clear that even the best planned strategies will not be sufficient to overcome organizational resistance.

Opportunities for success will be enhanced if employment equity practitioners negotiate a realistic job description supported by adequate resources and senior commitment at the outset. Effectiveness in the position will be improved by promoting and maintaining an overall vision for the outcomes of employment equity, a strategic plan for implementation, and the involvement of stakeholders internal and external to the organization. The outcomes of this approach are likely to be reduced levels of resistance to change, and greater understanding and acceptance of an employment equity corporate perspective. In Chapter 11, we will examine how the employment equity practitioner can use communication, education and negotiation to further enhance the success of the implementation process.

REFERENCES

Burack, Elmer H. "Linking Corporate Business and Human Resource Planning: Strategic Issues and Concerns," *Human Resource Planning*, 8, 1985, pp. 51-67

Devanna, Mary Ann, Charles Fombrun, and Noel Tichy. "Human Resources Management: A Strategic Perspective," *Organizational Dynamics*, Winter 1981, 51-67.

Hall, Douglas T. *Careers in Organizations*. Pacific Palisades, Calif.: Goodyear, 1976.

Harvey, Edward B. *Information Systems for Employment Equity*. Don Mills: CCH Canadian Limited, 1988.

Kanter, Rosabeth Moss. "Differential Access to Opportunity and Power." In Alvarez, Rodolofo, Kenneth G. Lutterman, and Associates, *Discrimination in Organizations*, San Francisco: Jossey-Bass Inc. Publishers, 1979

Kanter, Rosabeth Moss. *The Change Masters*, New York: Simon and Schuster Inc., 1983.

Kotter, John P., and Leonard H. Schlesinger. "Choosing Strategies for Change." *Harvard Business Review*. Vol.V. No.2, 1979, pp. 106-114.

McDonough, Edward F. "How much power does HR have, and what can it do to win more?" *Personnel*, 63, 1986, pp. 8-11.

Sept, Ron, Penny Westmacott, Carol Agócs, and Peter Suttie. "Human Resource Information Systems: Organizational Barriers to Implementation." *Journal of Management Systems*, 1989, 1(2), 23-33.

Somerset, Felicity. "The Employment Equity Process and Human Resource Management as an Agent for Change." *Industrial Relations Issues for the 1990's.* Proceedings of the 26th Conference of the Candian Industrial Relations Association, Quebec, June 1989.

11

Dealing
with
Resistance

I N CHAPTER 10 we presented the employment equity practitioner's role as that of a change agent who is a strategic planner, visionary, facilitator, and coalition builder. However, employment equity change agents almost always encounter resistance. It is now time to discuss several strategic approaches to dealing with resistance to change in an organization.

We will examine what resistance is and why it occurs; how to identify and diagnose it; how to analyze its strength; and how to develop preventative and remedial strategies to reduce it. We will describe how communication, training and negotiation can be used to respond effectively to resistance. A key premise of this discussion is that stakeholders need to be involved in changes in which they have an important interest.

What Is Resistance?

Resistance to organizational change might be viewed as behaviour that blocks or works against changes that are part of an organization's efforts to implement its own policies, or to comply with legal requirements to which it is subject. We would not consider neutrality, disagreement or criticism to be resistance; indeed, criticism is instrumental in identifying weaknesses of change proposals and making them more effective.

Resistance may manifest itself as active opposition, avoidance or denial. Active opposition can be vociferous at times and can come from many different directions. It might be expressed strongly and overtly in public and in private by those who cannot accept diversity in the workplace. Resistance can be expressed at meetings or training sessions devoted to employment equity issues, by graffiti in public places, through harassment of members of the designated groups or of change agents, or by the deliberate blocking of opportunities of individuals from the designated groups.

Resistance can be demonstrated by avoidance or refusal to participate in the process by individuals or groups who may not show up for meetings, refuse to respond to legitimate requests for assistance or information, or relegate employment equity issues to the lowest level in a hierarchy of priorities. Individuals may resist specific parts of the employment equity process, for example, by choosing not to respond to the work-force audit, or by not attending training sessions.

There may be refusal to admit that discrimination exists, or denial that people in one's own workplace experience it. For example, the study *No Discrimination Here* (Billingsley and Muszynski, 1985) found that almost half of the 199 employers interviewed emphatically denied the existence of discrimination or racial problems in their organizations. Some people may acknowledge that discrimination exists, but deny that change can happen, or that it is worth trying to implement. They may defend their positions with statements like: " That's just the way people are," or "That's what our customers expect." Individuals may deny any personal responsibility for eliminating discrimination or refuse to acknowledge their privileged positions and feel that any threat to such privileges would constitute oppression or unfair advantage. This attitude often reveals itself in comments about "reverse discrimination" or " political correctness."

What Are the Sources of Resistance?

Box 11-1
Some Sources of Resistance

- misunderstanding, lack of information
- attitudes and values counter to employment equity principles, and a perception of support for those values by the group
- self interest of those who are privileged by the existing system, and have something to lose by changing
- discomfort with change itself, and lack of sufficient rewards for changing
- divergent views on how change should be implemented
- lack of enforcement of sanctions for those who resist, or who fail to carry out policy or laws
- lack of credibility of change agents

Misunderstanding and Lack of Information

Resistance may be based on misinformation or inadequate information about the purpose or direction of change, which creates misunderstanding about what is going on, or about what is involved in implementing employment equity (Billingsley and Muszynski, 1985). Resistance is often based on fear about the consequences of change; some of this fear may stem from misinformation about what change involves and what the new picture will look like.

Attitudes and Values Counter to Employment Equity

In an increasingly diverse labour market and workplace, resistance may be based on feelings of difference between "them" and "us," and anxiety about contact with others who are different. For example, men may be concerned about reporting to a woman in management, or a wife may be concerned about her husband working closely with women. There may be discomfort with different cultural values or languages, or deep-seated stereotypical, prejudiced and racist attitudes about racial minorities and aboriginal peoples. There may be skepticism about the ability levels of people with disabilities, and feelings of discomfort about how to behave towards such employees. These attitudes are real to the people who have them, and need to be taken seriously. When there is a *perception of support* for values counter to employment equity principles by the group, then group norms will support resistance.

Members of the designated groups may resist out of a concern that attention to designated groups in the organization singles them out and makes them vulnerable to backlash or unfair treatment. There is also resistance if designated group members perceive themselves to be used as "tokens" or official representatives or spokespersons of their group.

Resistance to Change by the Privileged

As individuals or as members of groups, people are likely to resist change if they perceive that it threatens their interests and they may engage in various forms of collective resistance to protect their interests. Resistance may occur because organizational change within an employment equity context is a challenge to the status quo and to existing positions and relationships of power and influence within the organization. For example, individual employees may feel anxiety about the effect of employment equity initiatives on their future career development, or they may resist because they fear being challenged for promotion opportunities. When resistance is substantive, that is, based on interests that groups or individuals want to protect, rather than on misunderstanding, information will not dispel the problem. This kind of resistance to change is much harder to deal with.

Discomfort with Change and Insufficient Rewards for Change

Because change is seen as a threat to the way in which things are "usually" done, it is often resisted simply because it proposes a different way of doing things. There may be concern about not having the skills to do well in the new environment. For example, supervisors may not feel confident about supervising a more diverse work force.

If individuals do not perceive the benefits of change for themselves or for their group, if change does not have senior management support, and if there are no rewards for compliance or sanctions for failure to comply, behaviours that signify resistance to change may appear to be validated by the organization.

Divergent Views on How to Implement Change

Resistance may arise from a perception that change is too fast or too slow, or from concern with the ways in which the change is taking place. Members of designated groups, both internally and externally, may feel that progress towards equity is not visible enough, or that change is not moving fast enough or in a direction that is acceptable to them. If so, they may oppose the change process or choose not to participate.

Sometimes resistance to participation in change is encountered because a stakeholder is concerned about being co-opted into the process. This may be particularly true of representatives of the designated groups, who fear that they may lose their ability to act as critics of the process and the equity outcomes if they are part of it. Accepting the legitimacy of this kind of resistance may be a constructive response, and may create an important watchdog role for monitoring progress towards equity.

Lack of Credibility of Change Agents

If those who take on the role of change agent within the organization have little credibility because they lack power, resources, personal abilities, or commitment, the change process will not be taken seriously. In particular, if senior management does not prove its commitment publicly and by the allocation of resources, the credibility of its endorsement of the organization's progress towards employment equity is suspect.

Diagnosing Resistance

Disagreement is not necessarily resistance, and it can be functional and productive. It is important to identify whether the disagreement is over the best way to achieve employment equity objectives, or whether it is resistance to equity itself. Negotiation between the opposing views of different stakeholders may result in a pragmatic solution that contributes to effective equity outcomes. However, the practitioner needs to recognize non-productive resistance, realize that it prevents further progress, and examine means to counter or circumvent it.

Identifying who is likely to resist, why, and with what intensity is an essential first step in developing strategies for dealing with resistance. It is therefore important to identify stakeholder interests, which we discussed in Chapter 7, and to identify the resistance points for each group. Stakeholder mapping to record likely responses to the issues can be a useful step (Benick, 1989). However, it is important not to oversimplify the issues for any one stakeholder, and to recognize that there will be different views and interests within stakeholder groups, and that the issues are likely to change over time and at different stages in the development and implementation of an employment equity program.

Resistance can also develop into a self-reinforcing cycle. The diagnostic approach tries to predict when resistance will emerge as an overt impediment to the change process. There may be a critical point in the process where the strength of opposition to an initiative itself generates further resistance.

Developing Strategies for Preventing and Reducing Resistance

Diagnosing the sources, forms and potential impact of resistance allows the practitioner to develop appropriate strategies to deal with the different manifestations of resistance. Ongoing diagnosis may lead the practitioner to change the action plan.

A portfolio of strategies to deal with different kinds and sources of resistance will need to be developed. The type of intervention, and the timing, will be important components of strategy development. For example, effective communications that give clear, consistent and timely messages can dispel myths and misinformation about the process. Employees and supervisors need to be reassured that their concerns and anxieties will be addressed and that their education and training needs will be met so that they acquire the knowledge and skills to operate successfully in the new environment.

A change process involves real conflicts of interest. Dealing with conflicts of interest is not just a matter of information and communication, since the correct information, however well communicated, may still be unacceptable to some stakeholders. The negotiation and bargaining approaches discussed later in this chapter are essential here. In addition, rewards for implementation of equity processes, and sanctions for non-compliance with procedures that have been agreed upon, are important for dealing with entrenched resistance.

In the following paragraphs we will examine ways in which communication, training, bargaining and negotiation can be used to reduce resistance and contribute to effective employment equity implementation.

Communication Strategies

Essentials for Effective Communication

In any organization going through change, rumours run rife. The less information people have about what is happening, the more confused and uncertain they are, and the more morale will suffer and resistance to change increase. Uncoordinated, piecemeal communication attempts can make things worse.

It is important therefore to take a strategic goal-oriented approach to communicating about employment equity issues. The general goal for a communication strategy should be that it contributes to the effective implementation of equity within an organization.

Attention needs to be paid to informal as well as formal patterns of communication. Formal communication may be through messages from key sponsors in the organization, for example the CEO or the president of a union, using memos, newsletters, videos, bulletins and public address systems. Communication about change initiatives also takes place informally, for example, at the water fountain, over coffee breaks, through person-to-person telephone calls, in the elevator, or over lunch.

Making Employment Equity Visible

A communication strategy should enhance the credibility of the message and the message giver. Kanter (1979: 63) has suggested that visibility is one of the bases of power within an organization. Publicity and the extent to which activities are known and interesting to others affect visibility and power. It makes sense for the employment equity co-ordinator to make effective use of the communication channels within an organization to raise the profile of employment equity initiatives.

Communication on employment equity issues needs to be integrated into existing formal and informal communication arrange-

Box 11-2
Example: Middlesex County Board of Education

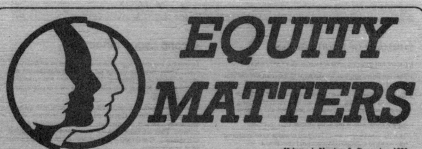

EQUITY MATTERS

Volume 1, Number 2 December 1990

BOARD APPROVES GENDER EQUITY ACTION PLAN

At its 1990 11 05 meeting, the Board of Trustees approved a comprehensive employment equity action plan. Subtitled "Towards Gender Equity--Responsible Management of Change," the plan is a blueprint for achieving employment equity for women in a manner that is proactive, reasonable and fair.

This issue of *Equity Matters* highlights the employment equity plan. If you would like more details, a copy of the plan is available in each school's equity resource binder, or can be obtained from your employee group's representative on the Employment Equity Advisory Committee.

Policy 400-26, Employment Equity

The Board, recognizing the importance of effective personnel practices and hiring procedures that develop and utilize the potential of all employees for the benefit of the pupils within the system, is committed to Employment Equity and establishes the following policy.

I The Board will seek out and remove systemic and attitudinal barriers to employment opportunities that have a discriminatory effect against any qualified individual, particularly women, aboriginal people, visible minorities and persons with disabilities.

II The Board will adopt special measures to seek out, support, and promote qualified individuals in these targeted groups in a results-oriented employment equity plan.

III The Board will extend the philosophy of this policy to benefit the pupils within the system.

This policy will be administered by the Director of Education or designate.

Approved 1989 07 10

AUTHORITY FOR THE PLAN

An action plan is a vital component of the employment equity management process, and also a requirement of the Board's employment equity policy, which was approved in July 1989. The policy affirms the Board's commitment to employment equity for women as well as other designated groups.

The Ministry of Education has directed school boards to develop employment equity policies for women and programs to increase female representation in supervisory officer, principal and vice-principal positions (by panel) to 50% by the year 2000. The goal for all other occupations is 30%. Policies and plans are to be submitted to the Ministry by the end of 1990.

KEY FEATURES OF PLAN

The plan presents gender equity goals which address four focal areas: employment policies and practices, women's status in the system, students, and the equity program's administration.

Strategies have been developed in support of each goal. These include special measures regarding the employment and promotion of women, and numerical hiring targets. Monitoring and evaluation procedures are also specified.

The plan is supported by data from a preliminary equity audit conducted last summer.

ments. Formal communication vehicles might include an employment equity logo, posters, newsletters, bulletin boards, videos, and direct mail. Personal contacts can promote the employment equity process and create interest in it.

Communication to Provide Information

Resistance to some employment equity initiatives may occur if people lack information and understanding regarding the activity. For example, the implementation of a work-force audit requires an appropriate communication strategy to deal with resistance that might produce a low level of participation and results that are of little use in planning an employment equity program.

There is often misunderstanding about why a work-force audit or census is being carried out, about what use will be made of the data, and about its confidentiality. There is also a need to stress the legality of the process of data collection, to counter misunderstandings that such data collection is against human rights codes.

Some of the companies and public sector organizations involved in data collection have rightly spent a great deal of time on communication, and have involved union and employee association representatives in the development of the communication plan in order to promote a high response rate (Box 11.3). One technique is to give the census a catchy name, such as "I Count" (Ontario provincial government), or "Count Me In" (GM Canada).

Involving Stakeholders in Communication

Different stakeholder groups need to be involved in communication where appropriate. For example, if an organization is developing a pilot project for outreach recruitment to aboriginal applicants, it will be important to involve key aboriginal stakeholders both inside and outside the organization in the development of internal and external communications about this project.

Two-way communication about change is important, hence communication approaches that are creative and new to a specific organization may need to be developed. Kleiman (1989: 110) suggests installing a hotline, holding small group meetings to disseminate information and running focus groups to give employees a chance to discuss their reponses to changes. Communication vehicles for the employment equity census may include a hot line to answer queries and concerns, information meetings to prepare employees for the census and to answer their questions, wide distribution of written information presenting commonly asked questions and answers, and the training of management and labour representatives to answer concerns within their areas. All these measures help to reduce anxieties and to produce a good response rate by taking employees' concerns seriously and dealing with them.

Delivering a Consistent and Accurate Message

Communication strategies should reflect the principles of equity that they promote, so that there is consistency between the message and the media by which the message is conveyed, as well as accuracy.

In communication to promote a work-force audit there will be a need to address potential anxieties about the use to which such data might be put. Communication should be more than symbolic: it is important that sound procedures are in place for the work-force audit, and these need to be explained. "Confidentiality" is more than just a word: employees need to know what is being done to ensure that confidentiality is being maintained. The fact that the census is "voluntary" needs to be emphasized, according to the regulations of human rights codes, yet the need for participation in data collection also needs to be explained in the communication package.

In published communications about the census, it is beneficial to strike a balance between messages that "this information is important," and an overly glossy presentation that may lead to accusations of excessive resources being given to employment equity at the expense of other projects.

All communication materials produced by the organization for any purpose should reflect the message of diversity within the workforce in a positive way, without any stereotypical, discriminatory or condescending overtones. Biased language should not be used, and pictures of people from the designated groups should portray them in an accurate and equitable manner, for example, in executive as well as support roles. However, if the organization is not diverse in its employee base it may be important not to communicate a misleading image, until some diversity has been achieved. Organizations implementing employment equity have been known to advertise in ways that promote an image that does not in any way acknowledge diversity either in its work force or its clientele (see Box 11.4). This can happen when an overall communication plan is lacking and the focus is on communication about single initiatives, or when employment equity is not integrated into the corporate communication system.

BOX 11-3
Census Questionnaire Introduction

The UNIVERSITY *of* WESTERN ONTARIO

March, 1990

This is the census questionnaire for Western's Employment Equity Program. Its purpose is to establish a data base determining the levels of representation in the university workforce of racial minorities, persons with disabilities, persons of aboriginal ancestry and women.

The university is required to gather and maintain this information under the terms of the Federal Contractors Program for employment equity. In addition, it will be used in the development and monitoring of equity programs here at Western. We are also asking for information on first language in anticipation of provincial legislation. As well, a separate questionnaire on each respondent's level of education is included.

The Census Makes Sense is the theme we have chosen. All the information which you provide will be treated confidentially, and will be used only by those given special access in order to implement and monitor equity programs. As you read further, you will find a Code of Confidentiality which describes the safeguards developed to protect your rights and confidentiality of the data.

The Executive Committees of each employee group at the university have approved this information-gathering exercise. Their statement of support appears on the next page.

This project has my strongest personal endorsement. It is an essential step in an important program of change in the management of human resources at Western. I urge you to take the time to complete and return the enclosed brief questionnaire.

K. George Pedersen
President and Vice-Chancellor
The University of Western Ontario

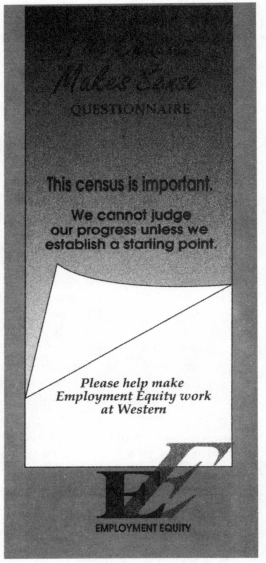

This census is important.

We cannot judge our progress unless we establish a starting point.

Please help make
Employment Equity work
at Western

EMPLOYMENT EQUITY

Communications should be made available in all relevant languages as well as in forms useable by the visually impaired. Communications may also need to be distributed to a much wider audience than the organization has traditionally tried to reach. For

Box 11.4
What Is This Ad Communicating?

The following text was part of a full page advertisement in the
Globe and Mail. It accompanied a photograph of a white male
executive in a busy office setting. He is looking confidently out at
the reader.

**THESE GUYS CAN
MAKE 500 DEALS
AN HOUR ON
WALL STREET.**

**BUT GUESS WHO
THEY RELY ON
FOR TRANSACTION
PROCESSING.**

For them seconds
mean the difference
between making a killing, or a dead loss. But,
whichever way the deal goes, they rush on to the next
'gentlemen's agreement'.

Code of honour or not, the deals aren't complete
until credit ratings are checked and transactions
processed.

That's where the dealers rely on us. Our lines feed the
boys in the States with data about Canadian clients.

Only our dealers are kept too busy making money to
have to worry about details.

---

example, organizations advertising jobs should not limit the posting to one daily newspaper but should communicate these opportunities through a larger number of outlets as part of their outreach efforts to recruit members of the designated groups.

Since all communication within and emanating from an organization should reflect diversity, and effectively demonstrate commitment to equity, staff will need to be informed and to understand the sources of bias in communication, whether using language or pictures, in order to prevent it. This requires linking complementary communication strategies with training and development in order to assist staff in learning to communicate without bias. Some organizations, such as Ontario Hydro, have produced resource materials to assist employees to communicate equitably.

Education and Training

Why Use Training and Development in Employment Equity?

Training and development issues are receiving more attention within organizations in response to the need for a more skilled and flexible work force. Bernhard and Ingols (1988) have suggested that training is a short term response to the needs of an organization and the individuals within it, and that staff development might be a more productive way of looking at organizational and individual needs: "Development is long-term and future oriented ... development broadens people and gives them new perspectives." The long range goal of employment equity training for individuals and the organization as a whole is the development of employees who are skilled in working in a diverse environment.

Attitudes of individual employees as well as values underlying the corporate culture need to be addressed by training initiatives. Employees typically lack knowledge and understanding of the disadvantage and discrimination encountered by members of the designated groups, and will almost certainly lack the skills and the organizational awareness needed to bring about employment equity change. Employees involved in employment equity need assistance in identifying and understanding systemic barriers and the opportunity to participate in developing new and more equitable employment practices. In addition, employees need to practice new behaviour patterns and skills until they become familiar.

There may be a perception that training is *the* answer to bringing about change in the organization. Yet training has its limitations. To expect that training can change employees' attitudes that have developed over a lifetime is unrealistic. These attitudes often reflect and are supported by the systems under which society and organizations operate, and organizational cultures often reinforce many of the stereotypical attitudes we hold. Nor can training by itself change systemic discrimination: remedies for systemic discrimination result from changing the systems that are discriminatory. Sometimes organizations use training as evidence that they are involved in "managing diversity," but when training is introduced as a stand-alone initiative without a context of commitment or structural support within the organization, its success is limited. It is unrealistic to expect that a "one shot training fix" will solve the problems within an organization, or be enough to ensure effective employment equity implementation. Such approaches achieve very little and can do more harm than good.

Appropriate training can be an important tool in employment equity implementation because it can raise awareness of the issues, provide information, impart skills, and allow the participants to work together to develop relevant organizational change measures. In order to do this, training needs to focus on changes in behavior and systems that will support and promote changes in attitudes and organizational culture over time. Done well, training can develop a shared understanding among employees of what employment equity means and a common language for dealing with implementation issues. Both communication and education can help to change corporate values to make the organization a more appropriate environment for a diverse work force.

Taking a Strategic Approach to Training

Rosenberg (1990:43-44) has suggested that "training for training's sake" is not generally effective. Rather, best results are obtained when training and development programs are related to identified strategic needs, and integrated with other human resources programs.

If training is to be used to support the major organizational changes required for the implementation of employment equity, then it is clear that the objectives of training must be directed towards organizational change. Training needs to be planned in a manner that recognizes the complexity of the task, the needs of the employees within the organization, the importance of the organizational commitment to the outcomes of training, and the limitations of the training initiative itself. Above all training is only one approach to organizational change: it should be closely integrated into the broader strategic plan for change. The goals and objectives of training, the participants, the trainers, the timing and duration of training and the content of training must all be placed within this wider perspective.

Identifying Training and Development Needs

A strategic approach to training includes an analysis of the training needs of the organization and the individuals within it. The first question to ask is, what does the organization want to achieve as a result of training? The responses to this question will dictate the shape and forms of the training approaches. How does the training fit into the overall development and implementation of the employment equity program? This will give guidance on the timing of the delivery of the various training components, who should receive training at various stages, and in what. Decisions might be made about what educational approaches are needed to introduce equity concepts within an organization, and about what training might be needed to support the collection of work-force data, the initiation of new recruitment measures, or the diagnosis and removal of systemic barriers for the designated groups.

Questionnaires, focus groups, informal interviews and meetings can be used to identify the concerns and fears of employees about employment equity. The needs analysis precedes and guides the development of strategies and agendas for training and development that are appropriate and relevant to individuals, and that address the key issues for the organization. A needs assessment can also assist in securing organizational and individual commitment to, and involvement in, the training process and outcomes. Before beginning the training it is important to develop clear goals and objectives and an evaluation process to measure its success.

Box 11.5
Defining Clear Goals and Objectives for Training

In 1985 in the United Kingdom, the Austin Rover Group companies and unions undertook a formal Agreement on Equality of Opportunity. This agreement included the phased-in implementation of a monitoring process, preceded by a training program for all employee representatives, managers and supervisors.

The objectives of this training were that by the end of the training, all participants would be able to:

- identify direct and indirect discrimination on grounds of race, sex or marital status;
- state the TUC and company policy on equal opportunity and the introduction of monitoring;
- outline the main provisions of the legislation on equal opportunity and the consequent obligations on individuals, companies and trade unions;
- understand the background to the Agreement between the companies and the trade unions;
- explain the purpose of monitoring and its introduction to the companies;
- outline the process and timetable for the introduction of monitoring to their plant;
- explain the role of joint plant-level committees and the companies' Joint Negotiating Committee in reviewing the results of the monitoring process;
- answer questions most frequently raised by employees concerning the introduction of monitoring, and know where and/or to whom to refer the more difficult questions; and
- state the role of the Joint Steering Committee in the introduction of monitoring to each plant.

The objectives of this training program are clearly stated and focus on the knowledge and understanding needs of the participants.

(SOURCE: Commission for Racial Equality, *Training: The implementation of equal opportunities at work*, Volume Two: Case Studies, London, 1989, 5-6. 11-4.)

Even if external consultants or other resources are used to deliver employment equity training, internal human resource departments and training units need to be involved in the development of the training process so that their "buy in" is assured. As far as possible, the training should be situated within the organization's overall approach to training and development, and build on the skills development already taking place. At some points the training may be specific to equity issues, and stand alone, while at other stages, equity issues may be integrated into every kind of training being delivered. Rewards for the completion of the training program can make it attractive for individuals to participate.

Who Should Train?

Clearly the training effort needs to have overall direction by those responsible for training, in consultation with those who have experience in shaping organizational responses to employment equity issues. However, the training itself can be delivered in several ways.

In-house trainers, members of the designated groups, consultants and trainers with specialized expertise in employment equity issues, and human rights officers are all sources of training expertise. In deciding who should train, there are a number of considerations to be aware of.

In-house trainers contribute knowledge and understanding of the corporate culture and organizational setting, but may not have the specialized knowledge, understanding and skills to deliver training on employment equity. The professional development of in-house trainers on these issues is a worthwhile long term investment for organizations. It may be more effective to focus on the development of the skills of the in-house trainers in designing training and development strategies and programs, rather than importing specialized trainers. It may also be advisable to avoid using "guest speakers" who deliver a message that does not fit into the overall training strategy for employment equity.

When a member of a designated group is invited to speak, there is a danger of suggesting to the training participants that this person is speaking for everyone in that group. It is also advisable to avoid training in the "specifics" of any particular group or culture, as this can lead to the creation of new stereotypes about the members of a designated group. The message of diversity within groups, as well as among groups, needs to be communicated to training participants. Approaches that promote an understanding of diversity could include the use of more than one member of a designated group and therefore more than one point of view, and group representatives who do not claim to speak for the group as a whole. Including members of the designated groups in the planning and design of training can help to integrate their contributions into a consistent and effective training plan.

External consultants and trainers can bring specialized expertise, including knowledge and experience of the ways in which disadvantage and discrimination affect the designated groups. Consultants and trainers should include members of the designated groups, and they should provide good role models for equity behaviour in their consultancy and training activities. For example, designated group representatives should be equal partners in the training, and should not be relegated to a supporting role. It is preferable to select trainers who carry out a needs analysis that will make the training relevant to the specific organization, and avoid those who deliver pre-packaged programs.

Federal and provincial government human rights officers and employment equity practitioners from other organizations may also be useful sources of training expertise. When training is done by human rights officers only, there is a danger that its focus will be on legal requirements to the exclusion of other training needs. It is important to integrate knowledge and understanding of human rights law into more general approaches to equity. Bringing employment equity practitioners from other settings into the organization to talk about their experiences, challenges and successes, can sometimes be very helpful.

A well planned training program should be able to make use of in-house trainers, designated group representatives, external consultants and trainers, human rights officers and other employment equity practitioners, in integrating the appropriate training expertise at the right time in the process of employment equity implementation.

Dealing with Resistance to Training

The decision to initiate training may also arouse resistance. In some organizations, training and development are not high on the list of priorities. For example, in an organization where taking the workers off the production line means a cessation of work, clearly the cost of training will severely limit the organization's commitment to training or educational programs. On the other hand, an organization may have a strong training department and an organizational commitment to training and development. But if the human resources or training department sees the initiative for developing training for employment equity as coming from outside their department, they may view it as an invasion of their territory and a threat to their training expertise.

Sugar (1987: 67) suggested that in the U.S., "EEO trainers too often face managers sitting back in silence and indifference to 'observe training'." Some employees may be resentful if they are pulled away from what they perceive as more essential duties. Employees may feel that the training process takes up too much time, or management may not be willing to incur the loss of production time for training. Others may see training simply as a way of avoiding the penalties arising from infractions of human rights codes or employment equity legislation or compliance requirements. A carefully planned approach to training will include consideration and effective management to minimize these sources of resistance, and help employees to see the benefits of training both to the organization and the individual.

Who Should Receive Training?

One of the issues to be considered is whether training should be mandatory for everyone in the organization. If it is not seen as relevant, or if there is considerable resistance to the content of training, mandatory training can arouse considerable resistance and backlash to the issues. On the other hand, voluntary participation in training can result in apathy and low attendance or in "preaching to the converted." However, in the long run a training program may have more success if it is aimed initially at those who support the issues, and who can become catalysts in the changes within the organization. Training for those who are to act as change agents will need to address skills and strategies that they will require to implement organizational change. Training should also be provided on specific behavourial changes that are required for the effective implementation of employment equity measures, for example, skills in bias free interviewing for those involved in hiring.

Over the long term everyone in the organization should receive training that supports the employment equity change process. As a minimum, all employees will need orientation to the principles of employment equity, the impact of disadvantage and discrimination on the designated groups and the organization's commitment and approach to employment equity implementation. We add further details about the content of such training later in this chapter.

In addition, employees will need job-specific training that develops their ability to work in a diverse work force. For example, union leaders, managers and supervisors need to feel confident that they have the answers to questions about employment equity that will be raised by other employees. They will need to receive information about employment equity legislation, regulations and principles, so that they can provide leadership in the employment equity process. Unions can play an important role in training that promotes equity in co-worker interaction.

It is essential to train reception and support staff, since reception staff give newcomers their first impression of an organization, and play a key role in its public image. They also often act as gatekeepers to the organization, and in this role can exercise a screening effect towards members of the designated groups.

Specialized training and development initiatives can also be used to adjust the imbalance of power encountered by the designated groups within organizations. Members of designated groups may need encouragement to strive for equity and training in personal goal setting and career planning to prepare them for success and promotion. There may be a need to empower members of such groups to stand up for their rights.

What to Give Training On

Awareness and Information

What kinds of training are appropriate for employment equity implementation? The needs analysis will identify areas of concern, although often employees are not aware of the extent of discrimination, and tend to fall into what might be called the "no problems here" syndrome. Practitioners should work to raise awareness of the more overt types of discrimination, which might include racial or sexual harassment. Often employees lack an awareness of the importance of language and the sensitivities surrounding designated group nomenclature. Training can enlighten people about the ways in which inappropriate language use can foster bias and stereotyping. We are all probably aware how the language used to refer to persons with disabilities, for example, has changed over the years. More generally, employees need training that addresses the issues of systemic discrimination and the ways in which it is historically embedded in the structure of society, as well as in organizational systems.

Employees often fear and resist the concept of employment equity. Sometimes this resistance is based on a lack of knowledge and understanding that needs to be addressed in an educational or training setting that allows for discussion of complex issues, dialogue and experiences that foster understanding. For example, employment equity in its Canadian context is often confused with U.S. affirmative action programs, and many employees express anxiety over the use of "quotas." Some employees confuse the concept of employment equity with pay equity and use the terms interchangeably until the differences are explained. Managers may express resistance because they feel threatened by the prospect of managing a diverse work force. They may need to discuss concerns about dealing with perceptions of unfair treatment, or with anticipated backlash. They may not be aware of their responsibilities and liabilities under human rights statutes. Faced with the prospect of a more diverse work force, supervisors are likely to be anxious about meeting deadlines, production quotas and service needs. There are many myths and uncertainties operating in the workplace about what employment equity means. Questions and concerns such as the following are typically raised:

> Why should we actively recruit? Why don't they apply? Aren't they interested?
>
> Will we have to drop our standards to meet our hiring goals?
>
> Will we have to use preferential hiring to meet our hiring goals?

What about special treatment because of designated group status?

What about my career and chances for promotion?

This is just reverse discrimination. Two wrongs don't make a right.

They are not qualified.

Questions and assertions such as these have to be dealt with and the myths dispelled if employment equity is going to be accepted within an organization. Training provides an opportunity to bring anxieties to the surface and to begin to respond appropriately. Training should also provide information about what needs to be done in an organization to promote equity, and explain such concepts as "special programs" and "reasonable accommodation."

Training can assist employees who may experience difficulties in responding to a changing environment. It can help people to develop confidence that they can work successfully with others different from themselves, and skills in accomodating the special needs of members of the designated groups. However, training will probably not change prejudicial and intolerant attitudes. In this case, the best that an organization may be able to do is to require behaviour that does not give expression to such attitudes.

Skills and Strategies

Training provides support for the development of new skills. What kinds of skills are needed? This may vary from one unit or type of job to another — hence the needs analysis is useful in identifying the specific training needs of groups of employees, supervisors or managers. For example, managers and union representatives will need skills for dealing with sexual and racial harassment.

In training, participants get the opportunity to move beyond theory and to practice skills in typical situations. The use of case studies, role play and other experiential training techniques contributes to knowledge, understanding and skill acquisition. Training can also assist in the development of employment equity initiatives. For example, an organization needs to recruit designated group employees, and training can allow and encourage employees responsible for recruitment to develop recruitment approaches that will help the organization to meet its equity goals.

Walton (1989) has suggested that the long-term effectiveness of training is enhanced when participants are assisted in developing self-direction and self-reinforcement. Trainees who act in a self-directed fashion "organize their environment to facilitate and support the changes they want to make. These employees implement routines, give themselves cues and build support systems with others to help establish and develop their new behaviours. They set specific behaviour goals and let others know what they are working to achieve" (Walton, 1989: 64).

It is clear that the training process will not be successful unless the desired outcomes are rewarded and supported by the organization. Training participants need support in order to implement behavioral changes and integrate what they have learned into their daily work.

Bargaining and Negotiation

No matter how effective communication and training strategies may be, it remains true that some stakeholders in the organization will be motivated by interests and values that are expressed in resistance to employment equity implementation. Bargaining and negotiation may be useful in accommodating these differing interests to the greatest extent possible, and in reducing resistance.

Negotiation is most effective when it is based on recognition and acceptance of the legitimacy of "interests," rather than on attempts to bargain over entrenched positions (Fisher and Ury, 1981). Negotiation on the basis of interests means identifying underlying interests and values brought to the table by the different stakeholders, and trying to find common ground. This ongoing process involves consultation with the different stakeholders at appropriate stages of employment equity program development and implementation.

In Chapter 10, we noted that organizational power tools include information such as data, technical knowledge, political intelligence, and expertise; resources include funds, materials, space, and time; and support in the form of endorsement, backing, approval, or legitimacy" Kanter (1983: 159).

The employment equity practitioner must access organizational power tools in order to be able to negotiate successfully when resistance seems very entrenched. Senior management can provide support for the employment equity practitioner by demonstrating a high profile commitment to employment equity in order to validate the practitioner's role. Senior management support is also needed to ensure line management accountability for employment equity performance and progress.

In the organizational change process required for employment equity implementation, resistance may be encountered from line managers for a number of reasons. The kind of hiring accountability implicit in employment equity can pose a threat to line managers' current areas of control (Devanna, Fombrun and Tichy [1981: 67]).

Frequent consultation with line managers can be useful when the development and exchange of information and technical expertise is of mutual benefit. Knowledge of how to access funding from government sources, for example, can be useful in negotiating. Funding programs that are aimed at giving employment experience to designated group representatives can be used to provide employees to meet line management's short term labour needs, and also to allow managers to recruit excellent potential long term employees to meet their employment equity goals. External funding may be available for expanding or upgrading equipment to make it accessible for use by persons with disabilities, or external sources of expertise regarding accomodation may be available. Employment equity practitioners may find that their knowledge of such possibilities is useful in their negotiations with line management. In addition, the employment equity practitioner or human resource manager can provide support in the form of approval and public recognition of line management's responsiveness to and success in employment equity initiatives.

A warning is necessary, however: employment equity or human resource managers should negotiate to influence decision making, rather than taking on a great deal of extra operational or technical work.

Conclusion

Communication, training and negotiation strategies should be linked in a strategic way that supports the direction of organizational change and helps to deal with resistance through the development of understanding, support and skills. However, it is unlikely that all resistance can be dealt with successfully no matter how effectively communication, training and negotiation are used to facilitate change. Some resistance will be so deeply entrenched that the employment equity practitioner will have to judge whether to move on to other areas of implementation, acknowledging that progress in some domains is unlikely. The practitioner needs to be able to discern when resistance encountered in one area may begin to link with other areas of resistance, thus undermining the overall employment equity implementation strategy. It may sometimes be effective to deal with resistance by calling attention to sanctions for non-compliance contained in employment equity regulations or legislation. The legal framework may ultimately be the most important resource available to the employment equity practitioner in dealing with resistance to change.

REFERENCES

Benick, Gail. *Employment Equity, Gaining Organizational Acceptance.* Sheridan College, 1989.

Bernhard, H.B., and C. A. Ingols. "Six Lessons for the Corporate Classroom." *Harvard Business Review,* Sept.-Oct., 1988, 40-46.

Billingsley, Brenda, and Leon Muszynski. *No Discrimination Here? Toronto's Employers and the Multi-Racial Work Force.* Toronto: Urban Alliance on Race Relations and Social Planning Council of Metropolitan Toronto, 1985.

Commission for Racial Equality. *Training: The Implementation of Equal Opportunities at Work.* Volume Two: Case Studies, London, 1989, 5-6.

Devanna, Mary Ann, Charles Fombrun, and Noel Tichy. "Human Resources Management: A Strategic Perspective." *Organizational Dynamics,* Winter 1981, 51-67.

Fisher, Roger, and William Ury. *Getting to Yes.* Harmondsworth: Penguin Books Ltd., 1987.

Kanter, Rosabeth Moss. "Differential Access to Opportunity and Power." In Alvarez, Rodolofo, and Kenneth G.Lutterman and Associates.

Discrimination in Organizations. San Francisco:Jossey-Bass Inc. Publishers, 1979, 52-68.

Kanter, Rosabeth Moss. *The Change Masters.* New York: Simon and Schuster Inc., 1983.

Kleiman, Marcia. "Ease the Stress of Change." *Personnel Journal,* September 1989, 106-112.

Middlesex County Board of Education. *Equity Matters,* 1991.

Rosenberg, M.J. "Performance Technology: Working the System." *Training,* February 1990, 43-44.

Sugar, Stephen. "Training's the Name of the Game." *Training and Development Journal,* December 1987, 67-73.

Walton, Jan M. "Training: Self-Reinforcing Behaviour Change." *Personnel Journal,* October 1989, 64-68.

12

Diagnosis of Discrimination and Disadvantage

B ill feels trapped. He is a labourer at a public utility — not a big plant, just about 100 employees. Bill is Black, as are thirteen of his co-workers. All the Blacks work in the labour department, one of two "outside" departments in the plant; the other is coal handling. Labour's hourly rate is lower than rates in the other departments. The three "inside" departments are operations, maintenance, and laboratory and test. Whites work as labourers too, yet many of them move on to other jobs in the inside departments, with better pay.

Some years ago, if you were Black, the only department that would hire you was Labour, and the transfer or promotion of Blacks into the other departments just wasn't allowed. All that has changed now, or so the company says, but Bill isn't sure he's any better off. To get into any of the other departments it is necessary to have completed high school. But few Blacks have completed high school in that part of the country. Bill hasn't, and neither have many of his Black friends or co-workers: Black students aren't encouraged to stay in school and get a good education, and those who do are streamed into vocational classes. Even Blacks at the plant who have a high school diploma do not get the good jobs; they seem to be blocked too. However, Bill has to admit that the company has recently started to help under-educated employees, both Blacks and whites, by financing two-thirds of the cost of tuition for high school courses. They call it a "special measure."

Recently, the company started to require everyone who wants to work in any department except Labour to pass two tests: an intelligence test and a mechanical test. Everyone, regardless of their race, has to pass the tests, and not everyone is successful. Some of the workers Bill used to work with in the Labour Department, and who transferred a few years ago to other departments, didn't have to pass any tests, and Bill sees that they seem to be doing O.K. They were lucky — they transferred before the tests were brought in.

What can Bill do? It's difficult and confusing for him to figure out whether he's being discriminated against. It doesn't seem fair that Bill is "stuck" in this job. Perhaps his children will break the cycle: stay in school, get a good education and a better opportunity for well paying jobs with a future. Or will they? Bill knows there are no guarantees, but he'd like to do something to help himself and his children have an equal opportunity for jobs they can do. He doesn't want to cause trouble in the company, and he doesn't want to lose his job, but Bill realizes that unless he does something nothing will change. How does Bill diagnose the problems of discrimination and disadvantage in his workplace? Where and how does he start?

Diagnosing Systemic Discrimination

Does Bill's problem sound familiar? Many employment equity practitioners, members of designated groups and employment equity advocates have experienced a similarly confusing mixture of facts and experience, hope and despair, in trying to unravel why some people and some groups are "stuck" when it comes to employment opportunities. It may appear that there are both "good" and "bad" practices at the workplace: employers have started some positive initiatives and good-faith measures, while at the same time continuing traditional, long standing practices that may act as barriers. It is often difficult to assess employer policies and practices in relation to equality in employment. Moreover, determining where and how to start an analysis of systemic discrimination may itself act as a barrier to taking action on employment equity.

If we look at Bill's situation we can start to outline how an analysis of systemic discrimination might begin. Initially, Bill has three important ingredients to help him identify and document discriminatory barriers: 1) information drawn from his own experience as an employee, 2) information about the company's employment practices, and 3) information on the number of Blacks and whites in the plant's work force (see Box 12.1). First, Bill can draw from his personal experience as a long-time employee of the company and his attempts to get a higher paying job in another department. Often an individual's job hunting, work and career experience will provide valuable information, especially as they relate to barriers in employment systems and organizational culture; we will discuss these issues in more detail in the next chapter. For example, Bill can describe his past efforts to obtain a transfer or promotion. He can gather information about the jobs he would like to transfer into, and how he is qualified or unqualified for them. He may be able to identify how and why his white co-workers progress into the better paying jobs. With this information, Bill, independently or with an advocate or champion for change, can begin to discover if there is discrimination, and if so, what forms it takes, how it operates and what might remedy it. He also needs to know if he is experiencing discrimination as an individual or as a "member of a class" based on his race and colour.

BOX 12.1
Initial Sources of Information for an Employment Equity Diagnosis

- Personal experience(s) of designated group members in seeking, getting and/or maintaining jobs in the organization (information may relate to employment systems and/or organizational culture).
- Information about the organization's formal and informal employment practices or policies.
- Information about work-force numbers: how many designated group members work in the organization and in what jobs. Data may also be available about job applicants and/or the availability of designated group members for jobs.

Second, Bill has worked at the plant for many years and has gained a lot of information through his observations of how people get jobs or do not get jobs, the stated and actual qualifications and requirements, and how these practices have changed over time. He knows both the formal and informal job policies and practices of the company, or at least some of them. Furthermore, he can ask questions and get information in order to know these "employment systems" better. Thus, generic information may be available about the organization's employment policies and practices — information that deals with "systems" and with the experience of groups of people, especially the designated groups. Such information often becomes evident though patterns of decisions and the outcomes of job policies and practices over a period of months or years.

Third, patterns may also be evident in an organization's work-force data that show who works in what jobs, at what levels and in which units of the company. For example, Bill knows or may be able to find out approximately how many Blacks and whites work in the plant, and in what departments and jobs. This information may provide a quick snap shot of the work-force representation and distribution of Blacks and whites. Since it is a small town with a cohesive Black community, it is likely Bill knows of Blacks who have applied for jobs, their qualifications, and whether they were successful or not. This investigation should also give an indication of the availability of Blacks for jobs.

What Bill needs is a framework to help him diagnose the inequities. He may also want the assistance of an advocate or champion to help him gain access to those with influence so that he might present his findings and trigger change. His immediate need is to gather enough information so he can assess whether he's responsible for being "stuck" himself, or if "systemic discrimination" is holding him back: is it Bill or the company that has to change? For example, if Bill knows about jobs openings and how to apply, but hasn't decided whether he wants to work in operations or maintenance, then Bill may want to try to come to a decision by seeking some advice from supervisors, co-workers or the employment office. On the other hand, if there is no way for Bill to even find out about openings and how to apply because only those in "the old boys network" know the "what, when and how" of job openings, then the company will need to open up its transfer and promotion practices. It might do this by changing its pattern of hiring "friends and old boys," providing job information through the employment office, doing outreach recruitment, and implementing job posting and bidding systems.

This chapter provides a diagnostic framework and guide to the information and evidence that can be used to identify and remedy barriers resulting from discrimination and disadvantage in an organization. We seek to understand and document the patterns and practices in organizational systems and cultures that result in systemic discrimination and barriers, and in the poor representation and distribution of designated groups in and through organizations.

A Canadian Analysis and Remedies

Bill's story is actually true. It is based on the experience of Willie S. Griggs, who worked at the Duke Power Company in North Carolina in the 1960s. Willie Griggs and twelve of his Black co-workers challenged the company's hiring and transfer practices and won, by a unanimous ruling of the U.S. Supreme Court in 1971. It is the decision from which we begin to understand what systemic discrimination is all about.

The following paragraphs are taken from *Griggs v. Duke Power*, U.S. 424, 91 S.Ct. 849 (1971) (U.S.S.C.) (p. 853-854):

> Congress has now provided that tests or criteria for employment or promotion may not provide equality of opportunity merely in the sense of the fabled offer of milk to the stork and the fox. On the contrary, Congress has now required that the posture and condition of the job-seeker be taken into account. It has — to resort again to the fable — provided that the vessel in which the milk is proffered be one all seekers can use. The Act [the Civil Rights Act of 1964, Title VII] proscribes not only overt discrimination but also practices that are fair in form, but discriminatory in operation. The touchstone is business necessity. If an employment practice which operated to exclude Negroes cannot be shown to be related to job performance, the practice is prohibited.
>
> We do not suggest that either the District Court or the Court of Appeals erred in examining the employer's intent; but good

intent or absence of discriminatory intent does not redeem employment procedures or testing mechanisms that operate as "built-in headwinds" for minority groups and are unrelated to measuring job capability.

The Company's lack of discriminatory intent is suggested by special efforts to help the undereducated employees through Company financing of two thirds the cost of tuition for high school training. But Congress directed the thrust of the Act to the consequences of employment practices, not simply the motivation. More than that, Congress has placed on the employer the burden of showing that any given requirement must have a manifest relationship to the employment in question.

The analysis of systemic discrimination has Canadian as well as U.S. roots. As discussed in Chapter 4, in 1987 the Canadian Supreme Court handed down a landmark employment equity decision in the Action Travail des Femmes case against CN Rail. The facts of this case are more detailed than those in *Griggs*, and its scope is broader, but the approach to identifying and documenting discrimination is similar in many ways. In *ATF v. CN*, a Montreal based women's group (ATF) gathered and documented sufficient information to formulate a complaint of systemic discrimination experienced by women in blue collar jobs at Canadian National Rail. Unfortunately, the company would not take the data seriously and act on it, so it was left to the Canadian government, through the human rights complaints process, to investigate the case.

The Canadian Human Rights Commission used three kinds of information to establish a finding of systemic discrimination. First, information on the experience of women blue collar employees and applicants at the CN Rail yards in Montreal was documented, including the resistance demonstrated by foremen, the personnel department, management, co-workers and the union to the women's desire to enter non-traditional jobs. This experiential data cast a spotlight on the organizational culture: it illuminated how much and what kind of support there was for what we now call employment equity, the difficulties women experienced in being integrated into blue collar jobs, the problems of retention, and the widespread existence of workplace harassment. The stories told by women applicants, employees and past employees also provided valuable information about recruitment, screening, selection, hiring, placement, job assignment, transfer, promotion and on-the-job treatment. Second, data were compiled about the number of women CN currently and historically hired, transferred and promoted into blue collar non-traditional jobs. These data were compared to census data showing the availability of women to work in blue collar jobs. There was a huge gap: 0.7% of blue collar jobs at CN were filled by women compared to approximately 13% in the labour market. Third, the experiential data were supplemented by evidence from the company and ATF describing CN's employment policies and practices. This evidence highlighted the many ways women, in comparison to men, were excluded, treated unequally, or negatively affected by the company's employment systems, including recruitment, hiring, orientation, on-the-job interaction, transfer, promotion and development.

The Diagnostic Framework: An Overview

To untangle the threads of discrimination and disadvantage such as that experienced by Bill and by members of Action Travail des Femmes, it helps to chart the stages in a diagnostic process (see Box 12.2).

BOX 12.2

Diagnosing Systemic Discrimination and Designing Remedies

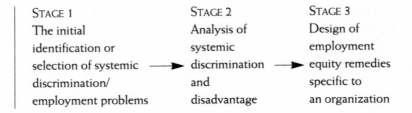

STAGE 1	STAGE 2	STAGE 3
The initial identification or selection of systemic discrimination/ employment problems	Analysis of systemic discrimination and disadvantage	Design of employment equity remedies specific to an organization

In a diagnosis of systemic discrimination we begin with the perceptions, experience and information of one or more stakeholders, in most cases members of the designated groups. The employment equity practitioner, community advocate or other equality seeker may check for signs such as "bad numbers," discriminatory or suspect employment practices, or complaints by individuals and groups. At Stage 1, it is wise to ask key stakeholders:

- What are your concerns and perceptions of disadvantage and discrimination? Of blockages in the organization?
- What barriers do designated groups face in this organization's culture, policies and practices?
- What barriers are presented or experienced in the attitudes, behaviours, norms, basic assumptions and decision-making of the people who work here?
- What information do you have that might shed some light on the equity problems we all have a stake in?

At Stage 2, we enter a phase of analysis:

- What is the nature of the problem, as indicated by the evidence and observations we have collected?
- Is it a type of discrimination — something we can seek legal remedy for if education, negotiation or persuasion does not lead to voluntary systemic remedies?
- If it is discrimination, what form does it take: unequal treatment, adverse impact or a lack of accommodation? We need to know because the remedies for adverse impact differ significantly from those for a lack of accommodation, which in turn differ from a response to unequal treatment discrimination, as discussed in Chapter 5 (see Box 5.3.)
- Even if a finding of discrimination cannot be supported by the analysis, are there patterns or conditions of disadvantage that might be ameliorated by employment equity initiatives?

At Stage 3, we seek the solution to this joint problem-solving process. Designing appropriate remedies causes us to consider alternatives, and perhaps to implement several measures in order to successfully address the problems and prevent future reoccurrences. For example, an analysis of a hiring process for a particular occupation in a company may lead to a remedy that deals not only with recruitment, screening and selection but also with job placement and assignment. It may also encompass the integration of designated group members with co-workers, supervisors and clients, and on-the-job issues such as uniforms, tools and equipment, and toilet and change room facilities. The guiding question is always how can we make this a successful change, in the long run as well as the short term? We will need to strategically plan the implementation of the remedies we have identified, working to prevent and deal with resistance. We will also need to ensure that remedies address the interests of various stakeholders, deal with the issues of integration and retention as well as recruitment and hiring, and build in monitoring, evaluation and feedback processes. Thus, the diagnosis of organizational barriers and the development of remedies reflects the organizational change strategies discussed in other chapters.

Box 12.3 outlines the analytical process in greater detail, and suggests the stakeholders whose involvement may be especially crucial at each stage of the process.

BOX 12.3
Key Elements and Stakeholders in the Diagnostic Framework

STAGE 1: SELECTING AND FOCUSING THE PROBLEM

The following information may be used to select and focus the problem:

- the personal experiences of designated group members in seeking, getting and maintaining jobs
- information about the operation of an organization's employment systems (policies and practices)
- work-force and/or applicant data and comparative (availability) data in order to address employment equity outcomes (or the lack of outcomes) regarding the organization's systems, culture and numbers.

Critical stakeholders to involve in Stage 1:

- Designated group members, internal and external to the organization

Also

- Employment equity and human resource practitioners
- Line managers, union officers and non-unionized employee representatives

STAGE 2: ANALYZING SYSTEMIC DISCRIMINATION

A 3-step "proof formula" for discrimination analysis may be used to identify whether findings of discrimination involving

- unequal treatment
- adverse impact, or
- lack of accommodation can be substantiated.

If discrimination is not identified, the findings may suggest patterns or conditions of disadvantage that might also be remedied by employment equity initiatives.

A strategic decision is taken to

- negotiate, or
- initiate legal action

in order to gain sponsorship for the initiation of employment equity remedies.

Critical stakeholders to involve in Stage 2:

- **Employment equity and human resource practitioners**
- **Designated group members and advocates**

Also

- **Internal change champions**
- **Government policy and compliance officers**

STAGE 3: DESIGNING SYSTEMIC REMEDIES

- all designated groups, or
- a single designated group

in the 3 key result areas of

- systems
- culture
- numbers

in order to work toward the three overall goals of employment equity:

- eliminating current barriers
- remedying past and preventing future barriers, and
- improving representation.

Critical stakeholders to involve in Stage 3:

- **Designated group members and advocates**
- **Employment equity and human resource practitioners**
- **Line managers**
- **Union officers and non-unionized employee representatives**

Also:

- **Top management**
- **Government policy and compliance officers.**

In Stage 1 of the diagnosis we select and focus the problems of employment inequality using the personal experience of designated group members, information about an organization's employment policies and practices (the "employment systems"), and the data and perceptions we hold about the representation and distribution of designated groups in an organization's work force.

Once the problem is defined, we enter into a fairly technical process of systemic analysis, using the concepts of discrimination outlined in Chapter 5. One objective of Stage 2 is to determine whether the problem we have selected is discrimination, disadvantage or neither. As discussed in Chapter 5, if it is discrimination, we need to decide what form it takes: unequal treatment, adverse impact, or a lack of accommodation. Even if it is not discrimination, the findings may suggest patterns or conditions of disadvantage experienced by one or more of the designated groups, something for which an employment equity (or special program) remedy may be appropriate.

As noted in Chapter 4, section 15(2) of the Charter and the special program provisions of human rights statutes allow employers to undertake employment equity initiatives in order to prevent, eliminate, or reduce disadvantage suffered by designated groups. Similarly, the legislative purpose of the federal Employment Equity Act focuses on correction of the "conditions of disadvantage in employment" experienced by the designated groups. These clauses allow employers to prevent and remedy disadvantage, in contrast to the non-discrimination clauses of human rights statutes, which require employers to prevent and remedy discrimination within their organizations. While employers are not required by human rights law to eliminate barriers that arise from general or societal disadvantage, these barriers nevertheless create inequities in the employment opportunities and experience of the designated groups within an organization. Remedies for disadvantage, then, are integral parts of an employer's employment equity strategy.

BOX 12.4
Disadvantage: An Example of Diagnosis and Remedies

A traditional recruitment practice of a medium size food processing company is the placement of an advertisement in one of the local newspapers when they wish to hire employees. The ad is not worded to exclude any designated group (that is, there is no unequal treatment), nor is there any evidence to suggest there may be adverse impact on any designated group because of a "neutral" selection requirement. As well, there are no known special needs or requirements of designated groups that would suggest an accommodation is required. Furthermore, the statistical profile of the employer's work force does not indicate gross statistical disparities between the work force and the availability of designated groups in the local recruitment area, although some gender segregation of jobs is apparent. Neither are there large samples of applicants and recently hired employees suitable for a statistical analysis since the level of hiring has been modest over the last several years. Consequently, the conclusion is drawn that there is no evidence of systemic discrimination.

However, even without evidence of discrimination specific to the company, a convincing argument of disadvantage experienced by the designated groups might be made based on data such as those summarized in Chapter 2. In response, the company might broaden its pool of applicants by undertaking some employment equity initiatives related to recruitment. For example, one or more of the following actions might be undertaken in addition to the traditional job ad:

- calling or sending a notice to local community groups and organizations with designated group interests and membership when the company has vacancies;
- using the personal information networks of current managers, employees and the employment office to encourage designated groups to apply;
- supplying outreach information (verbally or in writing) to designated groups, advocacy groups and others concerning the type and frequency of available jobs, when and how to apply, the qualifications sought, and the benefits of working for this company;

- communicating with local schools, colleges or universities and encouraging members of the designated groups to consider working for this company; and
- advertising in local or regional newspapers or newsletters operated by special interest groups of and for aboriginal peoples, women, people with disabilities and racial minorities.

Based on the analysis of discrimination and disadvantage, a strategic decision may then be taken by stakeholders to negotiate employment equity change or seek a legal remedy. The third stage and final stage of the diagnostic process is the identification of potential systemic remedies related to one or more key result areas: changing the organization's employment systems, its culture, or its numbers of designated group members. Chapter 13 discusses these three key result areas in detail.

Although it may appear that a linear process is described, this framework for employment equity diagnosis and remedies is not linear in reality. As we move through the analysis we are likely to perceive inequities in several areas, for example, in recruitment as well as selection, qualifications, or in training and development as well as in promotional practices. We will also come to perceive the issue from various stakeholder perspectives including those of the hiring manager, the human resource specialist, and the designated group member. At Stage 3, attention to recruitment and selection remedies may lead to the design of remedies that will not only ensure entry for designated group members, but also assist their integration and retention in the organization. Employment equity diagnosis does not begin and end, but once begun in a company it should become an ongoing, cyclical process. It is an important part of the research component of the action research process discussed in Chapter 8. It is also part of the ongoing monitoring, evaluation and organizational learning that is necessary to sustain change, as we will discuss in Chapter 14.

An employment equity diagnosis can be carried out from inside or outside the organization, from the perspective and experience of an employee or applicant, an employment equity or human resources practitioner, a representative of an advocacy group, a line manager, a union official, a government compliance officer, or a legal practitioner. All of the stakeholders discussed in Chapter 7 will have their own perspectives on equity issues. All of their views "count," yet in traditional employment equity programming and analysis, the only stakeholders who are likely to have influence are employment equity practitioners, government compliance agents, and senior management, especially senior human resource managers. In our diagnostic approach, the key stakeholders are members of the designated groups and their advocates since, ultimately, it will be their experience and definition of barriers and equality in the workplace that will define the end results of a successful employment equity process. Employment equity and human resource practitioners can work with the designated groups to carry out meaningful diagnoses, and to independently examine their organization's employment policies to identify discrimination and disadvantage. Government policy makers and compliance agents can also develop the expertise to diagnose inequities in specific organizational settings and in labour markets. The roles of union leaders and operating managers in the diagnostic process are strikingly similar: while they may play a role in uncovering some of the actual and potential problem areas, their expertise comes into play primarily at the third and final stage of diagnosis: designing (and implementing) remedies that eliminate barriers and address operational requirements (See Box 12.3).

While the diagnostic framework we set out here is complex, it reflects the complexity of both the problems faced by designated groups and the remedies for the systemic inequities they experience. The diagnostic framework will help chart a course and find ways to effectively identify and use information to uncover and remedy barriers. The technical analysis of systemic discrimination (Stage 2 of the diagnostic framework) is based on legal theories about the "burden of proof" in discrimination complaints and the evidence required to substantiate allegations of discrimination or perceptions of inequities. Stakeholders or change agents may avoid such a detailed and complex analysis by focusing instead on whether there are general patterns of disadvantage for designated groups. However, without a rigorous diagnosis of the problem it may be difficult to propose and negotiate a sound solution. This is especially likely when the problem centres on traditional human resource policies and practices that the organization may be reluctant to change. Remedies that aim to rapidly create a "critical mass" of designated group members may also be resisted by employers if a rigorous analysis is not first undertaken. The framework suggested here presents options for stakeholders to consider, and a diagnostic process to follow if an analysis of systemic discrimination is desired.

On the other hand, one of our guiding principles in diagnosing inequity is to direct our energies toward areas in which we can gain the most significant changes and remedies to systemic barriers. In other words, we want to focus on "fighting the ones we can win, and win big." The diagnostic framework set out here provides assistance in identifying such priorities and in amassing evidence to support arguments for change.

We now turn to an in-depth review of each stage of the process of diagnosing systemic discrimination and disadvantage, and designing appropriate remedies through stakeholder participation.

Stage 1: Selecting the Problems

Initially, stakeholders may see an equity problem in broad and general terms: "there are not enough minorities and women in policing." Or, they may identify a very specific problem: "When a 5 feet, 10 inch minimum height requirement, combined with a minimum 160 pound weight requirement, is used in screening and selection for applicants for the Middletown Police Service, it selects out significantly more women, some racial and ethnic minorities (specifically, aboriginal people, Asians and South Asians), and especially minority women, than it does men and whites."

The general example focuses on numbers only, while the specific example focuses on an employment system, in this case a specific selection requirement. Either can act as an effective diagnostic starting point. The general example states a concern about unequal treatment based on statistical disparities. The specific example illustrates adverse impact discrimination, and it implies that the numbers of applicants, hires and incumbent police constables are inequitable, and that the selection requirement is a systemic barrier. Moreover, the specific analysis identifies an equity problem, identifies the job (police constable), names the employing organization (the Middletown Police Service), tells how the inequity occurs (selects out designated group applicants), identifies the specific designated groups encountering the alleged discriminatory barriers (women, aboriginal peoples, Asians, and South Asians, and especially racial minority women), and identifies the comparator groups (men and whites).

Stakeholders may start with a broad, general perception or concern about inequality, perhaps focused on discomfort with the numbers or the culture (as suggested in Box 12.2), or personal examples of unequal treatment. However, substantive remedies dealing with specific systems, culture and numbers, such as those contained in the tribunal/court order in *ATF* and listed in Box 1.5, will more likely result if the diagnosis focuses on specific problem areas within an organization. To illustrate this point let us turn again to the police examples given above. The general concern about numbers needs to be supplemented by further probing about the reasons for under-representation. What features of Middletown's recruitment and selection of police officers — currently and historically — might have caused such low numbers? Questions related to the systems and culture of the organization will supplement the perception of "bad numbers," leading to a more systematic assessment of the causes and effects of systemic barriers affecting the designated groups.

On the other hand, a focus on the height and weight requirement — an example of potential adverse impact discrimination — would, on its own, produce a narrow, although substantive, remedy: cessation of the requirement and its replacement by a requirement that does not adversely impact women, minorities and minority women, or failing that, a requirement that has a lesser adverse impact. The Griggs case illustrates this: the court imposed remedy was the removal of the high school diploma requirement since it was shown to have an adverse impact on Blacks, yet was not job related or a business necessity. Even though the Duke Power workforce data showed exclusions of Blacks in most departments and jobs, the remedy did not focus on numbers, but on the selection requirement. Similarly, it can be argued in our police example that the appropriate remedy is not to "hire more women and minorities" — although that may be a desirable goal — since the analysis does not assess work-force and comparative data, and thus we do not have an indication of how many more women and minorities to hire, nor do we have a diagnosis of the problem. Yet, as in the *ATF* case, a collection of systems problems at the Middletown Police

Service, including the height and weight requirement, can be viewed in combination with "bad numbers" and other evidence of a discriminatory organizational culture. These observations would produce a very strong argument for wide-spread employment equity change, including numerical remedies, leading to the hiring of substantially more women, racial minorities and aboriginal peoples as entry-level police constables.

Ideally, a stakeholder will begin to make a case using perceptions and supporting information concerning all three key result areas: systems, culture and numbers. Legally, this enquiry is called "establishing reasonable grounds to believe discrimination exists," and may lead to the establishment of a *prima facie* case of discrimination. We will discuss this further in the next section of this chapter. However, it is not unusual for a stakeholder to start with only one area, often general perceptions of "bad" numbers, or complaints about the organizational culture that cite harassment, marginalization, tokenism of designated group members, or poor integration. In such an instance it is desirable to widen the search area to include perceptions and information about one or both of the other areas.

Box 12.5 suggests a grid that might be used to organize and summarize the selection of problems in the stage one diagnosis: the perceptions of designated group members based on their personal job seeking and employment experience, and information various stakeholders have compiled related to the organization's systems, culture and numbers. The discussion of systems, culture and numbers in Chapter 13 will help the reader interpret some of these components. A similar grid might be developed to summarize the findings from Stage 2 and suggested remedies from Stage 3 in relation to the designated groups and the key results.

Stage 2: Analyzing Systemic Discrimination and Disadvantage

One of the general goals of employment equity is to remedy systemic discrimination and disadvantage found in organizations. The identification of specific discriminatory barriers generally requires a rigorous analysis, whereas an assessment of disadvantage may not. Nevertheless, if employment equity initiatives and remedies (Stage 3) are to reflect the unique characteristics of a particular

BOX 12.5
Grid Summarizing Stage 1 of the Diagnosis

		DESIGNATED GROUPS			
		WOMEN	ABORIGINAL PEOPLES	RACIAL MINORITIES	DISABLED PEOPLE	ALL DESIGNATED GROUPS
STAGE 1: Identifying the Problems	DESIGNATED GROUP PERSONAL EXPERIENCES • seeking jobs • maintaining jobs • promotion and career development					
	EMPLOYMENT SYSTEMS					
	• getting in					
	• being there					
	• moving through					
	• moving out					
	ORGANIZATIONAL CULTURE					
	• workplace environment					
	• integration					
	• retention					
	• support for employment equity					
	NUMBERS					
	• zeros					
	• near zeros					
	• concentrations					
	OVERALL OBSERVATIONS OR CONCLUSIONS					

organization, then our diagnosis must enable us to precisely identify what needs to be remedied.

We have seen how the *ATF* decision ordered CN Rail to implement strong remedies. It was able to do this because the remedy was based on solid evidence and detailed analysis of the barriers women faced in getting and keeping blue collar jobs. Similarly, we noted that the U.S. Supreme Court decision in *Griggs* identified the barrier for Blacks at the Duke Power Company as a high school diploma selection requirement, a qualification that had an adverse impact on Blacks and could not be justified as a business necessity. The barrier was remedied by the removal of the high school diploma as a selection standard; it was not remedied by the implementation of an "accommodation" or "special measure," such as two-thirds tuition assistance from the company. Thus, *ATF* illustrates how a detailed systemic analysis can lead to comprehensive remedies, while *Griggs* shows the need for good problem identification in order to bring about an appropriate remedy. The analytical process described here will enable stakeholders to achieve these aims.

Stage 2 is the most complex and technical part of the diagnostic process because the analysis of systemic discrimination is based on legal proof formulas, definitions and evidence. Hence we will develop the Stage 2 analysis based on the discussion of legal definitions and analysis in Chapter 5. Our experience suggests that making such legal concepts accessible and understandable to more of the employment equity stakeholders is essential if a truly cooperative, stakeholder based approach to employment equity is to become a reality. We begin by attempting to make this information and knowledge available to those who are not human rights lawyers and investigators. Our aim is to make the analysis of systemic discrimination and disadvantage — using qualitative and quantitative data — a more common and visible element of employment equity planning and implementation. We hope that the framework set out here will encourage practitioners to experiment with this analytical process, seeking legal advice and systemic discrimination expertise as required. Box 12.6 situates the "legalistic" components of Stage 2 within the overall diagnostic framework.

By the end of Stage 2, we will have analyzed each of the concerns and perceptions that surfaced during Stage 1. Based on the findings of our analysis we will be able to decide whether these concerns fit a legal understanding of discrimination, or a more general definition and assessment of designated group disadvantage. The Stage 2 diagnosis is based on a three-step "proof formula" that is used to organize the evidence of discrimination, and to diagnose each of the three forms of systemic discrimination discussed in Chapter 5: unequal treatment, adverse impact and lack of accommodation. Then we will decide on a strategy: do our findings encourage us to negotiate the employment equity changes we wish to achieve, or might it be more effective to take legal action? This second option might include filing complaints of discrimination, or seeking a remedy under employment equity laws, regulations or policy.

Box 12.6
Situating the Stage 2 Analysis within the Diagnostic Framework

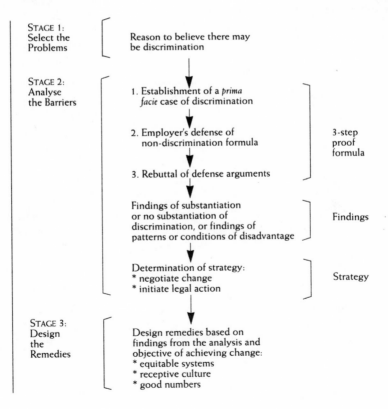

STAGE 1:
Select the
Problems

Reason to believe there may
be discrimination

STAGE 2:
Analyse
the Barriers

1. Establishment of a *prima
facie* case of discrimination

2. Employer's defense of
non-discrimination formula

3. Rebuttal of defense arguments

3-step
proof
formula

Findings of substantiation
or no substantiation of
discrimination, or findings of
patterns or conditions of disadvantage

Findings

Determination of strategy:
* negotiate change
* initiate legal action

Strategy

STAGE 3:
Design
the
Remedies

Design remedies based on
findings from the analysis and
objective of achieving change:
* equitable systems
* receptive culture
* good numbers

Three-Step Proof Formula   Simply put, the three-step proof formula moves from establishing a *prima facie* case of discrimination, to whether a legitimate defense to the *prima facie* case can be offered. It ends by determining whether a rebuttal to the defense can be made. If the *prima facie* case is maintained, either because no defense is forthcoming or because it is successfully rebutted, then discrimination is substantiated. If not, no discrimination is found. Unlike a human rights complaint, in an employment equity analysis one then has to determine if a case can be made for disadvantage. If not, and even though perceptions of unfairness may remain, it may be difficult for external advocates or internal champions of change to argue for an employment equity remedy, or for a tribunal or court to order it. A decision tree illustrating this three step process is presented in Box 12.7.

BOX 12.7
The 3-Step Proof Formula

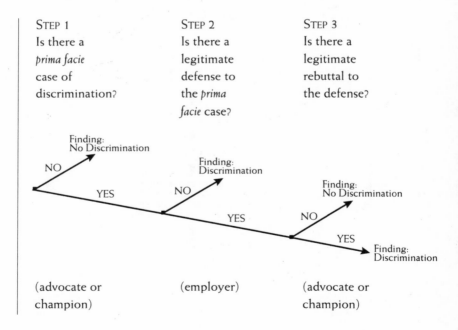

STEP 1	STEP 2	STEP 3
Is there a *prima facie* case of discrimination?	Is there a legitimate defense to the *prima facie* case?	Is there a legitimate rebuttal to the defense?

Finding: No Discrimination — NO (Step 1)
YES
Finding: Discrimination — NO (Step 2)
YES
Finding: No Discrimination — NO (Step 3)
YES
Finding: Discrimination

(advocate or champion)   (employer)   (advocate or champion)

In Chapter 5 we suggested that discrimination might be seen as two types — intent and results based — and taking three distinct forms: unequal treatment (intent based), adverse impact (results based), and lack of accommodation (results based). Boxes 5.1 and 5.3 discuss and illustrate these distinctions. In this chapter we integrate these concepts and definitions of discrimination with the three-step proof formula. Box 12.8 contains many of the essential components of the proof requirements for each form of discrimination. However, given that definitions of systemic discrimination vary and that the case law is constantly evolving, it may be necessary to adapt this analytical tool as needed for the purposes of a specific analysis.

As noted in Chapter 5, our definition of systemic discrimination includes adverse impact, unequal treatment and the lack of accommodation. Each of these three different forms of discrimination requires a distinctive analysis, and each is associated with different evidence and remedies. Yet all are related to human resource decision-making, policies and practices that "operate to limit a group's right to opportunities or to exclude a group from participating in an activity" (CHRR, "Thesaurus of Human Rights Terms").

BOX 12.8
Overview of Proof Formula Applied to Discrimination in Treatment, Impact and Accommodation

	UNEQUAL TREATMENT	ADVERSE IMPACT	LACK OF ACCOMMODATION
PRIMA FACIE CASE	• Direct or comparative evidence of discriminatory motive	• A specific job requirement or qualification has an adverse and disproportionate impact	• Steps not taken to accommodate a known need or special requirement
DEFENSE	• Legitimate non-discriminatory reason given for differential treatment	• *Bona fide* occupational requirement (BFOR) or business necessity	• Undue hardship based on safety, cost, or practicality

REBUTTAL	• Pretext (the defense offered is not true)	• An alternative practice or policy with no impact (or a lesser adverse impact) is available	• Undue hardship is not substantiated, or no rational connection to job performance is shown

As noted in Chapter 5, the case law provides little guidance about using statistical work-force evidence to make a case of systemic discrimination requiring an employment equity remedy. Although statistical evidence alone is unlikely to prove adequate or persuasive, it may be possible to create and maintain a *prima facie* case of discrimination based only on numbers. Such evidence would likely follow the proof pattern given for unequal treatment, focusing on statistical comparisons. The case might hold if gross statistical disparities are shown between the employer's work force and the applicant pool.

Solid cases of statistical disparities usually depend on 1) large samples, which may occur if there are large numbers of people being hired or promoted into occupations with comparably large applicant pools to draw from, and 2) the ability to draw an inference that the actual hiring results have come about for reasons other than chance. In other words, if a gross statistical disparity is unlikely to have occurred by chance then an inference of discriminatory decision-making can reasonably be made.

Statistical judgements based on two to three standard deviations might guide the assessment of such evidence. Less stringent tests are also sometimes used, such as the "80% rule" or "four-fifths rule." However, a statistical likelihood of less than one percent to five percent (the two to three standard deviation rule) is more persuasive.

Given the wide-spread and fundamental inequalities in the Canadian workplace, gross disparities might not be difficult to uncover. Nevertheless, mindful of the need to do more than "hire more members of the designated groups" if we aim to make employment equity a success, we would recommend that such a case be supplemented with evidence of discrimination in employment systems and in the organizational culture. If the statistical disparity as such is so gross, then such evidence will be available.

The combination of evidence regarding numbers, systems and culture would lay the ground work for an effective remedial plan to dismantle barriers and create a critical mass of designated groups in the work place.

Stage 3: Developing and Implementing Remedies

Once we have analyzed each of the concerns and perceptions arising from our Stage 1 diagnosis using the proof formulas for discrimination, we will have findings from which we can draw conclusions. Specifically, we will be able to conclude whether the barrier is "discrimination" or not. Given this, how might we make a strong argument for changing the systems, culture or numbers of an organization based on our analysis?

If we are external advocates and there is substantiation of discrimination, we have two main strategic options: 1) present our data to the organization's decision-makers, demonstrate that a discriminatory barrier exists, and negotiate a remedy, or 2) proceed with legal action under human rights laws or employment equity statutes and regulations. Of course, we may combine these two options, either by beginning with negotiation, and if unsuccessful, then proceeding with legal action, or by commencing legal action and then opening discussion with the organization to negotiate a remedy.

If we are internal champions of change, or if our findings suggest disadvantage but not a clear case of discrimination, we will probably need to use negotiation and persuasion to effect change. Such an analysis may be carried out in an employment systems review and work-force analysis that is legally required as part of a mandatory employment equity or contract compliance program. The barriers analysis may become public owing to reporting, feedback and audit mechanisms. In addition, sponsorship for change may more easily be attained if the diagnosis is backed by a strong legal argument. Thus, employment equity change is most likely if there has been a well documented analysis, especially one that clearly shows what the problem is, why it is a problem, and what the remedy might be.

We believe that many employment equity remedies currently proposed and sometimes implemented are simplistic, merely "quick fixes" demonstrating only surface commitment. Such remedies may include a single appointment of a designated group member, employer participation in job fairs and sporadic mailings of notices of available jobs to community organizations, and education for managers about workplace harassment. A systemic problem requires more than tinkering, however well intentioned it may be.

Our framework makes it clear that "systemic" problems stem from the employer's systems. Hence the remedy applies to the organization, not the members of the target groups. Women, aboriginal peoples, people with disabilities and racial minorities do not need "fixing" and improvement; the organizational systems and cultures they encounter or in which they work do. Employment equity is not unlike occupational health or environmental medicine that seeks to address what in peoples' environments endangers their health. Employment equity is directed toward organizational change, not individual change. Of course, many aspects of employment equity require developmental and enhancement activities that affect individuals, such as training, upgrading, mentoring, and career planning. Yet such activities are part of a carefully planned organizational change process aimed at removing or reducing disadvantage and discrimination faced by the designated groups, preventing future barriers, and acting to increase their participation over time in the employer's work force.

Conclusion

Each stakeholder in the employment equity change process has a wealth of information and experience to draw upon to assist the diagnostic process. In particular, the designated groups and their advocates can help identify and select what, in their view, are the important equity problems in an organization. Thus, the diagnostic framework suggested here begins with stakeholders' perceptions of discrimination and disadvantage in an organization's employment systems, organizational culture and the numbers of designated group members it employs and in what jobs. The perceptions and information of stakeholders allow them to identify and select the key problems for further analysis. A complex process of systemic discrimination analysis is then used to determine whether the problems and barriers might be defined as discriminatory, and if so, what form of discrimination is involved: unequal treatment, adverse impact or a lack of accommodation. Based on these findings, the stakeholder then must make a strategic decision to negotiate change, or perhaps seek legal action to force change. Finally, remedies for the barriers uncovered in the diagnostic process are designed to appropriately address the discrimination and disadvantage faced by designated groups. These remedies, in conjunction with standard components of employment equity programs and an organizational change strategy, lead to the design of an employment equity action plan. This plan will be discussed in the next chapter.

References

Action Travail des Femmes v. CN Rail, [1987], 40 D.L.R. [4th] 193 {S.C.C.]
Griggs v. Duke Power, 401 U.S. 424. 91 S.Ct. 849 (1971) (U.S.S.C.)

13

Systems, Culture and Numbers: A Framework for Employment Equity Planning

A DELLE BRENNER, manager of employee relations for CDI Technologies, a medium size high technology firm, is preparing for a meeting of the company's employment equity committee. The committee, formed six months ago, represents many of CDI's employment equity stakeholders: managers from key departments, union and employee representatives, recruitment and labour relations staff, senior management, and resource people from within and outside the company who are helping the committee address the needs and views of the designated groups. The committee is now preparing to develop an employment equity work plan for CDI, a participant in the Federal Contractors Program.

Adelle knows that in order for the work plan to contain appropriate goals and action initiatives directed toward change, the committee needs to develop a simple planning framework. Next week the committee will meet to discuss and decide on the guidelines CDI will use to plan and set corporate and departmental employment equity goals and action plans. Thinking ahead to what the designated groups, government agencies and company insiders are likely to see as necessary outcomes, Adelle drafts a lengthy list of employment equity activities and desirable results. Scanning the list she begins to see a pattern. On her writing pad she doodles the words: Systems — Culture — Numbers. Then, thinking of the Olympic logo, she draws three intersecting circles:

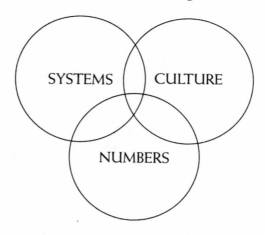

At the meeting, Adelle discusses her ideas with the committee. "Maybe this will help us focus on the problem. What are the barriers in our employment systems that need changing? What would equitable employment systems look like, and how would they respond to the needs of the different designated groups? How does our corporate culture help or hinder equity? What constitutes a supportive organizational culture for designated groups and for the changes employment equity aims to bring about? We have lots of work-force data: what does it tell us about where CDI ought to be focusing its efforts? And, what are the good numbers we ought to be able to point to if we were truly an employment equity employer?"

In Chapter 1 we discussed some ways in which the purpose and goals of employment equity have been defined, and suggested a way to think about the general goals of employment equity. In this chapter we translate these goals into a planning framework focusing on three key areas: employment systems, organizational culture, and the "numbers" or numerical representation of designated groups in an organization's work force. We have found that the "three circles" — systems, culture, and numbers — help organizations and employment equity stakeholders to develop a vision of what to aim for and focus on so that they can take action to make employment equity happen in their organization. This approach to employment equity planning and goal-setting differs from that used by many others, and especially the American affirmative action model. It is broader than an approach that defines the problem and the solution as "bad numbers," that is, the absence or marked under representation of designated group members. This three-part framework includes analysis and remedies concerning the representation and distribution of designated groups, yet also addresses the influence of organizational culture on the quality of work and work environments experienced by members of designated groups once hired or promoted, and the effects that human resource decision-making and employment systems have on designated group members' access to employment and their experience in the workplace. The interlocking circles offer a visual image that helps people remember the key result areas, and at the same time it is an image that reflects the overlapping reality of the three arbitrary categories. For example, workplace harassment might be seen an issue of organizational culture, yet employment policies, practices and the decisions based on them may contribute to an harassing, unequal and discriminatory work environment. Similarly, if certain employment systems are put into place they may help to prevent or remedy workplace harassment, and in turn help recruit, integrate and retain members of the designated groups, thus improving representation and distribution.

The three part image can help an organization focus its goal setting on both qualitative (systems and culture) and quantitative (numbers) outcomes. Keeping a focus on what might be changed in the organization not only helps us identify actual or potential problems in the organization; it may also help us use limited resources efficiently.

Translating Goals into Results

Once the key results of employment equity are specified, it is then possible to plan how to make the desired change happen. Unfortunately, employment equity stakeholders often remain unclear about both the goals and key results they aim to achieve.

Clearly defining and linking the goals of employment equity with outcome statements of key results can aid both our understanding of employment equity (what it is) and the goal-setting process (how to make it happen). This is especially true if employment equity is seen as a change process, whereby an organization moves from a present to a future state. That future state must be named and defined. The three ideas of equitable employment systems, a supportive organizational culture, and "good" numbers of designated groups in and throughout the organization, gives managers, employment equity practitioners and designated groups a simple framework with which to organize their thinking, action and evaluation of an organization's employment equity efforts and results.

It is also helpful to think of employment equity as problem-solving. If a stakeholder approach is taken, then employment equity becomes a joint problem-solving process. What is the problem? The problem is barriers caused by discrimination and disadvantage experienced by the designated groups. What is the solution? It is a process and actions to eliminate, remedy and prevent these barriers, and to improve representation. Box 13.1 shows the linkage between general employment equity goals discussed in Chapter 1 and the key result areas: systems, culture and numbers.

BOX 13.1

Translating Employment Equity Goals into Key Results

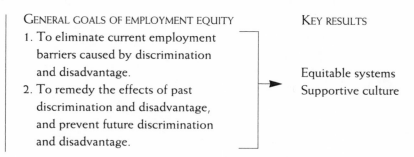

GENERAL GOALS OF EMPLOYMENT EQUITY

1. To eliminate current employment barriers caused by discrimination and disadvantage.
2. To remedy the effects of past discrimination and disadvantage, and prevent future discrimination and disadvantage.

KEY RESULTS

Equitable systems
Supportive culture

3. To improve the representation, access and distribution of designated groups in the work force and labour market.  Good numbers

What Do We Mean By Systems, Culture and Numbers?

An organization's policies, practices, procedures and programs that govern employment decision-making are described as **systems**. Employment systems include recruitment, selection and hiring; training and development, transfer and promotion; conditions of employment, pay and benefits, leaves; disciplinary action, dismissals, lay-offs and recalls. Employment systems may be formal or informal, including what is written down or stated as the "standard operating procedure," as well as what is understood, experienced, or known to be the way decisions are made and policies and practices are implemented. Each organization is unique in both the components of its employment systems and the language used to describe them. Some examples of the "employment systems" found in organizations are listed in box 13.2.

BOX 13.2
Examples of Employment Systems

GETTING IN
- recruitment
- screening
- testing
- interviewing
- reference checking
- selection
- negotiating offers
- job assignment

BEING THERE
- work environment
- information access and networks
- pay
- benefits
- grievance procedures job training
- performance assessment
- job accommodation
- work and family responsibilities

MOVING THROUGH
- training
- development
- career management
- secondment
- acting assignments
- succession planning
- transfer
- promotion

MOVING OUT
- dismissal
- lay-off
- re-calls
- downsizing
- discipline

A key result employment equity aims for is equitable employment systems. To begin to discover inequities in a particular employment system, one might ask:

- What policies, practices, procedures or programs seem to hinder or block job opportunities for minorities, aboriginal peoples, women, and people with disabilities? How are these impacts shown?
- Why are white, able-bodied men not hindered by these aspects of the system?
- What kinds of barriers occur in the system regarding:
   getting into the organization — recruitment, selection and hiring?
   life in the organization and on-the-job treatment — pay and benefits, the workplace environment, information networks, training and performance assessment?
   moving through the organization — transfer, promotion, development and succession planning?
   moving out of the organization — discipline, dismissal, lay-off and recall?
- Where, specifically, do such barriers occur?

Organizational culture is embodied in the basic assumptions and beliefs understood or articulated by the organization. The culture determines the atmosphere and workplace environment within which the designated groups are received, integrated and retained, successfully or unsuccessfully. A key result that employment equity aims for is an organizational culture supportive of employment equity and the designated groups. To identify barriers to this supportive culture in the organization one might ask:

- In what way do the values, norms and organizational culture block the designated groups from attaining full and equal employment opportunities? How is this shown?
- What attitudes, behaviours, symbols, activities, basic assumptions or organizational practices seem to cause problems and blockages?
- How might any of the target groups experience the organization differently than do white, able-bodied men?
- How does the organizational culture support or hinder the employment equity change process? The integration and retention of designated groups? Is workplace harassment prevented? Is it remedied when it happens?

The representation of the designated groups in the organization — the jobs they occupy, in what numbers, and at what levels — is referred to as **numbers**. In assessing representation, we ask, "Are there members of the designated groups working for the organization?" In considering distribution we ask, "In what jobs and at what levels do members of the designated groups work?" The distinction between representation and distribution is important and can be illustrated in the employment of women by banks. As noted in Chapter 2, while there is good representation of women in banks, their distribution is a problem: women are concentrated in lower level clerical, teller and customer service jobs. There is a need for employment equity initiatives to hire, promote and develop women (and members of the other designated groups) in managerial, professional and technical occupations. A key result employment equity aims for is "good" numbers, defined in terms of representation and distribution, and in comparison to indicators of the availability of the designated group. To identify problems in the numbers, one might ask:

- Where are the numbers "bad"? In what way do they fall short of expectations or perceptions of what they ought to be? Why?
- Are there certain jobs or occupational groups where the numbers should be different? What would these numbers be?

There are many more questions that might be asked. Box 13.3 lists some typical questions stakeholders might ask about systems, culture and numbers.

BOX 13.3

Typical Equity Issues and Problems as Perceived by Stakeholders

PERCEPTIONS ABOUT SYSTEMS

- "We [the designated groups] never hear what jobs are open, and when they become available."
- "Sure, we can apply, but we never get the jobs."
- "Unionized jobs aren't open to the designated groups: seniority systems relegate designated groups to entry level jobs, lateral entry is prevented, and hiring halls operate on the 'old boys and their sons' network."
- "Employers should help their women employees with day care and the pressure of family responsibilities."
- "They [the management] say the workplace is accessible; what they mean is that they put some braille numbers on an elevator, retro-fitted one washroom, and put in a ramp. It's not good enough."

PERCEPTIONS ABOUT CULTURE

- "Sure they [the management] do employment equity: for white, middle-class women who want to get into management. What about the rest of us?"
- "Workplace harassment is a real problem for women, minorities, disabled people and aboriginal people. The women are patronized, accused of taking jobs away from men with families to support, stereotyped and put down. Racial minorities are called names, subjected to "jokes" and slurs, and stereotyped. People with disabilities are patronized and treated as if they are the problem if they ask for accommodation. Aboriginal peoples are stereotyped and marginalized; their skills and cultural heritage are not recognized."
- "I don't want to be a clone of a white, able-bodied male. This is not how I define success."
- "Employment equity in this company is just lip service and window-dressing: senior management is not really committed, supervisors just ignore it and do what they want, the human resources department doesn't do anything but fill in government reports, and the unions resent it."
- "Sure there is training, but all of the examples used in the sessions are about white, able-bodied males. The analogies given use North American sports and military illustrations. The language is sexist and Anglo. There is never any attention to the needs of

disabled employees concerning accessible training facilities, materials and instruction."

PERCEPTIONS ABOUT DESIGNATED GROUPS — NUMBERS

- "There are not enough..." or, "There should be more..."
- "They are ghettoized."
- "They aren't getting promoted."
- "They get hired as casuals [or, part-timers, or contract workers], not permanent workers."
- "It's a revolving door: they get hired, then laid off or fired, or they just quit."

Reviewing Employment Systems

In our view, information about employment systems is essential to carrying out a convincing diagnosis of systemic discrimination, whether it takes the form of unequal treatment, adverse impact or a lack of accommodation. In building a body of evidence pointing toward specific discriminatory barriers and remedies, information about systems is also critical for making fundamental, long-term organizational change, and for addressing two of the three goals of employment equity: removing current barriers, and remedying past barriers and preventing future barriers, as discussed in Chapter 1. Diagnosis of the employment systems gives the stakeholders an understanding of specific remedies that may be necessary and possible, as discussed in Chapter 12.

Much of the information about systems will come from the stakeholders' experiences. Of course, examining the written or formal employment policies, practices and procedures also provides information about systems.

Criterion 5 of the Federal Contractors Program regulations is intended to address systemic discrimination in employment policies and practices:

It is important, therefore, that a review be undertaken of all procedures used in the recruitment, selection, training, promotion and termination of employees. Any policy, practice or system, whether formal or informal, which is found to have or is likely to have an unfavourable impact should be eliminated or modified to prevent recurrence of that impact.

(SOURCE: Employment and Immigration Canada, *Federal Contractors Program: Information for Suppliers*. Minister of Supply and Services Canada, 1987.)

The employment systems review required by the FCP may yield insights into how decisions are made and what employment practices are in operation.

However, many employment systems "reviews" are technical exercises that fall short of a true and comprehensive analysis of an organization's employment policies, and practices. As noted in Chapter 5, the systems review has become part of the employment equity tool kit and jargon. But often the systems review is superficial and static. A systems review is superficial if:

- it examines only the formal policies and procedures, for example, how an organization says it recruits and selects, but not actual practices, or
- it deals generally with jobs and promotions at a company or in a government department, but not specifically with the variations in employment systems between and among different occupational groups. For example, at CDI Technologies where our fictional Adelle Brenner works, there may be a need to differentiate between entry and more senior level production jobs, between supervisory and management jobs, or clerical, administrative and sales jobs. There may also be a need to examine differences among bargaining units or employee associations, such as the plant unions and the office employees. It may also be important to look at employment systems within different organizational units, for example, departments, divisions, plants and facilities, and geographic locations.

Each organization is unique in the extent to which employment policies, practices and procedures apply "across the board." A comprehensive systems review will recognize and build on the variations and diversity of employment systems operating within an organization.

In our view, an authentic employment systems review is never complete, since change is always occurring in an organization's hiring and management of people. This is particularly true of organizations that are growing or undergoing downsizing, restructuring or mergers. Thus it is nonsense for a government funding or compliance agency to review employers and ask: "Have you done an employment systems review?" — implying that it can be done once and completed. In our experience, a systems review is a process, not a finite task. Yet, in the interests of efficiency, arbitrary decisions must be taken by stakeholders concerning the boundaries one might place on each component of the systems review. Box 13.4 suggests considerations in drawing the boundaries for an employment systems review.

BOX 13.4

Questions to Guide Decisions About the Boundaries of an Employment Systems Review (ESR)

1. What employment systems will be reviewed?
   - In — recruiting, selecting and hiring people into the organization
   - There — treatment on the job, the work environment, terms and conditions of employment, including benefits and compensation, grievance processes
   - Through — mobility through and within the organization, including transfer and promotion, development and succession
   - Out — moving people out of the organization, dismissals, downsizing practices, disciplinary action
2. Will formal and informal employment systems be reviewed?
3. For which occupational group(s) or jobs will these systems be reviewed?
4. For which bargaining group(s) or employee association(s) will these systems be reviewed?
5. Will systems be reviewed for all designated groups, or selected designated groups (women, racial minorities, aboriginal peoples, people with disabilities), or combinations of designated groups (e.g.: disabled women)?
6. On which organizational units will the ESR focus, for example: corporate, departmental, divisional, branch or plant?
7. Will the geographic focus of the ESR be: Canada-wide, provincial, regional, municipal, etc.?
8. To what time periods will the ESR give attention: current barriers, past/historical barriers, or future barriers?

Various stakeholders will often bring different perspectives and concerns to an employment systems review. "Fresh eyes" will help, not hinder, the process. Organizations will benefit from the involvement of various stakeholders, including those external to the organization as well as internal stakeholders who are on the "front lines" of management or work units. Stakeholder participation is helpful in 1) deciding what systems to examine (drawing the boundaries), 2) examining and assessing barriers, 3) drawing conclusions based on the findings of the analysis, and then 4) designing remedies and making change to employment systems.

It is understandable that one might become bogged down or confused during the process of examining the employment systems of an organization, or have a difficult time getting started with the review. If this happens, then refer to the examples of employment systems listed in Box 12.5 and ask the following two questions:

1. For each of these systems, what happens?
2. What gets in the way?

In looking at "**what happens**" we must also consider how things happen. How do people find out about jobs? What is the first thing they will do, experience, encounter? Then what takes place? Describe everything in detail; do not ignore anything, or leave anything out. Look for patterns in all the "bits and pieces" that describe how employment systems work in practice, not necessarily how they are supposed to work. Also describe and then assess the formal policy, practice or procedure, including how information is made available to employees and applicants, how decisions are made by managers, and on what basis.

The second question "**What gets in the way?**" prompts an identification of the actual, perceived or potential barriers for designated groups. Do not begin to analyze these barriers now; a more technical analysis will take place in part 2 of the diagnostic process. Simply list and describe in detail. Patterns may begin to emerge, or you may need to go back and methodically develop a picture of what may cause barriers for the designated groups. Somewhat like the analysis of work-force data, a systemic analysis needs comparisons. For example, if aboriginal peoples encounter difficulty with a specific employment practice or policy, then go a step farther and ask what may create a barrier to success, a problem or difficulty for aboriginal peoples compared with non-aboriginal persons? Or ask, how does the system work for non-aboriginal peoples, yet get in the way for aboriginal peoples?

Culture: Workplace Values and Environment

In the 1980s the popular management literature began to pay a great deal of attention to identifying and modifying organizational culture to improve job satisfaction and morale, productivity, product quality, customer service, communication and a host of other objectives. Here we use the term organizational culture to refer to the values, norms and principles that become expressed in the attitudes and behaviours of people in the organization, as well as the basic assumptions, standards, symbols and customs of the organization that develop over time. An understanding of the impact of organizational culture on the workplace environment as it is experienced by designated groups is important for those involved in the employment equity change process.

Edgar Schein (1991: Chapter 1) proposes that organizational culture has three interrelated levels:

1) **artifacts and creations**: technology, written and pictorial communications, observable behaviour patterns, and other features of the organization's physical and social environment;
2) **values**: shared understandings about what is real, what is true, what is right or wrong; and
3) **basic assumptions**: the underlying and unexamined guides to behaviour, perceptions, and interpretation of experience that are widely held by organizational members.

Schein argues that the third level — basic assumptions — contains the essence of organizational culture, and forms the foundation of the other two levels. The basic assumptions and beliefs that operate in an organization are learned responses on the part of organizational members to problems of organizational survival and integration. These assumptions are widely shared and taken for granted, and are not ordinarily acknowledged or subjected to scrutiny. An organization may have a common culture, and in addition, a number of sub-cultures specific to occupational groups, such as different professions, or regions, or distinctions between managers and workers, or sub-cultures rooted in gender or ethnicity. For example, the top executive group may constitute a white male and highly privileged sub-culture with distinctive assumptions about its own legitimacy and about who is acceptable as a member of its "inner circle." Some of these and other basic assumptions may be part of the culture of the organization as a whole. For example, it may be generally assumed that certain jobs are "women's jobs," or that people with disabilities are suited only for certain types of work, at certain rates of pay. Hiring and promotion discussions may be guided by basic assumptions — often undefined — about "merit," "excellence" and "best qualified." Such assumptions are often deeply rooted in the organization's historical experience.

Culture is an important focus of employment equity initiatives because a receptive organizational culture helps to implement remedies to reform employment systems and designated group representation. For example, policy statements committing the organization to employment equity can become a part of the organizational culture, not merely another human resource policy. Evidence of commitment may be reflected in everyday life in the organization, for example,

- in how senior, line and human resources managers talk of employment equity,
- in the attitudes and behaviours they and other organizational members demonstrate and model, and
- in the way the organization communicates internally and externally, formally and informally.

What kind of culture helps employment equity? To answer this, we must identify what underlying processes make designated groups feel welcome to apply for jobs or comfortable working in certain organizations, as opposed to "chilling out" their interest. What positively affects the interview and selection process? What helps the effective integration of people who either have not been included in a particular work-force, or have not been visible in great numbers? How do co-workers or supervisors and workers communicate with each other, or in groups? How do they share, withhold or trade information? These are some of the cultural issues that the perceptions, experience and information of various stakeholders will address in an examination of barriers faced by the designated groups.

Three essential components of employment equity implementation involve organizational culture: 1) the successful integration of designated groups into jobs and workplaces in which they have not previously worked, 2) designated group retention in jobs, careers and organizations, and 3) the creation and maintenance of an harassment-free workplace. A focus on cultural change usually leads to the strategies and issues of communication, education and training discussed in Chapter 11.

Numbers: Zeros, Near Zeros and Concentrations

Often, "numbers" are seen as the critical, if not the only, employment equity issue. Specifically, "bad numbers" — that is, the lack of designated group representation relative to availability — are cited as evidence of systemic discrimination. In our view, it is rare that bad numbers alone will make a solid or convincing case of discrimination and a strong argument for large-scale organizational change. Nevertheless, work-force data reflecting inequities experienced by designated groups can be a powerful tool in developing evidence of discrimination, and can help to develop momentum for fundamental and highly visible employment equity change. As well, numbers are an important, although not the only, benchmark against which we can determine whether fundamental change has taken place over time.

Thus, an analysis of numbers will help us decide where to focus our efforts to identify where the systemic problems may lie, or where remedies are most urgent. Numbers are one of the three important sources of information used to focus stakeholder perceptions of employment equity problems as part of a diagnosis, as well as one of the three key result areas for employment equity outcomes. Employment equity practitioners often use their analysis of work-force data to begin their review of employment systems. With the increase in government legislation, regulations, incentive funding and policy requiring the collection and reporting of data, many employment equity stakeholders now have unprecedented access to the work-force numbers of a wide range of organizations.

Let us now turn to some of the key considerations in a diagnosis of work-force numbers.

It is important to keep in mind that numbers are only helpful for employment equity diagnosis when comparisons are made. Thus, an organization's work-force data (the jargon often used is "stock data") are compared to "outside availability" data or to "feeder group availability" data. Here the percentages are compared, not the actual work-force numbers. Percentages of designated group and majority group members in an organization's work force may be compared against:

- applicant data
- labour market data
- other "feeder group" data, such as statistics on new graduates from relevant university or college programs, or internal promotional pools, and population data, such as the "representation in the community" defined in the Ontario police employment equity regulations (Box 7.1).

Let us illustrate some of the potential comparisons using the *ATF vs. CN* case:

Representation of women in blue collar jobs at CN Rail:	0.7%
Percentage of women in the Canadian population:	52%
Percentage of women in the Canadian labour force:	45%
Percentage of women working in blue collar jobs in Canada:	13%

It would also be relevant to consider applicant data, that is, the representation of women in the blue collar applicant pool in CN's St. Lawrence region. If appropriate comparative data are not available, one might make use of organizational data alone, looking for "zeros," "near zeros" and "concentrations."

Zeros

Zeros indicate an absence or exclusion of the designated groups from certain occupational groups or specific jobs. Data reflecting "zeros" can help build a compelling argument for employment equity change. For example, a finding of no Native people in teaching occupations with a board of education in northern British Columbia, or in supervisory and managerial classifications in a federal government department, may prompt a further search for comparative statistical data, as well as employment systems information.

Near Zeros

Near zeros indicate those occupational groups or specific jobs where designated groups are very few in number. These "near exclusions" should be checked for historical trends: for example, have designated group individuals only recently been hired or promoted into these jobs? Is there high turnover? The *ATF* example built a case for progressive numerical employment goals on the basis of a minuscule representation of 0.7 % women in blue collar jobs in the region.

Concentrations

Concentrations indicate large numbers of designated groups members in certain occupational groups or specific jobs, compared with their absence from other jobs. For example, in banks women may be predominant in bank tellers' positions and absent from senior management. Again, examine the historical hiring and employment patterns in jobs and occupational groups, keeping in mind that, as discussed in Chapter 2, concentrations of white males are not considered a problem that requires an employment equity remedy.

Pay data are often required for government reporting. These data supplement the employment equity census or work-force data and may be useful in analyzing compensation and benefit patterns and practices as part of the employment systems review. They may provide clear evidence of how women, and in particular minority women, disabled women and aboriginal women, are disadvantaged relative to men.

Without work-force and labour market data that are timely, accurate, valid, and most of all, relevant, even the most expert analyst will have difficulty in making a solid case based on numbers alone. Relevancy includes comparability in terms of designated group and majority group status, job or occupational group, and definitions of "qualified" or "qualifiable" persons in the availability pool. Using timely data is also important, especially for designated groups that may be growing, for example, racial minorities in large urban areas such as Metro Toronto, or for certain occupations that a designated group might be entering, such as women in non-traditional jobs. Availability data are further discussed in Box 13.5.

BOX 13.5
Availability Data

Employers covered by the Federal Contractors Program are required to compare the representation of designated groups in their employ with their representation in labour markets from which the employer might expect to recruit. These counts of designated group members in external labour markets are known as "availability data."

Availability data for women, racial minorities and aboriginal peoples are drawn from the 1986 Census of Canada. Availability data for people with disabilities are derived from the 1986-87 Health and Activity Limitation Survey (HALS) of a national sample.

Data for all four designated groups are provided to employers by the Technical Services section of the Employment Equity Branch of Employment and Immigration Canada, in the form of reports, as hard copies and DBase III files. These reports, entitled *Employment Equity Availability Data* contain data for fairly large geographical entities (the nation, provinces and territories, and census metropolitan areas), and large occupational groupings, and may not always be useful to employers who draw from small local areas or from very specialized labour markets. Data on persons with disabilities are particularly limited. The availability data underestimate the numbers of qualified designated group members in the labour market, since the data reflect the effects of systemic discrimination, and are out of date.

For further information on employment equity availability data see Edward B. Harvey, *Information Systems for Employment Equity: An Employer Guide*, Don Mills: CCH Canadian Ltd, 1988; Edward B. Harvey, Eric J. Severn and John H. Blakely, *Computing for Equity: Computer Applications for Employment Equity* Don Mill: CCH Canadian Ltd., 1990; and *Employment and Immigration Canada, Employment Equity Act and Reporting Requirements*, Ottawa: Supply and Services, 1986.

Diagnostic Results and Employment Equity Planning

The prime objective of the planning framework we have been discussing is to identify barriers specific to an organization and its occupations, bargaining groups, stakeholders and the designated groups, and to set realistic goals for change in order to get results.

Consequently, in order to develop a comprehensive employment equity plan, we need to relate the design of remedies to the results of an organization specific diagnosis and goal setting process. We suggest that an organization use the systems-culture-numbers framework for developing employment equity initiatives as part of a work plan or action plan that specifies: 1) the barriers unique to an organization, 2) the standard activities that have become associated with employment equity programming or required under legislation or government policy, and 3) a strategy of organizational change. Box 13.6 summarizes this.

Box 13.6
From Diagnosis to Employment Equity Action Planning

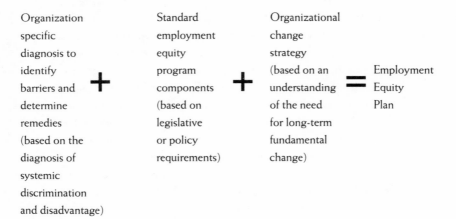

| Organization specific diagnosis to identify barriers and determine remedies (based on the diagnosis of systemic discrimination and disadvantage) | + | Standard employment equity program components (based on legislative or policy requirements) | + | Organizational change strategy (based on an understanding of the need for long-term fundamental change) | = | Employment Equity Plan |

The challenge for those involved in action planning and goal setting is to select those ingredients that best fit both the needs of designated groups and the organization. Then we must determine what might make employment equity happen within the operational constraints of available time and resources, as well as the political realities of shared and conflicting interests and priorities of multiple stakeholders.

We also need to consider the level of organizational commitment to act in order to attain equitable outcomes. Our planning framework orients the analysis to goals for employment equity actions related to the three key results: equitable employment systems; an organizational culture supportive of employment equity, designated group integration and work force diversity; and representation of designated group members in and across all occupations and levels in the organization. Box 13.7 introduces a continuum of remedies or actions toward each of these three key results, suggesting various degrees of progressive action.

BOX 13.7
Continuum of Actions Toward Key Results for Systems, Culture and Numbers

EQUITABLE EMPLOYMENT SYSTEMS:

Non-discrimination	Outreach	Giving advantages to designated groups

SUPPORTIVE ORGANIZATIONAL CULTURE:

Non-discrimination	Managing diversity	Valuing diversity

GOOD NUMBERS:

Within 2 standard deviations of availability	Meets availability	Exceeds availability to create "critical mass"

├─────────────────────┼─────────────────────┼─────────────────────┤

Conclusion

This chapter suggests a planning framework to help employment equity stakeholders and organizations develop a vision of what to aim for and focus on, so that appropriate goals and action initiatives are directed toward employment equity change. The general goals of employment equity are translated into a planning framework focusing on three key result areas: equitable systems, supportive organizational culture, and the numerical representation of designated groups in an organization's work force. This framework can be used to examine inequities and then to set realistic goals for change and action initiatives. The result is an employment equity work plan or action agenda.

REFERENCES

Employment and Immigration Canada. *Federal Contractors Program: Information for Suppliers.* Ottawa: Minister of Supply and Services Canada, 1987.

Schein, Edgar. *Organizational Culture and Leadership.* San Francisco: Jossey-Bass, 1991.

14

Tracking Progress Toward Equity: Monitoring, Evaluation and Organizational Learning

R ECENTLY, CANADIAN FINANCIAL SERVICES INC.
(CFS) has worked hard to develop plans
for employment equity and implement
change projects. CFS has introduced more equitable approaches to
recruiting, interviewing and selecting job applicants; sexual and
racial harassment policies with procedures for dealing with complaints; and flexible scheduling and parental leave programs. There
have been modifications, such as reducing the height of some customer service counters, to improve accessibility for people with
disabilities. As part of a human resource planning strategy, CFS's
departments evaluated their management development process.

This evaluation resulted in departmental targets to increase the representation of women, racial minorities and people with disabilities in middle management within five years. The goals are part of a broader management development and career planning program for all supervisory and middle management personnel in the company.

At the last meeting of CFS's Board of Directors, questions were raised about what the company is doing to improve its representation of the designated groups. Top management has asked the employment equity manager for a status report. Many of the human resources staff are pleased with the employment equity process and feel that it is more advanced than those of most other companies in the same industry. But many of the employees are sceptical and suspect that nothing is really changing because CFS's top management is not serious about employment equity. Others, resistant to the change process from the beginning, are saying that white able-bodied males are no longer promoted in the company.

How can these questions and concerns be addressed? What are the facts about what is happening as CFS begins to implement employment equity? Only a systematic collection and evaluation of information can shed light on the results and impacts of the company's employment equity initiatives over time, and give a clear picture of the company's progress, or lack of progress, toward equity. In this chapter we examine the importance of monitoring and evaluation — the set of procedures that are used to:

- find out whether a change program is actually doing what it is supposed to be doing — getting results!
- keep an employment equity program "on track," and
- make effective and efficient use of peoples' time and other resources to accomplish the equity goals the organization has set.

Monitoring and evaluation should be seen as an integral and ongoing component of a goal-oriented change strategy. In the preface to this book we suggested that employment equity is both a process and a set of goals — visions of desired results — established through consultation with the primary stakeholders. In developing procedures for monitoring and evaluation, we attempt to see if and how the change process is working. To answer this question we must judge what is real change: what truly indicates progress toward equity in the workplace? In addressing these and other issues our change model directs attention to the needs of various stakeholders for information obtained from monitoring and evaluation, and to reasons and ways to involve the users of information in the processes of collecting and interpreting data.

Why Monitor and Evaluate?

Monitoring and evaluation for employment equity resemble the other systems the organization uses to keep track of its resources and accomplishments — its inputs and outputs — and to ensure a focus upon its business or service goals and objectives. Systematic monitoring and evaluation are the feedback loop in the system. Their purpose is to help keep the organization's activities "on track" and directed toward its goals.

Organizations implement monitoring systems in order to ensure that actual results of activities conform to planned results of those activities (Wholey et. al., 1975:195). Organizations must monitor and evaluate themselves continuously to ensure improvement and success in their business operations and service delivery. Quality and inventory control systems, productivity analyses, monthly sales reports, status reports on cases opened and closed, analyses of data on absenteeism, turnover and grievances, and budgeting, accounting and auditing systems, are all required in order to evaluate and improve organizational performance in the service, business, financial and human resource management functions. These control systems are considered essential to the management of the business or service, not extra cost items or add-ons to the "real" administrative decision-making process.

In the same way, organizational change strategies for employment equity must be monitored and evaluated. Too often, monitoring and evaluation are tacked on to the end of an employment equity or other organizational change program as an after-thought. We suggest that they should be built into the design of the organizational change strategy from the very beginning, and recognized as essential components to include in the initial planning and allocation of resources directed toward the achievement of equity of outcomes in the organization.

We are unable to assess equality of results unless we are able to measure and evaluate outcomes. In Chapter 8 we examined employment equity as a process of strategic planning that involves setting goals and identifying ways to attain them. In Chapter 12 we discussed a framework for diagnosis that can guide us as we identify and document sources of discrimination and disadvantage that must be addressed if we are to attain our goals. This diagnostic process is a necessary step toward planning effective remedies for inequitable practices, as discussed in Chapter 13. In this chapter we are looking at ways of measuring the success of the employment equity change projects we have initiated to deal with the inequitable practices we diagnosed. (The sequence is outlined in Box 14.1.) In evaluating the effectiveness of employment equity policy, whether at the national or provincial levels or at the level of the workplace, it is useful to remember that policies, as guides to action, may be seen as hypothetical solutions to some perceived problem. The definition of the problem, therefore, is the heart of the policy, the key to deciphering its meaning and logic (Pal, 1987: 10).

Box 14.1.
Monitoring and Evaluation as Part of an Employment Equity Change Process

SETTING GOALS

How do we define equity in our organization?

For each designated group, what are our objectives for improving:

• numerical representation and distribution ?

• employment systems ?

• workplace culture ?

What are our targets and time-frames for attaining these objectives?

DIAGNOSIS OF DISADVANTAGE AND DISCRIMINATION

For each designated group, what are the barriers to equitable access, distribution, retention, integration, career development, and rewards? For each designated group, is there unequal treatment ? Adverse impact ? Failure to accommodate ?

DESIGNING AND IMPLEMENTING REMEDIES

What change initiatives will we undertake to address the issues identified in the diagnosis ?

Who needs to be consulted? Informed? Involved in designing remedies?

Who is accountable for implementation ?

What are the time-frames and resources required ?

MONITORING AND EVALUATING PROGRESS TOWARD GOALS

How will we measure the results of our change initiatives ?

Who is involved in tracking and assessing results ? How ?

Are we moving toward the goals we have set ? At an appropriate pace?

How is information from monitoring and evaluation communicated to all who need to know ?

How is this information used to make employment equity more effective in getting the desired results ?

Organizations covered by the federal Employment Equity Act are required to conduct a limited program of monitoring in order to supply numerical data in a standard format to the government on an annual basis. Organizations that participate in the Federal Contractors Program are expected to provide the results of an acceptable work-force census, regularly updated, in the event of a compliance review. Businesses covered by the City of Toronto's contract compliance program, and police services in Ontario, must also collect and report numerical data. Organizations in other provincial and municipal jurisdictions face similar requirements.

Hence many organizations are required to undertake at least some form of monitoring in order to comply with legislation or government regulations. If collecting and reporting numerical data on the distribution of designated group members is the only employment equity requirement to which sanctions are attached — as has been true under the federal Employment Equity Act — then this may be the primary or only employment equity activity undertaken by the organization. We have argued in previous chapters that data collection and monitoring in themselves do not constitute an employment equity program.

We are suggesting, however, that **monitoring and evaluation are important not just to comply with regulations or legislation:**

they are central features of an effective strategy for organizational change that is intended to get results. For example, we need to keep a record of the numbers and distribution of the designated groups over time in order to see whether the remedies we have introduced have resulted in increases in their representation. Similarly, we need to track organizational processes, especially the equity measures we have implemented, to see whether human resources decision-making is indeed becoming more equitable and moving us toward the equity goals we have set.

Are the outreach recruitment activities we have developed producing more applications for employment from members of designated groups? Are our new procedures for interviewing and selection resulting in more hires of designated group members? If not, why not? Is there a difference between the proportion of applicants and the proportion of hires that are designated group members ? If so, why? Are the policies and procedures for dealing with harassment, and the training of supervisors in dealing with diversity, paying off in the form of a higher rate of retention and improved job satisfaction of designated group members in the work force? Is there evidence that designated group members feel they are receiving acceptance and support from co-workers and supervisors?

Procedures for monitoring and evaluation enable us to measure outcomes such as these over time. This information then becomes the basis for making improvements in our employment equity strategy and program components in order to get better results and use our resources more effectively in the future. It may also be important in providing a rationale and justification for resources that are allocated to employment equity, or for increasing the organization's level of commitment.

Most important, perhaps, information derived from monitoring and evaluation is a necessary foundation for ensuring accountability for results of the change program. Policy researchers have noted that there is frequently a gap between the intentions of policymakers and the sponsors, agents and champions of change, on the one hand, and the activities and results of a change program, on the other (Morah, 1990a). It is important to the credibility of a change program to be able to identify this gap, and to assess its nature and size, in order to determine whether the measures taken are only cosmetic, or whether change is actually occurring.

The organization as a whole, the employment equity practitioner, top management, and line managers responsible for results at the departmental level, cannot be held accountable for failures to make progress, nor rewarded for successes, if there is no yardstick with which to measure outcomes. An employment equity program will lack credibility with both internal and external stakeholders if there is no systematic assessment of its successes and failures, and therefore no way for the organization to hold decision-makers accountable. In any event, internal and external stakeholders will make their own assessment of the validity of organizational claims of making progress toward employment equity, from information and impressions available to them.

In this chapter, then, we are looking at the role of monitoring and evaluation in the organizational change process. We are not interested solely in the data-collection activities that must be undertaken in order to comply with government requirements, although these may be important elements of a broader monitoring and evaluation capability that is designed to assist the organization to get results from its employment equity process.

What's Involved in Monitoring and Evaluation?

To monitor is to watch or observe in order to check, test or adjust ongoing activities. To evaluate means to appraise or assign a value to those activities. Monitoring and evaluation, then, are the processes through which observations are made and recorded, and the results are interpreted.

Several assumptions underlie organizational steering and control systems, no matter what specific purpose they serve. Because these considerations are the foundation of any set of monitoring and evaluation procedures, in the pages that follow we will discuss them in relation to employment equity applications.

Of Course We Have Goals... But What Are They?

First, there is an assumption that the organization has engaged in *planning to set goals and objectives*. The primary purpose of an evaluation of a program's impact is to see whether it is reaching the goals for which it was established, so the evaluation process must begin with an understanding and assessment of those goals (Morah, 1990b: 9). It may not be immediately evident what the actual goals are, since there are typically many operational goals that are assumed or unstated in addition to the formal, explicit goals. For example, an employment equity coordinator's role may be established to provide a focus for developing an effective change program. Or the role may have been created to prepare the organization for an impending audit by the Federal Contractors Program, or to provide a job for an employee who needs a position but for whom no other job is currently available in the organization. In addition to clarifying both explicit and operational goals, it is important to identify goal conflicts, or areas of disagreement over goals, since these can give rise to implementation problems and resulting difficulties in attaining desired outcomes.

BOX 14.2:
On the Gap Between Policy and Practice...

> Discussions of equity programs pay insufficient attention to the distinction between the official and unofficial, the formal and informal, head office decisions and local plant behaviour. Philosophical commitments, policy statements, and contract language represent only one level of reality. The actual implementation of policy, commitment to change, and the interpretation of issues represent another...
>
> (Sugiman, 1987: ii-iii)

As discussed in Chapter 12, any program of change is based upon an underlying theory of causation that specifically relates a problem that has been diagnosed to a remedy that is believed to be effective in dealing with the problem (Poister, 1978: 55). Part of the assessment of goals, then, is to evaluate whether the means selected to attain the goals are appropriate, and whether the conceptual link between problems and remedies has at least face validity. If this is not the case, it may be that a lack of results is due not to inadequate implementation of the program of change, nor to an inappropriate diagnosis, but to a lack of fit between the problems and the remedies adopted.

Goal-setting is to some degree a data-driven process that involves the monitoring of trends both inside the organization and in its environment. (We discussed some of the issues involved in strategic planning and goal-setting for employment equity in Chapter 8.) Realistic planning and goal-setting for employment equity involves the use of internal human resource planning data, as well as various kinds of externally generated data with which the organization will compare its own results. For example, employment equity goals are typically set with reference to "availability data" (Box 13.5). The quality of these data and their adequacy as a basis for goal-setting, then, is also an issue in the evaluation process.

How Will We Measure Progress Toward Our Goals?

A second assumption underlying any system of organizational steering and control, including monitoring and evaluation procedures, is that standards of performance have been set that reflect the organizations's goals. A process of measurement of performance, based upon these standards, is then developed to **systematically collect observations about where the organization is in relation to its goals**.

Monitoring is designed to be useful, not to intrude upon or hinder the organization's operations. Measurement is not an end in itself, and its importance may not be immediately evident to line managers and other decision-makers who may resent any extra burden involved in maintaining records for employment equity purposes. It is therefore important to involve these decision-makers in developing appropriate measures and data collection procedures and to communicate clearly the need for them. For example, systematic procedures may need to be developed for collecting information about job applicants, the nature of offers made, and responses to offers of employment. In large organizations where hiring is done at the department or other sub-unit level it may be important to compile and analyze this kind of information in order to identify barriers to the designated groups. In the absence of such data it may not be possible to assess the organization's success in attracting applicants from the designated groups and in making equitable offers to them. For example, there is evidence that women in management jobs receive lower salaries than do men with similar qualifications at the same level (Morrison and Von Glinow, 1990). Because it is likely that the inequality begins with offers of starting salaries, tracking these offers may be useful in identifying a systemic barrier that contributes to under-representation of women in management.

The choice of indicators for measuring program outcomes may require considerable thought. Measures of inputs are often easy to confuse with measures of results. The organization's employment equity budget, or numbers of managers trained, are not in themselves evidence of progress toward goals. However, it is also important to evaluate the adequacy of resources devoted to the change effort. If funds, personnel, or time allocated to the process fall short of requirements, we might expect that outcomes will be limited accordingly. The following considerations (adapted from Morah, 1990b:14) may be helpful in thinking about what kinds of indicators or measurements to include in an employment equity evaluation. Examples are provided in Box 14.4.

1) Indicators should follow from, and relate to, the goals of the process.
2) Indicators should reflect the causal theory that is contained in the link between the diagnosis of disadvantage and discrimination, and the remedies that were designed to correct these conditions.
3) Indicators should be valid. That is, they should be true measures of what they are intended to measure. For example, we may not be able to assume that performance appraisals by supervisors are accurate and unbiased sources of information about the performance of members of designated groups, or about whether they are receiving appropriate opportunities for training, professional development and promotion.

BOX 14.3.
Performance Appraisals:
A Systemic Barrier to Promotion?

A number of studies have suggested that women and racial minorities are not treated equally in performance evaluations, and in decisions about advancement that take performance appraisals into consideration. For example, a study of managers in three U.S. companies found that Black managers had the same job-related characteristics as white managers, but were rated lower by their supervisors on both relationship and task components of performance. Consequently they were given lower assessments of promotability. Black managers were also more likely than whites to be dissatisfied in their jobs and to be plateaued in their careers. Performance appraisals were found to directly affect promotability assessments and plateauing (Greenhaus, Parasuraman and Wormley, 1990).

Pettigrew and Martin (1987) suggest that white supervisors may have low expectations of Black employees, which may result in their giving Blacks less opportunity for challenging assignments or training that can lead to promotions. If performance appraisals are biased and lack credibility with employees, they are not useful as guides to future behaviour and success in the organization. The minority employee, then, is disadvantaged by not having accurate feedback, and the organization's productivity suffers as well.

Women encounter similar systemic barriers to promotion. A study in a large Canadian public sector organization found that among clerical employees, women were as likely to be promoted as men. Yet women were significantly less likely than men to be promoted into administrative positions from clerical jobs. Men and women had equivalent job related characteristics and performance evaluations, but they were not judged in the same way. Women were held to "different and tougher promotion criteria" than men (Swimmer, 1990: 308; also Olson and Becker, 1983).

These findings suggest the importance of monitoring both promotions and performance appraisals of employees to check for the existence of bias and unequal treatment.

4) Indicators should be reliable: they should produce consistent or stable results at different points in time. For example, the percentage of women in middle management may increase in a year not because their numbers in that category improved, but because of layoffs of women in other job classes.

5) Indicators should be part of an appropriate overall research design or strategy that is capable of identifying impacts of the change program and distinguishing them from impacts of other influences in the environment. For example, a company has hired several women, and no Natives or racial minorities, into skilled trades jobs in the past year. A closer examination reveals that this was also true in other local companies. The improvement in women's representation was not due to better recruitment or selection methods in the company, but to a government-funded

apprenticeship and placement program for women in trades in the local community college, combined with a general labour shortage in the trades.

6) Data collection should include indicators of the process — what has been done — as well as outcomes.

7) Indicators should take the views of various stakeholders into account.

We will discuss the last two items in some detail, and give examples, in the pages which follow.

BOX 14.4.

Examples of Indicators of Employment Equity Success for Each Component of the Equity Strategy in CFS Inc.

	GOALS	INDICATORS
NUMBERS	Recruit 5 women for sales management trainee jobs within three years and move them into permanent sales positions.	Annual counts of applicants, interviews, offers, hires and terminations for sales management of trainee jobs, and of promotions into permanent sales positions by gender.
SYSTEMS	Develop a training, mentoring and coaching program to prepare people with disabilities and racial minorities to move from technical and clerical jobs into entry level management positions over a five year period.	Trainee, trainer and management evaluations of the program and of job preparation of participants. Number, duration, and content of developmental assignments Number and types of promotions of target groups and others. Number of trainees ready for promotion.

SYSTEMS	Over the coming year, develop and communicate a policy on management's responsibility to accommodate disability Develop processes for employees and applicants to voice needs for accommodation.	Numbers and kinds of accommodations and requests for accommodation for existing and new employees.
CULTURE	Over the coming year, train all employees with supervisory responsibilities about effective ways to prevent and deal with sexual, disability, and racial harassment.	Annual counts of recipients of training. Trainee evaluations of program. Annual assessment of climate by representatives of designated groups. Counts of complaints filed and their disposition, and of preventive actions taken

What Are We Actually Doing About Equity?

A third basic element of monitoring and evaluating is that **information needs to be collected about the implementation process itself — about what people are doing to put employment equity initiatives into practice.**

Employment equity is not a "program" that has a specific end point after which it ceases to exist: it is a new way of thinking and doing things that gradually becomes part of the organization's culture and employment systems. In this sense, employment equity is a process, an on-going set of activities that change over time as the organization's environment, resource base, employee population, task mix, and market or clientele change, and as organizational members come to understand and practice employment equity principles. That is why it makes sense to think of monitoring and evaluation as on-going components of the total organizational change strategy involved in employment equity — not as something that occurs once, at a particular point in time.

Program and policy evaluation are often viewed as one-time activities that provide information useful in deciding such questions as whether a program has been successful, whether it should be continued, or whether its budget should be increased or cut. We are viewing monitoring and evaluation as having an additional purpose — that of providing information on a periodic or continuing basis that will help change agents and other decision-makers to develop new change initiatives, and to fine-tune, alter or scrap existing ones. The purpose of this kind of evaluation is to make an on-going change process as useful, efficient and effective as possible so that the intended results are more likely to be attained. This use of information corresponds to what has been called formative or process evaluation, as distinct from product, outcome or summative evaluation (Poister, 1978: 16). Taken together, process and outcome evaluations can shed light not only on whether goals are being attained, but why or why not, and how. Unless the process of implementation is documented and assessed, we are measuring the outcomes of events that themselves remain a mystery (Morah, 1990b:37-38).

Viewed in this way, the process of monitoring and evaluation involves collecting and evaluating information about specific employment equity activities — the details of what actually gets done in the organization — not just about the goals that have been set and whether or not they have been attained after a specified period of time has elapsed. The purpose of monitoring and evaluation, then, is not just to decide whether employment equity has been "successful" in attaining its goals, but how — in what ways — the various change projects that form part of the employment equity process have made a difference, and how they could be improved in order to move the organization closer to its goals.

How Do We Measure Up?
A fourth element of any system for monitoring and evaluating performance is that information collected in the monitoring process must be interpreted. This is usually done by comparing what the measurements show about the organization's performance with its goals, and with various kinds of comparative data, in order to **assess the gap between actual and expected accomplishments**. An

evaluation based on this comparison provides a basis for identifying both successes and failures, or areas of inadequacy.

Our change model implies that we should expect various stakeholders to assess this gap in different ways when they look at the same employment equity outcomes. Moreover, stakeholders will probably vary in their goals and priorities for change, and in identifying issues that have not been adequately addressed by the change process. For example, organizations representing people with disabilities and advocates of the interests of racial minority women have been critical of the general tendency for first generation employment equity programs to concentrate on measures that may benefit white middle-class women. However, many white feminists have also been disappointed in the results so far attained under employment equity legislation and regulations.

Who Gets the Credit? How Can We Do Even Better?

A fifth consideration in monitoring and evaluation is that assessment of the discrepancy between actual and expected results becomes the basis for **allocating rewards and taking corrective actions** to ensure that the organization continues to move toward its goals as efficiently and effectively as possible. If the allocation of rewards and sanctions is to have the desired effect of reinforcing effective change-oriented measures, the process must be seen as solidly based and equitable. For example, the practice of giving out "employment equity awards" to employers will be met with scepticism if the awards go to organizations that appear undeserving, in terms of the results they have demonstrated. The use of internal rewards and sanctions can be crucial to reinforcing accountabilities for results and for recognizing the contributions of people who have taken risks and worked effectively for employment equity. But again, if they are to serve their purpose, rewards and sanctions must be assigned equitably, and this requires a credible evaluation process.

Who Should Monitor and Evaluate?

Traditional views of management often include the assumption that the control functions in organizations are always performed by management — that it is management's job to plan, set goals, assess performance, detect and correct error, and evaluate. In today's organizations the need for steering and control systems is almost universally accepted. There is also a growing recognition that control — monitoring and evaluation — need not, and perhaps should not, be performed unilaterally by management. Japanese and Scandinavian management approaches, quality circles, statistical quality control systems, and self-managing work teams are all concepts that give a role in monitoring and evaluation — and as a result, in steering and controlling — to workers at all levels of the organization.

New management thinking recognizes that when management alone has authority to monitor and evaluate performance and exercise control, disadvantageous consequences tend to follow. First, there may be considerable conflict between workers and management, and resistance on the part of workers to management's unilateral authority, which is perceived as oppressive. Such adversarial social dynamics are less likely to be present in the workplace when control is truly shared, through joint union-management structures, employee involvement processes, or other arrangements that assure that employees have the right to participate in decision-making.

Second, management alone cannot do as good a job of monitoring and evaluating performance, since workers directly involved in operations have a deeper and more detailed knowledge that can make an essential contribution to the assessment process.

Third, a preoccupation by the management with control as an end in itself tends to focus attention and resources on maintaining stability and existing power relations, and away from encouraging innovation and flexibility in response to a changing environment.

Fourth, steering and control systems tend to be costly; the resources consumed by specialized measurement and evaluation activities might be more effectively spent in ways that will contribute more directly to attaining the outcomes of a change process. An example is the trend toward doing away with inspection and quality control specialists and giving production workers the authority and responsibility to ensure product quality. An employment equity example is reporting on a three year rather than an annual cycle, which would free up resources for change activities.

Like today's participatory theories about management, our model of organizational change stresses the importance of involving all the key stakeholders in decision-making throughout the change process. This is also true of the monitoring and evaluation that is an on-going part of a mature program of organizational change, whether that change is directed toward employment equity or some other organizational goal. In the following paragraphs we will consider ways in which the collection and interpretation of information, for purposes of monitoring and evaluation, can be enriched by involving stakeholders.

What Kinds of Information Are Needed for Evaluation?

A broad approach to monitoring and evaluation is needed through which information is systematically and regularly collected about the representation and the experiences of designated group members working in various kinds of jobs, and about the results of specific employment equity initiatives. A plan or strategy for monitoring and evaluation will help ensure that all the information that is needed is collected, while restricting data collection to information that will provide useful feedback about the program's results.

The Federal Contractors Program and some provincial regulations provide employers with guidelines that specify what kinds of employment equity initiatives are required. Guidelines such as these are commonly used as a framework for orienting an employment equity program, and its monitoring and evaluation component. The result is likely to be an organizational emphasis on three types of information for purposes of monitoring and evaluation:

a) the employment equity census or work-force audit,
b) the organization's quantitative goals and timetables for the representation of the four designated groups, and
c) the work plans or action plans, and the specific initiatives that have been established in order to move toward the attainment of goals.

These are essential components of the information base needed to evaluate the employment equity process, but they are not sufficient in themselves. A more balanced and complete view of the change process is possible if, in addition to these types of information, the evaluation also includes:

d) information about how the work plans are actually implemented;

e) qualitative and contextual information that aids in the interpretation of quantitative data; and

f) perspectives of members of the designated groups, both within and outside the organization.

We will now consider the contributions and limitations of each of these six types of information in relation to the process of monitoring and evaluation.

The Work-Force Audit or Census

The employment equity census provides data on the representation and distribution of members of the four designated groups in the organization's work force. It is a one-time survey with some arrangement for updating with the passage of time. The validity and hence the utility of the survey results depend heavily on the rate of response, and on the types of questions asked.

Federal regulations suggest that the census involve voluntary reports by individual employees about their own status as designated group members. If participation in the survey is poor or uneven, for example, if people with disabilities do not feel comfortable about reporting that they have disabilities, the data will not be useful and the census will have been wasted. It is therefore essential to communicate clearly to all employees the reasons for the census and what will be done with the data. It is particularly important to provide credible procedures to protect the confidentiality of respondents, and to communicate widely about those arrangements. Otherwise employees may fear that supervisors, co-workers or others may have access to the information or that it will be used inappropriately.

The quality of numerical data on the distribution of designated groups in the workplace is likely to be viewed in various ways by different stakeholders. The most obvious situation is one in which an organization publically reports the results of its work-force audit, as will occur if it is regulated by the federal Employment Equity Act. Advocacy organizations representing the designated groups may respond with criticisms of what the numbers show regarding the organization's lack of progress. They may also question the way in which the numbers were collected, interpreted and reported. In other words, the validity of the organization's employment equity data may be called into question. If this criticism is well-founded, the organization has spent resources on a monitoring and evaluation process that is not helpful in assessing progress toward equity, and that is damaging to its image in the community.

BOX 14.5
Validity Issues: Data on Disability

Disabled People for Employment Equity, a coalition of 24 advocacy groups representing people with disabilities, organized to prevent companies required to report under the Employment Equity Act from continuing to inflate their counts of people with disabilities. Major banks and other companies were including employees who, for example, wore eyeglasses or who had gout, in their counts of employees with disabilities. The coalition claimed that only one major bank — the Bank of Montreal — complied with reporting requirements. Its level of representation of people with disabilities was very low, 0.7 percent. The coalition's coordinator noted that while this was not a good record, "at least they were honest."

The coalition attempted to get a federal court order to require the government to "issue guidelines instructing employers to use the correct definition and directing the [employment and immigration] minister to enforce the act by prosecuting offending employers." The court did not decide in their favour, but the coalition called off further court action when Employment and Immigration Canada issued a directive on the proper definition of disability.

The directive, issued in March 1991, specified that counts of members of designated groups can include only those individuals who identify themselves or who agree to be identified as members. People classified as having disabilities are those having an impairment that is "long term and on-going," and the impairment is such that "the individual considers that he or she is likely to encounter barriers in employment, resulting in employment disadvantage" (*Globe and Mail*, March 26, 1991: A7).

The Toronto-Dominion Bank and the Bank of Nova Scotia have asked the Federal Court to declare null and void the requirement that a person must consider themselves to be disadvantaged by their disability in order to be counted. The banks are seeking a broader definition of disability so that more of their employees will be included in counts of persons with disabilities. Until a decision is handed down, the regulation stands (*Globe and Mail*, Aug. 16, 1991: B1).

Goals and Timetables for Increasing Representation

Targets are usually based upon the work-force audit and availability data, together with internal human resource planning data (such as anticipated retirements) where available. It is difficult to set goals in the absence of knowledge about the availability of employees with the skills and experience the organization requires. Evaluation of progress toward employment equity involves comparing organizational data on the changing representation of designated groups over time. It also involves comparisons of organizational data with its own targets, which in most cases are set by referring to external availability data. Finally, evaluation involves comparisons of organizational data with external availability data at a point in time.

One of the frustrations faced by employment equity practitioners is the lack of relevant and up-to-date availability data for many jobs and organizational settings. Statistics provided to employers by Employment and Immigration Canada, for example, are largely drawn from the last census (after the data have been processed, which takes several years). These data are not only likely to be seriously out of date; they may not be available at a useful level of disaggregation or detail, or for all the designated groups. For example, a Vancouver employer who wishes to hire more women for civil engineering jobs may find that the only data available are counts of all engineers, with no details as to area of specialization, for 1986, for the province. Furthermore, this employer may be unsuccessful in finding relevant availability data for engineers who are members of racial minorities, who are aboriginal peoples, or who have disabilities. It appears questionable at best to use the available numbers as a basis for recruitment goals for a five year planning period.

In most organizations, goal-setting is done by the employment equity coordinator or officer, often with little or no consultation with line managers and other decision-makers. Although such a goal-setting process meets government requirements for compliance, it is highly likely to be a "paper exercise" that gives decision-makers little incentive to take the resulting goals seriously.

With appropriate training it would be feasible for the decision-makers in each unit of the organization to use data relevant to their operations to set their own goals that are specific and relevant to each unit. The unit goals can then be aggregated into goals for the organization as a whole. A decentralized and participatory approach such as this may be more likely to elicit the commitment of decision-makers to the goals. Moreover, targets set by each unit may be more realistic, since they would reflect specific knowledge about the labour market and staffing conditions within specialized occupational groups. In turn, the process of monitoring and evaluation is likely to be taken more seriously if the goals themselves are perceived as "real."

Work Plans: Documenting Inputs

Work plans are required to demonstrate that the organization has fulfilled government requirements. For a federal contractor this documentation would include public statements of commitment to employment equity by top management, an employment equity policy statement for the organization, the appointment of an employment equity manager, descriptions of how employment systems are reviewed to identify and eliminate systemic barriers, and descriptions of special measures. In Chapter 13 we discussed ways in which work plans can be developed, with stakeholder involvement, in order to provide remedies for problems identified in the diagnosis.

Documenting Implementation

Work plans provide important information, but they do not give us insight into what is actually happening — what people are actually doing — as distinct from what is supposed to happen. There have been cases in which change programs that were never really implemented were nonetheless evaluated (Morah, 1990b:32-33). For example, a federal contractor might develop corporate goals and timetables for employment equity that are never used by managers to guide their hiring, training and promotion decisions. An evaluation that looks only at goals, plans and outcomes, and does not examine what actually takes place as the program is implemented, provides no basis to explain the success or failure of the program. Morah (1990b:35) notes that when a change program is evaluated and found ineffective, unless we have adequate information about the implementation process, we don't know whether it failed to attain its goals because it was a poorly designed change program, or because it was not carried out according to plans.

It is possible that by comparing how various departments or other units within an organization implement employment equity activities we may gain very useful information about the relative success of these activities. In any organization some units will pursue change activities with enthusiasm while others do little, or resist change. It may be difficult to draw conclusions about the effectiveness of a change strategy within the organization as a whole unless these internal differences in implementation are acknowledged. This kind of analysis is also needed if there are to be meaningful arrangements for accountability and equitable provisions for rewards and sanctions.

BOX 14.6
How Does Your Organization Stack Up?

Jain and Hackett (1989) developed an Employment Equity Index based upon an organization's claims to have implemented requirements of the Federal Contractors Program. This index is useful in comparing organizations in order to study differences among them in level of employment equity activity. The index score is based on the following components:

CRITERION:	WEIGHT:
1. accountability	20
2. numerical goals and timetables	20
3. monitoring and control mechanisms	20
4. on-going publicity	10
5a. special target group recruitment efforts	5
5b. special target group training efforts	5
6. employment practice review	10
7. employment equity committee or employment equity coordinator	5
8. resources or budget	5
TOTAL	100

Interpreting Data
Numerical data need to be interpreted in context, and supplemented by qualitative and experiential information in order to obtain a balanced and complete picture of the employment equity implementation process and its outcomes. Quantitative goals and data produced by work-force audits are important components of a

monitoring and evaluation process, but they are only the beginning. Without interpretation, analysis and evaluation, the utility of work-force census and other numerical data is open to question. Such data are costly to collect, yet numbers alone do not tell the whole story, and can even be misleading in the absence of contextual information to guide their interpretation.

For example, the representation of women in middle management in our hypothetical company, CFS, increased by one percent over the past year. Is this a "good" or "bad" result? We need to know that CFS is downsizing and was only able to fill half of the management positions that became vacant, and that CFS's representation is slightly better than the proportion of women in comparable middle management jobs in the province. However, we also need to know that women are concentrated in the administration, human resources and customer service areas at CFS, and are absent from investment and sales management positions. There have been women in sales management but there have been many complaints of a sexually harassing work environment, and difficulties in combining family and work responsibilities. Consequently, CFS has not attracted or retained women in the sales management jobs

In another kind of organization, a university, many of the women teaching in one of the professional faculties feel that they face a sexist organizational culture, both in the classroom and in their interactions with colleagues. Some women have said that they mistrust the processes and criteria used to make decisions about hiring, contract renewal and promotion — perceiving that these processes are arbitrary and tend to favour men. Yet the numbers are not "bad": there is a larger representation of women teaching in this setting than in many of the other faculties of the university. Clearly, numerical data alone will not document and clarify what is going on.

It is of course important that government and political stakeholders responsible for policy making and compliance, and external advocacy groups attempting to monitor how much real movement employers are demonstrating, have access to numerical data about the representation of the designated groups, and information about the employment equity measures the organization claims to have undertaken. These stakeholders need to be able to study change over time, and to compare sectors and organizations within sectors, with respect to the representation of designated group members at all levels of the organization. They also need to know what actions organizations are taking to implement regulatory guidelines. But these kinds of information alone are inadequate as a basis for determining what kinds of employment equity initiatives are effective in getting results, both within a particular organization and in general.

It may also be useful to communicate a broader range of information to external stakeholders in order to enlarge their information base beyond the reports available to the public under the federal legislation. Numerical data will be the focus of responses by advocacy groups if this is the only kind of information available to them.

Perceptions of Designated Group Members

Perceptions of designated group members within and outside the organization are also important to include when monitoring and evaluating an employment equity change process. Data from the employment equity census, quantitative goals, and work plans, present a profile of the organization largely from the perspective of the employment equity office. The perspectives of other stakeholders, including the designated groups, top and line management, union officers, employees, and the community, are missing.

It is important to provide for feedback from members of the designated groups to ascertain whether employment equity initiatives are meeting their needs. We need to get a sense of the nature of the organizational climate, and whether it is changing, from those directly affected. Is more or less racial and gender harassment occurring? Is racist and sexist language being used? Are complaints dealt with in a timely and effective fashion by line management? Are requests for accommodation given an appropriate response? Is there a sense that top management is committed to employment equity? Is there a feeling of confidence on the part of individual members of designated groups that their performance will be appraised fairly and that they will have access to career development opportunities? How are selection, job assignment and promotion decisions actually made, when compared with how they are supposed to be made?

Questions such as these indicate the need for monitoring procedures that permit the collection of qualitative as well as quantitative data. Work-force counts do not provide insight into people's experiences of what actually happens in the workplace. A variety of means might be considered for collecting this kind of information.

BOX 14.8
Qualitative and Experiential Data for Employment Equity Monitoring and Evaluation: Some Examples

- Open-ended questions on the employment equity census questionnaire.

  > EXAMPLE: questions from The University of Western Ontario's employment equity self-identification questionnaire:

  > Are you female? ☐   or male? ☐

  > As an employee at Western, do you feel you have experienced disadvantages based on gender?

  >   no ☐   yes ☐

  > If you answered "Yes", please summarize your major concerns:

  > _____

  > _____

  > _____

  [The same question format was also used for the other three designated groups.]

- Arrangements for individuals or groups to talk about their experiences with the organization's employment equity committee or its subcommittees, or with individual members of these groups, and to have this information summarized as a resource.

  > EXAMPLE: The Employment Equity Policy of the University of Western Ontario created a President's Standing Committee for Employment Equity. The Committee consists of a representative selected by each of the

employee associations (faculty, staff, unions and graduate students), an appointee of the President to represent each of the four employment equity designated groups and part-time faculty and staff, two members of the senior administration, and the employment equity officer. Employees of the university are encouraged to discuss their concerns and questions with anyone on the Committee. In addition, the Committee hears testimony from individuals and groups *in camera* sessions, which provide valuable sources of insight and understanding which assist the Committee in its policy-making function. The Committee has also created several working groups, one of which is mandated to gather information about actual practice, as opposed to policy, in relation to human resource decision making.

- Reporting by unions or advocacy organizations on their members' workplace experiences and assessments of employment equity initiatives.

    EXAMPLE: At the University of Western Ontario, an independent advocacy organization for women faculty and staff — Western's Caucus on Women's Issues — developed a "report card." Members of Caucus were asked to grade the performance of the University administration, the President's Standing Committee for Employment Equity, their own faculty, and their own department, on several employment equity indicators. This information was compiled and submitted to the Committee with recommendations as to members' priorities. In addition, Caucus sponsored a survey of its members regarding their experiences of discrimination and perceived threats to their safety during their employment at Western. A report on this survey was provided to the Committee.

- Reports from focus groups of stakeholders, conducted by unions, advocacy organizations, the employment equity officer, or others.

- Inclusion of employment equity items on existing employee survey instruments.

- Special surveys or studies of employees or subgroups of employees.

    EXAMPLE: At the University of Western Ontario, four faculty members interviewed 35 other women faculty members in various departments regarding their experiences. The interview materials were compiled into a report that documented a "chilly climate" for women faculty, including the use of sexist language, exclusion from informal networks where career-related information is passed on and decisions are made, failure to give women credit for their achievements or contributions, failure to include women on committees where important decisions are made, unequal treatment in regard to compensation and access to research support, course assignments, and other working conditions, and a variety of other inequitable practices.

This report provided insights that assisted the President's Standing Committee for Employment Equity in planning change projects designed to retain women faculty and assist them in developing their careers. One of these projects was an educational video and training manual about the chilly climate for women in universities and colleges, produced jointly with Western's Caucus on Women's Issues, and funded by the Ontario Women's Directorate and the Ontario Ministry of Colleges and Universities. Another project was a career information and support initiative, or mentoring program, again jointly sponsored with Caucus.

- Annual summary reports on complaints and counselling related to workplace harassment, and on responses to complaints, with appropriate safeguards to protect the confidentiality of all participants.
- Annual summary reports on exit interviews;
- Confidential follow-ups of new hires and promotions from designated groups by the employment equity officer.
- Annual summary reports of appraisals of management performance on employment equity, to provide a general overview of the extent of accomplishment and accountability of managers at various levels and in various functions.

No single source of information in itself is sufficient as a basis for evaluating the progress of an employment equity change program, but together they form a composite picture of what is happening. Each type of information requires interpretation within a broader context. For example, data on incidence of complaints of workplace harassment may show an increase in the number of complaints since a harassment policy was implemented. This could be interpreted to suggest that the climate is getting worse and that the policy is not helpful. However, it is much more likely that the number of cases is increasing because there is now a policy and a procedure for dealing with complaints, so that those who experience harassment are now willing to raise the issue in the expectation that appropriate action will be taken and complainants will not suffer reprisals.

Organizational Learning for Equity

Data collection and monitoring systems are important only if they are used. The potential benefits of monitoring and evaluation will be lost if organizational decision makers are not committed to analyzing and interpreting the information, acting on what it shows, and ensuring accountability for results. The information produced by monitoring and evaluation needs to be taken seriously whether or not it coincides with the political agenda of key decision makers; otherwise the employment equity process will lack credibility. If decision makers have a clear vision of their goals, and a commitment to act, then monitoring and evaluation provide feedback that can aid in continuously improving the effectiveness of the employment equity change process.

Improvements can come through learning from the experience of working toward equity. Learning requires the critical examination of what is changing and why, of where and why resistance is occurring, and of the assumptions and theories that lie behind action. This kind of enquiry must be informed by valid information from monitoring and evaluation. As theories about what works are continuously tested, refined or transformed, and as assumptions are examined in light of evidence, change strategies can be revised to take into account what has been learned from putting theories into practice. The learning experience inherent in large-scale organizational change is a collective process, shared by all of the stakeholders who have an interest in its progress and results.

A process of change that is based on the critical examination of shared experience, as described in the preceding paragraph, might be called "organizational learning". Harrison (1987: 120) defines organizational learning as "changes in the body of interpretations and accepted responses that guide members in their treatment of problems and challenges." If we think of the employment equity change process as a form of organizational learning, we might consider the following three points.

First, employment equity is a form of learning because it requires us to see things in new ways. Employment equity is to a large extent a new way of thinking that calls into question the traditional assumptions about women, racial minorities, people with disabilities and aboriginal peoples, and replaces outmoded perspectives and stereotypes with more informed, accurate and unbiased views. Developing a collective understanding of the meaning of social diversity in the workplace means that we acknowledge that there are many different ways of experiencing and interpreting reality, and we grow in our capacity to understand and live in an increasingly complex world as we become aware of the standpoints of others whose experience is very different from our own. We learn to realize that their perceptions, while not traditionally acknowledged as important and legitimate, have much to contribute to the pluralistic community of the workplace.

Second, the process of employment equity change is on-going and never "finished," like learning itself. As realities change around us we engage in a continuous process of observing, interpreting and trying to understand what is happening so that we can take appropriate and effective action. Hence it is not possible to learn to "be equitable," as we might learn to skate, and then never have to think about it again. Learning equity, like learning democratic participation, is an ongoing process of discovery. It is a way of being.

Third, employment equity change, like learning, involves questioning, asking why, and searching for patterns and relationships in the world we observe and live in. Seeing patterns and relationships instead of discrete and unrelated events means developing hypotheses, models and theories about why and how things fit together, and using those theories as guides to action. In employment equity change, we begin with the analysis of systemic discrimination in the workplace in relation to systems, culture and numbers. To analyze discrimination we observe and listen in order to understand what the rules are that guide behaviour and decision making in the workplace, and how those rules affect different groups of people in different ways. We realize that some of the rules that have traditionally worked effectively for the dominant group in the workplace — white ablebodied males — do not work well for women, racial minorities, people with disabilities, or aboriginal peoples. The origins of some of the rules embodied in employment policies and practices may be lost in the past; they may have developed to deal with conditions that are no longer present (see Box 14.9). As a form of organizational learning, the practice of employment equity develops in individuals and groups the capacity to think critically about accepted practices and to solve equity problems in their immediate environments.

BOX 14.9

Some Rules Are Made to Be Changed

"...there are some written and unwritten rules which absolutely must be adhered to. Then there are many rules, written and unwritten, which were put there for perfectly good reasons and were made by people for people like themselves, and at one time the rules worked, but these rules don't work for the people who work there today and have nothing to do with bottom-line productivity. They are strictly rules of comfort and habit which worked well for one group and now don't work for another group and need to become flexible enough to accommodate differences. It's amazing when you ask about every one of those rules, written and unwritten, how much of it can be flexible and how much of it is not necessary. Examining corporate culture is a critical process that covers every aspect in the system — recruiting, training, hiring, promoting, competition, holidays, workspace, sales, customer service..."

(SOURCE: Interview with Lewis Griggs in B. Leonard, "Ways to Make Diversity Programs Work," *HR Magazine*, 36 (4), April 1991, 39.)

For example, if we track numerical representation over period of time we may see that women, racial minorities, aboriginal peoples and people with disabilities are being hired in increasing numbers, in part as a result of outreach recruitment and more equitable interviewing and selection practices. Human resources staff and line managers have had to learn new approaches to hiring. Yet we might see that the overall representation of the designated groups in the workplace is staying the same. There is a need to understand why the recruitment and selection initiatives are not moving the organization toward its goals for numerical representation.

Further analysis might reveal that the organization has failed to address issues of organizational culture, and to examine and change employment systems that influence career progression and job satisfaction. Perhaps co-workers are practicing harassment and are not accepting the new hires as equals, or supervisors are not giving them opportunities to learn the skills needed for advancement. As a result, employees who are members of designated groups are leaving the organization.

It is clearly not enough to bring members of the designated groups into the organization as it is. They must be integrated, and for this to happen, both individual and organizational learning must occur. There need to be new policies and practices that assure freedom from harassment, accommodation of diversity, and equal opportunity for all to progress. Patterns of exclusion from informal social interaction, and stereotyped expectations about members of the designated groups, will have to change. Individuals in the organization need to learn more equitable ways of treating their co-workers and subordinates, and in addition, some new organizational rules and norms of behaviour need to be developed, learned and applied.

The learning involved in employment equity implementation is a collective, organizational process as well as an individual experience. Individuals learn best when the organization of which they are a part provides a supportive, reinforcing context that rewards them for practicing new behaviours. Moreover, employment systems and culture are collective products: individuals follow the rules and norms of informal social behaviour that apply to all members of their work group. Changing those rules and norms to create and maintain a more equitable workplace is therefore a collective process of organizational learning. Individuals learn to practice equity when corporate policies, operating procedures, reward and accountability systems, information flows, power relations, and organizational culture all reinforce each other in promoting equitable behaviour. Ultimately, this will occur only when organizational decision makers at all levels, with the participation of all employment equity stakeholders, develop these new and more equitable systems and cultures and make them the standard operating procedures of the organization.

Organizational learning is an inherently participatory process through which people develop skills and understandings that assist them in continuously monitoring, evaluating, and revising in order to improve organizational practices. People learn by participating, and in organizations that have developed the capacity to learn, there are structures that permit everyone to become involved in diagnosing problems and in devising and evaluating solutions. Organizational learning does not simply involve "replacing one set of structural arrangements with another set," but instead, it is a "process of continuous active adaptive learning by which alternative designs are discovered, maintained, elaborated, and modified as conditions and needs change" (Williams, 1982: 163).

In this way, employment equity change becomes a process of continuous learning based upon information available from monitoring and evaluation. This information can itself become a force for change if it is publically reported and available to the various stakeholders who have an interest in employment equity in the organization. In this framework, the role of the employment equity practitioner is that of a facilitator, coordinator, and resource person, not the expert who "supplies clients with completed solutions" (Harrison, 1987: 123). Employment equity practitioners cannot learn "for" people in the organization: people have to do this themselves, with expert assistance

The organizations we have, and their human resource management systems, were created by the choices and decisions of people who had problems to solve. In the words of Peter Senge, "today's problems come from yesterday's solutions" (Senge, 1990:57). If these solutions no longer work for us they can be changed. Organizational learning involves people in making choices, on the basis of valid and relevant information, about what kind of organization they want to create, now and in the future. In organizations that have developed the capacity to learn, people are not helpless victims of "the system." They can invent new and more equitable ways of doing things that meet the needs of those who are in the workplace now, and in the years to come. In the long run, organizational effectiveness "depends on the ability of members to adjust to future states and solve problems that have not yet arisen" (Harrison, 1987: 120).

If implemented through a participatory process, employment equity change brings together two fundamental currents of change in contemporary organizations — protection of human rights and democracy in decision making. It also moves the organization toward a more open, harmonious relationship with its community and society. The practice of employment equity challenges entrenched structures of power and opportunity and contributes to the realization of democratic values in the workplace. Given the emerging demographic composition of the workplace and of society, as well as the values that are cherished by people around the world, these changes are long overdue.

REFERENCES

Argyris, Chris, and Donald Schon. *Organizational Learning: A Theory of Action Perspective.* Reading, Mass.: Addison Wesley, 1978.

Greenhaus, Jeffrey, Saroj Parasuraman and Wayne Wormley. "Effects of Race on Organizational Experiences, Job Performance Evaluations, and Career Outcomes." *Academy of Management Journal,* 33 (1), 1990, 64-86.

Harrison, Michael. *Diagnosing Organizations: Methods, Models, and Processes.* Beverly Hills: Sage, 1987.

Jain, Harish, and Rick Hackett. "Measuring Effectiveness of Employment Equity Programs in Canada: Public Policy and a Survey." *Canadian Public Policy,* 15 (2), 1989, 189-204.

Morah, Erasmus. "Why Policies Have Problems Achieving Optimal Results: A Review of the Literature on Policy Implementation." Vancouver: University of British Columbia, School of Community and Regional Planning, Discussion Paper # 20, July 1990 (a).

Morah, Erasmus. "A Comprehensive Approach to Public Policy Evaluation: The Implementation-Outcome Connection." Vancouver: University of British Columbia, School of Community and Regional Planning, Discussion paper # 21, July 1990 (b).

Morrison, Ann, and Mary Ann von Glinow. "Women and Minorities in Management." *American Psychologist,* 45 (2), 1990, 200-208.

Olson, Craig, and Brian Becker. "Sex Discrimination in the Promotion Process." *Industrial and Labour Relations Review,* 36 (4), 1983, 624-641.

Pal, Leslie. *Public Policy Analysis.* Toronto: Methuen, 1987.

Pettigrew, Thomas, and Joanne Martin. "Shaping the Organizational Context for Black American Inclusion." *Journal of Social Issues,* 43 (1), 1987, 41-78.

Poister, Theodore. *Public Program Analysis: Applied Research Methods.* Baltimore: University Press, 1978.

Sugiman, Pamela. "Affirmative Action and Work: The Case of the Canadian Auto Workers and General Motors of Canada." Queens Park: Ontario Women's Directorate, 1987.

Swimmer, Gene. "Gender Based Differences in Promotions of Clerical Workers." *Relations Industrielles* 45 (2), 1990, 300-309.

Wholey, J.S., J.N. Nay, J.W. Scanlon, and R.E. Schmidt. "If You Don't Care Where You Get to, Then It Doesn't Matter Which Way You Go." In Lyons, Gene (ed.), *Social Research and Public Policies*, Hanover, N.H.: Dartmouth College, Public Affairs Centre, 1975: 175-197.

Index

benefits
  improve human resource management
    outcomes, 80-82
  keep pace with government regulation,
    88-90
  meet challenge of demographic
    change, 73-79
  participate in changing social climate,
    85-88
  summarized, 89, 90
  understand diverse marketplace
    needs, 84, 85
  use potential of entire workforce, 79,
    80
Bilingualism and Bicultural Commission,
  111
Bill 172, 110
Bill C-62. see Legislated Employment
  Equity Program: bona fide occupational requirement, 129, 130
budget requirements, 290
buy-in, 256, 266

Canada Employment and Immigration
  Commission
  Affirmative Action Branch, 122
  Employment Equity: A Guide to
    Employers, 13, 14, 154
  free consultation at regional offices, 294
Canadian Auto Workers
  affirmative action clause, 207
  award, received, 87, 194
  generally, 86
  position against collaborating with
    employers, 153, 154
Canadian Human Rights Commission
  Bell Canada, complaint laid against, 101
  CBC, complaint laid against, 101
  generally, 99-102
  procedure for ensuring compliance,
    101, 102
  Royal Bank of Canada, agreement
    with, 103
  voluntary review agreements, 101
case law, effect of, 105, 106
cases
  Action Travail des Femmes v. CN
    Rail. see ATF case

Brooks v. Safeway, 120
Central Alberta Dairy Pool, 141
Griggs v. Duke Power Company,
  140, 333, 334, 347
Roberts v. Ontario (Ministry of
  Health)
  examined concept of affirmative
    action, 14, 15
  generally, 107
Singh v. Security and Investigative
  Services, 141
Turpin v. R., 117
CEIC. see Canada Employment and
  Immigration Commission: census data
  basis for availability data, 372
  documents disadvantages, 38
champions, 257-265
change. see also organizational change
  accountability, importance of,
    261, 262
  basic reasons for, 270, 271
  created gradually over time, 250
  different than management of
    routine affairs, 220
  examples, 255
  focused around fundamental values,
    221
  not result of rational linear process,
    219
  not smooth flow of activity, 219
  value-driven, 220-222
change agent
  all are key stakeholders, 257
  defined, 156
  role changes over time, 263
  stakeholders who may act as, 258,
    259
  strategies, 291-295
  types
    distinctions between different
      chart, 260, 261
      generally, 261, 265
    listed, 257
    roles of different, not mutually
      exclusive, 259
change model, stages of building understanding and momentum
  generally, 246-249